HIGH HULLS

HIGH HULLS

FLYING BOATS OF THE 1930s AND 1940s

CHARLES R. G. BAIN

FONTHILL

To my parents, Randall and Janice, who give me everything in love, support, and advice, and to my grandparents, George and Anne Shaw, the best and most loving grandparents I ever could have had—my four pillars.
And to Lori, who I hope will become my fifth.

Fonthill Media Language Policy

Fonthill Media publishes in the international English language market. One language edition is published worldwide. As there are minor differences in spelling and presentation, especially with regard to American English and British English, a policy is necessary to define which form of English to use. The Fonthill Policy is to use the form of English native to the author. Charles R. G. Bain was born and educated in Ontario; therefore Canadian English has been adopted in this publication.

Fonthill Media Limited
Fonthill Media LLC
www.fonthillmedia.com
office@fonthillmedia.com

First published in the United Kingdom and the United States of America 2018

British Library Cataloguing in Publication Data:
A catalogue record for this book is available from the British Library

ISBN 978-1-78155-691-7

Typeset in 10.5pt on 13pt Sabon
Printed and bound in England

Preface

An easy way to describe my childhood would be "lucky." I was blessed with loving, attentive parents, and I was within close proximity to loving grandparents. It was this love and openness from them and my parents that, above all, shaped who I am today; in specific relation to aircraft, this is relevant since I saw my grandparents all the time and they lived a scant few blocks from the local airport.

Here some context may be necessary. I was raised, and still happily live, in Windsor, Ontario. It is a small, frequently maligned corner of a vast nation, and in the most southern region of Canada—contrary to much popular belief, further south than a significant chunk of the United States. Despite popular jokes, it was a quiet and peaceful place to grow up—and one filled with history. Essex County, of which Windsor is the regional seat, has a significant amount of history to its credit. The War of 1812 rolled through the area, and schools, roads, and towns still bear the name Tecumseh—the proud name of an even-prouder Shawnee warrior who fought here. The area was, owing to the Hiram Walker distillery and its physical proximity to Detroit, a major center for bootlegging during the Prohibition era in the United States.

Windsor also bears the names of Canada's sacrifices in both world wars in its streets, and in its parks. Words like Somme, Vimy, Dieppe, and Normandy—these and more are quietly borne, often unnoticed in the general hustle of day to day life. It is, in the final analysis, a city acutely shaped by its history, though it lamentably never seems to support that history as much as one might want. Nevertheless, history could and indeed can still draw a crowd. For me growing up, this was encapsulated by the local air show.

Windsor's airport first opened in 1928 and was a part of the Commonwealth Air Training Plan during World War II. Indeed, our small but dedicated aviation history group is based out of a hangar used for that program, with a wonderful little museum attached in a small building where parachute packing used to occur. Anybody visiting the area today, with any interest in aircraft, will be fascinated by the artifacts on display. Moreover, the airport and associated museum is now home to Windsor's Avro Lancaster—long on display on a plinth in nearby Jackson

Park. Years of mistreatment by city plans to repaint or care for the aircraft have left her in a bad way, but the staff of the Canadian Historical Aircraft Association are labouring uphill to restore her. In her place in Jackson Park, a pair of pillars now proudly display a replica Hawker Hurricane—always a personal favourite of mine—and a Supermarine Spitfire. A complete replica of a de Havilland Mosquito also draws nearer to completion, a thrilling prospect for the future.

I mention this aside simply because it is worth noting that this is, in many ways, where Canadian history truly lives: in dedicated volunteers, fighting hard to preserve both historic aircraft and history in general. The people working on the Lancaster labour uphill, pitting the sweat and effort of volunteers against a massive cost, relying on what government help, donations, and visitors' fees they can acquire. It is, in short, a labour of love. It is the staff and volunteers of these small museums that keep Canada's past alive, and in a larger sense help to keep aviation history on the wing.

This is where I have ended up after years of study and museum visits. Yet when I was little, all this still lay ahead. To me, in those days, the aviation world was a trip to Winnipeg on Air Canada, and the annual air show. The air show was always a wonder to a small child, and Windsor pulled in aircraft of a variety and type that did not reflect a relatively small city. We would see the aircraft up close, then retire from the crowds to my grandparent's home, and the close proximity of their yard to the show made for wonderful summer days, watching planes wing by and having family meals. One moment on one of these lovely days became the first event that would set me on a winding path that would eventually lead to here. A small historical lesson here is that an eventual end can come from small, unexpected starts. I remember distinctly one clear, warm day at my grandparents. The barbecue had been going, and it was time to come in and eat. I lingered outside, hoping to see a few last aircraft flying by, and I caught a glimpse of a replica Fokker Dr.I triplane fly past in the distance, and the black shape of a distant F-117 Nighthawk—by itself a combination that in retrospect reveals much about the headlong speed with which aviation technology had grown.

Finally, it all looked to be over, but as I moved towards the house, a rumbling took over from the background noises and an Avro Lancaster flew over the house at low altitude. It looked like it was low enough to almost clip the television antenna, and it was the largest vehicle I had ever seen up until that point in my life. It was gone in seconds, but those seconds changed my life.

So much has happened since then, and so much has passed, but each step saw me moving deeper into a love of history and a desire to learn about the history of aviation in particular. The more I read and the more I learned, the more information I wanted to consume. As may be rather obvious from these words in this book, this fascination has not faded in the many years that have passed since.

Along the way, I discovered flying boats. They are particularly fascinating to me, for reasons that I have some difficulty putting into words. There is, simply, something about them. Perhaps it is just how thoroughly their world has disappeared, and how strange and alien the concept seems now, in a world of massive airports and trans-oceanic jet airliners. Perhaps, and I suspect this has a larger role to play, it is their frequent grace. These were aircraft that were also ships—ships meant to fly—and they had to have qualities of both to succeed. There is something strange and wonderful in their grace, and their frequent beauty. The romance of the flying boat is perhaps a third reason. These were aircraft meant to stitch the world together, and they helped to usher in the golden age of air travel that we all benefit from to this day.

I admit fully that I am extremely curious what reason you, the reader, have for picking up and reading these words, for delving into this subject as I did long ago. Whatever your reason, I hope this book strikes a chord for the amateur or the professional alike. It is your passion for history that will keep events alive, which will preserve our knowledge and ensure that memory endures. History lives in each of us, both the events and the lessons they teach, and we are shaped by it. For me, that journey started with a single plane overhead when I was a child. Perhaps that journey will start here, for someone else. I certainly hope that will prove true.

Acknowledgments

The author wishes to express his thanks to the following people and organizations for their help in the writing of this book: Dr. Funke Aladejebi, Jeanette Anderson, Michael Bajcar, Michael Baldock, Ashley Bissonette, Andrew Bomberry, Nico Braas, Jerilyn Buresh, David Colamaria, Ray Crupi, Paul Cuny, Reid Dennis, Christian Doerk, Ron Dupas, Gord Emberley, Bill Ewing, Sophia Gleuel and the Blohm und Voss Corporation, David Gardner, Brian and Doug Green, Philip Hayes, Bruce Hinds, David Horn, Greg Howard, Jeremy Hughes, Lars Kambech, Fred Kullas, Philo Lund, John MacDonald, Paul Marchwica, Bill McBride, Eric McClure, Stephen C. Mestler, Heath Moffatt, Davide Montebruno, Jerry Murbach, Fred Nicolau, Barry O'Kelly, John Olafson, Kieth Olsen, Christopher Pinn, Bill Pippin, PoorOldSpike (Username), Steinar Saevdal, Debbie Seracini, Margaret O'Shaughnessy, Dan Shumaker, Max Smith, Baldur Sveinsson, Van S. Swindelle, John Thomson, Jacques Trempe, Joleen West, Ferenc Varga, Johan Visschedijk, and Eric Yamasaki.

Special thanks to Lori Brake for her help with photograph editing.

Special thanks to Kate Fathers for her editing help and writing advice.

Special thanks to Lindsy Fish for her legal help.

Special thanks to Kitty Moore for her extensive research assistance.

Special thanks to Jay Slater, Alan Sutton, and the staff of Fonthill Media.

Contents

Introduction

Shortly before the Wright brothers changed history, with implications beyond their wildest imaginings, someone tried to launch an aircraft from the water. It was not a flying boat in any sense of the word, nor did it bear much resemblance to any aircraft we know today. If anything, the project was an attempt to launch an airplane from a houseboat, an aberrant event without precedent and without connection to anything that has come since.

The name Samuel Pierpont Langley has been sadly overshadowed by the triumph of the Wrights. In the annals of early flight, there is little irony to match the tale: Langley was Third Secretary of the Smithsonian Institution, then an enormously influential and resourceful scientific entity. He was also a highly accomplished astronomer who began experimenting with flight in 1887. The Wrights, in part inspired by Langley's early efforts, took an interest in their own experiments in 1899. Unfortunately for Langley, all his brilliance, resources, and a tremendous head start would count for little arrayed against a superior method and a better idea for a design held by the two bicycle repairmen from Dayton, Ohio.

Nevertheless, for a time it appeared as if Langley might crack powered flight: his steam-powered, unmanned model, *Aerodrome No. 5*, had flown for three-quarter miles in 1896—a flight witnessed and photographed by his good friend Alexander Graham Bell. It is difficult to see in the highly competitive aviation world today, but the leading minds in the development of flight were not so much rivals as distant colleagues, at least until the Wrights succeeded and new paradigms began to evolve.

In 1898, Langley received a total of $70,000 in grant money from the War Department and Smithsonian to create a piloted airplane, with the U.S. military even then seeing glimmerings of what aviation might mean. This then-staggering sum was poured into a major venture for a strange aircraft. It had tandem wings, one pair set behind the other, and while it had a tail that could provide pitch and yaw control, it had no roll control whatever. After seemingly endless engineering frustrations, it also came with a 50-horsepower engine—in contrast to the 12-hp engine the *Wright Flyer* would use.

All seemed well, but Langley's attention had been soaked up by the engine, whereas the Wrights had concentrated on control. Their aircraft could fly against a strong wind and land on solid ground, whereas Langley's craft had to be catapult-launched, with the intention to land softly in the Potomac River. In two attempts, in October and December 1903, the craft was launched from a modified houseboat. The first time, Langley insisted that it clipped part of the catapult, though the true cause of its failure is not known with certainty. On the second launch, the craft simply fell apart as it left the catapult, though the pilot—and designer of the engine—was successfully rescued.

Langley's well-funded effort had drawn much press attention in a world that presumed his objective was impossible, and with consummate pettiness, newspapers bashed away at what they made into an expensive flop, without any merit. The project became a political football, and Langley's dreams of flight were crushed.

So it was that, without much ceremony and almost no press—the secrecy with which the Wrights worked did not aid in this regard—that it was up to the men working at Kittyhawk to make the first powered flight, though it took several years for the full measure of their achievement to become clear to the world. Even if Langley's claims that his craft could fly were true, the aircraft was too big to be controlled by the weight of a pilot's body, but he nevertheless made a profound contribution to the science of flight, and it was with some irony that the first American aircraft carrier, converted from a collier in 1920, was named *Langley*. In short, the Wrights could make their idea work. Langley, in the moment, could not. Though Langley did not in any way envisage the flying boat, his water launch was a harbinger of things to come, events tied inextricably to the early days of aviation.

Here as well there had been considerable history leading up to those moments. The first patent for something resembling a flying boat was filed by Alphonse Pénaud in 1876, though nothing came of it, even though Pénaud's tail design would be taken up by Langley. There were other attempts at seaplanes in the years that followed, but it would take until François Denhaute's pioneering flight in 1912 for the first actual flying boat to rise into the air. The concept was so new that it was not even named a "flying boat" until Glenn Curtiss named it such the next year during his own experiments.

From here, history and aviation evolution stepped on the accelerator. Glenn Curtiss had been an early admirer of the Wright Brothers, who became a bitter enemy as the Wrights' patents required all aircraft manufacturers in the United States to pay a royalty to the brothers. Curtiss was himself a brilliant designer, and friend to Alexander Graham Bell. He had worked on Bell's flight experiments before going off on his own—the product of a remarkably collegial early competition in the name of science. This was rapidly becoming something other than the scientific pursuit Bell wanted, and much more about the potential profit, which Curtiss in many ways represented. Curtiss founded his own company in 1916, benefitting greatly from the war then engulfing the globe.

The government of the United States, fearful they would soon be embroiled in the war raging in Europe, invalidated the Wrights' patents in order to allow aircraft manufacturers to ramp up production. Curtiss, who already had an excellent relationship with the U.S. Navy, responded with the famed JN-4 Jenny trainer, one of the most ubiquitous aircraft of the era, and by itself well worth the government's efforts.

In 1917, Curtiss was commissioned to build a large, four-engined flying boat, which would eventually become the NC series. By this point, the capabilities of aircraft had expanded at an astonishing pace from what was possible in 1903, and the NC series looked ahead to the future. The NCs had been designed for anti-submarine warfare and patrolling, but the end of the war left an opportunity for one of them to carry out a spectacular aviation first.

The NC-4, the "Nancy Boat," was chosen to make the world's first transatlantic crossing via airplane, along with the NC-1 and NC-3. The four Liberty engines, each with 400 hp, would carry a crew of five at a maximum speed of 95 miles per hour. All of this seems painfully slow and underpowered considering what was to come, but in a mere sixteen years since Kittyhawk, this was a staggering advance in design and capability. In the event, only the NC-4 would successfully finish the long, hopping flight—in sum, a five-leg journey covering 3,875 miles. Along the route, U.S. Navy ships were strung out every 50 miles to aid with navigation, a total of twenty-three warships in all.

The success of the flight astonished the world, although it was overshadowed in short order by the first non-stop crossing made by British aviators John Alcock and Arthur Brown in a converted Vickers Vimy bomber a mere two weeks later. Here, already, the eventual demise of the flying boat was written.

In the meantime, the spectacular flights opened new vistas for passenger aviation, and it would be flying boats that were perfectly positioned to take advantage. The root of their success lay in the engineering and physics involved in aviation at the time. In order to lift larger numbers of passengers, aircraft had to become correspondingly larger. To lift these larger aircraft, more powerful—and, by necessity, heavier—engines were required. The larger the aircraft, the larger its capability, the higher the number of engines needed to power it. So with inadequate power, the aircraft might not get in the air, but adding more engines only added more weight. It was a thorny problem for designers, to balance weight and power *versus* performance and capacity. This was then compounded by the simple problem of space.

If adequate power could be applied to a sufficient capacity to make an aircraft profitable in civilian use, this meant that the heavier take-off weight would require longer runways and these were a highly expensive rarity in the early decades of aviation—an alien concept to modern eyes. The ideal solution, it seemed, was the water. The reasoning was that a calm waterway was essentially an unlimited runway, without the need to find an adequate space. A very large aircraft, taking off from the water, would have all the room it needed to get airborne. As an added bonus, this would come at a fraction of the infrastructure cost. Under this logic, a golden age of flying boats and seaplanes began that functioned differently in different classes of aircraft. For the smaller boats and seaplanes, it was all about utility. Flying in a remote country, a small flying boat or a seaplane could put down on lakes and rivers without having to worry about rough terrain, and to this day, the seaplane is a major presence in this particular niche. For the big aircraft that were to come, there was the potential to carry out significant feats and create regular passenger travel.

This world was envisaged early, and it did not hurt the development of the flying boat that many of the early winners of the famed Schneider Trophy were flying boats. As early as 1921, Italian designer Giovanni Caproni tried to create a massive passenger flying boat. The result was the Caproni Ca.60 Noviplano, a nine-winged monster meant to carry 100 passengers across the Atlantic. This particular design, fantastic and alien, managed to take-off in tests. It did not make it past them, as a crash, followed by the strains of trying to rescue the massive hulled air vessel, wrecked it beyond repair. Reflecting on the end of the titanic craft, Caproni remarked:

> So the fruit of years of work, an aircraft that was to form the basis of future aviation, all is lost in a moment. But one must not be shocked if one wants to progress. The path of progress is strewn with suffering.
>
> "The castle door, the mooring pylon and the Transaereo—Part 1"
> *WW1 Aero—the Journal of the Early Aeroplane*, p. 194
> Gregory Alegi

Yet even as he said it, his prophetic vision was coming to pass. By the early 1920s, there were companies in multiple nations that specialized in flying boats; some of these companies will be noted later on in this book, though other companies turned out the occasional such aircraft. As technology and design progressed, Caproni's vision rapidly became reality. By 1930, there were large passenger flying boats in service, and they kept growing. By the middle of the decade, flying boats had reached the apex of their existence, straddling the globe, with their only real competition being the enormous passenger Zeppelins built by Germany. In the Pacific, the graceful flying boats were making the world a little bit smaller, and at the same time, military designs had been proceeding apace. When war erupted again, the flying boat stood at an apogee of its evolution, and more than ready to serve. In combat, flying boats would be seen in the hands of practically every combatant nation, performing a variety of duties with varying degrees of success.

After 1945, many declared the flying boat obsolete, a verdict some historians have echoed and enlarged. Larger, land-based runways and growing airports were matched to vastly more powerful engines, and the full swing of the jet age had begun. Certainly, flying boats could not maintain their dominance as passenger aircraft or even as military aircraft under these circumstances. It is unfair, however, to argue that their era ended altogether. Many older flying boats lingered on, and indeed still do, in private hands—cherished possessions and a reminder of a golden age long past. Others evolved to fulfil specific niches, though in many cases, seaplanes proved a more cost-effective option in the long run. At least one of the titanic flying boats of yesterday, discussed later, looked obsolescence and the passage of decades square in the face and simply defied them, and is still capable of heavy work as these words are written.

So the golden age may be finished, but the concept lives on. Far from being dinosaurs doomed to extinction, flying boats have survived in private hands and, indeed, in our memories. Yet it is to the golden age that this work is dedicated, to a time when it looked like the flying boat was set to conquer the air outright. In civilian and military service, the two decades of deep challenge, dark tragedy, and tremendous achievement were the pinnacle of the flying boat era. The history that follows, the stories of many of these fascinating and varied aircraft, will cover the globe and the passage of time. These high hulls, these graceful ships of the air, were never bigger and never better.

1

Beriev MBR-2, Be-4, Be-6: The Long Line of Russian Flying Boat Evolution

The Beriev name is one well worth beginning with since, unlike many other entries, the manufacturer still exists—more than that, Beriev is still in the business of manufacturing flying boats. The Beriev style has evolved with the decades, filling several niches for the Soviet and, later, the Russian state and private interests. The three chosen flying boats for Beriev demonstrate the evolution of flying boat design across twenty years, each fulfilling a role for the Soviet Union. In war and peace, these three flying boats well represent what might be termed a medium flying boat, with an ample demonstration of the capabilities such a craft possessed before and during World War II.

Specifications (Beriev MBR-2)

First Flight: 1932
Powerplant: M-17B inline piston engine, 680 hp
Armament: One ShKAS 7.62-mm (0.3-inch) machine gun in nose, one in mid-ship ring mounting, up to 500 kg (1,102 lb) of bombs or depth charges on underwing racks
Top Speed: 124 mph (200 kph)
Range/Service Ceiling: 404 miles (650 km), 14,435 feet (4,400 metres)
Dimensions: Length 44 feet 3½ inch (13.5 metres), height 14 feet 9 inches (19 metres), wingspan 62 feet 4 inches (19 metres)
Number Built: 1,365

Beriev Be-4

First Flight: 1940
Powerplant: Shvetsov M-62 radial engine, 1,000 hp
Armament: One fixed, forward-firing ShKAS 7.62-mm (0.3-inch) machine gun, one similar for observer, up to 400 kg (800 lb) of bombs or depth charges.

Top Speed: 221 mph (356 kph)
Range/Service Ceiling: 716 miles (1,150 km), 26,575 feet (8,100 metres)
Dimensions: Length 34 feet 5 inches (10.5 metres), height 13 feet 3 inch (4.05 metres), wingspan 39 feet 4 inches (12 metres)
Number Built: Approximately forty-seven

Beriev Be-6

First Flight: 1949
Powerplant: Two Shvetsov ASh-73TK radial engines, 2,400 hp each
Armament: Five 23-mm (0.9-inch) Nudelman-Rikhter NR-23 cannon, mounted in three remotely controlled turrets, bombs of various weights, two 1,000-kg (2,205-lb) torpedoes, or eight mines
Top Speed: 257 mph (414 kph)
Range/Service Ceiling: 3,100 miles (5,000 km), 20,013 feet (6,100 metres)
Dimensions: Length 77 feet 1 inch (23.5 metres), height 25 feet 1 inch (7.64 metres), wingspan 110 feet (33 metres)
Number Built: 123

Georgy Mikhailovich Beriev was, as the 1930s dawned, a young engineer of the Central Design Bureau of Seaplanes Manufacturing. At the time, he was a leading figure in Work Team No. 5, and he turned his team's attention towards addressing a deficiency in Soviet military for patrolling the U.S.S.R.'s vast coasts. Beriev would prove to be a natural choice for this work, since his design team had been working on seaplanes since the 1920s. Beriev himself had begun work immediately after graduating from the Aviation Department of the Leningrad Shipbuilding Institute, and his first aircraft had been developed in 1931–32. His arrival on the scene came at a fortuitous time.

The Soviet Air Force in the 1930s was suffering through both a laggardly pace of development and a process of changing their strategic mission, which, ultimately, would help win the war that was to come, albeit at titanic cost. The Soviets had put much emphasis in the post-Civil War period on heavy bombers, developing innovative—and to the eyes of the observer, frequently strange—methods of projecting air power. By the 1930s, however, the heavy bomber program was beginning to suffer. Indeed, only one modern heavy bomber would enter the Soviet arsenal throughout World War II. The force was shifting towards the battlefield weapon it would become, and one consequence of this was that there was little room in strategic thinking for maritime aviation, let alone a flying boat.

Flying boat development had a very low priority, and only Beriev and his team were able to attract official attention with a modern design for a small flying boat—though, in time, Beriev would become a name associated quite extensively with the concept.

The immediate result of their labours would be the MBR-2 (the "MBR" standing for *Morskoi Blizhnii Razvedechik*, or "short range maritime reconnaissance plane"), which was completed in December 1931 after an extremely rapid design and construction period. Originally meant to carry the M-27 engine, plans had to be redrawn as the M-27 had not yet passed tests, and the M-17 would be used initially. As it stood, the prototype would fly with an imported BMV VI.Z engine of 500 hp, and in any event, the M-17 was a license-built development of this engine. The powerplant was mounted high over the fuselage with a pusher propeller, a somewhat unusual feature for the era. The aircraft began its tests for the Soviet State in May 1932. Flying from Sevastopol, with pilot B. L. Bukgolts at the controls, aircraft behaviour was deemed to be excellent. The result was the immediate acceptance of the aircraft for production by the Soviet Navy.

Part of the secret to the aircraft's success was in its construction, which was undertaken with an eye towards making both production and repair an easier task—namely in the deep concave bottom of the two-step hull. The construction was mostly wooden, with the hull predominantly constructed with a 3-mm plywood skin. The bottom was 6 mm on the first step and 2.5 mm on the tail section. Over this, all the external surface was covered with fabric and lacquered. The tail structure was metal, but fabric covered. Interestingly, Beriev reversed the building methods then in use in other nations by making the hull wooden but the wings metal. In other countries, the hull was becoming metal because it avoided an increase in gross weight as the hull soaked up water over time. Why Beriev made this decision is debated and could possibly have to do with ease of acquiring materials, an attempt to preserve metal for other aircraft, or, as John Batchelor and Louis Casey put it, "possibly the Soviet designers had learned something new in wood preservation, or operated with the same load regardless of the gross weight."

MBR-2 of the Soviet Navy on take-off run. (*Photograph courtesy of Dan Shumaker*)

The aircraft was designed for a crew of four or possibly five, with the pilot and co-pilot sat side by side in what was initially an open cockpit, though this was later enclosed. For defence, the aircraft had two 7.62-mm PV-1 machine guns, one in the bow and one in the mid-upper fuselage, both on moveable mountings. Additionally, the aircraft could carry up to 661 lb (300 kg) of bombs, depth charges, or mines. Interestingly, the aircraft was designed for quick conversion for unusual conditions and could be given a non-retracting wheel or ski landing gear so it could operate from land or, more importantly, from ice-covered waters and other winter conditions.

Series production of the aircraft began at Factory No. 31 in Taganrog, near Rostov on the Sea of Azov. The series production aircraft, known in Russian parlance as the TsKB MS-1, mounted a more powerful engine, an upgrade of the M-17; though, later still, the aircraft would apparently receive the M-34 engine. By 1937, the MBR-2 was the main seaplane of the Soviet Navy, and versions for cargo and transportation had been developed to enhance the type's range of abilities.

The aircraft was in production from 1934 until 1940, and it also found a home in Russian civil aviation as the MP-1. The MP-1 could carry a total of eight passengers, and otherwise differed very little from its military siblings. One notable example of the aircraft was the one crewed by three women: Marina Raskova, Vera Lomako, and Polina Osipenko. With these pilots, the aircraft would set no fewer than six world records, one of which stood for twenty years. Even here, in its relatively lesser-known commercial service, Beriev's flying boat did its work and took part in the interesting role for women in aviation that was part of the Soviet Union's history at the time, which would blossom into all-female air regiments during the war—of significant and deserved fame. Moreover, it also took part in the highly important role for aircraft envisioned by dictator Joseph Stalin: each achievement in aviation trumpeted the modern, proficient industrial state he was so brutally constructing. After the war, MP-1 aircraft (and the MP-1T freighter sub-variant) and surplus military aircraft would find themselves a new niche for some time thereafter—as fisheries' protection aircraft and in other related roles. In terms of its overall importance, some authors have declared the MBR-2 to be the Soviet equivalent of the Supermarine Walrus, staying in production for a significant amount of time and having a long and varied career. It is entirely possible that some examples were still in use as late as the 1970s.

In both military and civilian service, there were excellent reasons to use the MBR-2. It was known for its reliability, as well as being comfortable for pilots. In addition, it was well-constructed and good at absorbing punishment in combat, which was apparently a feature of Taganrog-constructed aircraft. This durability was further enhanced by the fact that the aircraft was easy to fly and just as easy to maintain.

When the Germans launched their invasion in 1941, the MBR-2 was obsolete technology, but like much of the Soviet stockpile, it would be required to soldier on regardless. Contrary to what one might expect, the 560 MBR-2s on hand with

MBR-2 being examined by her Finnish captors. (*Photograph courtesy of PoorOldSpike*)

A view of the MBR-2 that shows details of the skis for winter use. (*Photograph courtesy of PoorOldSpike*)

A crewed and operational MBR-2, being towed in to dock. (*Photograph courtesy of PoorOldSpike*)

Soviet naval aviation proved more than adequate to the task. During the war, it carried out many roles, such as reconnaissance and night bombing, but also forayed into daytime bombing—despite its slow speed—and as an anti-submarine aircraft. It also served as an artillery spotter, a transport, and perhaps, most importantly, as a rescue aircraft for downed airmen. The MBR-2 went everywhere the navy needed it and did all that it was required—obsolescent or not. The situation was dire enough in the early days of the war that every aircraft was required, no matter how obsolescent it might appear. As a result, for three years of war, the MBR-2 was the mainstay of the Soviet Union's short-range maritime capacity. All the roles that the MBR-2 took on were missions that exposed it to Luftwaffe fighters that had vastly superior performance, and the MBR-2 would suffer accordingly. It would also serve valiantly as an anti-submarine aircraft and a reconnaissance platform. In the ASW role, the MBR-2 was chosen because the naval air arm simply did not possess any dedicated ASW aircraft; despite the best efforts of pilots and crews, the MBR-2 was not particularly successful at harrying German submarines, mainly because the aircraft was not well suited to flying low and slow.

The onset of war brought a hurried desire for a replacement, which in the immediate sense would be the MBR-2bis. This was given an 860-hp AM-34N engine to replace the M-17. The MBR-2bis also received a new fuel tank, and the range was extended from 597 miles (960 km) to 870 miles (1,400 km). This was a more than adequate range to cover the main battlefields for Soviet maritime aviation: the Baltic and Black Seas, and the northern arctic seaboard. In addition, a manually operated turret was added with a 7.62-mm ShKAS machine gun, and some structural changes were made in terms of larger vertical tail surfaces. Most importantly, an enclosed crew cabin was provided. In 1942, over 1,500 aircraft were delivered to the VVS-VMF (Soviet naval aviation), this despite the disruption of much Soviet production by the rapidly advancing Germans.

Over time, the MBR-2 would slowly be supplanted in service by newer aircraft, like the Chetverikov Che-2 or either American- or Soviet-built Catalinas. Despite this, the MBR-2 soldiered on until the end of the war, with the last unit to operate them likely being the 115th aviapolk in what became the U.S.S.R.'s Pacific Theatre, with the unit using their MBR-2s to attack naval targets in Korea when the Soviet Union declared war on Japan.

Beriev had already started work on a successor aircraft before the MBR-2's production run ended. Work on an aircraft meant to be launched from Soviet warships had begun in 1939, and the aircraft first flew in the autumn of 1940. The aircraft was part of a massive modernization program for the Soviet fleet that had originally begun in the 1920s. Perhaps surprisingly, the Soviet Navy was very late to develop ship-based aviation, and as late as 1929, the fleet had not mounted Soviet aircraft as a part of policy. To rectify this, the Soviets initially ordered German-made catapults and Heinkel HD 55 two-seater reconnaissance aircraft. This arrangement was quickly to be supplanted by Soviet-based designs. The navy rapidly developed its own domestic solution, deploying their own catapults (known as *Boyevaya Chast'*, or "battle unit") by 1939, and turned to Beriev to design a native aircraft to go with it. Specifically, Beriev was responding to a 1938 requirement for ship-borne aircraft for the newly projected *Sovetskii Soyuz* battleships and *Chapayev*-class cruisers.

Initially, the result of Beriev's efforts was the KOR-1, in 1937. It was a two-seater, all-metal, single-float biplane. While it had some performance advantages in the air over the available flying boats, it proved rather unseaworthy. In addition to handling badly on the water, the KOR-1's M-25A engine was so inadequately cooled that it would overheat while in the process of taxiing. The KOR-1 actually failed to meet official tests but was pressed into intermediate service anyway as the only available aircraft. The handful of KOR-1s, later relabelled Be-2s, lingered on until early in the war. The initial desperation of Soviet forces is well illustrated by the fact that, despite its deficiencies, a wheeled version of the KOR-1 was still employed against the Germans. In the meantime, Beriev had turned his eyes back to flying boats to replace the flawed KOR-1.

The resulting aircraft has been compared to a small Catalina, and in some ways, the aircraft does look like a single-engined little brother to the famed PBY. The aircraft that resulted was almost entirely metal, aside from a fabric-covered aileron and rudder. The hull was built with two planing steps, with the main step being angular and the boat's bottom being heavily dished. It was equipped with the M-62 engine, which developed between 850 and 1,000 hp. The aircraft carried a single stationary machine gun, a ShKAS model, on a turret deck mounting to the rear of the cockpit and wing. In addition, the new design could carry a total of 400 kg. In practice, it could also be armed with a total of four RS-82 rockets, carried in pairs beneath the wings.

The prototype flew for the first time on October 8, 1940, and by February of the following year, the aircraft had entered official testing. Two experimental copies were handed over to the Black Sea Fleet's LII VVS BMF (this heavy acronym was for the heavier *Letno-Ispytatel'ny Institut Voenno-Vozdushnykh Sil Voenno-Morskogo Flota*, or Flying Test Institute of the Naval Air Force) at the great fleet base at Sevastopol. The prototypes had been given the newer M-63 engine and had a speed near the water of 192 mph (310 kph) and 221 mph (356 kph) at altitude. This aircraft was superior in every way to the KOR-1 in terms of speed and maximum altitude, achieving a ceiling of 26,574 feet (8,100 metres). To the undoubted relief of the Soviet Navy, it was also found that the KOR-2 had vastly superior water-handling qualities to the KOR-1 and could land and take-off in choppy waters and into lateral winds. The only flaw was one that would, tragically, only become apparent later: the aircraft had a steep glide path, which would cause fatal accidents and crashes in service. This was certainly not an obstacle at the time, and given the nature of the Soviet military's fatalism, likely not a critical flaw at any time, and serial production was recommended.

Development of the Be-4 (otherwise known as the KOR-2) was temporarily disrupted by the German invasion. Taganrog, for instance, was overrun and production of aircraft there had to be rapidly moved. This was part of a massive,

Rear view of a Be-4 mounted on a Soviet ship. (*Photograph from Wikimedia Commons, all credit to original poster and creator for this public domain image*)

sometimes chaotic, but ultimately effective movement of Soviet industry out of range of the enemy. Every piece of equipment that could be moved was moved, and efforts were made to destroy everything else—though the Germans frequently captured entire factories intact. This movement process included shipping the workers from the plants in peril, often on arduous journeys to the far side of the Ural Mountains. It was an exhausting, sometimes brutal process, but the result was successful. Work on the newly redesignated Be-4 had started in the village of Savelevo outside of Moscow, but in the event, it was moved first to Omsk, and ultimately on to Krasnoyarsk, over 2,400 miles to the east. It was in Omsk that Be-4 production would truly begin, despite the disruption of war. The small number of Be-4s built would mostly be used as short-range reconnaissance aircraft on the Black Sea and the Baltic, though it was also used as an anti-submarine aircraft and, like its forebear, as a rescue aircraft.

The first of the production aircraft was finished on August 11, 1941, and plans called for twenty aircraft initially. The production version differed from the prototypes, for a start coming with the M-62 engine. Though it was less powerful than the M-63, the engine was significantly more reliable and had a greater engine life. In addition, a new canopy that could be jettisoned was added for emergencies, with an armoured plate mounted in the cockpit to protect the flight crew.

This first aircraft did not end well. On its sixth test flight, on September 9, 1941, the aircraft crashed into the water at high speed. The cause of the crash had nothing to do with the aircraft itself, but rather something known as the mirror phenomenon, where a pilot without a reference point finds it difficult to determine the flight attitude and glide path. The second aircraft would be completed by late September, but the third example and all subsequent ones were delayed by the need to evacuate production out of range of the Germans.

Further delays occurred in both production and deployment because of the lack of suitable catapults. The Be-4 was heavier and faster than the KOR-1, and the first of the ZK-2B catapults that could launch the aircraft were not ready for testing before the summer of 1941, with the first test carried out on July 23 by a navy pilot recorded as "S. Reitel."

The first aircraft produced at Omsk were assemblies of aircraft that had been built at Taganrog before the evacuation. The aircraft repair plant Beriev production was assigned to (No. 166) had a small hydro-launching facility built on a bank of the Irtish River, but the location was ultimately entirely unsuitable to serial production. Omsk lacked sufficient apartments to house the workers, and there was no industrial base from which to grow. Beriev's solution was political, and he attended a reception in Moscow hosted by P. Dementjev, the First Deputy of the People's Commissar of Aircraft Industry. Here, he was able to wrangle an order to transfer his design bureau to aircraft factory No. 477 in Krasnoyarsk. It was May 1943 when the transfer occurred, and Beriev was appointed the factory's chief designer.

Here work on refining and finishing production of the Be-4 continued, with the armament upped on some models to eight RS-82 rockets, or reinforced armour. A dive-bombing variant was also produced in mid-1942, carrying four of the high-explosive PLAB-100 bombs. Starting in the latter half of 1943, the Be-4s were equipped with auxiliary fuel tanks, giving them a new flight radius of 357 miles (575 km). Responding to crew observations, defensive armament was also increased, mounting a large-caliber 12.7-mm (0.5-inch) UBT machine gun in a VUB-3 turret. These upgraded versions would be produced between 1944 and 1946. All these upgrades and production were handled by a total of forty people at the factory.

The Be-4 would see service from the Arctic to the Pacific, and in the hotly-contested Black Sea. They would be based at Poti on the Black Sea as part of a coast guard unit, and at Tuapse, Riga, Leningrad, Archangel, Murmansk, and Vladivostok. In actual service, an irony occurred that effected many other aircraft meant for ship-based reconnaissance: the Be-4 was never used for its primary design purpose. In fact, the Be-4 would only ever be launched from a ship in exercises, flying off the *Kirov*-class cruiser *Lazar Kaganovich* in 1946. It is to be noted here that some sources disagree as to the date and place of this use, with others stating that the first such flight was in 1944 from another *Kirov*-class cruiser, the *Molotov*. In actual wartime service, the Be-4 mainly saw combat in the Black Sea, with its main tasks being spotting German submarines, guarding the coast, and searching for floating mines.

Sources vary on how many Be-4s were ultimately built, but in any event, the production total doubled from the initial order. Between forty-four and forty-seven of these aircraft were likely completed. The roles the aircraft had been used for, or at least tested for, were a surprising turn of events for an aircraft originally meant as a spotter. Even more surprisingly, it was apparently successful in its unusual dive-bomber testing, though there is no indication in the sources found for this book that the aircraft was used operationally in this role.

Beriev and his design team would return to Taganrog in 1946 after the Soviet victory, but before it left Krasnoyarsk, the team started to develop a flying boat that was labelled LL-143, which would become the Beriev Be-6. The aircraft grew out of a previous project, known as the MBR-5, but the Be-6 that emerged was an altogether more capable aircraft. Intended from the start as a maritime patrol and antisubmarine aircraft, the aircraft has often been compared to the Martin Mariner because of some similarities in appearance. The most noticeable feature about the design was the high gull wing, which, just as in the case of the Mariner, was an excellent way of keeping the engines high and away from the spray without sacrificing aerodynamics as had previous Beriev models and other flying boats of the 1930s. Unlike previous designs, the Be-6 would be an amphibian, greatly increasing the overall utility of the project.

The aircraft began the design process in 1945 before the company returned from its wartime location and would emerge in 1947. At this stage, physical work had begun on the project still known then as LL-143, which first flew in September 1945. Sources differ as to whether the flight took place in Krasnoyarsk or back "home" at Taganrog. Regardless, development of the aircraft continued at Taganrog thereafter from 1947–1949, although before the project left Siberia, the initial aircraft was fully armed with six 12.7-mm (0.5-inch) machine guns and various bombloads. This can be relatively confusing as some sources will list a first flight in 1945, others in 1949 as a result. The simplified version is that the LL-143 first flew in 1945, but the production version of the Be-6 only flew in February 1949, with M. I. Tespilov at the controls. Essentially, the LL-143 was modified enough and enlarged enough that it emerged as the Be-6, a substantially different aircraft. For a start, the production Be-6 had more sophisticated equipment, including a retractable radome to the aft of the hull's second step, and ultimately a redesigned nose without the cannon armament. After three rounds of minor revisions, the aircraft was accepted for production.

The "final" aircraft was an all-metal, high-wing monoplane driven by a pair of Shvetsov Ash-72 radial engines, and the armament was completely changed. The Be-6 emerged with twin NS-23 23-mm cannon in a tail turret behind the twin rudder and fins and two more in a remotely controlled dorsal barbette, with a fifth such cannon in a bow turret initially that, as stated before, was later deleted. This was a much heavier and more capable armament than the 1945 LL-143, reflecting the lessons learnt during the Great Patriotic War. It is worth noting that at a later stage, the tail armament was replaced by what, to many eyes, would look like a very strange protuberance, but what was, in fact, an elongated housing for magnetic anomaly detection equipment, used to detect submarines. To carry out attacks on the submarines it was meant to hunt, the Be-6 came with various heavy offensive loads up to 8,800 lb (3,991 kg) including combinations of depth charges, mines, and torpedoes—mounted on pylons under the wings, outboard of the engines. It is lastly worth noting that the engines changed during the development process, eventually becoming the Shvetsov Ash-73TK eighteen-cylinder, air-cooled engines, which could generate 2,400 hp each.

Though the aircraft was designed to haul a relief crew, or up to forty troops as an assault transport, it was mostly used for patrol and ASW work as originally conceived, but also found a role as a search and rescue aircraft. It entered service with the Soviet Navy in September 1951, and remained in production until 1957, with a total of 123 aircraft being built. It was given the NATO reporting name of "Madge," and was a somewhat rare encounter for intercepting aircraft. Nevertheless, the Be-6 soldiered on until the early 1970s in naval service before being phased out, and even after that, a handful lingered in service as transport or fishery patrol aircraft into the late 1970s before finally being retired. A passenger version, known as the PLL-144, reached the stage of full-scale mock-up before it was cancelled. Along this long path, some of the Be-6s had their armament removed and replaced with additional fuel between 1955 and 1957, being thereafter known as Be-6K aircraft.

Around twenty Be-6s were sold to the Chinese in 1959–1960. These aircraft served in the same roles even longer than in the Soviet Union. Long enough, in fact, that the Shvetsov engines wore out long before the aircraft did and were replaced with Chinese-made Wopen WJ6 turboprop engines; they became known as the Qing-6. A dozen of these aircraft were still on hand with the Chinese People's Liberation Army Navy as of 1999, and at least two of these aircraft were still reported as active from the base at Qingdao in 2003.

Even as time and development moved on, the increasingly obsolete Be-6 would serve as the genesis of its own successor. In the late 1950s, it is believed that Beriev fit a Be-6 with turboprop engines in a test, and the successor aircraft would retain the gull wing and tail of the Be-6. This would ultimately result in the Be-12, which first flew in October 1960—continuing Beriev's propeller-based flying boats while the design bureau was pursuing jet development. In both regards, Beriev flying boats would continue to serve the Soviet Union; indeed, the company is still active today. Here, at least, the flying boat still finds a home. The Be-12, for instance, has soldiered on in service since the 1960s, continuing to operate today in small numbers. The latest aircraft from the company is the Beriev Be-200 Altair, which was introduced in 2003. As of 2016, these aircraft were leased to Portugal to help in combating forest fires.

This trio of Beriev flying boats forms an interesting circle of development that covers the entire period of this book from the early 1930s to the late 1940s. In this regard, taking the three aircraft as a cohesive whole is a good way to illustrate the process of development the flying boat underwent in this time. At the start, one must consider the MBR-2, with its high-mounted single engine—if not elegant to the eyes of a modern reader, this was nevertheless "state of the art" for the early 1930s. The Be-4 that followed was a much sleeker version of this concept, streamlined for the 1940s. Finally, the Be-6 adequately demonstrates the flying boat model that has worked successfully ever since: it was a highly influential design that continues to inform Russian military and civilian aviation to this day.

These aircraft served in different times, in different ways, and in different places, yet they all illustrate both the great uses and limitations of their designs and their times. Each was a necessary step in development that not only reveals what flying boats were meant to do in different decades, but also traces the origins of how they are still used today.

As a final aside to the interested reader, Beriev also has a fascinating history as part of Soviet development of Ekranoplanes—vehicles using ground effects to fly that take on strange and fascinating designs. This is well worth further investigation by anyone interested in the strange and unusual aspects of aviation. Moreover, Beriev is one of the key modern designers of flying boats.

2

Blériot 5190: Pioneer's Legacy

The name Blériot is one that has been written grandly across the early history of aviation. It is, of course, the name of the man who first flew across the English Channel in 1909, proving that the still-nascent aviation industry could create marvels. This single flight demonstrated that aircraft were more than just toys capable of short hops. Blériot's achievement also proved that aircraft could achieve increasingly great things. Naturally enough, Blériot himself was very much concerned with not just his own profit, but with advancing the science, and indeed the art, of aviation. His famous flight pointed the way towards aircraft ranging further and further afield with the passage of time. It was perhaps only a matter of time until his mind turned to flying boats.

Specifications

First Flight: 1933
Powerplant: Four Hispano-Suiza 12NBr engines, 650 hp each
Armament: None.
Top Speed: 131 mph (210 kph)
Range/Service Ceiling: 3,100 miles (5,000 km), 16,730 feet (5,100 metres)
Dimensions: Length 141 feet (43 metres), height 22 feet 8 inches (6.9 metres), wingspan 85 feet 3 inches (26 metres)
Number Built: One completed, three under early construction

Though it is a distantly forgotten fact today, there was a time when the Blériot 5190 was one of the world's largest aircraft—mentioned in the company of famed past aircraft like the Dornier Do X and the Sikorsky S.40, representing the state of the art for the time. Unlike those aircraft, however, the 5190 was created by a very different impetus. Those aircraft represented dreams of technology and the regular flying of passengers over large distances, and the 5190 was designed entirely to carry something different and, at the time, perhaps more lucrative: mail. The story of the Blériot 5190 helps to underline a paradoxical process in which the French, despite possessing excellent designs, frittered away any advantage through bureaucratic incompetence. The Blériot 5190 was to form a triumvirate with the Couzinet 70 and the Latécoère 300, the latter of which is described in more detail in a later chapter. The corruptive process that ended up benefitting the Latécoère 300 is also described there.

To build a competitive aircraft for a potentially lucrative market, the company made use of the talents of Italian designer and engineer Filippo Zappata, who designed a unique four-engined aircraft that remains unusual to the observer even today. For a start, the aircraft's engines were installed three across in the front, with the fourth as a pusher behind the central front engine. Overall, it was a high-wing monoplane, made of duralumin, with a strongly-built hull meant to be very seaworthy. The hull and pontoons were both of a two-step design to facilitate easier take-off. The pontoons were given what essentially amounted to double bracing, being attached both to the wing and the hull. Above the hull, the design took on its most obviously apparent unique feature, with the high wing being connected to the hull by a ship-like central superstructure. This was by itself over 13 feet long (4 metres), and over 8 feet high (2.5 metres), though only just under 4 feet wide (1.2 metres). This tall, long, but thin structure had to contain the four crew members: commander, pilot, co-pilot, and mechanic. The pilot did at least have excellent visibility, being installed at the very front of the superstructure. Inside the hull were sixteen separate fuel tanks, carrying a total of 3,086 gallons (11,684 litres). The aircraft had an aluminum colour all over, shining silver in life—apart from the lower portion of the pontoons and fuselage, which were rust-brown.

The top of the superstructure also formed part of the wing, making them essentially one solid piece. The main wings were joined to this centre section and braced by two steel struts mounted on each side of the superstructure. There were two main wing spars, with interior bracing, and the exterior of the main wings was fabric-covered, typical of the time. In a fairly typical move for these large, ocean-going flying boat designs, the wing was made thick enough to effect in-flight repairs of the engines.

The first flight was carried out at Caudebec-en-Caux, on August 3, 1933. At the controls were Lucien Bossoutrot, the company's chief test pilot, and Zappata himself. The aircraft lifted off from the Seine—not precisely an ideal launching ground for a large flying boat—in a mere seventeen seconds, with a total weight of 35,718 lb (16,200 kg). Interestingly, it was flown in this first test flight without the design's elliptical wing tips, which when installed would have brought the wingspan up to a width beyond that of the hangar it emerged from.

Four and a half months of tests followed for the aircraft, not only at Caudebec-en-Caux, but also at Cherbourg, before completion was successfully achieved in early January 1934. The aircraft was given the name "Santos-Dumont," after the famous early aviator; Blériot was, in effect, paying tribute to a fellow pioneer—a gesture full of gallantry that was typical of an aviator of the era.

F-ANLE at rest on the water. (*Photograph from the Johan Visschedijk collection, 1000aircraftphotos.com*)

The same aircraft at her moorings. (*Photograph from the Nico Braas collection, 1000aircraftphotos.com*)

Though the aircraft had been created to fulfil the need of *Aéropostale*, its service would prove to be something else entirely. In 1933, several French airlines were merged together. *Aéropostale* was one of them, and the effort created a name that is still familiar in the present day: Air France. There were some major advantages to the amalgamation. Each company built in to the new company already had a well-developed set of routes that spanned France's empire and beyond. All told, the new airline inherited an existing route structure of 27,000 miles (43,452 km). Another advantage was it inherited all the aircraft, a grand total of 259. The majority were land-based aircraft, but at least thirty-three were seaplanes of various descriptions. The 5190 would be finished and flown under these new auspices.

The French Air Ministry loaned the aircraft out to Air France by November 1934, and the aircraft was soon ready for its first operational test. It was to carry the mail from France to Natal in Brazil via Dakar. With Bossoutrot again at the controls, the aircraft made its first jaunt across the South Atlantic from Dakar on November 27, 1934, arriving without incident in Brazil after a total time of sixteen hours and fifteen minutes. Another trial crossing followed the next month, and the reliable aircraft then was put into regular, weekly service, carrying out nine more flights between February and April 1935. A three-month break followed, then the aircraft began the pattern all over again, with the aircraft making thirty regular delivery flights in all, without any hiccup worth recording.

This accomplished, it was time for a lengthy and complete overhaul. The aircraft was moved to Étang de Berre, near Marseilles, for this purpose where it would stay for a year before returning to the Natal run. The aircraft would be withdrawn from service in June 1937 after completing a total of thirty-seven mail flights. More aircraft were ostensibly meant to join it. The 5190 had, after all, proven more than adequate to the task and in fact had established a reputation for reliability. However, it was at this point that internal forces within the French bureaucracy took a hand—forces that had little reference to objective standards. These will be discussed in detail later in the chapter on the Latécoère 300 but suffice to say that there was definite favouritism at play.

The tragedy of the bureaucratic processes was that Blériot himself—a French national hero—would pay the price, rather than anyone else. La Société Blériot Aéronautique received a contract to build another three 5190 aircraft from the French government in 1935, given the aircraft's success on the transatlantic route. Louis Blériot borrowed a major amount of money to be able to engage in what would be a massive construction process, amounting to a total of 5 million francs. Almost at that moment, the contract was withdrawn, and Blériot was left with nothing save his reputation. No explanation was given for the cancellation, nor was any compensation forthcoming. He would die of a heart attack in 1936, the position of his company unrecovered, while Air France still flew his aircraft. The firm would never recover and the Blériot 5190 would prove to be the last aircraft to bear the name of one of France's greatest aviation heroes.

The story of the Blériot 5190 at first glance appears to be nothing more than that of a single aircraft that served for a while before being taken out of service and promptly forgotten as events overtook France both in peace and war. What the story instead reveals is that even an unusual, unorthodox aircraft could be more than sufficient to a task, and the 5190 certainly was that. The history of French aircraft in the 1930s is one replete with unusual designs, some more successful than others. Yet the story of Blériot's last aircraft is also one that reveals a trend that would in peacetime ruin the company of a French hero and would, in different ways, continue into the war and the Fall of France. The issue for the French in the 1930s and into 1940 was not that their companies could not produce serviceable and even stellar designs—they certainly could—but that issues in the bureaucracy and industry, having nothing to do with design, would undermine France in subtle and not so subtle ways.

In the end, the Blériot 5190 was the last of a lineage, and but for the decision of bureaucrats, it might have become a regular sight over the South Atlantic. Perhaps, had the contract been kept and had the French government kept their promise, this unusual design could have become better known, and perhaps there could have been more aircraft bearing the proud name Blériot.

3

Blohm und Voss BV 138: Germany's Trimotor Flying Boat

Blohm und Voss started life in 1877 as a shipbuilder, which remains a role that it fulfils to this very day. Some of their earliest work included the "Flying P" liners, four of which have survived to the present: the *Passat* remains at Travemünde in her native Germany; the *Peking* lies at anchor as a museum in New York City, in the United States; the *Pommern* can be found in Mariehamn, Finland; and lastly, and most interestingly, the *Padua* is still in active service—taken as a war reparation by the Soviet Union in 1946, she serves the Russian navy to this day as the *Kruzenshtern*. This last is perhaps an apt sort of irony, for the war that brought the *Kruzenshtern* to Russia was one that built up the aircraft wing of Blohm und Voss considerably, and planes with the prefix 'BV' would ably serve the German Luftwaffe throughout the war. The company was one in crisis in the early 1930s, but the sudden restoration of the German arms industry under Hitler's Nazi Party bore up their fortunes. The company would in many ways mirror the darkness that engulfed the German state. By the end of the war, they would be using inmates of a concentration sub camp as labourers, one of many German companies that actively participated in the brutal exploitation of enslaved people—many of them still quite active today. The post-war Blohm und Voss, long since shed of its wartime past, no longer makes aircraft of any kind, but for a time, their flying boats were not only a major component of the Luftwaffe's maritime strength, but in some cases grew enormous.

However, it is instructive to start much smaller. The Blohm und Voss BV 138 was, and remains, a strange-looking design at the outset. While officially called the *Seedrache*, or Sea Dragon, it was known as the "flying clog"—a reference to its unusual profile. Yet this unusual aircraft did sterling service, taking on a multitude of forms.

Specifications

First Flight: 1937
Powerplant: Three Junkers Jumo 205D opposed piston diesel engines, 868 hp each
Armament: Two 20-mm MG 151 cannons, one in nose turret and the other in the rear fuselage, one 13-mm (0.51-inch) MG 131 machine gun in open position

behind the central fuselage, up to three 7.92-mm (0.3-inch) MG 15 machine guns as an option, and six 50-kg (110-lb) bombs or four 150-kg (330-lb) depth charges under the starboard wing root

Top Speed: 177 mph (285 kph)

Range/Service Ceiling: 2,670 miles (4,300 km), 16,400 feet (5,000 metres)

Dimensions: Length 65 feet 1½ inches (19.85 metres), height 19 feet 4 inches (5.90 metres), wingspan 88 feet 4½ inches (26.94 metres)

Number Built: 297

When the time came to build aircraft for German military service, Blohm und Voss used its subsidiary Hamburger Flugzeugwerke to spearhead the project. The origin point for the BV 138 can be found in design studies that the company carried out as early as 1934. The impetus for military designs came from even before this. Importantly, the BV 138 would be designed from the start to not just be a military flying boat, but also reveals important facts about pre-war Germany. While civilian designs were another matter, it was illegally designed as a military aircraft long before the resurgent German Luftwaffe was formally announced in February 1935. This points to two facts: first, German military designing did not stop in the Weimar period, as some might believe; in most cases, corporations simply hid their work or moved it to neutral third countries, such as the Krupp firm moving their submarine building operations to the Netherlands. As a result, military design remained current, and so did German air practice and theory, through thinly-disguised air clubs, "mail" planes, and secret pilot training agreements with the Russians. Thus, by 1934, Blohm und Voss was able to hit the ground running, without having to catch up on years of research.

Secondly, Blohm und Voss, like most of Germany's major corporate concerns, correctly read the direction that their bellicose, and increasingly monstrous, government was heading. Long before Hitler formally declared the Treaty of Versailles repudiated, the conditions were in place—both industrially and in design—to rapidly create full fighting arms for the German state. In essence, the companies had the know-how and were ready and eager to fulfil the demands for a war machine they knew was coming.

The BV 138, as a result, was already being created as a military reconnaissance aircraft a year before it was openly required; though it would not make its first flight until 1937. Despite knowing well in advance which way the wind was blowing, the project would have a difficult birth. This was unfortunate from the German point of view, because as early as 1938, the choice had been made that the project would be used to replace the Dornier Do 18 for long-range reconnaissance.

Development officially began as a project dubbed Ha 138, under the control of Hamburger Flugzeugwerke's chief designer, *Dr. Ing.* Richard Vogt. Originally, the aircraft was designed for two engines, though there was some ambiguity as to what the powerplant would be. Three prototypes were to be constructed, each utilizing engines from a different manufacturer, each rated at 1,000 hp

The Ha 138 V2 aircraft, in pre-war colours. (*Photograph from the Ron Dupas collection, 1000aircraftphotos.com*)

so comparative evaluations could take place. Delays in the development of engine programs—a fairly common problem that would increasingly impact the Luftwaffe—necessitated a change, and the design was reworked to carry three of an already fully-developed engine, the Junkers Jumo 205C, rated at 650 hp each. This accounted for the two-year delay between the first mock-up and the first powered flight. On July 15, 1937, the first prototype, Ha 138 V1, flew, closely followed by V2 in November. The V2 prototype had a modified hull design, and both were tested at the Travemünde test center. Major problems quickly became apparent, both in terms of airborne and waterborne handling.

Initially, it was felt that a redesign of the tail section would suffice to handle the aircraft's issues, and the vertical tail surfaces were modified. This did not solve the problem, and a radical redesign proved necessary. The hull shape itself was flawed, being prone to excessive drag in the water. The solution to such a flaw was extensive, of necessity. The hull was enlarged significantly, the planing surfaces were refined, and the new tail surfaces were to be carried by more substantial booms. This aircraft was given the "BV" prefix, and emerged as the BV 138A, with five aircraft following the initial prototype.

As a result of all the modifications, flight testing of the pre-production aircraft did not get under way until April 1940. Here, coincidental timing took a hand in the aircraft's development. By that point, German forces were invading Norway and Denmark, an operation that required reconnaissance flying boats, and the Germans certainly believed they needed more than were available. Owing to this, the BV 138A was hurriedly pressed into service after a shortened evaluation time. The aircraft that was thrown into combat featured a single 20-mm cannon in a bow turret and two 7.92-mm (0.31-ichn) MG 15 machine guns in open positions behind the centre engine nacelle, at the rear of the hull. A total of three aircraft were available for this operation, which was hardly enough to fulfil the need for transport, but it emphasizes the urgency of that same need.

This was, as logic and common sense may reveal, hardly the best possible move for the Germans. Problems were encountered in the 138A with both the engines and propellers. The result was an extensive redesign program that resulted in the version the Germans should have pursued in the first place with more thorough testing, the BV 138C. The 138C was the end result, but the first improvement was the BV 138B. The 138B resulted from hull strengthening and the installation of new Jumo 205I engines developing 880 hp. A 20-mm MG 151 cannon was added to the rear hull position in addition to the bow weapon, along with provision for up to 150 kg (331 lb) of bombs beneath the starboard wing root. Including the BV 138B-0 prototype, a total of nineteen aircraft designated 138B-1 were built before further strengthening was added and a 13-mm (0.51-inch) MG 131 gun was installed behind the engine centre nacelle. The main variant was the BV 138C-1. This aircraft had a pair of 20-mm MG 151s, keeping the rear gun and adding one in a nose turret. It could also have up to three optional MG 15s, but also carried a 13-mm (0.51-inch) MG 131 that covered the top rear area, being situated in an open position behind the central engine. It could also carry up to six 50-kg (110-lb) bombs or four 150-kg (330-lb) bombs under the starboard wing root. The BV 138C formed the vast majority of the production run, comprising 228 examples.

There is one other production variant worthy of note, and that is the unusual, or even more unusual, considering the BV 138's design, BV 138 MS. Built specifically as a minesweeping aircraft, the aircraft came with a large degaussing loop of dural installed around the airframe, with field-generating equipment equipped and all armament deleted. All the aircraft put to this task were converted from the BV 138B.

The BV 138 was deployed briefly in the Atlantic but would make most of its contribution in the northern reaches of that body of water, as well as be seen in the Baltic and North Sea. In early engagements against Allied aircraft, the "flying shoe" did quite well: it downed a Bristol Blenheim and a Consolidated Catalina, one of the very rare occasions upon which a flying boat downed another flying boat in combat. The BV 138C was well-suited to these operations, having a maximum endurance in the air of sixteen and a half hours. While its main duty was maritime reconnaissance, the 138 also took on the task of attacking convoys, blowing up acoustic mines, radar reconnaissance, and even troop carrying.

In terms of hunting convoys, the crews of the BV 138 developed a dangerous tactic to increase their effectiveness: they would land their aircraft on the open ocean and wait for convoys to come along. In this role, they could wait for up to three days. Owing to its range, endurance, and this "boost" in terms of how long it could be on patrol, the BV 138 became a major part of German anti-convoy operations. They took part in several sharp convoy battles, and the most famous of these was the mauling of convoy PQ-17 to the Soviet Union. Hounded by both the *Luftwaffe* and submarines, the convoy would lose two thirds of its ships.

A production BV 138 being winched aboard a seaplane tender in Norwegian waters during the war. (*Photograph courtesy of the Naval History and Heritage Command*)

Wartime photograph of a German seaplane tender with BV 138s aboard, off of Tromsø, Norway. (*Photograph courtesy of the Naval History and Heritage Command*)

Early on, there was relatively little chance of interception. Aircraft like the BV 138 and the Focke-Wulf Fw 200 Condor could range freely, challenged only rarely by other aircraft. Yet the arrival of aircraft carriers in the convoy battle radically shifted the balance of power in the air. Initially, this involved Royal Navy Hawker Sea Hurricanes, and when they first encountered a BV 138C in September 1942, they mauled it severely, subjecting it to an hour and a half of hounding.

From 1943 until the end of the war, the "flying shoe" (a name given to it by its opponents) suffered more and more heavily. It had a relatively low air speed, and Allied fighters were only increasing in numbers and abilities. Much like its larger Blohm und Voss cousin, the BV 222, the BV 138 could not operate as boldly in its small overall numbers. One interesting incident around this time did break radically from this pattern. In the summer of 1943, some BV 138C aircraft operated for three months from a secret base set up in Soviet territory by German U-boats. Given their range and this far advanced post, the seaplanes flew as far as the Yamal peninsula—1,000 miles east of Moscow and were believed to operate at least that same distance to the north of it. The BV 138s used for this purpose thus held the distinction of making the furthest penetration into enemy territory of any Axis aircraft. The flying boats would support extensive German operations in the Arctic Circle to set up and maintain meteorological stations, but these far-ranging secret flights were unique.

This was not to be the last unusual achievement of the BV 138. The last would come in the most unlikely of places: the final stages of the Battle of Berlin. One of the last surviving BV 138s dodged a hail of Soviet fire on May 1, 1945, under the control of Wolfgang Klemusch, and set down on one of Berlin's lakes. His mission was to take on two sealed envelopes, but in the chaos of the Reich's final moments, he refused to take them on as the bearer could not say what they were. Instead, he flew out ten wounded soldiers, taking them to Copenhagen. As it transpired, the documents were the final words of Adolf Hitler: his last will and testament.

No part of the BV 138 program remains today, no sign of one of the strangest-looking flying boats of the war, but for a time, it was the eyes of German might at sea, a capable hunter and attacker of Allied convoys. As will be demonstrated, all Blohm und Voss' major—and increasingly gigantic—flying boat programs during the war resulted in nothing save photographs and sparse documents today.

A BV 138 being pulled out the water for servicing at Kirkenes, Norway. In the background, a Heinkel He 115 can be seen. (*Photograph courtesy of the Naval History and Heritage Command*)

A BV 138 picking up her mooring buoy at Kirkenes. Note the deployment of weaponry under the inboard wing, and also the four-bladed propeller on the inboard engine. (*Photograph courtesy of the Naval History and Heritage Command*)

4

Blohm und Voss BV 222: Powerful Viking

By the 1940s, flying boats were reaching an apex in size and power. As their capabilities grew, so did the roles for which they were designed, which necessitated larger and larger sizes. The later years of World War II would see flying boats successively claim the title of largest aircraft in the world, some of them with a capability that matched their size. For Germany and the Luftwaffe, Blohm und Voss would turn out two titanic flying boats. The first was the BV 222 *Wiking*, or Viking.

This titan was a demonstration of the practical power of the flying boat in specialized roles, as by this time land-based aircraft had long since dominated primary air combat roles. An aircraft of prodigious size, the *Wiking* was in the main a transport—a role that, in the late war years, was one that flying boats could excel at.

Specifications

First Flight: 1940
Powerplant: Six Junkers Jumo 207C twelve-cylinder inline diesel engines, 1,000 hp each
Armament: Three 20-mm MG 151/20 cannons, one each forward and wing turrets, five 13-mm (0.51-inch) MG 131 machine guns, one in the nose and four in beam positions
Top Speed: 205 mph (330 kph)
Range/Service Ceiling: 3,790 miles (6,100 km), 23,950 feet (7,300 metres)
Dimensions: Length 121 feet 5 inches (37 metres), height 35 feet 9 inches (10.9 metres), wingspan 150 feet 11 inches (46 metres)
Number Built: Thirteen

Given the secretive military birth of its smaller cousin, it is perhaps a bit ironic that the BV 222 began life not as an ambitious project for the Luftwaffe, but for Germany's premier civilian carrier, the Lufthansa. In 1937, the company issued a requirement for a long-range passenger transport, capable of flying between Berlin and New York within twenty hours with sixteen passengers in sleeper berths, or to accommodate up to twenty-four passengers for shorter routes (the specifics regarding passengers were added as a later detail, in December 1937, after the aircraft had already been ordered). Three companies were in the running for the contract. Heinkel would submit a design labelled as the He 120 (then later He 220), believing four engines more than adequate. Dornier, also in the running, submitted the Do 20 proposal, which in many ways was an evolved Dornier Do X, featured later in this book. This modernized design would feature four paired sets of engines, so a total of eight engines would drive four propellers—a concept that in other aircraft proved very difficult in execution. For Blohm und Voss, the design was undertaken by *Dr. Ing.* Richard Vogt and *Herr* R. Schubert, Blohm und Voss's chief of aerodynamics and hydrodynamics. Vogt's proposal was quickly taken up as having the most potential, with its rivals never getting past the model stage.

The design had some noteworthy features in addition to sheer size, though even at this early stage, construction began with six 1,000-hp BMW-Bramo Fafnir 323R radials just to power it. For a start, the design featured an extensive unobstructed floor area. This was achieved by having a beam of nearly 10 feet (3.05 metres), with no obstructing bulkheads above floor level. The wing was built around a tubular main spar, and contained fuel and oil tanks. The stabilizing floats at the edge of the wings were innovative, too, splitting in halves to retract sideways into the wings—a rare feature for any flying boats.

The BV 222 V1 aircraft, possibly on tests. (*Photograph from the Bill Pippin collection, 1000aircraftphotos.com*)

Lufthansa formally issued a contract on August 19, 1937, and three aircraft were ordered in September, with design work on the first example beginning in January 1938 and construction following in September. Work on the second and third prototypes began a few weeks after that.

The war would overtake the project, however, and the military applications of the design would overtake this initially civilian project. Yet in the immediate sense, the war caused a slowdown in work on completing the giant. Skilled labour was most notably drawn away to try to speed the BV 138 program, now considered critical. This exacerbated an already slow development process since the Germans had precious little experience to draw upon in terms of designing an enormous, modern flying boat. The V1 aircraft first flew on September 7, 1940, under the command of *Flugkapitän* Helmut Wasa Rodig, having already successfully completed flotation testing and taxi trials.

The testing process proved that the flight handling characteristics of the giant were more than adequate, but the flying boat did tend to become unstable in horizontal flight. On the water, there was also the significant issue that it would begin to lurch from side to side when taxiing. These problems would be worked on as the prototype aircraft made its way into service. For the moment, extensive flights and tweaks were performed until December 1940, when ice on the Elbe River precluded further work. Here, the air force stepped in.

Even by the time the aircraft flew, it was obvious that the Lufthansa would never receive its aircraft. The military potential of the design had been clear from the beginning, and the Luftwaffe was in significant need of heavy transport aircraft. The military proposed setting up a transport testing program between Germany and Occupied Norway, to combine experimental work with practical duties and thus save precious fuel. Soon afterwards, the V1 was fitted with enlarged doors and a military camouflage scheme for these duties and made its first test flight as a military transport on July 10, 1941, flying between Hamburg and Kirkenes in Norway. By August, the program had been deemed a success, with the V1 having completed seven flights. In 120 hours of flight time for the program, it carried 143,300 lb (65,000 kg) of supplies to Norway and flew back 221 wounded personnel to Germany. The aircraft was then given a general overhaul and put into immediate formal service.

This first aircraft wandered far in its service, having started its career on the Germany–Norway route before being transferred to the Mediterranean to ferry supplies to German soldiers of the *Afrika Korps*. The prototype flew the route between Athens and Derna seventeen times between October 16 and November 6, 1941, ferrying 66,138 lb (30,000 kg) of supplies and carrying out 515 wounded personnel. In this role, the BV 222 V1 was escorted at all times by a pair of Messerschmitt Bf 110 heavy fighters as, since she was so new, she had not yet received armament. In this capacity, the huge flying boat had several lucky escapes from Allied fighter aircraft, and the need for defensive armament became clear. One of these escapes involved the aircraft surviving an attack by three heavily-armed Beaufighters on a flight between Taranto and Tripoli.

The BV 222 V3 aircraft on operations. (*Photograph courtesy of Dan Shumaker*)

Armament was first fitted to the second and third prototypes, which had first flown in August and November 1941. The third aircraft received very light armament at first, carrying only a 7.92-mm (0.31-inch) MG 81 machine gun in the bow, but this was augmented by gun turrets on top of the wings between the outboard engines, which each came with a 20-mm cannon. By comparison, the second aircraft had other MG 81 weapons mounted in four waist positions, and in two upper turrets, but also carried a pair of 13-mm (0.5-inch) MG 131 guns, installed in two gondolas located beneath the centre section. Retroactively, the first aircraft was armed with an MG 81 in the nose, a pair of DL 131 turrets firing MG 131s were placed in the upper fuselage, and four more MG 81s were installed in side stations.

The V1 was naturally the first aircraft officially adopted for service, being delivered to *Lufttransportstaffel* (*See*) 222 on May 10, 1942. The second prototype would follow in August, having been put through her paces at Erprobungsstelle Travemünde, which resulted in the addition of a modified planing bottom to improve her handling on the water. Overall, water handling would be improved utilizing propeller reverse thrust on the middle engine on each wing. Performance was also finally assessed and found to be acceptable. The BV 222 in service could fly, if it was so required, from Hamburg to New York without stopping, with a maximum range of 4,349 miles (7,000 km). It was further intended that it could also carry ninety-two fully equipped soldiers or seventy-two wounded on stretchers. All told, these three prototypes and the next two aircraft were brought into Luftwaffe service as the BV 222A. Even before receiving its formal designation and acceptance in August 1941, the V1 had covered a distance of some 19,000 miles (30,000 km). All told, by the end of 1942 the handful of aircraft have been noted by some sources to have carried a total of 3,478 tons of supplies, along with 37,528 soldiers, and as many as 5,169 wounded.

By March 1943, seven of these gargantuan transports had been completed and delivered to service, becoming part of *Lufttransportstaffel* 222 in the Mediterranean. In combat usage, the aircraft still proved vulnerable, despite its armament and size, when caught by enemy fighters, with two being shot down by fighter aircraft. One of these was the V6, struck down by Beaufighters south of the island of Pantelleria on its way to Tripoli. The Germans altered their flight routes, but since the 222s flew according to a precise plan, the British soon figured out where to intercept them again, striking them only on the way to Africa when they were carrying supplies, and leaving them be on the return flight when they carried wounded soldiers.

A third, the original V1, was lost in mid-February 1943 when it struck a buoy on landing at Piraeus Harbour outside Athens. The aircraft had been forced to set down in total darkness owing to an air raid alarm and the hull was ripped open and the aircraft sank in a few minutes. By this time, it had already made seventeen successful flights in its supply role. The remaining aircraft (the V2 through V5) were converted over to maritime reconnaissance aircraft and four of them were equipped with FuG 200 Hohentwiel search radar before being transferred to Fliegerführer Atlantik with 1.(Fern)/*Seeaufklärungsgruppe* 129. These aircraft also took on more state-of-the-art equipment: FuG 16 radar for command guided target approach, FuG 25A Identification Friend or Foe (IFF) radar, and the FuG 101A radio altimeter. These aircraft were found to be very well suited to the Atlantic, as long as they stayed away from aircraft carriers. At a reduced speed, these aircraft could remain airborne for up to thirty-three hours.

They also received revised armament, which comprised three power-operated dorsal turrets, with two more at quarter-span positions above the wings. Two of them, the V3 and V5, would be destroyed at their moorings at Biscarosse by Allied fighters in June 1943. In a somewhat unusual situation, a third (V4) was supposedly destroyed in October 1942 by a U.S. Navy B-24 Liberator over the Bay of Biscay under the command of one Lieutenant Evert—one of the "biggest" air-to-air actions that could have occurred in terms of the size of aircraft involved. Sources are not in agreement on this point. Several found by the author contradict this story, with some claiming it was an Avro Lancaster that shot down the V4, and others that it was the V4—working in conjunction with the V2—that brought the Allied aircraft down. Given later listed incidents involving the V4, the author is inclined to believe it at least survived the incident. It is further described as being damaged in combat on December 10, 1942, when the V1, V4, and V8 were flying just over 16 feet (5 metres) over sea level. British aircraft flew under them at just under 7 feet (2 metres) over a smooth sea before pulling up into their formation. The V4 was given a mauling but stayed airborne. The V1 escaped unharmed, but the V8 was forced down and exploded on contact with the water.

At this point, the Germans also considered using the BV 222 to make flights to Japan, since after the invasion of the Soviet Union, standard flights to the Far East were impossible. Making these journeys via surface vessel was near impossible, and it was nearly as deadly for German U-boats since, by this point, the Allies had regular access to German codes. Blohm und Voss's titanic flying boat was one of three aircraft considered for this, with a route planned from Kirkenes to Tokyo via Sakhalin Island in an aircraft modified for very long-range flight. The BV 222 had drawbacks in this capacity, aside from the fact that it was not in any way designed for this operation. The Navy High Command, *Oberkommando der Marine* (OKM), realized that Blohm und Voss would have an extremely low rate of completion for these enormous aircraft, which could be no more than one per month. In *Luftwaffe over America*, Griehl states that the Luftwaffe's command staff summarized their view for the 222 thusly: "The difficult supply and transport situation means we have to employ all long-range aircraft, including large flying boats, as transports, though we do so with reservations." Ultimately, the Junkers Ju 290 was chosen instead. The third aircraft considered was the Heinkel He 177, and this decision in the Junker's favour was likely for the best given the 177's unreliability owing to frequent engine fires—though the project ultimately came to nothing in any event.

The V7 aircraft served as prototype for the BV 222C production series (the designation BV 222B was given to a civil version of the aircraft that was planned but never produced). The 222C series introduced either the Jumo 205B (only one aircraft was fitted with these—later changed for 205D models) or 207C engines as well as additional armament. These diesel engines were chosen because they opened up the possibility of refuelling these aircraft at sea via U-boat. Five pre-production examples of this were built as a planned prelude to a production series, but the RLM decided to end the use of diesel engines, and ultimately no more than thirteen aircraft were completed in sum. They also suffered further losses in operation, with one shot down by a night fighter near Biscarosse, and another destroyed by strafing P-51 Mustangs at Travemünde. According to one source, the aircraft downed at Biscarosse was the V3, which had been evaluated in the Bay of Biscay for the maritime reconnaissance role of locating convoys and then passing that information on to bomber aircraft and the U-boats.

One interesting aside is the role that a single BV 222 took on in supporting one of Germany's secret meteorological stations in the high arctic. The Germans had set up a manned station on the island of Alexandra Land, which was being supplied by an Fw 200 Condor. In the spring of 1944, some of the men fell sick from eating raw meat, suffering from serious pain and high fever. The men were diagnosed as suffering from trichinosis, a type of roundworm infection. On July 7, a physician was dispatched on a Condor. Rather than insisting that he parachute out, as he had for previous missions, the pilot landed, and in the process, one of the main landing wheels collapsed. An urgent message was sent to the base at Banak in the extreme north of Norway, and a BV 222 that was ready as a standby aircraft at Bille-Fjord was dispatched to drop the replacement wheel and parts; as a result, the Condor was able to take-off, carrying away the station's sick crew.

By war's end, what aircraft of the series remained could only be found in the comparative calm of the Baltic, flying out sick and wounded soldiers until the end of the war. It is remarkable that apparently six aircraft remained in flying condition come the war's end, in part because they lived such a dangerous life for a large aircraft. Operating in at best very small numbers, they were in near-constant danger from fighters, with the additional nerve-wracking procedure (which wrecked the V1) of having to suddenly and dangerously set down at night in order to avoid British bombers. Of course, when the war ended, the Germans who operated and maintained the aircraft were loath to let them fall into enemy hands, which resulted in the scuttling of some of them. Two of the remaining aircraft would be sunk by their own crews rather than have these aircraft captured, and the V2—by now a veteran aircraft—was destroyed during the Allied liberation of Norway, being scuttled by the British in 1946.

Sources disagree as to what precisely happened to the remaining BV 222s at the end of the war. According to one account, two aircraft were captured after the German surrender, with one going to the United States and the other going to England—being sent on to the Marine Aircraft Experimental Establishment at Felixstowe for testing. Ultimately, it would be passed on to No. 201 Squadron for testing before being scrapped in 1947. Another account holds that three aircraft were captured (separate from the V2), with two going to the Americans and the remaining aircraft heading on to England as otherwise told.

The American aircraft had one of two fates. Some accounts hold that at least one was still flyable, though airtime was brief owing to engine fires stemming from substandard materials used by the Germans at war's end. This aircraft was supposedly sunk by a destroyer, but other accounts hold that both aircraft were either flown or shipped to the United States where at least one was earmarked for Convair's hull design studies as part of the R3Y Tradewind program, after which they disappear from the record. Other sources claim that at least one BV 222 was used for information that may have wound up in the Hughes Hercules program before it was scrapped.

The enormous aircraft was test-flown by Captain Eric "Winkle" Brown, easily one of the most accomplished pilots in the history of aviation based on the sheer variety of types and experiences he was involved with. Brown noted the control system: "… in the huge BV 222 flying boat they used servo-tab controls on all three axes, which in my opinion made them almost dangerously light for that particular aircraft."

Brown was given the opportunity to test the giant before it was sent on to Calshot for further evaluation. Brown "worked his way up" to the task with practice on smaller German flying boats, including the aforementioned BV 138, before arriving in Trondheim to fly what was as far as he was aware at the time the only airworthy BV 222 remaining in the world. Brown himself tells the story of what happened best:

> I made another request for the loan of a German pilot to help me learn the taps, and was given a Luftwaffe major, who sat in the first-pilot's seat, with me at his side. He seemed to have been expecting me.
>
> He started the engines and, with everything going flat-out, we were soon tearing up Trondheim Fiord. We roared on and on over the gleaming water. When we had gone what seemed for miles and were still flat on the surface, going very fast and taking a tremendous buffeting from the water, I realized that something was very wrong.
>
> I grabbed the stick from the German and tried to ease it back. It was locked solid. He had not taken any of the control locks out. He was deliberately trying to wreck the boat. I cut the throttles.
>
> I heaved him out of the seat, yelled to the crew to hold on to him, and got the control locks freed. I couldn't waste time taking him all the way back, so I taxied her a little way back down the fiord and started again.
>
> *Wings on my Sleeve*, p. 125
> Eric Brown

This dangerous moment aside, Brown found the enormous boat pleasant to fly, taking particular notice of the enormous cockpit compared to some of the other innumerable aircraft he would test fly in his remarkable career.

Interestingly, one of the likely aircraft flown by Brown—possibly the V2—was supposedly filled with BV 222 spare parts from the Ilsvika base to weigh her down. The British then scuttled the aircraft, where according to some sources, she rests in excellent condition owing to the low oxygen content of the water. There are, apparently, plans to raise the aircraft.

The BV 222 ultimately was never used for the peaceful purpose for which it was originally ordered, but it did serve extensively as a heavy transport aircraft wherever it was required. The range and heavy capacity of such aircraft were huge attributes, but no matter how heavily defended they were, these giants proved vulnerable in combat conditions to much smaller, land-based aircraft. Somewhere in that is a decided metaphor for what was happening to the flying boat in general by the mid- to late 1940s, but in a more specific sense, it showcased the vulnerability of small numbers of large aircraft operating on their own, with, at best, light fighter escort.

The BV 222 remains one of the titans: among the largest flying boats ever to be constructed, and certainly the largest to see regular military service. It certainly did its duty, whatever its vulnerabilities to other aircraft, and remains a potent symbol of both the achievements and limitations of German air power and design.

5

Blohm und Voss BV 238: Germany's Last Titan

The second of Blohm und Voss's titanic designs, the BV 238, never existed beyond the prototype phase, but the design was the largest flying boat to take to the skies during World War II, and easily one of the largest flying boats ever. The brief life of the BV 238 provides an ample demonstration of size and power, but the story of this aircraft is one with significant controversy attached—well worth the study of the reader. Physically, it was the largest Axis aircraft of the entire war, and one of the heaviest of the conflict overall, outweighing even the mighty Boeing B-29 Superfortress.

Specifications

First Flight: 1944
Powerplant: Six Daimler-Benz DB603G inverted V-12 liquid-cooled piston engines, 1,900 hp each
Armament: None mounted on prototype
Top Speed: 264 mph (425 kph)
Range/Service Ceiling: 4,113 miles (6,620 km), 23,950 feet (7,300 metres)
Dimensions: Length 142 feet 3 inches (43.35 metres), height 42 feet (12.8 metres) wingspan 197 feet 5 inches (60.17 metres)
Number Built: One, with two incomplete prototypes

Dr. Vogt had, as early as 1940, begun design work on a massive eight-engined flying boat for Lufthansa, meant to carry 120 passengers a total distance of 5,343 miles (8,600 km). This dovetailed nicely with design work being undertaken to eventually replace the BV 138. This project was tentatively designated P.200, but it never progressed beyond the design stage. By 1941, the RLM put a stop to this civilian designing in order to feed the emergency needs of the German war machine.

They instead wanted a large multi-role flying boat that was to be powered by four Junkers Jumo 223 diesel engines, each meant to develop 2,500 hp. These troublesome engines never reached a reliable form, which meant that the project had to be dropped. As a result, Dr. Vogt went back to the drawing board and, in the final analysis, submitted what was in essence an enlarged BV 222. The initial plans called for six Daimler-Benz DB 603 engines in the first three completed aircraft, with the fourth to carry six BMW 801 engines. The designation BV 238 was attached to the project. The first three aircraft were to fulfil what was termed the BV 238A production model, with subsequent models with the air-cooled BMWs to be the BV 238B model.

While it did start life as an enlargement of the Wiking, The BV 238 was even bolder in conception. The two-step hull in fact had eight small steps after the first one, an unusual feature. More revealing is the bold length-to-beam ratio. The BV 238's ratio had a factor of ten, much more than the six to eight of the BV 222. This would pay dividends in the aircraft's water handling and aerodynamic performance, suffering none of the teething problems of her smaller sister. Other notable features included the hull opening at the front to allow direct loading of the lower deck, a major convenience. The massive wing was built around a welded tubular spar that held fuel, with flaps running along the trailing edge all the way to the ailerons. The wing was big enough and thick enough that, like most of the largest flying boats, it could contain a passageway for an engineer or mechanic to reach the engines during flight.

Given the limited resources available to expend on the program—with Blohm und Voss fully committed both to the BV 138 and 222 programs—an attempt was

Front view of the BV 138 V1. (*Photograph courtesy of the David J. Gauthier Memorial Collection, 1000aircraftphotos.com*)

made to avoid difficulties in the prototype's construction by building it first as a small-scale flying model. It was built at the Flugtechnische Fertigungsgemeinschaft GmbH based at Prague, in Occupied Czechoslovakia. This working miniature was specifically referred to as the FG 227.

Construction on this scaled aircraft was meant to be carried out by Czech students working with *Dipl.Ing.* Ludwig Karch, one of the best glider pilots of the era. The FGP 227 was, like the full-size Wiking from which it was derived, a cantilever, shoulder-wing design with a keeled hull and similar raised tailplane. It was given some power by the use of six ILO FL.2/400 engines, each with the relatively miniscule output of 21 hp each. Flight testing was supposed to take place over land, and so the aircraft was fitted with tricycle landing gear.

All these efforts to have the aircraft take to the air swiftly were ultimately for naught. In early tests, the model simply refused to take-off from the grass airfield. The model was then to be transported to Travemünde to try again, but this was frustrated, as sabotage prevented the first test flight from occurring until September 1944. The model had been disassembled to be loaded onto trucks for transport, and according to some sources, it was at this point that French POWs being used as forced labour took a hand. The prisoners were loading one of the wings and deliberately allowed it to be dropped from a crane, causing major damage. Even when the damage was repaired and the model was once again ready, the result was hardly a desirable one: it resulted in a crash-landing. Almost immediately after getting into the air, all six engines seized up, apparently due to fuel starvation. This resulted in a heavy landing on the water, causing further damage that required extensive repair work. The model only ever flew a few more times. Consequently, the FGP 227 (listed in some sources as the FG 227), for all the effort put into it, played no real role in the development of the BV 238.

Preparation to build the actual BV 238 had begun as early as 1942, with the jigs for parts having been assembled. As a result, construction of the first prototype was ready to begin in January 1944 at Finkenwerder. The construction process moved at a snail's pace because Allied air raids were increasing in frequency, and the final construction was not finished until March 1945. However, what emerged from this delayed process was a superbly prepared aircraft that benefitted from the practical lessons learned on the Wiking program. The flight trials that began immediately after construction were extremely promising, and after a mere four flight tests, the prototype was deemed ready for front-line testing, despite not having been fit with any armament whatsoever.

How much the aircraft's own abilities played into this decision, as opposed to the needs of the emergency Germany found herself in, is debatable. By this stage of the war, the BV 238 project was a decided rarity—rapidly dwindling resources had been increasingly concentrated into fighter production and the design of new emergency aircraft. Bomber production had in fact ceased almost entirely after mid-1944. Moreover, all flying boat production was halted soon thereafter, at the start of October. Given these circumstances, it is logical that the BV 238 was either exceptional—or believed to be still necessary—to be given fuel to fly at all, let alone to maintain the program.

Certainly, the figures stemming from the program may have been enough to justify continued development. The aircraft's empty weight was 120,593 lb (54,700 kg); the aircraft's wing alone was 197 feet (60.17 metres), carrying engines that each developed over 1,700 hp. That power was believed to be able to potentially push the aircraft to 277 mph (446 kph) as a maximum speed, flying as high as 23,950 feet (7,300 metres) and as far as 4,474 miles (7,200 km).

There was also some consideration given to the idea of using both the BV 222 and 238 in coordination with U-boats at sea. Studies regarding cooperation between large flying boats and Germany's sea wolves had been done as early as 1941, with the initial idea that the seaplanes would be used to refuel the submarines. The idea of mutual refuelling became established as studies unfolded, and there was apparently consideration given to using the BV 222 exclusively to ferry fuel, supplies, and crew members to submarines, and for shipping wounded men or prisoners back to France. In the event, the Wiking was considered to not have the capacity wanted to be ideal in this role. The BV 238, which was slated to have a 20 per cent higher fuel reserve, could transport a payload of over 12 tons. This could translate to being able to transport eight torpedoes up to 900 miles (1,450 km) out, or four torpedoes to 1,553 miles (2,500 km) out. Given this, the idea was that two BV 238s would be fitted with refuelling equipment to help increase the endurance of U-boats deployed in the Caribbean or near the coast of the United States.

The V1 photographed from a boat. (*Photograph courtesy of Dan Shumaker*)

Other sources point to the project having been essentially abandoned. One author, an editor for *Flight* magazine, in conversation with Vogt after the war, quoted Vogt as saying that production plans had been officially abandoned, though development apparently continued. According to Vogt, Field Marshal Erhard Milch said metaphorically that since the house was burning, the Germans had to put the fire out first. In this conversation, Vogt claimed that the prototype had first flown in 1943, not 1944 as noted in other sources.

All of this planning came to nothing, as in the end, neither aircraft was used in any capacity for either refuelling operations or for long-range bombing. This may have stemmed in part from a report by an engineer named Wahl from the Travemünde test centre that was created as the BV 238 prototype was slowly working along. He estimated four aircraft would be completed by the end of the year, followed by a series run of fifteen. By the end of 1945, this would be supplemented by eighty-six BV 222s that were theoretically to have been produced, which would be replaced in service by BV 238s. In any event, this rate of production was well out of reach of the overstretched and hammered German industry—such numbers would be impossible from the outset, and these likely would be insufficient for any sustained campaign, given the sheer number of Allied aircraft to oppose them. Supposedly, this finding reduced official interest in the project, which was reflected in a decision to put off choosing between the DB 603 and BMW 801 for the aircraft.

The project was at least slated to receive armament. It was meant to comprise an HD 151 twin-gun turret containing two MG 151/20s, with another two HL 131 V turrets meant to carry four MG 131s each, with another two MG 131Zs in side stations—a heavy total of twelve guns. In the final analysis, it is difficult to believe that even had an armament been fitted it would have made much of a difference to the prototype's fate.

Over the course of the 238's development, a further idea for armament was floated for a land version of the BV 238 (discussed later in this chapter). In this paradigm, the aircraft would carry a payload of up to six SC 2500 bombs, which weighed 5,291 lb (2,400 kg) each. This was to match a RLM requirement in 1942 for transport with a range of over 4,300 miles (7,000 km) with 20 tonnes of bombs, with further ranges specified for partial loadouts and as a purely reconnaissance aircraft.

After those four flights, the prototype BV 238 was destined never to fly again. It became imperative to try to hide the aircraft after the Blohm und Voss Wenzendorf industrial works at Hamburg were destroyed in air raids. The trouble was finding camouflage for an aircraft that massive that late in the war. The aircraft, camouflaged inadequately on the Shaalsee near Lübeck, was discovered by Allied fighters and sunk by gunfire. There has been some historical disagreement over just who did the sinking, under what circumstances, and even when it occurred. Both the Americans and British have laid claim to striking down this particular titan, and sources cannot even agree as to when the aircraft was destroyed. Some point to an American strike in September 1944, others to a British strike four days before the war's end.

According to the American version of events, a flight of P-51 Mustangs from the 361st Fighter Group happened upon the massive boat during her testing program on September 18, 1944. The leading P-51, *Detroit Miss*, was piloted by Lt Urban "Ben" Drew. Drew and his wingmen destroyed the aircraft on the water. Drew was told that he had destroyed a BV 222, and believed this until 1974, when he was approached by the BBC, who were researching a documentary and had uncovered evidence that he had instead demolished the prototype BV 238.

The other version of the story is taken primarily from German sources and can be traced to the testimonials of Blohm und Voss employees, and states that the British discovered the massive craft sometime in late April 1945 and were concerned it was an escape aircraft for high-ranking Nazis, and sent in either Hawker Typhoons or Tempests. Both theories ultimately have merit, and choosing either one or the other colours many of the other facts reported about the BV 238 program—creating a plethora of mysteries around the giant aircraft.

Regardless of who did the sinking, the program had come to a sudden end in a fiery catastrophe that matched the ending of the war. What was left of the BV 238 was blown up in 1947 or early 1948 to make dismantling it easier. The individual parts remaining were finally scrapped in Hamburg between 1948 and 1949. The V2 and V3 prototypes, under construction at war's end, had their hull and wing parts scrapped after the end of hostilities, bringing the program to a complete and inglorious end. Some sources denote that a V4 had also begun construction. All three were likely scrapped in 1946. In addition, there were parts being created and assembled for prototypes V5 through V8, all of which were also likely scrapped in 1946.

There are persistent stories that the BV 238 was finished and meant to be kept ready as a method of escape for high-ranking Nazis to flee the collapsing Reich. According to some versions of the tale, Martin Bormann—one of the highest-ranking of Hitler's inner circle—wanted the aircraft kept ready as a means of escape from Berlin.

Interestingly, in some ways, the Germans may have anticipated the trend in aviation technology that would see flying boats eclipsed. Both the BV 238 and the BV 222 had landplane versions projected, which were different only in terms of adding multi-wheeled landing gear. In addition to details mentioned earlier, for the BV 222, this was given the project number P.187, with the BV 238 getting the project designation Bf 250 (sometimes this is written as BV 250 in sources). Neither of these progressed beyond the design stage. The land version of the BV 238 was slated to receive a heavy armament of twelve MG 151/20s. Originally, it was planned that this version would get Junkers Jumo 222 engines, but these were not ready by war's end, and it would have been fitted with the same DB 603 engines that equipped the 238's prototype. Total crew was to have been eleven men, and it was theoretically thought to be capable of carrying 150 fully equipped soldiers.

The BV 238's history is one filled with contradictions and frankly one which raises more questions than it answers. It is difficult to say how or even if these questions can be answered, or the discrepancies at least explained. Many of the records involved have long since been lost, including much of Blohm und Voss's own records. Much of their documentation was destroyed during the war or during flooding disasters, and what portion of it remains is now held by the Bundesarchiv in Freiburg. Much has been lost about this project, the biggest and heaviest flying boat of World War II. What remains is the leviathan itself, an aircraft more elusive than anything of its size should be.

The BV 238 was Germany's last titan, and it is almost natural as a result that so much mystery should attach to it. Conceived for a clear purpose, its story becomes less and less clear as the nation that birthed it slid progressively further into the chaotic death throes of a tyrant empire. It pointed the way both to how large flying boats could be while still being effective, but in trying to retrofit it for land use, it also spelled out very clearly the doom that was coming for the same giant aircraft.

6

Boeing 314: The Golden Age Takes Wing

Of all the aircraft contained in this volume, the Boeing 314—the famed Clipper—is perhaps the flying boat most associated not only with the concept of large, vintage flying boats, but with aviation's golden age. The Clipper has come to be associated with the romance of flying in a bygone era, of fabulous travel across oceans, and is a frequent staple of fiction whether written or on film. The true story of this aircraft is no less remarkable, for the Boeing 314 was a major technological achievement for its day, and a superb design in a number of ways. If there are two stories of the flying boat, peace and war, the Boeing 314 Clipper is emblematic of the peace side, fulfilling a role as a premier passenger aircraft, and a graceful and beautiful one at that, until war interrupted its history forever.

Specifications

First Flight: 1938
Powerplant: Four Wright R-2600-3 radial engines, 1,600 hp each
Armament: None
Top Speed: 210 mph (340 kph)
Range/Service Ceiling: 3,685 miles (5,896 km), 19,600 feet (5,980 metres)
Dimensions: Length 106 feet (32.33 metres), height 20 feet 4½ inches (6.22 metres), wingspan 152 feet (46.36 metres)
Number Built: Twelve

The Boeing 314's reputation is not merely down to fond remembrance or the beauty of its lines. The 314 was a leap forward in passenger air travel, superior in many ways to even the large, relatively comfortable passenger flying boats that had preceded it. Its performance, carrying capacity, and level of comfort would all be vast improvements over anything else in service. The aircraft was meant from its original conception to be superlative, in many ways to be a crown jewel in the already illustrious collection of the then-dominant Pan American Airways.

In 1935, Pan American was looking to solicit a majorly new design. Today, a company might cast its eye on existing designs or production aircraft looking to what best suited their needs. In the 1930s, however, Pan American's needs were to conquer air routes that were still in the process of development. If not precisely trailblazing, instituting regular service across vast swathes of the globe was a tremendous challenge that very few aircraft of the time could meet. It must be remembered that transcontinental travel was not the common place occurrence of today, but a new, cutting-edge aspect both of air travel and indeed of technology.

Pan American was also being bold: their target was the North Atlantic, a traditionally harsh environment that had punished sea travellers since human beings first ventured across its cold, and frequently unforgiving, waters. Pan American's vision was a route that would run from the coast of the United States to England, with stops in Newfoundland and Ireland. At the time, Pan American already possessed the capable Martin M.130 for its Pacific routes, but the company deemed the aircraft unequal to the heavier task of the North Atlantic. In short, they wanted something bigger and better that could carry more passengers in safety and comfort.

The company solicited design proposals, but in December 1936, they selected Boeing to proceed with development of the model dubbed 314, with delivery of the first aircraft expected within a year—a very quick pace. Boeing immediately threw itself into the task. The company was fortunately able to save some time by utilizing elements from a design that had already been built in prototype form, one that proved very influential to the company's design future.

The XB-15 first flew in 1937, and at the time it took to the skies, it was the most massive aircraft ever to be built in the United States. It would prove to be a record setter, including achieving one for the heaviest air cargo to date. Though it never entered production as a bomber as it was intended, the experience Boeing gained with the XB-15 helped the company's design progress towards a bomber that did: the B-29 Superfortress.

That event was still years off, but at that moment, the XB-15 had much to give to the 314 project. Namely, the majority of the wing design and engine nacelle placement of the XB-15 were moved wholesale into the design for the new flying boat. The wing was assembled in five sections, coming in with a 152-foot wingspan. The wing was designed with care and complexity. As one author puts it:

> The wing spars were made up of channels of square tubing and bolted and riveted duraluminum to support the ... wing span. The wing was constructed with Pratt-trussed spars, square tubing, and channel ribbing. The area of the wing was an impressive 2,867 sq. ft. Split trailing-edge wing flaps were employed to provide minimal air resistance in flight. The wing tips were sealed and acted as small flotation tanks in the event the aircraft tipped over in rough seas. Trim and control tabs, constructed of aluminum tubing and doped canvas, were used on the flight

control surfaces. Four Frieze ailerons were employed to reduce yaw, each having a trim tab.

"A Detailed Look at the Fabulous Boeing 314"
Airpower Magazine, p. 17
Jared Zichek

A small fact can illustrate the scale of the wing in real terms: the wing chord was so thick that the in-flight mechanic could actually crawl along the leading edge of the wings right to the engine nacelles, so small repairs to the engines could be carried out mid-flight. With such a complex and advanced wing, it is easy to see in retrospect how the knowledge gained from the XB-15 would lead to bigger things. Nor was the flying boat project quite done with the XB-15, since the 314 design also took on the bomber's light-alloy structure overall, being designed to have stressed aluminum skin.

The hull, too, was ambitious. It was made to be deep enough to accommodate an upper flight deck that would contain all the essential flight components such as the cockpit, navigation and radio rooms, and engineering spaces. The upper deck also was where the baggage spaces were contained and had the space to accommodate ten crew members. The end result of this smart decision to make the hull deep was that there could be a lower deck completely devoted to passenger space. By contrast, the M.130 had to make do with a single deck, limiting the total number of passengers it could carry. The 314's design would carry a total of seventy-four passengers in a "day" setting, or forty in sleeper berths. The tail was designed to be high and clear of any spray on landing or take-off, and the designers chose a twin fin and rudder system on a horizontal stabilizer. The total weight of the aircraft was 82,500 lb.

Atypically, the designers did not select a fairly standard design element of wing floats, but instead went with two sponsons, one on either side of the fuselage. Apparently, these were inspired by the Dornier Wal flying boat, and they provided greatly increased structural strength and, in the bargain, better taxiing characteristics. There were some downsides, too: these increased weight, drag, and made the aircraft porpoise in certain sea conditions. In the end, the main advantages outweighed the downsides in Boeing's mind. In addition, the sponsons served as a convenient boarding ramp for passengers, and each carried 3,525 gallons of fuel. This fuel would power the most capable aircraft engines then available, Wright R-2600 engines—superb radial engines that would power multiple combat aircraft in World War II, including the Brewster SB2A Buccaneer, the flawed Curtiss SB2C Helldiver, Douglas A-20 Havoc, Grumman TBF Avenger, and the North American B-25 Mitchell. They also would power the Martin Mariner, discussed later in this book, and many others. In short, the Wright engines were the right choice—and would continue to be throughout the 1940s for many others.

The structure of the aircraft was mainly Alclad aluminum, with electric spot welding used in low-stress areas, and the aluminum panels then coated with cadmium and anodized to resist saltwater corrosion. Varnish-infused industrial flannel was used to make the hull watertight, and the assembled aircraft was painted in stunning aluminum lacquer.

Even the propellers would be revolutionary, with Pan American rejecting the first ones and tasking Boeing and Hamilton Standard to produce new, varied-pitch propellers that were also full-feathering and had braking; the new propellers would become a standard of aviation design. Every aspect of the airplane was state-of-the-art, and in some cases revolutionary. Boeing's plan was to produce a marvel, and in an engineering blink of an eye.

Despite making use of an existing wing design and engines, the ambitious time frame for the project proved to be entirely too optimistic on the part of Pan American. Boeing ended up being a total of five months behind schedule, hardly surprising given the size and complexity of the task at hand, as well as the quality of the overall project. In the event, from commissioning to prototype took a mere seventeen months, an astonishingly fast pace. The delivered aircraft was the most expensive civil aircraft completed in the U.S. until that time—each unit would cost $550,000. The tremendous risk of such a cost was off-set by it being a state-of-the-art machine when it was completed, and so luxurious they were often termed "flying hotels," with everything from soundproofed cabins, carpeting and upholstery, and even fine china for meals. The aircraft could cruise at 175 mph, and depending on the configuration, it had a range between 3,100 and 4,000 miles. All these figures were remarkable, but when the first machine was completed, all of this still needed to be proven beyond the drawing board.

The first stage in proving the 314's capability came with taxiing tests in Washington State's Puget Sound at the end of May 1938. The first test flight came on June 7, and subsequent tests revealed that the tail design lacked a sufficient total area for effective directional stability, so a third fabric-covered fin was added, which gave the type its definitive triple-tailed look.

This was the only major change made to the aircraft, and the first production aircraft was delivered to Pan American in late January 1939. Named *Honolulu Clipper*, the aircraft was sent to Pan American's Pacific base of operations at San Francisco, California. *Honolulu Clipper* was placed on the San Francisco–Hong Kong route, and the subsequent 314s were allocated between two oceans.

California Clipper came next and was also assigned to the Pacific route. The remaining four aircraft—*Yankee Clipper*, *Atlantic Clipper*, *Dixie Clipper*, and *American Clipper*—were all earmarked for the Atlantic route. Pan American was close to realizing its most cherished dream.

The passage of time has lessened what was, for Pan American, its crowning glory. Getting these aircraft into transatlantic service had been the company's dream since the 1920s. In 1925 alone, a million people had crossed the Atlantic. Moreover, the quantity of mail that did so was vast and was at the time the keystone to any airline's revenue stream—passengers being a secondary bonus. Express freight was also a lucrative enterprise. Pan American, already successful

Pacific Clipper in the air. (*Photograph courtesy of the David L. Gauthier Memorial Collection, 1000aircraftphotos.com*)

in Latin America, assumed it could expand into Atlantic operations at well. Here, however, they ran into an absolute stone wall: the British government.

The British were well aware both of American productive capacity and also their burgeoning air capabilities. They did not want the Americans to have a head start on the air routes across the Atlantic, and certainly not to allow American volume or aircraft to achieve dominance over the Atlantic. The method of preventing American success was simply to deny them access to British territories such as Atlantic Canada or Bermuda, making either a northern or southern route to Europe difficult. The British demanded reciprocity, insisting that they would not grant landing rights to any American airline until British aircraft operated by Imperial Airways were able to commence a similar service.

This long, frustrating impasse had only one possible solution, and it was not one Pan American would have preferred. In 1936, Juan Trippe, Pan American's founder and Chairman, made a deal with the Managing Director of Imperial Airways, George Woods-Humphrey. Frankly, it had more in common with a treaty between rival powers than it did with an agreement between companies. The deal created a new monopoly, but between Pan American and Imperial Airways. It locked out other airlines from other nations from British stepping stones, but also ensured that Pan American could not commence its own operations until Imperial Airways could do the same. It would take until 1939 for Pan American aircraft to fly across the Atlantic.

In the meantime, as they planned the future, Pan Am built a series of bases and opened up service to Bermuda, since the Short Empire had come into service in mid-1936 and had the range to get there from England. Small wonder that when the time came to begin service, Pan American wanted a brand-new flying boat at the ready. *Yankee Clipper* would be the pioneer, beginning a survey flight of the North Atlantic in late March 1939. This flight encompassed both the planned routes. The northern route flew through Shediac, New Brunswick, then on to Botswood in Newfoundland before leaping across the Atlantic to Foynes in Ireland. Finally, the route terminated in Southampton, after a stop in Bermuda along the way for good measure. The southern route flew to Lisbon and Marseilles via the Azores. The next step was to inaugurate mail service, for which the choice was also *Yankee Clipper*, which carried a ton of mail to Europe along the southern route on May 20, 1939, with the northern route following a month later.

Dixie Clipper would make the first transatlantic passenger flight of a heavier-than-air aircraft on June 28, flying out of New York along the southern route with twenty-two passengers. The one-way ticket for that flight cost $375 dollars, a large sum but for a pioneering service. Within a month, *Yankee Clipper* had done the same along the northern route. Pan American had a long history of long-distance travel over water, which meant that the ultra-modern 314 was being used in an experienced and highly efficient operation. The cost, in other words, could be justified by the comfort, efficiency, and overall safety of the service.

The long dream of Juan Trippe and Pan American had finally been realized, but events would make the dream somewhat short-lived. When the war began, the air routes were an early casualty. In October, the routes across the Atlantic for passenger air travel were cancelled. Pan American kept *Yankee* and *Dixie* flying along central routes to Brazil and then on to West Africa, but their grand plans to dominate the routes to England were dust. Yet Pan American's pre-eminence came to their rescue. The U.S. Government saw an opportunity in the continuing operation of the airline, since it ensured their access to strategic countries. The Chief of Naval Operations, Admiral Leahy, even insisted that Pan American's service be increased, and the Civil Aeronautics Authority more than tripled the mail revenue per mile on some routes. At the barest minimum, the rate went from $2 dollars to $3.35, with a maximum on some routes of $7.12. Some of the 314 flights were coming in with 8,000 lb of mail per flight. This and the long lines of war refugees trying to gain flights to North America meant that Pan American was making a fortune from the war.

From the time they entered service until the United States entered the war, the clippers would carry over 25,000 passengers in safety. In 1939 alone, profits hit $20 million dollars. The airline was the "chosen instrument," reaching a peak of its glory that it would never reach again. The necessities and scope of the war would ultimately help to eclipse them, but for the moment the Boeing 314 was the brightest symbol of an unparalleled dominance for a single airline.

Under these circumstances, it is hardly surprising that Pan American carried on the order for six more aircraft, and Boeing began to deliver them in late September 1939. These were an improvement, the 314A. The main changes were uprated versions of the R-2600 engines, larger hydromatic propellers, which could change

One of the passenger Clippers before the war. (*Photograph courtesy of Dan Shumaker*)

Maintenance being performed on the tail of the one of the Clippers. (*Photograph courtesy of Dan Shumaker*)

The Boeing 314 "Berwick" that carried Winston Churchill. (*Photograph courtesy of the David L. Gauthier Memorial Collection, 1000aircraftphotos.com*)

pitch faster and had a wider range of pitch control, and a better fuel capacity. The first three were *Pacific Clipper*, *Anzac Clipper*, and *Cape Town Clipper*. The last three, however, became part of another agreement with Britain and were sold to the British Purchasing Commission and put into service with the British Overseas Airways Corporation. These aircraft were known as *Bristol*, *Bangor*, and *Berwick*.

For a short time, the graceful 314s continued their passenger service unabated. With the United States' entry into the war in December 1941, however, these giant and capable flying boats were simply too useful to keep out of military service. Four of the remaining aircraft were pressed into service with the U.S. Army Air Forces Air Transport Command, where they were redesignated as C-98 aircraft and put to work transporting personnel on long distance flights. Others went into service with the U.S. Navy.

On the outbreak of war, one of the still-civilian 314s was put in immediate danger, however: *Pacific Clipper* was on the way from New Caledonia to New Zealand when the Japanese Navy struck at Pearl Harbor. Flying back across the Pacific was deemed to be too dangerous, so *Pacific Clipper* had to engage in an epic long-distance flight the long way around the world. From Australia, the plane flew to Java, then Ceylon, and through India, Bahrain, Sudan, the Belgian Congo, Brazil, and Trinidad before finally reaching the United States—an epic total journey of 8,500 miles in complete safety thanks to the Pan American crew, with Capt. Robert Ford at the helm. It was an impromptu flight around the world, a test of the 314's capabilities and the endurance both of the aircraft and its crew, and both passed with flying colours.

In military service, the 314s performed well, transporting even President Franklin D. Roosevelt, and the B.O.A.C. controlled 314s would transport Prime Minister Winston Churchill on many occasions. Three would be lost in service, all in accidents. Though Pan American continued to operate four of these magnificent aircraft, all the 314s that remained stayed in military service until the end of the war, when they were returned to Pan American civilian operations. With land-based aircraft rapidly taking over the realm of the giant flying boats, they lingered in charter services until all but one was scrapped in 1950. The three B.O.A.C. aircraft were sold after the war to General Phoenix Corporation but were never used commercially again. The last 314, *Anzac Clipper*, was sold to a private owner but met her end a year later in an accident. In a few short years, all trace of the remarkable and beautiful Boeing 314 had vanished.

Thanks to the efforts of an Irish museum, this was not the end of the Clipper experience. The Foynes Flying Boat & Maritime Museum in Ireland engaged in a massive ten-month project to build a full-size replica, ensuring that the beauty and elegance of the Boeing 314 continues to inspire visitors to this day. In discovering this project, the author of this work was fortunate enough to be put in contact with Margaret O'Shaughnessy, the founder, managing director, and curator of the museum. Foynes had a significant local history with the glory days of aviation, and there was no local historical presence for it, not even a plaque—leaving no sign of the community's significant role in the development of passenger air travel.

The museum itself is built into a building from 1860, with the small rooms now hosting a rapidly increasing stream of visitors, and the museum has grown from four rooms with the same number of staff to now occupy the entirety of the old airport terminal building and having twenty-five staff members. Another reason for necessary expansion is the museum's large archive and collection of memorabilia, much of it donated by Conor Beau Fitzsimons, the belongings of his grandmother—patron of the museum and movie star Maureen O'Hara Blair.

The genesis of the replica project came from the irony that though they had a flying boat museum, they did not in fact have a flying boat in that museum. Finding a large-scale flying boat was near impossible, and there certainly were no pieces of the Boeing 314 available, let alone a whole aircraft. The initial idea was small, with the museum being introduced to a man named Bill Fallover (thanks to Jack Harrison & Associates) to build a single cabin, to give visitors a sense of the luxury and scope of the time period. Fallover's response was, in simplest terms, "why not build the whole thing?" This vision carried the day, and Curator O'Shaughnessy and the other directors approached Minister John O'Donoghue, T.D., the Minister of Arts and Heritage. Minister O'Donoghue was as taken with the project as anyone else, helping to provide funding to get started.

Budgets were a difficult process, since nothing like this project had been done, and thus no comparisons could be made. Indeed, financing the project was perhaps the greatest difficulty in the entire process; ultimately, the available cash came up far short of the cost. Mr. Fallover agreed to help split the costs, and local banks stepped in to provide the remaining necessary cash.

Mr. Fallover began construction of the replica at his home in County Wicklow with the aid of his sons, Harry and Joe. The construction process took a total of nine months, and the project was fortunate enough to receive significant help from Boeing in Seattle, which provided dimensions, photographs of the interior, drawings, and other materials. Along the way, another challenge had to be solved: sourcing and weaving cloths for the seats and beds. The end result was thrilling, and the replica 314 had to be shipped by road to Foynes during the night, then lifted in over the building with cranes and assembled on site.

The replica 314 was unveiled by Minister O'Donoghue, owing to his role in getting the project rolling, in 2006. A few hundred people were in attendance, including people who remembered and had been directly involved with the flying boat days in Foynes. Since then, the replica has been a major draw for people from all over the world, and a funeral was even held on board for a former pilot and his wife. This unique attraction has certainly garnered unique reactions. People respond very well to the replica, with modern visitors remarking—undoubtedly with some wonder—on the luxury of air travel in the golden age of flying boats. When the cost of the ticket at the time is revealed, there is some understanding as to where the luxury came from, but visitors are still rather wistful for the amount of leg room—unheard of to most air travellers today.

When asked about the overall importance of the Boeing 314, Margaret O'Shaughnessy had this to say:

> Well we feel very strongly that this aircraft the Boeing 314 was the first great aircraft used to cross the North Atlantic with passengers and we must never forget that. Also it really was the first Air Force One as in 1943, President Franklin D. Roosevelt travelled to the Casablanca Conference in a Pan-Am crewed Boeing 314 Dixie Clipper. Today the world is a much smaller place and we must preserve aviation history for the generations of the future.

Thanks in no small part to the museum staff and the dedicated people behind recreating the Foynes Museum's 314, the legacy of this impressive and unforgettable aircraft seem very secure going forward into the future. The aircraft's history is remarkable in and of itself, and the legend of the aircraft only grows as the decades have passed by. The Foynes Flying Boat Museum has provided posterity with a living, vibrant reminder of a long-gone world when transoceanic air travel was just beginning, an era that has taken on a patina of romance ever since. In this era, the Boeing 314 Clipper stands tall as one of the signal aircraft of its era not only advancing the science of aviation, but helping to create a world of travel unlike anything the world had ever seen before.

7

Breguet 521: The Bizerte

Breguet Aviation, otherwise known as the Société des Ateliers d'Aviation Louis Breguet, was originally founded in 1911 and made a number of aircraft for French and British service during World War I. After 1918, the company began to look to passenger travel and developed a series of airliners, alongside continued military development. All of these planes were land-based, until Breguet began to modify a Short flying boat from England, under license. The result was the Breguet 521 Bizerte, an aircraft that would come to have an interesting history under her original masters, and then as part of the Luftwaffe after France's defeat in 1940.

Specifications

First Flight: 1933
Powerplant: Three Gnôme-Rhône 14Kirs fourteen-cylinder radial engines, 900 hp each
Armament: Five 7.5-mm (0.295-inch) Darne machine guns, 300 kg (660 lb) of bombs
Top Speed: 151 mph (243 kph)
Range/Service Ceiling: 1,305 miles (2,100 km), 19,685 feet (6,000 metres)
Dimensions: Length 67 feet 2 inches (20.48 metres), height 24 feet 6 inches (7.50 metres), wingspan 115 feet 4 inches (35.18 metres)
Number Built: Thirty-seven

The Bizerte would start its life by being derived, essentially, twice over. Originally, it was developed from the Bizerte S.8/2 Calcutta, which itself was a license-built copy of a British aircraft, the Short S.8 Calcutta. The Calcutta had been a trimotor biplane flying boat that had first taken to the air in 1928, and a handful had been built.

The aircraft that became the Bizerte would be created to meet a specification issued by the French Navy in 1932 for a long-range flying boat. There would be stiff competition for the role, with Breguet being one of four competitors in the race—the other three being Latécoère, Loiré et Olivier, and Loire Aviation (Latécoère produced the Latécoère 582, which was only built in prototype form, and Loire Aviation produced the Loire 70, a strange trimotor combination with two puller and one pusher engine configuration. Eight would ultimately serve the French Navy. Loiré et Olivier designed but never built the unusual LeO H42 seaplane).

The design was meant primarily as a reconnaissance aircraft, but it could carry a punch as well, and was designed to carry four 165-lb (75-kg) bombs. The design was also very modern in that it was an all-metal construction. The engines were mounted in a line between the lower and upper wing and initially had a much smaller cockpit with an open gun position forward of it.

The Bre 521-01 prototype first flew at Le Havre on September 11, 1933. It was powered at the time by three uncowled Gnôme-Rhône 14 Kdrs radial engines. Flight testing proceeded for most of the rest of the year, and it was not until April 1935 that the aircraft would begin its operation service tests for the French Navy, being sent to *Escadrille* E1, at Cherbourg.

While tests were still proceeding, and showing some confidence in the design, three pre-production aircraft had already been ordered. The second of these differed from the aircraft that came before, extending the cockpit enclosure forward to the end of the nose, giving the aircraft a very distinct look. This cockpit had the benefit of giving the aircraft superb visibility. Further, the originally-used open gun position in the nose was replaced by a more unusual configuration of gun blisters on either side of the aircraft at the rear of the cabin, each housing a forward-firing 7.5-mm (0.295-inch) Darne machine gun. Two more similar guns were installed to the rear of the wings, meant to fire laterally through sliding hatches. A fifth gun was installed in the extreme tail.

These aircraft were meant to carry a fairly heavy crew of eight, consisting of the pilot, co-pilot, bombardier, and five gunners. In actual production, they were ordered by the French government in small batches. The first aircraft produced entered service with *Escadrilles* E2 and E3 in late 1935. A total of a dozen aircraft had been produced by the end of 1936, and the last of these was experimentally fitted with Hispano-Suiza 14AA radial engines and was designated the Bre 522. It was the only aircraft so equipped, and the standard production Bizerte aircraft came with Gnôme-Rhône 14 Kirs I engines.

By 1938, a total of twenty-eight aircraft had been delivered from Breguet's Le Havre factory, which was being incorporated into SNCA du Nord—part of an amalgamation and reorganization of France's air industry undertaken with an eye towards smoothing and increasing production with war looming. The outbreak of that war would see the ordering of another dozen Bizertes, to be completed with 900-hp Gnôme-Rhône 14N engines and a few minor detail changes to the aircraft. Owing to the Fall of France in 1940, only three of these aircraft were ever completed.

In wartime service, the Bizerte equipped *Escadrilles* E1, E2, E6, and E9 over both the Atlantic and Mediterranean. They were mostly confined to their reconnaissance duties. After the Fall of France, two squadrons of Bizertes were

A Breguet 521, but in her transport life as the *Saigon*. (*Photograph courtesy of the San Diego Air and Space Museum*)

A Bizerte at rest. (*Photograph courtesy of Photo Industrielle et Maritime, via 1000aircraftphotos.com*)

kept on—equipping 1E and 9E (the letter-number designations were reversed in 1941), the other two squadrons being dissolved. Ultimately, the aircraft of 9E, plus four other aircraft assembled from stores, would be taken over by the Germans and utilized as part of the Luftwaffe as air/sea rescue aircraft. The German units used in this capacity frequently used the Dornier Do 24, but the Bizerte was an excellent aircraft for them to acquire in this role as well. The Germans liked it enough that they ordered eight more from the Vichy authorities, and ultimately operated a total of twenty-one aircraft as part of *Seenotstaffel* I.

To say the Germans liked the aircraft could be considered an understatement. It was given a sea state 5 (rough) capability designation, meaning it could operate in weather that would imperil or even wreck daintier aircraft. While its speed was noted, according to one experienced German pilot, the aircraft's seaworthiness was unmatched by any other similar aircraft. In German use, six Bizertes were based at Brest, with two more at Hourtin.

As part of their German service, a quartet of Bizertes ended up becoming an ancillary part of the Battle of Britain. Four of them were assigned to *Luftflotte* 3, stationed at Brest as part of an ASR centre established there. Each of the German centres controlled a subsidiary ASR Command. The centre at Brest was responsible for a command at Royan, where a further two Bizertes were stationed.

The Bizerte was also present for one of the most regrettable actions of the war, the British attack on the French fleet at Mers-el-Kebir, where the British attacked their former allies in an effort to keep the French fleet out of German hands. Bizertes, fairly vulnerable at this point owing to their light machine guns, were on hand to keep an eye on the movements of the English fleet, though their presence made no difference to the eventual open conflict between servicemen who had, until just a short time before, been allies.

After the fall of the Vichy collaborationist state, and the liberation of France, at least one Bizerte was returned to service in French colours. The French raised *Flotille 9FTr* on November 1, 1944, part of the Aéronavale that was slowly beginning to be reconstructed. The unit was brought into being at Saint-Mandrier-sur-Mer near Toulon, with the assigned role of providing transport between naval bases in France and the French Empire in Africa. The unit received what flying boats and seaplanes could be assigned, and as a result, its initial equipment consisted of the prototype for the Latécoère 611, the first Breguet 730, and a single surviving Bizerte. The unit later took on captured German Dorniers. In these later capacities, the Bizerte did run into enemy aircraft on occasion, and some losses occurred. There is also some indication that the Bizerte did wind up being captured or passed on to the Italians, who at the very least evaluated it and may have used it further, though at the time of publication, the author has been unable to trace this particular branch further.

The Bizerte also had a civilian "double life," as it were. The French airline Air Union had ordered a civilian version of the Bizerte, known as the Bre 530 Saigon. By the time the civilian version of the Bizerte was ready, Air Union had become a unit of Air France. Only two of these civilian aircraft were ever completed, designed to carry a crew of two and up to twenty passengers. There were three cabins in the aircraft: a deluxe compartment in the rear for two or three people, an amidships cabin for six first-class passengers, and a second-class cabin further forwards for eleven more. There was also a toilet and baggage hold at the rear of the aircraft's hull. These aircraft did not carry Hispano-Suiza engines like the sole Bre 522 but got a trio of 765-hp Hispano-Suiza 12 Ybr twelve-cylinder V-type engines. The first aircraft, F-AMSV *Algerié*, flew for the first time in May 1934. Joined by her sister, F-AMSX *Tunisie*, the two aircraft began service across the Mediterranean in January 1935. There were plans to introduce a larger, long-range development of the Saigon, to be called the Dakar, for transatlantic mail and freight purposes, but this was never built.

Few things in the history of aviation are more indicative of the rapid development of aircraft in the 1930s. The Bizerte was considered a large, very modern aircraft when she debuted—yet, in under a decade, she was hopelessly obsolete compared to larger, much more capable aircraft—and vulnerable to fighters far more powerful and fast than anything she had been designed to face. This was part of a cycle that occurred in the era that effected different nations at different times, where their aircraft were rapidly outpaced by rivals; this prompted either hurried efforts to address the issue or led to serious strategic deficiencies.

The Bizerte has little overall legacy today: war service and a lack of spare parts used the aircraft up relatively rapidly, and no physical trace of the aircraft remains. Regardless of this, it remains a fascinating part of France's complex and varied flying boat programmes that, at one point, projected French power and served as the eyes of the fleet. The Bizerte is an interesting "in between" example of flying boat technology. The first generation that stocked air forces during and immediately after World War I were surpassed by a larger, more capable generation of aircraft that began to range further afield, such as the Supermarine Southampton seen later in this volume. The third generation could be defined—albeit with undoubted debate—as the large, increasingly monoplane aircraft designed to cross oceans. The Bizerte could, under this definition, be called a "2.5" aircraft: it was a decided improvement on the biplane flying boats that had preceded it, but still possessed the limitations of the biplane form and the engines of the early 1930s.

Aircraft like the Bizerte trace the evolution of the flying boat form in the early years of the 1930s, demonstrating the ever-rising capability of these aircraft that came with a commensurate increase in size. As their design, construction, and engines improved, flying boats became more and more capable, a fact proven quite readily by the next chapter in this book, which deals with an aircraft of the same manufacturer, designed and flown only a few years later than the Bizerte, which nevertheless had over triple the range.

As for the Bizerte itself, for an aircraft built in relatively small numbers, it was very successful at what it did. Designed for reconnaissance, it proved more than adequate to the task—if somewhat vulnerable to newer fighter aircraft, a common suffering for many reconnaissance flying boats—and found an unexpected role in enemy hands as a rescue aircraft. This unusual looking flying boat more than fulfilled its designer's intentions, and once upon a time, in either civilian or military hands, was a proud sight for the French.

8

Breguet 730: Interrupted Development

The Breguet 730 was a very different aircraft to the Bizerte, so much so that while many companies show a visible evolutionary line to some of their designs, the world of difference between the two aircraft is remarkable. This flying boat, serving far later than many owing to France's strange and unfortunate circumstances, also amply demonstrates how quickly the technology behind flying boats advanced in the 1930s, and how French military flying boats only grew in their capabilities.

Specifications

First Flight: 1937
Powerplant: Four Gnôme-Rhône 14N-44/45 fourteen-cylinder radial engines, 1,120 hp each
Armament: None
Top Speed: 205 mph (330 kph)
Range/Service Ceiling: 4,300 miles (6,923 km), 19,700 feet (6,000 metres)
Dimensions: Length 79 feet 11½ inches (24.38 metres), height 28 feet 2 inches (8.60 metres), wingspan 132 feet 5 inches (40.37 metres)
Number Built: Five

The Breguet 730 was originally intended to be the successor aircraft to the Bizerte. Its initial impetus came from a specification issued on May 10, 1935 by the French Admiralty. The specification called for a new 20-ton flying boat. Replacing the Bizerte was explicit in the specification, as was a modern construction, long range of operation, and a strong defensive armament consisting primarily of 25-mm guns. Breguet was not alone in submitting an entry to replace its previously successful aircraft; Latécoère and Potez-CAMS designed their own contenders as well. Breguet's engineers met the French requirement to the letter with an aircraft designated Br 710, which had a gull wing.

In December, the navy changed its mind and revised its requirements to encompass a larger aircraft, and Breguet's engineers went back to the drawing boards and crafted a 23-ton boat, which was accepted for prototype construction, along with entrants from Breguet's rivals (Latécoère's design would become the Late 611 and the other the Potez-CAMS 141, both of which would be accepted for service but never go beyond the prototype). Breguet's design was that of an all-metal aircraft with a high cantilever wing and a large two-step hull.

The wing itself was designed to carry the fuel, a total of 18,000 litres (4,755 gallons). The wing beam was used as a supporting structure, and it was three sections: a rectangular inner section, a trapezoidal outer section, and the rounded wingtips. As was the case with many large flying boats, there was a tunnel in the wing core that could be used to reach the engines in flight. Beyond the wing, the designers made some unusual choices. The tailplane structure rested on top of a single pylon rising high over the hull, appearing disjointed. Stranger still were the wing floats, which unusually came with a supporting profile, making them appear almost a solid part of the wing. A very similar enclosure to that of the Bizerte was also used in the new aircraft, which was designed for a crew of six to ten. Also unusually, the design utilized two different kinds of engines in the construction of the prototype—Gnôme-Rhône N-2 and N-3 engines, with the N-2 on the right and the N-3 on the left to eliminate torque influence.

To meet the navy's requirements for armament, it was planned to equip the aircraft with one or two rotating gun turrets in the rear fuselage with a single 25-mm weapon each. Gun stations were also planned in each section of the hull to hold Darne machine guns of 7.5-mm (0.295-inch) calibre. Five machine guns were also, in a more unusual move, apparently to be installed in a downward shooting position in the rear of the fuselage. In addition, the aircraft was to take on the offensive punch offered by carrying four 440-lb (200-kg) bombs. In the event, none of the aircraft built ever received any armament.

The prototype, officially designated Br 730-01, was to be built in two places. The main work was to be carried out at Breguet's Le Havre facility where the fuselage, tailplane, and floats were to be built, with the wings built at Villacoublay. This was, in many ways, to be where the news stopped being good for the type, and indeed for Breguet. Events both internal and external would hereafter plague the program and ultimately mean that the Bizerte would be forced to "carry on" without a successor.

Even before it flew, the prototype aircraft played its small part in the upheavals of French society in the 1930s. The Great Depression had hit the French economy hard, which in turn made a fertile ground for labour activism and radicalism. The rise of the far-right in Europe, and in Germany in particular, fed into the growing unification of various left-wing groups in France, which would result in the "Popular Front." These developments had a central effect: the groups that would become the Popular Front (which would eventually form the government) were unified in their resistance to fascism, and the French government wished to combat the growing strength of Adolf Hitler in Germany. As a result, both groups called for a major increase in aviation manufacturing, creating one of very few industries in France in the time period that was growing. A consequence of the expansion was a larger, more unified labour activist core.

A Breguet 730 being tended to. (*Photograph from the Nico Braas Collection, 1000aircraftphotos.com*)

These growing numbers, and their growing importance, had forced concessions from lord-like company owners for the first time since World War I, and labour militancy increased with time. Part of the consequence of the rearmament drive was exposing how ill-prepared France's aviation companies were to deal with the demands for increased production of modern aircraft and attempts to speed up often ran into resistance from workers who disliked the chaos and had little reason to trust their employers.

When France went to the polls in 1936, the Popular Front became—to the surprise of many—the government of France. The two years of this government represent a complicated period in French history, which is beyond the scope of this work but is well worth the study of anyone with an interest in French history. The relation to this work is that when strikes erupted again in the summer of 1936, the Breguet works were not exempted. The Breguet works in Le Havre were a genesis point for a far wider movement, as the city had a strong history of labour activism. The crisis erupted on May Day, which fell between rounds of the French election—workers walked off the job to try to maintain momentum for the Popular Front. A total of 90 per cent of the workers at Breguet did not show up to work that day, and Breguet's factory manager responded as many such owners did (and indeed still do): with reprisals. Two workers were fired for their politics, though some believed they were fired also for workers opposing the spreading of

A closer view of a 730 that displays the unusual tail to full effect. (*Photograph from the Nico Braas Collection, 1000aircraftphotos.com*)

far-right newspapers on behalf of the personnel director. Whatever the intent, the result was a call for the workers' reinstatement, and a forty-hour week to avert the perennial layoffs that plagued the French aviation industry.

A strike call spread afterwards (this was not discussed at the initial meeting to avoid it coming to the ears of the police informers in the audience—the French government before the Popular Front was as deeply suspicious of labour activism as many others in the period) and all 500 workers in the prototype and production shops downed tools and refused to work until the men were rehired. The plant director refused to negotiate, and the workers occupied the factory. While an improvisation, the men and women quickly organized a durable effort, and the director asked the police to clear the factory. The mayor of Le Havre tried to calm the situation, knowing the potential consequences of an assault.

The incomplete 730 prototype was then undergoing static tests, and was sitting in the factory fully fuelled. In the event of an assault, the workers had vowed to retreat into the prototype, which, as one worker put it, could have "serious consequences." With a potentially explosive situation—quite literally—on their hands, and with the company's future prototype on the line, some calm was restored to the situation. The police did not storm the factory. The strike was ultimately arbitrated, and the workers had a victory. In this small way, the Breguet 730 prototype became a part of the labour movement, a long-forgotten symbol of the power a unionized worker could possess in opposition to unfair or pernicious treatment by an employer.

With the labour unrest out of the way, the prototype was finally ready for its testing either on February or April 4 (sources disagree), 1938, on the River Seine. With these initial trials out of the way, the aircraft was transferred to Cherbourg for further testing work. Disaster struck soon afterwards. On July 16, the prototype was brought in for a landing in water that was too shallow to accommodate it, and two crew members were killed and the prototype wrecked. The French government nevertheless authorized construction of three more aircraft in 1939. This good news was followed by even more good news: when France went to war in September, they told Breguet to prepare for unlimited production of the 730. Given the state of the French aircraft industry, only four boats were started right away, with construction taking place at the former Latécoère (by now property of SNCAN) factory outside Toulouse at Montaudran.

Then catastrophe enveloped France. The German armies swept in, and none of the aircraft had been completed by the time the French government surrendered. The aircraft languished for a time until the Vichy government authorized their completion in 1941. The first two "production" aircraft were completed as the Br 730, with alterations to the wing and fuselage. In addition, new engines were fitted, this time Gnôme-Rhône N-44 and N-45s. The first aircraft was completed in 1942, when catastrophe overwhelmed development again. Fearing growing Allied success and the buildup of enemy strength in the Mediterranean—including Free French forces—the Germans occupied the rest of the Vichy-controlled France, taking over the Breguet program. As will be seen in the chapter on the Dornier Do 24 later, the Germans were willing to take on whatever flying boats they could, or indeed make use of any aircraft they could. As a result, the testing of the aircraft at Berre was continued, and the Germans began production of what they thought would be eleven examples of the Br 730. This production moved along slowly, but the Allies had little intention in letting them finish: the Montaudran facility was bombed on April 6, 1944. Only three of the aircraft survived the attack.

As German power retreated, the program could get back underway. The Germans began pulling out of Southern France in August 1944, and by December, the first aircraft, named *Vega*, was finishing its testing at Berre. The other three were to be completed at Biscarosse. In February 1945, *Vega* was belatedly delivered to the French navy's *Escadrille 9Ftr Aéronavale*. The aircraft available to the French for naval use at this point were a very mixed lot indeed, and essentially, the French had to make use of any floatplanes or flying boats they could get their hands on. It is not out of the realm of possibility to state that had the 730 had the flying characteristics of a thrown brick, it still would have found a home in French service. It is likely, of course, that the aircraft did significantly better than that. *Vega* was ready for service, and *Sirius* (the second aircraft) was ready for testing in mid-June 1946. By then, naturally, the world of the flying boat was contracting nearly everywhere—but, in slowly-rebuilding France, there was some mileage left to be covered.

Breguet 731 after the war, with modified cockpit. (*Photograph from the Nico Braas Collection, 1000aircraftphotos.com*)

Indeed, the next two aircraft would be extensively modified. A new, more modern cockpit design was fitted as were different Gnôme-Rhône engines, this time R-24 and R-25s. These "new" aircraft were designated Br 731, with the first called *Altair* and the second *Bellatrix*. The former began its testing at the start of September 1947, with *Bellatrix* to follow later. All four completed Breguet boats were assigned to Squadron 33S for transport flights between Metropolitan France and her North African territories.

Vega was lost in a crash in North Africa in 1948, continuing the program's bad luck, and *Sirius* would meet the same fate in Morocco in June 1951, in a crash that killed seven. By then, it was one of an increasingly endangered species. *Altair* had been assigned to the route between Toulon in Southern France and Dakar, a route it followed until 1950 when it was withdrawn. *Altair* and *Bellatrix* might have soldiered on longer, but the first helicopters were arriving with the squadron, pushing them out of their niche. *Altair* was withdrawn first in 1953, and *Bellatrix* followed the next year. Thus, ended a program plagued by delays and difficulties from the start.

The history of the Breguet 730/731 is an excellent example of what can happen to any aviation program, no matter how promising. The type was plagued by labour unrest, production delays, two German invasions, a disastrous bombing attack, and then by the passage of time. Each of these provided progressively more difficult obstacles to overcome, and the last proved fatal as indeed it does to most

Put out to pasture—behind the 731 is a PBY Catalina. (*Photograph from the Nico Brass Collection, 1000aircraftphotos.com*)

things. That any aircraft ever flew at all reflects the determination of her designers and builders, and despite all the difficulties France encountered, the program not only continued, but even improved itself with time. While it may never have set records or carried out great deeds, the Breguet 730/731 program is still very deserving of study by any aviation enthusiast.

9

Canadian Vickers Vedette: The First Bushmaster

There was once a vast little-known world to the north. It was not that the land had not been explored, *per se*—the First Nations and Inuit had known these lands for untold thousands of years, and then French, British, Canadian, and other nationalities had explored them once again—but owing to a combination of fantastic vastness and often daunting terrain, the lands remained little known and inaccessible. The possibilities posed by aviation were tantalizing as a result: aircraft might open up travel routes, make resources easier to access, and make it possible to get to remote communities. In short, the future seemed like nothing but opportunity for aviation, and the more aircraft developed, the more profound the effect on Canada's north, and indeed Canada itself. A tumultuous and risky period began that lasted for many years, where the north of Canada and Alaska became territory to conquer from the air—a process not without its peril.

The Canadian and provincial governments also had objectives to fulfil, albeit carried out in a far more prosaic fashion. One of the most crucial tasks for aircraft was survey work—getting to know the land with all the tools available to modern technology. Another objective was to guard against forest fires, something that private companies would take on in the decades to come. To achieve the objectives of conquering the vast Canadian interior by air, the flying boat was admirably suited to an enormous task. The Canadian Vickers Vedette was one of these pioneering craft, only finding retirement in the 1940s—after nearly twenty years of mastering Canadian skies.

Specifications

First Flight: 1925
Powerplant: Depending on model, one Wright J-4 nine-cylinder radial (200-hp) engine, Wright J-5 (220-hp) engine, or Armstrong-Siddeley Lynx IV seven-cylinder (180-hp) engine.
Armament: None

Top Speed: 92 mph (153 kph)
Range/Service Ceiling: Approximately five hours' endurance, 13,000 feet (4,000 metres)
Dimensions: Length 32 feet 10 inches (10 metres), height 11 feet 4¼ inches (3.359 metres), wingspan 42 feet (12.80 metres)
Number Built: Sixty

The Canadian Vickers Vedette has always held a unique place in Canadian aviation. Other Canadian-built aircraft have been better known, and to the vast majority of Canadians today, the name 'Vedette' would spark no knowledge or memory. This should absolutely not be the case, since the Vedette was the first aircraft designed and built in Canada. It was a pioneer in more than one way.

In 1925, the further reaches of Canadian territory were still unknown in large part, at least to some. While the First Nations, Métis, and Inuit had both lived in and known the land intimately for many thousands of years, their knowledge was neither prized nor sought by the Canadian state or Canadians in general. Indeed, they had long since been displaced from their ancestral lands. Today, this same prejudice and bigotry—or sometimes general ignorance—of the history, culture, and struggles of the Indigenous Peoples of Canada remains unfortunately strong. This work cannot even begin to address such important topics, but it is to be hoped that improved education about their vibrant cultures and long history will help to lessen Canada's many sins towards the country's indigenous population. Beyond these vast and pressing issues, the immediate effect was to limit practical knowledge of Canada's remote regions.

There was precious little to help with this monumental task. The coastlines were well known, and the railways had provided some knowledge, but vast tracts were unexplored. Aircraft offered a useful way not only to chart the interior officially, but also to provide access to the resources held within. Canada had been built on the exploitation of natural resources, a process which (more controversially) continues to the present day, and it seemed only natural that aircraft could be used to further economic development. It was this economic motive that prompted their use in surveying since the Canadian government had no interest in maintaining air strength after World War I.

In any event, they did not exactly have aircraft that were up to the task. What was left over after the war were aircraft of the Imperial Gift, a donation of surplus British aircraft to the Dominions after 1918. These aircraft formed the backbone of the post-war Canadian Air Force (today the Royal Canadian Air Force) and were put to use for mapping as well as to aid in forestry patrols, geological surveys, air ambulance services, air spraying, fire suppression, and other activities. The aircraft being used for this were not well-suited to the rugged conditions and hard labour they were put to. What was needed was a specialized aircraft suited to Canadian needs, and so the air force approached Vickers in 1924 to see if they would be willing to build a flying boat in Canada.

A flying boat made particular sense. There were few enough airfields in and around major Canadian centers, the interior was completely devoid of such things.

The flexibility of a flying boat was the only practical solution at the time. Vickers was willing, but possibly sensed the urgent need for the aircraft since they wanted to charge $15,000 for each aircraft, an enormous price at the time. Despite this, Vickers employee R. K. Pierson had already been working on a design, and it was turned over to Canadian Vickers. Chief Engineer Wilfred Thomas Reid set up a facility in Montreal to produce the aircraft that he modified to suit the Canadian environment, which they said would be ready in six months. Reid had already made basic plans for a flying boat, and as a result the first mock-up was ready for wind tunnel testing at the University of Toronto by the summer of 1924. The idea, already named Vedette, was given more substance when the air force signed the contract for it in August, and the first prototype—true to Vickers' word—was ready to fly in November.

The design was for a two or three seat pusher aircraft, originally powered by a 200-hp Rolls-Royce Falcon III engine in the prototype—a feature that would change twice as testing continued. The aircraft, typically for the period, was to be built primarily of wood and canvas. The design was also fairly typical of flying boats of the period, with a lattice-like construction to the wooden hull. This did not denote strength, as the Vedette would prove somewhat fragile in service, and unusable in winter. This fragility is amply demonstrated by the fact that a common problem when a Vedette landed too heavily or crashed was that the engine, mounted high over the cockpit, would fold or crash down into it, injuring the crew. It also carried three in total: the pilot, engineer, and an observer/photographer in a forward position in a bathtub-type seat. The positions for

A Canadian Vickers Vedette in RCAF service, at Victoria Beach in Manitoba. (*Photograph from the Bill Ewing Collection, 1000aircraftphotos.com*)

both the pilot/engineer and the observer/photographer were both open to the elements, making it all the better for them that the Vedette was not suited to winter operations.

The aircraft flew for the first time on November 4, 1924, with Flight Officer W. N. Plenderlieth of the R.A.F. at the controls. Over time, the prototype would switch out the Rolls-Royce engine for the 210-hp Wolseley Viper, and then the 200-hp Wright Whirlwind J-4 before finally receiving the 215-hp Armstrong-Siddeley Lynx engine. The prototype (c/n 9) comprised the Vedette I variant. The Vedette II would prove to be the production version. The testing had revealed that while the aircraft might be fragile—hardly a unique complaint for aircraft built in the 1920s—it was lighter and more maneuverable than the Curtiss HS2Ls, one of the few other aircraft that might be acquired. The Vedette II would make only minor changes to the design, namely modifying the rudder. The engines would be standardized in the production version, with the RCAF using the Lynx, while the commercial versions took on the Wright J-4. The first of these was produced for Fairchild Aerial Surveys Limited, labelled G-CAFF. When the aircraft was completed on May 10, 1926, it was the first commercial aircraft to be built in Canada.

Flying the aircraft was not always a joy, as one account recollects about a Vedette V. The III and IV models were never built but were supposed to have had an enclosed cabin. The V model was an improved amphibian version, but many were never built with wheels. Former air ace Don MacLean had opened his own company called Pacific Airways, a small business that thrived on aerial spraying and fisheries patrols. The Vedette V was one of their aircraft, a far cry from others that had such luxuries as an enclosed cabin or upholstered seats. Flying a Vedette meant the pilot was, as he put it, "sat out there where God meant airplane drivers to sit; out in the noise and wind." This had its disadvantages, namely the cold but also the chance for injury, nor did it help that the Vedette apparently did not do too well in rough air. The chance of injury was likely foremost on pilots' minds as illustrated by an incident in the summer of 1928, when one flying from Prince Rupert to Queen Charlotte City hit the trees when the pilot became lost in clouds between two islands. The Wright J-5 this particular Vedette had mounted fell forward into the cockpit, injuring the pilot. All three of the crew were eventually rescued, but the Vedette was unrecoverable.

Another incident reveals another small way in which the Vedette was a Canadian first, and also relates the overall danger of aviation in the time period. On May 17, 1929, Colin Jack Caldwell was test flying a Vedette over Montreal when the engine failed and it went into an unrecoverable spin. He baled out, becoming the first Canadian to have his life saved by a parachute. Unfortunately, he would be killed just over a month later when his aircraft hit wires over the St. Lawrence River. Flying was still a very hazardous business in the late 1920s and improving aviation safety would be a major task over the coming decades.

The vast majority of produced Vedettes were taken over by the RCAF, where they became a well-liked aircraft despite a temperamental nature and a leaky hull.

This was a common problem for all wooden-hulled flying boats, and there was an additional problem for hulls of this type: water soaked into the wood over months of operation, making the aircraft heavier with the passage of time. The RCAF made great use of their Vedettes as photographic aircraft, mapping the Canadian interior and producing topographic maps that remained in use for decades. In fact, the Vedette carried this duty out until the outbreak of World War II, working on a vast coast-to-coast survey project. This survey would only be completed after 1945, using other, newer aircraft. It also carried out forestry patrols under government service. Both the RCAF and Western Canada Airways used their aircraft for other patrol duties, carrying out fishery patrols and anti-smuggling operations on both coasts of the country. They were also put to excellent use on mercy missions, and in a unique twist, were used for aerial goose hunting. This apparently went on until a pilot was hit by one.

In addition to the use of the prototype, the RCAF purchased thirteen Vedette V aircraft in 1929. In addition to the potential for amphibious use, the V model also had a higher gross weight. They also acquired eleven Vedette VA aircraft, which came with Handley Page wing slots. There were also two metal-hulled versions of the Vedette built, both with only single examples. The one and only Vedette VI was one of these two aircraft and also received an enclosed cockpit, and its fate has not yet been traced. The other was a Mk V that was refurbished at the factory and emerged as the metal-hulled Vickers Vam, known in the RCAF by its call sign "ZD." It was, in fact, the last Vedette produced.

These RCAF aircraft were durable and useful enough to serve through the 1930s and all the way into World War II. A total of eight Vedettes were still plying the skies by then for the RCAF, all Vedette VA models, as well as a single Vedette VI. These flew with No. 4 (BR) Squadron and as part of the Seaplane and Bomber Reconnaissance Training School, based in Vancouver. (The latter became No. 13 Squadron.) These last, elderly survivors remained in service until May, 1941.

Vickers also exported a total of six Vedettes to Chile, where they became part of the *Servició de Aviación Militar de Chile*, serving the Chilean air force well. At least one of these, and possibly all six, met with a fate no Vedette—indeed no aircraft of the period—could survive: being caught by hurricane-force winds, in an incident that caused two fatalities. In addition, Vedette experts believe that at least one aircraft made it as far as China, though its service history and fate are unfortunately unknown.

Over the Vedette's service life, the RCAF began to give up its forest fire patrol duties, and provincial governments took the type over for their use. The RCAF, after 1929, was seeking to trim its sails in light of the financial crisis, and Civil Operations was scaled back significantly. Passing on the Vedettes made excellent sense. The main users were the provinces of Manitoba (Manitoba Government Air Service), Ontario (Ontario Provincial Air Service), and Saskatchewan. These governments were able to purchase the aircraft at nominal sums (Manitoba paid $1 for each of the five aircraft they received, for instance), a major boon in the 1930s when provincial governments were also feeling the pinch of the Great

A Canadian Vickers Vedette rests at left, with a Vickers Varuna to the right. (*Photograph courtesy of Dan Shumaker*)

Depression. The Government had a caveat in that former RCAF pilots should be employed. In this service, the aircraft proved quite adept at transferring firefighters to deal with blazes, though stacks of stone weights had to be kept on hand to rebalance the aircraft after it dropped off its human cargo, since their weight altered the aircraft's center of gravity. The center of gravity had, according to one of the men involved in restoring the aircraft, always been something of a problem. In the case of Manitoba, they kept piles of flat rocks on the dock along the shore of Lake Winnipeg. Rocks had to be loaded and unloaded either from docks or sand beaches to keep the aircraft balanced as it went about its firefighting duties. Manitoba's use of the Vedette centered around Lac du Bonnet, where many aviation services centered their operations, and the community definitely remembers the Vedette very well indeed.

Not many Vedettes were produced to begin with, and they were slowly used up by the passage of time, the rough conditions, and their own fragility. The arrival of the war and the subsequent post-war boom both served to dim the memory of the Vedette, though it was not entirely forgotten. In 1994, the Canadian Mint began to issue a series of ten coins to honour and remember aviation achievement in Canada. The second coin released had the Vickers Vedette, and also honoured Wilfred Reid's role in Canadian aviation in the 1920s. The coin itself was designed by Ontario artist Robert Ralph Carmichael, who created the design for Canada's iconic dollar coin, known as the "Loonie" owing to the Loon that has adorned the coin since it was introduced.

By that time, there were no Vedettes that were intact, and a group that would grow into a Western Canadian museum aimed to fix that. The idea was to rebuild a Vedette from parts of aircraft that were found either in storage or in the

A Vedette in provincial service, in this case the Government of Manitoba. This picture taken *circa* 1930 at Lac du Bonnet. (*Photograph from the Bill Ewing Collection, 1000aircraftphotos.com*)

bush. A huge part of this effort was finding the remains of an aircraft originally labelled CF-AIS. This aircraft was bought by the Manitoba government in 1934 and re-designated CF-MAG. On a flight in 1937, its engine failed, and it was lost in a swamp; it was from aircraft like these, retrieved by something akin to archaeological expeditions, that the world's only rebuilt Vedette would be crafted.

In this respect, the author is indebted to the Royal Aviation Museum of Western Canada for discussing the project. This primarily took the form of an interview with one of the main restoration team members, Gord Emberley. The original form of the Vedette rescue group consisted of Al Hansen, Murray Clearwater, Gord Emberley, his son Doug Emberley, and (later) Keith Olsen. Perhaps expectedly, it grew out of a love of aviation. Gord Emberley was a bush pilot starting in the 1950s, and after he left commercial flying, he has pursued personal aviation ever since. He had made a presentation about the Manitoba Air Service, and his son asked what happened to the Vedettes; this opened up a process of seeking out wreckage in the bush of not only Vedettes but other aircraft of the period lost to time. This led to the formation, between the five men, of the Manitoba Aviation Restoration Group. In 1973, they formed into the museum association, which was formally opened by Queen Elizabeth II a decade later; today, it is the Royal Aviation Museum of Western Canada. Their collection continues to grow, especially regarding early aviation in Canada, and the Vickers Vedette began all of it.

A friend of Mr. Emberley knew the rough location of the wreckage of CF-MAG near Cormorant Lake in Manitoba, and after a twenty-minute dive, they found the remains of the airplane, which had been burnt down to the waterline. However, they found the oil and fuel tanks, and retrieved parts that had been salvaged by others in the area. This did not immediately translate into a restoration because there were no drawings to work from; whatever was left at a national level had either been lost or ruined by water damage. After salvaging the hull of another partial Vedette from around Prince Rupert, they added a nose section from Ottawa and the center section with the engine mount and the wing mounts. In the 1980s, the group added the help of engineer Doug Newey—who had been a Vickers engineer in the 1920s working on wing designs—to draft blueprints and make new drawings. All told, it took nearly twenty years to restore the Vedette—a process totalling thousands of hours. Mr. Emberley himself designed and built the engine mount and installed the engine and fuel and oil system. It took five years just to make the drawings, based on the pieces that had been salvaged from all the sources. After that, they manufactured the frames and templates, had to make everything from exhaust studs to the oil and fuel tanks, and according to Mr. Emberley, had to use their imagination a little bit to get it done completely.

He spoke of the airplane in very interesting terms:

> It's quite a remarkable little airplane ... Vickers were boat builders ... so it's built like a boat ... it has mahogany [diagonally] on the hull, and two layers of fabric ... then it's doped and there's another layer of wood, then another layer of fabric, and this made it supposedly watertight. But they were much heavier by the fall after sitting in the water all summer—they were literally removed and hung out to dry. They took on quite a bit of extra weight, possibly up to 150–200 pounds.

Another interesting aspect about the Vedette's service life that Mr. Emberley related was that the airplane had no rudder, so they had to have a rigger on board to make it turn on the water. If you wanted the aircraft to turn to starboard, the rigger would get out the right side of the cockpit and walk the starboard wing until he dipped the sponson float. That would cause drag and turn the airplane right. If the captain changed his mind, he had to climb back through the strutting and past the engine all the way to the port wing to repeat the process.

At the end of his conversation with the author, Mr. Emberley demonstrated the continuity to preserving aviation history, where knowledge is passed from hand to hand. He related how the museum benefitted from knowing Air Vice Marshal Ralph McBurney, who had flown Vedettes in the late 1920s and answered all the questions Mr. Emberley had for him. When he came to get an award at the museum, he said he could not remember much from seventy years ago, but when he sat in the airplane, he immediately could tell them where things were correctly placed and where other things were out of position. From his original hands, the knowledge passed to the restoration team, and from there to future generations.

The museum, always geared mainly towards preserving the history of civil aviation, has always sought to restore its aircraft as faithfully and completely as possible. Though the Vedette restoration is far too precious to ever allow back into the air, it nevertheless is "the whole package," as it would have been in its glory days. The restoration was completed in 2002.

Another Vedette has been restored by the Western Development Museum in Saskatchewan, using some of the drawings that were so painstakingly created by their colleagues in Manitoba, and this second Vedette was finished in early 2017.

The history of the Vedette is one that is well remembered but by relatively few in the nation of its birth. It was a genesis point for much of the bush flying that in many ways has knit the distant regions of the country together over the passage of decades. This first Canadian-built bush plane might have been physically lost forever were it not for the dedicated work of aviation enthusiasts of all varieties—a message that this book will return to time and again. Their passion and long dedication helped to restore not one but two Vedettes, which proudly stand as a testament to those early days and the important role of the Canadian Vickers Vedette in Canada's aviation history.

Monument to the Vedette and her pilots at Lac Du Bonnet, Manitoba. (*Photograph courtesy of Davide Montebruno*)

10

CANT Z.501: Italy's Wooden Angel of Mercy

Caproni, as previously discussed, was an early and visionary proponent of the flying boat. His native Italy would pursue this vision with vigour in the 1930s, producing a stable of graceful and capable flying boats that would perform feats that dazzled the world—all of it to promote the greater glory of Mussolini's attempt at a new "Roman Empire." This propaganda would mask long-term strategic vulnerabilities within Italy's *Regia Aeronautica*, but for a time the illusion would hold. Throughout the war, the Cantieri Aeronautici e Navali Triestini concern would be at the forefront of both flying boats and bombers during the war, creating perhaps Italy's best bomber of World War II, the Z.1007 *Alcione*. In the 1930s, though, they would produce an aircraft meant to scour the Mediterranean and perform the feats that Mussolini so desperately craved. Long after fascist glory faded into a dark warning from history, the image of Italy's flying boats of the 1930s would endure.

Specifications

First Flight: 1934
Powerplant: One Isotta-Fraschini Asso XI.RC RC2C.15 liquid-cooled twelve-cylinder engine (producing either 880 hp or 900 hp depending on source cited)
Armament: Three 7.7-mm (0.303) Breda-SAFAT machine guns, some models with only two when the nose position was removed, and 640 kg (1,400 pounds) of bombs on external racks.
Top Speed: 170 mph (275 kph)
Range/Service Ceiling: 1,500 miles (2,400 km), 23,000 feet (7,000 metres)
Dimensions: Length 46 feet 11 inches (14.30 metres), height 14 feet 6 inches (4.40 metres), wingspan 73 feet 9¾ inches (22.50 metres)
Number Built: Approximately 454

One of the chief drivers behind the development of Italian air power in the 1930s was the Minister of Aviation, Italo Balbo. A small part of his work was, in the early 1930s, working to persuade *Ing.* Filippo Zappata to become the chief designer for the newly reorganized company (known as Cantieri Riuniti dell'Adriadico (CRDA), the company had been merged with other shipyards, but retained the CANT designation for aircraft, though a reader will sometimes see the "CRDA" label affixed in some sources) and his first of many designs would ultimately become the CANT Z.501 known as the Gabbiano, or "Seagull."

The aircraft was, typically of both many Italian designs and also CANT products, designed to incorporate significant wooden construction. In this case, the hull was fully wood, while the upper hull was fabric-covered; wood featured throughout the rest of the design wherever possible. Fabric also was used to cover the wing and tail structures. The high parasol wing had a single engine, mounted above the centerline. Originally fitted with a two-bladed wooden propeller, a metal three-bladed unit would equip later examples. What made the Gabbiano's design unique was the fact that the engine nacelle was extended to create a cockpit for the flight engineer, who was also expected to serve as a gunner for a 7.7-mm (0.303-inch) machine gun, with the aircraft having two more such weapons being mounted in the bow and a dorsal position. Inboard of the floats, bomb racks were fitted at the intersection of the wing and float struts, allowing the aircraft to carry up to 1,411 lb (640 kg) of bombs. The total crew capacity of the aircraft was five: the pilot and co-pilot in the cabin, two gunners, and the strangely isolated flight engineer.

The intended purpose as a reconnaissance and bomber aircraft was still secondary to the immediate goal, however. To demonstrate Italian prowess and technical achievement, and none too long after the prototype's first flight on February 7, 1934, the fascist government set a task for the new aircraft. CANT's chief pilot, Mario Stoppani, took the aircraft on a record-breaking 2,560-mile

A CANT Z.501 beginning her take-off run. (*Photograph from the Dan Shumaker Collection, 1000aircraftphotos.com*)

(4119km) flight from the company base at Trieste on the Adriatic all the way to Massawa, in Italian Eritrea. The record did not hold for long, with the French seizing it in July of 1935. Undeterred, Stoppani simply took the record back, with a 3,080-mile (4,957-km) flight from the same starting point to Berbera in British Somaliland.

As a natural result of this, the Z.501 began to enter squadron service in 1937. This was the path for other record-breaking aircraft built by the Italians, though with varying measures of success. Some, like the Savoia-Marchetti SM.79 *Sparviero*, could look forward to a major career with a certain amount of success. Others, like the Breda Ba.88, were unmitigated disasters. The CANT Z.501 would fall somewhere in the middle, through no fault of its own.

By the time war came for Italy in 1940, the Z.501 equipped a full seventeen squadrons, and four flights, with a total of 200 already built and in service. Some foreign service had by this point already occurred, with the Z.501 being sent to Spain. As part of Italy's efforts to aid General Francisco Franco's Nationalists, Z.501s had been sent to Majorca as part of the Aviazione Legionaria. A small number of Z.501s would also end up serving under Romanian colours, as part of a coastal defence unit, equipping a squadron that operated in the Black Sea region against Soviet forces.

In combat usage, the Z.501 was to suffer a certain deterioration in performance—again a common factor among Italian record breakers, since the astounding feats were accomplished before military equipment was added on. The Z.501, most noticeably, saw a major drop in its effective range, according to some sources being downgraded to 620 miles (998 km). Most sources denote a range of around 1,500

A Z.501 about to lift off. (*Photograph from the Dan Shumaker Collection, 1000aircraft photos.com*)

miles (2,400 km), however—still well short of its previous reach. The aircraft did have its positive qualities. It was well-liked by its crews for its easy-going nature in the air, and because it was a simple aircraft to maintain. More serious issues developed, however, that would rather outweigh these positive features.

There was a greater difficulty that came with the shift from peace to war, and that had to do with the aircraft's structure. The graceful, even elegant, design was slower and far less agile than any fighter aircraft it might encounter, a situation that was only going to get worse with the passage of time. Moreover, that same beautiful structure, which in peacetime meant low wing loading and a high level of reliability, became a liability. Designed as a marathon runner, it was not suited to quick dashes or, for that matter, being durable enough to withstand heavy amounts of enemy fire. Nor were the maximum of three machine guns (often the Z.501 had only two mounted) adequate to protect it from aircraft that could outrun, outmaneuver, and outgun it.

Worse still, the strains of combat usage revealed the limitations of the type's structural strength. Its seafaring properties had never been stellar, and in rough seas, the fuselage was known to break up—a process that also only deteriorated as wartime materials and construction quality worsened. Perhaps the worst part was that in rough landings on the sea (far more likely in times of war), the propeller tended to crash down into the cockpit, only a short distance behind and below.

Perhaps naturally enough, combat operations against France and then Britain predictably did not go well. It was planned that the aircraft could take on reconnaissance, anti-submarine duty, and engage in searching for mines, but ultimately it would be relegated to a role as a rescue aircraft, though this was limited by a small amount of available space on board. In practical terms, it would end up searching out and reporting shipwrecks to naval units of the Italian Fleet.

The course to this outcome happened rapidly. Italy declared war on France and England for two primary reasons. The first was to gain glory for Italy in a conflict that looked to be swiftly going Germany's way. Second, both France and Britain were perceived as potentially vulnerable targets—France owing to her imminent collapse, and Britain's Mediterranean and African possessions potentially for the taking as they were (the Italians hoped) consumed with the fight against Germany. Italy's plans did not work out. For a start, Britain would prove more than capable of defending and even going on the offensive in the Mediterranean, and despite France being struck mortal blows by the German military, what the French had available against Italy proved more than capable of striking back fully against Italian efforts.

Very quickly, the French destroyed seven Z.501s during an attack on their base on Sardinia, with another being lost in a crash the next day. Thereafter, encounters with fighter aircraft of the Royal Navy's Fleet Air Arm began to take their toll; by the end of 1940, sixty-two aircraft had been lost, and other operational problems reduced the number of available aircraft to a mere eighty-seven. A grand total of forty recorded incidents took place in which enemy aircraft encountered the Z.501 in the air, and many of them resulted in the aircraft being shot down.

Z.501s flying in formation over either the *Conte Di Cavour* or *Giulio Cesare* at a 1938 naval review. (*Photograph courtesy of the Naval Aviation and Heritage Museum*)

New orders had to be placed to bring the numbers up, and the type ultimately equipped fifteen of the twenty-seven squadrons being used for reconnaissance, the *squadriglia da ricognizione marittima*. There was some success, too, in attacking submarines, with Z.501s damaging perhaps half a dozen enemy vessels and participating in the destruction of two others. In this role, the Z.501 was significantly hampered by the fact that though it could carry depth charges, it carried no detection equipment of any kind with which to locate its targets. Even with the relatively clear waters of the Mediterranean—that could often reveal a submarine travelling at shallow depths—this was a severe brake on their potential effectiveness.

In service, the type was nicknamed "*Mammaiuto*," or "mamma help me!" owing to its dedicated role as a search and rescue aircraft. Interestingly, the aircraft also participated in rescuing its tormenters, picking up downed R.A.F. aircrews. Efforts to arrest its structural deficiencies ultimately added to the weight, and despite equipping a slightly more powerful engine, overall performance still declined. This, coupled with its already stated vulnerability and a reduction in defensive firepower, meant that like most Italian arms during the war the Z.501's abilities and numbers dwindled consistently. By 1943, the type was out of production and numbers were dropping steadily owing to its combat vulnerabilities and structural problems in regular service. After Italy's surrender, the type continued service with both the Axis-allied *Aeronautica Nazionale Repubblicana* and the Allied Italian Co-Belligerent Air Force. The last examples would linger in Italian service until 1949–1950, but the handful of remaining aircraft were all scrapped shortly thereafter.

The Z.501 was nowhere near the worst Italian aircraft fielded during the war (a dubious title that, this authour contends, belongs to the Breda Ba.88 rather handily) but neither was it a stunning success. Designed for the marathon, it was not at home in the rugged world of World War II but it was far from a failure. Indeed, it found a specific niche that suited it, soldiering on despite its deficiencies to the benefit of many sailors and airmen who it would find in the waters of the Mediterranean. The Z.501 also had one, final distinction: it was the only flying boat to see service with the *Regia Aeronautica* during the war.

11

Consolidated PBY "Catalina": America's Ubiquitous Workhorse

The Consolidated PBY is easily the most recognizable aircraft in this work, a legend that is perhaps the most well-known flying boat of World War II, and some would argue of all time. The British named it Catalina, and this name has not only stuck, but become a nearly universal part of the aircraft's lore. Consolidated built an aircraft that became a ubiquitous sight in World War II, serving everywhere that there was water to land on and in every role, it was possible for such an aircraft to serve. The legacy has endured, too, with a warplane becoming a very popular civilian option in the post-war years, and indeed still an enormously popular aircraft today. In its heyday, the Catalina was one of the most versatile aircraft ever produced, let alone flying boat. It has created an enduring legend that is unlikely to come to an end any time soon.

Specifications

(Except for first flight and number built, all figures are for the PBY-5A version)

First Flight: 1935
Powerplant: Two Pratt & Whitney R-1830-92 Twin Wasp radial piston engines, 1,200 hp each.
Armament: Three 7.62-mm (0.303-inch) machine guns, two in the bow and one firing aft, two 12.7-mm (0.5-inch) machine guns, one in each beam position, up to 1,814 kg (4,000 lb) of bombs or depth charges.
Top Speed: 179 mph (288 kph)
Range/Service Ceiling: 2,545 miles (4,096 km), 14,700 feet (4,480 metres)
Dimensions: Length 63 feet 10½ inches (19.47 metres), height 20 feet 2 inches (6.15 metres), wingspan 104 feet (31.70 metres)
Number Built: 3,305

The Consolidated Aircraft Corporation was doing well long before it received the go-ahead to start the Catalina project. The Corporation's previous commercial success with the Commodore civilian transport had gotten them a crack at a navy contract, and the response had been the P2Y Ranger. Forty-seven of these aircraft had been ordered in May 1931, and these were followed by other developments. The Ranger would be the last aircraft program that Consolidated undertook in its Buffalo location; the firm decided to relocate to San Diego, California. The reasons for this, according to some sources, are self-explanatory: the lake by the company's Buffalo factory would freeze in winter, hardly a conducive environment for a company building flying boats. Regardless of the why, the change in scenery was accomplished by October 1935—just in time to start producing the Ranger's replacement.

In 1933, the U.S. Navy Bureau of Aeronautics (BuAer) issued a design specification asking for a new type of patrol aircraft that was meant to eventually replace the U.S. Navy's existing stockpile of such aircraft, namely Consolidated's previous P2Y or Martin's P3M. Consolidated built on its previous experience to ensure they won the competition. In October 1933, Consolidated received a development contract to create a single example of what was theoretically designated the Model 28. The initial designation was XP3Y-1. They were not the only winner of the competition, with Douglas given a similar contract to produce a prototype designated XP3D-1, which later became the P3D. Both were supposed to be delivered to the Navy in early 1935 for competitive trials.

The XP3Y-1 was a logical next step from the company's previous flying boat development, but the engineering staff led by Isaac M. Laddon sought to create a much more efficient design. Early emphasis was placed on reducing drag, first through a streamlined pylon that would support the wing to removing all miscellaneous strutting, sticking to a single pair of diagonal lift struts on each side. The only other concession to necessity would be the wingtip pylons, but the team also aimed for a significant power upgrade over previous models. The initial engines specified were Pratt & Whitney Twin Wasp radials, developing 850 hp each. The overall design was all metal aside from the then-standard fabric coverings on control surfaces, as well as on the wing section aft of the main spar.

Construction of the prototype was undertaken in Buffalo, New York, and it was completed in early 1935. From there, the prototype was delivered by train to the Naval Air Station at Anacostia, where it flew for the first time on March 21, 1935. The company's "next step" proved to be exactly that; the early test flights demonstrated a significant increase in capability over their previous patrol flying boats. Douglas had created an aircraft that could compete on these grounds, and the two prototypes were roughly comparable. The decisive factor in the Navy's decision was ultimately not on the grounds of capability, but of cost. The new Consolidated flying boat came with a lower per-unit cost of around $90,000 per aircraft. As far as the Navy was concerned, this was the end of the matter, and a contract was issued for sixty aircraft designated P3Y-1.

As the production line took shape, the prototype was returned to the factory for some modifications and improvements. Namely, the nose was lengthened by a total of eighteen inches to include a forward gun turret. In addition, the design team also altered the vertical tail surfaces and installed even more powerful 900-hp engines, this time the R-1830-64 model of the Twin Wasp. Between these relatively small alterations and production, the designation was changed to PBY-1, which reflected a shift in navy thinking away from the patrol concept and towards a more active conception of a naval patrol aircraft. The bombing role was henceforth to be emphasized, meaning that the PBY's job would not just be to spot enemy ships but to carry out active hunting patrols.

The newly upgraded prototype was sent back for testing, taking to the air for the first time midway through May 1936. It was in this early testing that the new XPBY-1 would post a record-setting non-stop flight of 3,433 miles. The first production deliveries were arriving, too, being posted to Pearl Harbor in Hawaii. The first two squadrons equipped with the aircraft were VB-11 and VB-12, in that order.

Douglas had not been sitting inactive in this time and tried again with a revised version of their flying boat. Consolidated was more than ready to meet that particular challenge: despite major modifications, the XP3-D2 was trounced. Consolidated received another contract as a result in July 1936 to produce fifty more aircraft designated PBY-2, which had only minor changes. A handful were also sold for civilian purposes as the Model 28. Five were initially sold in 1937–38, including one to an explorer who re-sold that aircraft on to the Soviet Union for a rescue mission. The aircraft must have made an impression, since the Soviets purchased three more Model 28s, along with a license to build their own. The only difference of note about the first Model 28s sold to the Soviets were that they were powered by Wright R-1820 Cyclone engines.

Consolidated PBY-1 in flight. (*Photograph courtesy of the Naval Aviation and Heritage Museum*)

The PBY-2s began delivery in late 1937, and all were in place by February 1938. This success was just the beginning, as the navy made the decision to upgrade its entire existing fleet of flying boats, with the PBY to form a central core of this program. Even before the PBY-2 started to be delivered, sixty-six PBY-3s had been ordered, arriving with a slightly newer set of Twin Wasp engines. These PBY-3s started to arrive in late 1937, and by the time the last one was delivered in the late summer of 1938, the PBY was equipping a total of fourteen naval patrol squadrons, including five at Pearl Harbor and two in the Panama Canal Zone. Already, the PBY was tasked with defending two of the most important strategic sites the United States possessed.

The navy's requirement for more PBYs seemed insatiable, and once again the process repeated itself. Before the first PBY-3 was even delivered, another thirty-three PBY-4 aircraft had been ordered. These came with 1,050-hp R-1830-72 Twin Wasps and arrived soon after their PBY-3 compatriots. The last three of these came with blister type enclosures over the waist gunner's position, a change that would become both standard and iconic of the type.

As 1939 progressed, the PBY was in extensive service with the navy, and civilian interest continued to grow apace. One Model 28-4 that was sold to Great Britain even became the first aircraft delivered by transatlantic flight. As this was happening, the PBY kept being upgraded, with the past PBY-4 sent back to the factory to have tricycle landing gear installed, making the aircraft into a true amphibian. This aircraft first flew in late November 1939 as the XPBY-5A.

The arrival of the war in Europe, combined with ever-increasing tensions with the Japanese, meant that the PBY was becoming more and more essential to the American military. In December 1939, the navy laid down its largest single order of aircraft since World War I, calling on Consolidated to deliver 200 new PBY-5 aircraft. In addition to the landing gear that would come with the PBY-5A, the main PBY-5 was a substantial upgrade over previous models. It had a new, squared off rudder and once again featured an engine upgrade, this time to 1,200-hp R-1830-82 engines. The waist blisters were given heavier M2 Browning .50 caliber guns to give the PBY a heavier defensive punch.

Britain, hard pressed for aircraft, also had taken note of the PBY and the Model 28's capabilities, as had other Allied nations. Some 174 were ordered by Australia, Britain, Canada, and France. The French never received their PBYs, being overwhelmed by the Germans before they could be delivered but Britain would absorb these, too. The PBY was simply too useful not to take as many as could be acquired. In British service, they received the iconic name Catalina, the first generation designated Catalina I. The British model had different engines, the R-1830-S1C3G, and instead of the Brownings received twin 0.303-inch mounts in the aircraft's blisters. They were also built with durability in mind, with an additional 225 lb of extra armour and self-sealing fuel tanks. The British expected their Catalinas to both give and take a punch.

Back in the United States, the first naval PBY-5 was accepted in September 1940, with the second going to the Coast Guard soon thereafter. By December 1941,

167 PBY-5 aircraft were in service with the navy, with an additional thirty-three PBY-5A aircraft on-hand. The United States' entry into the war resulted in these numbers skyrocketing. Orders poured in, with the U.S. Navy's order rising to 1,533 aircraft, a mix of PBY-5s and 5As. Great Britain received more, too. They ordered 225 non-amphibious models that were designated Catalina IB, and seventy Catalina IVAs with amphibious capabilities. All of these were supplied under Lend-Lease.

For the company, this was a glorious boom—and by 1943, demand for more Catalinas was so high that they had to construct a second factory in New Orleans, Louisiana. Other production lines opened, too. The Naval Aircraft Factory was called upon to start production on a variant model, so as not to disrupt the production of the PBY-5 series. The variant was a further eighteen inches longer, with a more pointed bow and longer rear step as well as a taller fin and rudder. This version was called the Nomad, and officially designated PBN-1. Only a handful of these ever saw naval service before the rest were allocated to the Soviet Union.

The Soviet Union's production of the Catalina may have lasted as late as 1948, as the aircraft proved useful in military service everywhere it went. Estimates vary on just how many Soviet-produced Model 28-2s were built, but the number of license-built aircraft in the Soviet Union was no lower than 400 and may have been as high as 1,000. The Russian version, too, had its own name: the Amtorg GST. This stood for *Gidro Samolyet Transportnyi*, or hydro aircraft

Resting in Colder Seas: A PBY in Soviet service. (*Photograph courtesy of PoorOldSpike*)

transport. Soviet versions had their own engines, either Milukin M-62 or Shvetsov ASh-62IR engines.

In addition, Canadian Vickers also began to produce the aircraft, contributing 732 PBYs, and Boeing Canada produced another 362. These sported a confusing array of designations since they would receive new ones whenever they arrived in service under another flag. So it was that a Canadian Vickers-built Canso A (its Canadian designation) would become the PBV-1 under the BuAer system, and OA-10s in naval service. The sheer usefulness of the Catalina meant that they frequently changed hands between branches of service and even Allied nations, making the task of figuring out the precise distribution of these aircraft difficult.

The reason for this snarl of transfers, production lines, and designations is that the Catalina was an astonishingly effective and useful aircraft, and Catalinas would be found in various air forces everywhere Allied planes went in the Atlantic and Pacific theatres. The Catalinas ran the gamut from being reconnaissance aircraft to search and rescue planes, transports, surface attack, and anti-submarine attackers.

As a reconnaissance aircraft, the Catalina could list some spectacular successes. It would be a Catalina working for the R.A.F. Coastal Command that spotted the Bismarck on March 2, 1941, as she attempted to slip away from watchful British eyes. An RCAF Catalina would, on April 4, 1942, detect a Japanese fleet attempting to attack the British fleet in the Indian Ocean. Perhaps most critically of all, on June 4, 1942, a U.S. Navy Catalina would detect the Japanese fleet steaming towards Midway, and a pivotal moment in the war in the Pacific ensued. The Catalina was everywhere eyes in the sky were needed, and for a relatively small flying boat, its fantastic range made it an excellent pair of eyes indeed.

In the Atlantic, the Catalina was also employed as a U-boat hunter, and Catalina crews would by war's end be credited with forty U-boat kills. These were daring attacks carried out in daylight and into the teeth of a U-boat's potentially heavy hitting anti-aircraft armament. Despite this, the main limitation seemed to be the slow overall speed of the Catalina, which often gave the U-boat time to dive. Other times, pitched combat erupted, and at least two Victoria Crosses were awarded for Catalinas operating under British or Commonwealth pilots, one of them posthumously.

In the Pacific theatre, the Catalina was also put to a very original and daring use that would see it achieve great success in a role it was never designed to take on: night raider. The first to recognize the potential of the Catalinas in this role were the Australians of the Royal Australian Air Force. Americans had used Catalinas in a night-time raid on the occupation force of the Japanese Fleet during the Battle of Midway, but the Australians used four squadrons of them as minelayers from April 1943 until July 1945. These mine-laying activities ranged deep into the Japanese-held southwest Pacific and forced re-routing of merchant shipping into deeper waters where they were vulnerable to roving American submarines. The minelaying slowed the shipment of oil, bottled up Japanese combat forces, and mined Japanese ports on the Chinese coast as far north as Wenchow. They also, as did the Americans, used their flying boats to carry out night-time nuisance raids to cause light damage and keep the Japanese from resting, even throwing empty beer bottles with razor blades in their necks out of the airplanes just because of the whistling noise they created on the way down.

The Americans took these activities further still by creating the 'Black Cat' squadrons, carrying out night-time bombing raids on Japanese shipping and naval targets. The aircraft would often fly so low to hit unsuspecting targets that there was a very real potential that the bomb blast would damage or envelop the aircraft itself. The secret to their success was the mounting of radar units in the Catalinas. Though primitive, these sets still allowed them to seek out Japanese ships in the dark that often did not manage to fire back until the Catalinas had already dropped their payload of bombs or a torpedo. Multiple squadrons ranged over Japanese holdings sowing havoc against merchant ships and smaller targets. Proof of their success can be recounted by looking at the one-month total for a single Black Cat squadron: VPB-33. In just over a month, these black-painted flying boats had sunk forty-three ships totalling 103,500 tons of shipping, mauling another twenty.

One spectacular incident involved a pilot named William B. "Wild Bill" Sumpter. Searching Davao Gulf on Mindanao in the Philippines, he came across

A "Black Cat" Catalina of VPB-34 off of Samar Island, in the Philippines. (*Photograph courtesy of the Naval Aviation and Heritage Museum*)

a *Chitose*-class seaplane tender in the process of refuelling two destroyer escorts. Flying in at masthead height and completely surprising the Japanese, he dropped his four bombs and all four scored a hit—one each for the escorts, and two on the tender. The escorts sank rapidly, and after strafing runs against the burning and listing tender, she too went down. Three warship kills in a single mission is a spectacular result for any aircraft, let alone a flying boat operating in a role it was never designed for.

These Black Cats carried out rescue operations and teamed up with PT boats to hammer away at small Japanese transport barges, raiding essentially anything they could, on land or sea. It goes almost without saying that this was dangerous work against a determined, mercurial foe; it was not without casualties for the raiders. Nevertheless, the story of the "Black Cats," which has received book-length treatment elsewhere, will likely fascinate many readers.

The end of the war meant a swift end to the use of most of the non-amphibious Catalinas, though several PBY-5As and PBY-6 aircraft continued on in U.S. Navy and Coast Guard service as rescue aircraft. Many of these were configured to carry droppable life boats, and in this useful role they soldiered on until the 1950s. The very last Catalinas in U.S. service, PBY-6As, were retired from the Coast Guard in 1954, and from the Navy in 1957. As they were "put out to pasture" in the United States, Catalinas found themselves sold off or transferred to other forces around the world in great numbers—still a versatile and useful craft. The list is extensive: Brazil, Chile, Columbia, Denmark, the Dominican Republic, Ecuador, Iceland, Indonesia, Israel, Mexico, Norway, Peru, the Philippines, South Africa, Sweden, and Uruguay. Many of these would continue to fly in government service for decades, possibly as late as the 1970s when most of their compatriots had long since been replaced and scrapped.

Most of the time, this would be the end of the story, where a writer would turn to a discussion of the handful of museum or display aircraft still on-hand after the decades had passed. Not so the PBY Catalina. The aircraft proved enormously popular in commercial and civilian hands after the war. Starting in 1951, for instance, Northern Consolidated Airlines of Alaska operated the type. These Catalinas flew out of Fairbanks into the challenging terrain and weather of Alaska with regularity, carrying passengers, freight, and mail. Other airlines, such as Transocean Airlines, would operate it as a passenger aircraft until the 1960s, and others would use them for charters, government surveys, geological surveying, and as firefighters—a role in which the aircraft lasted for decades. By that point in time, one might expect that the official role for the Catalina would have disappeared as well, but it was not so. Even in the 1960s, the reconnaissance role was still being filled by Catalinas in Argentina, Brazil, Chile, Ecuador, and Mexico; Nationalist China, the Dominica, Indonesia, and Peru were still making use of their Catalinas for rescue missions. France and Israel, too, still had Catalinas on hand for various duties.

The list of surviving Catalinas is rather extensive, which befits the type's versatility and popularity. A number are still in flying condition and remain a

A post-war PBY Catalina. (*Photograph courtesy of Michael Bajcar*)

common sight at air shows and museums around the world. The legacy and the legend of the PBY Catalina has certainly not dimmed, nor is it likely to do so in the future. This incredibly useful, versatile flying boat may no longer be in active service but once she was a critical weapon of war and aided peaceful human endeavours around the world. The Catalina is, perhaps, the first thought that many aviation enthusiasts, historians, and authors have when the words "flying boat" are uttered—reflective of the type's well-earned and enduring fame. Consolidated's engineers and technicians could scarcely have known any of this when they rose to that challenge back in 1933, but they produced a world-beater that deserves as much fame as a Spitfire or a Mustang.

12

Consolidated PB2Y "Coronado": Heavyweight out of Time

The difference between Catalina and Coronado is like that between night and day. The flying boats of World War II were immensely capable, and their range of abilities is demonstrated amply by the comparison between an aircraft designed for light maritime patrol and its potentially lethal bigger brother that was designed to carry a heavy tonnage of bombs; perhaps surprisingly though, the Coronado only rarely served in the role for which it was designed. Like most of the big flying boats, a giant capability meant a giant lifting capacity, and a combat aircraft would spend most of its service life as a transport, spanning oceans in aid of the Allied cause.

Specifications

First Flight: 1937
Powerplant: Four Pratt & Whitney R-1830-92 Twin Wasp radial piston engines, 1,200 hp each
Armament: Six 0.5-inch (12.7-mm) M2 Browning machine guns in twin nose, dorsal and tail powered turrets, with a further two in manual waist mounts, and either two Mk 13 torpedoes (600-lb torpex warhead), or up to 12,000 lb (5,400 kg) of bombs, housed in the wings.
Top Speed: 194 mph (310 kph)
Range/Service Ceiling: 1,070 miles (1,720 km), 20,500 feet (6,250 metres)
Dimensions: Length 79 feet 3 inches (24.2 metres), height 27 feet 6 inches (8.4 metres), wingspan 115 feet (35 metres)
Number Built: 217

The U.S. Navy, in the mid-1930s, not only had correctly denoted that flying boats would make superb patrol aircraft, they also looked to a concept that was known as the "Sky Dreadnought." The basic idea was that a large combat flying boat would serve as long-range bombers from widely dispersed sea bases. The

Consolidated Coronado began life in response to this concept, as did the Martin Mars which will be discussed at length later.

In late July 1936, Consolidated received a contract to create a prototype four-engine flying boat to be designated XPB2Y-1. Their attempt to fulfil the Sky Dreadnought concept had some family resemblance to the smaller PBY, namely in having folding wing floats and a similar tail, with a bow projecting in front of the nose turret. The similarities ended here, however. It did away with the supporting pylon that mounted the PBY's wing, opting instead of a much deeper hull that mounted the wing directly atop the fuselage. The entire structure was covered in stressed aluminum, aside from the moveable control surfaces. A further effort was made to streamline the aircraft by housing all its droppable munitions in flush bays under the wings, rather than being mounted on standard hard points.

The nearly eighteen-month construction period for the prototype was followed by a rocky start for the future Coronado, after its first flight in December 1937. Within the first three flights, it was demonstrated that the prototype had serious directional stability problems, and engineers hurriedly added finlets to the horizontal stabilizers at this point. To their undoubted grave disappointment, this did not solve the problem, and a further issue came to light when it became clear that the hull planing surfaces meant that the aircraft had issues with its hydrodynamic characteristics.

Clearly, something major had to be done. The prototype was returned to the factory for a major upgrading process that lasted until mid-1938. The changes were extensive, with the empennage—the complete arrangement of tail surfaces—being entirely redesigned, adding twin circular fins and rudders at the ends of a new horizontal stabilizer that was arranged with a six-degree dihedral orientation. The rear step was also extended nearly halfway to the tail to improve the hull's performance on water. The suitability trials demonstrated that Consolidated's engineers had solved the problems, and the prototype was accepted but no immediate order was forthcoming. Instead, the prototype was assigned to the Aircraft Scouting Force and designated as the "flagship" of that force's admiral.

Consolidated went back to the drawing board to secure a better future than a single flagship, and by March 1939, they had once again essentially redone the hull. This time, the result was an order for six aircraft designated PB2Y-2. The wing was moved down to a shoulder position, as the hull had been deepened enough to accommodate it. The hull's streamlining and water performance were both improved with a newly faired bow, which came with a smoother, reshaped nose turret.

The improvements went far deeper. The fins and rudders were enlarged, and the engines were approximately 15 per cent more powerful, mounting R-1830-78 models. In addition, three new gunner's positions were added to give the aircraft more punch, with the positions being installed in a dorsal blister behind the wing and in circular windows on either side of the plane's waist. The first of these better designed, more capable aircraft were handed over to the Navy on New Year's Eve

A Coronado on a postcard! From the early, pre-war days of the program. (*Photograph from the Ron Dupas Collection, 1000aircraftphotos.com*)

Early Coronado in flight. (*Photograph from the Jacques Trempe Collection, 1000aircraftphotos.com*)

of 1940. The factory had dubbed them "Coronado," and by mid-1941, a total of five of these aircraft were on hand in Navy use.

The increased capability certainly helped. While the new empty weight was a full 7,500 lb higher than it had been, the better-designed hull and more powerful engines resulted in a performance increase to 255 mph, the fastest the Coronado series would ever fly. The range of this new heavyweight was almost double that of the already long-legged Catalina, even in its later developments. The five Coronados were, before the war, mainly used for evaluation and training. The sixth ordered aircraft was produced to a revised production standard and was designated XPB2Y-3, flying in December of 1941. One of the existed PB2Y-2s received modifications as well and was fitted with Wright R-2600 Twin Cyclone engines and dubbed XPB2Y-4.

At this stage, the Navy had some concerns about their Coronados. The reason for this had nothing to do with any doubts about the airplane's capabilities. Before the war in the Pacific began, the Navy had far more restrictive budgetary concerns to be aware of, and the Coronado cost like the devil. The cost of a single Coronado could be put towards a total of three Catalinas, which were in high demand in the pre-war navy.

Nevertheless, before the aircraft even arrived in their hands, the Navy bit their Coronado-shaped bullet and ordered 210 of these Sky Dreadnoughts from Consolidated. With Lend-Lease coming into effect, 177 were to go to the Navy as the PB2Y-3, and the remainder were to go to Great Britain as the PB2Y-3B. The production aircraft the two nations received was even more capable than its predecessors. Weight increased again by a further 5,700 lb, a full ton of it dedicated to armour protection, with self-sealing fuel tanks and twin-gun power-operated turrets in the bow, dorsal, and tail positions, with two more flexible waist guns. This better-protected aircraft, with its improved teeth, began to reach patrol squadrons in the summer of 1942.

By then, in a twist of irony, their design role was already disappearing. The Sky Dreadnought concept had been dropped in favour of building a fleet of fast aircraft carriers using smaller aircraft to bomb targets. It appeared to the navy's planners that the Coronado—with their excellent range and huge hulls—could be put to better use as transports. As a result, the last forty-one aircraft to be built were handed over to the Rohr Aircraft Corporation to be completed as unarmed transports, the PB2Y-3R. Once again, the Coronado proved more than adequate to the task: the transport versions could carry forty-four passengers or 19,000 lb of cargo. Of some note is that given the war situation, only ten Coronados were ever actually delivered to England and all of them were used as transports.

Even the 136 Sky Dreadnought Coronados found themselves pushed slowly out of their role. Some were converted over to reconnaissance aircraft, being fitted with ASV radar mounted in a fairing that was placed just behind the cockpit. This was not enough to save them. Land-based Liberator aircraft increasingly supplanted them during 1944, and these suddenly displaced Coronados were also converted over to transports. While the Coronado did see service in its originally intended role, it was so rapidly overtaken that it had little time to leave a considerable mark on either the air war or combat aviation history.

One last variant of the Coronado bears discussion, and that is the version that was modified as a dedicated medical transport. Some of the PB2Y-3s were modified with low-altitude R-1830-92 engines and re-entered service as PB2Y-5Rs, and some of these were further modified to carry twenty-five medical litters, being known as the PBY-5H.

The Coronado was very quickly withdrawn after the war, and herein lies the tragedy of the aircraft—at least to those who love the romance and beauty of the flying boat era. The Coronado is one of the clearest examples of the arc of history that both raised and then doomed the flying boat. It was caught very quickly into its service life by land-based aircraft and pushed out of what had been originally conceived of as a central role in naval strategic air operations. A further tragedy is that this process ensured that there was almost no demand for the aircraft in the post-war world. Howard Hughes purchased one of them, but otherwise the Coronado was both swiftly withdrawn from Navy service and then disappeared from the pages of history. Today, only a single example is known to survive: a PB2Y-R, which spends its retirement in Pensacola, Florida, part of the collection of the Naval Aviation Museum.

13

Dornier Do 24: From the Past to the Present

The name Dornier is perhaps best-known today for its land-based combat aircraft. The Dornier Do 17, known as the "flying pencil," would carve out a famed role for itself in the Battle of Britain and the Luftwaffe's other early campaigns. There is also something to be said for all the derivatives of this line, improved throughout the course of the war. To those who are most fascinated by Germany's late war aircraft concepts and designs, the name will be known for the Do 335 "Pfiel," or Arrow—the strange pusher-puller design built in the final days of Hitler's dark empire. In many ways, however, looking first to these two aircraft is to do Dornier a disservice. The history of Dornier that is most frequently told is one that forgets the vast achievements of the company in the field of flying boats. Most famed of these, perhaps, is the Dornier Do 24—a craft that has enjoyed a strange, second life in modernity.

Specifications (For Do 24T)

First Flight: 1937
Powerplant: Three Bramo 323R-2 Fafnir nine-cylinder radial engines, 940 hp each (1,200 with water injection)
Armament: One 20-mm Hispano-Suiza HS 404 cannon, two 7.92-mm (0.312-inch) MG 15 machine guns
Top Speed: 211 mph (340 kph)
Range/Service Ceiling: 1,678 miles (2,700 km), 26,670 feet (6,300 metres)
Dimensions: Length 71 feet 9¾ inches (21.89 metres), height 18 feet 10⅓ inches (5.75 metres), wingspan 88 feet 7 inches (27 metres)
Number Built: 330 (including French construction)

Given the fact that many of the aircraft associated with his name have become ubiquitous with the German Luftwaffe, it might surprise many to know that Claude (often written as Claudius) Honoré Desiré was only half German by birth, being born in Bavaria to a German mother and a French father. He would gain his initial aircraft experience working on Germany's early Zeppelins before striking out on his own.

His company's first major success was the Dornier Do J *Wal*, which proved popular and spread widely around the world with over 250 examples ultimately being built. It became standard reconnaissance equipment in some countries, built outside of Germany to avoid Allied restrictions imposed by the treaty of Versailles.

The aircraft was so successful that in 1934 Dornier set forth to build a replacement to it. The first outcome of this effort was the Do 18, which became part of the still-nascent Luftwaffe. Interestingly, the aircraft was only meant as a stop-gap. Both the German RLM and the Dutch Navy both wanted to develop a better successor aircraft. The Dutch wanted a maximum speed of 196 mph (315 kph) with three or four engines, so the aircraft would still have good performance if one engine broke down or was knocked out in flight. As an aside, this ruled out the Consolidated PBY, which was available but did not fit the engine requirement, despite meeting the speed requirement.

The Dutch were willing to purchase over seventy aircraft, so this was a lucrative contract that naturally attracted competition. Sikorsky submitted a design that did not impress the Dutch, and it ultimately went nowhere. A much more serious competitor was from a native Dutch company, Fokker. They submitted the BV, which fulfilled the requirements. The problem for Fokker was that the company's resources were stretched thin and the company had yet to make the transition to manufacturing with monocoque metal. As a result, the Dutch Naval Air Service (MLD) came to favour Dornier's submitted P.14 project, and it was duly declared the winner of the competition August 1935. The Dutch gave over an initial contract the next year for six aircraft and a production license. Ironically, by this time the German RLM had lost interest in Dornier's design, and had instead come to look at the Blohm und Voss BV 138.

Dornier laid down four prototypes in total. These were given the designation Do 24K, and the first two laid down were the V3 and V4. These two aircraft were meant for the Dutch, with the V1 and V2 built for Germany, to be evaluated against the BV 138. The Dutch aircraft—based on a guaranteed order—got priority, and so it was that the V3 was the first aircraft completed. This aircraft engaged in its first taxi tests on Lake Constance on July 2, 1937, with pilot Erich Gundermann at the controls.

The design featured what was by now Dornier's standard: *stummeln*, or stump wings joined to the lower portion of the hull which removed the need for floats. It also featured a curved fuselage and a high, twin-fin tail which in similar form would feature on the well-known Dornier Do 17 bomber. The aircraft was powered initially by three Wright R-1820-F52 Cyclone radials fitted on the high parasol wing, fed by fuel tanks in the sponsons and central wing section. The fuselage itself was divided into nine watertight compartments and was designed to fit a crew of up to six. This would include two pilots, a radio operator, navigator, engineer, and an optional tail gunner. Five bunks were provided, and some seating could be provided for passengers; all could be fed by the on-board galley.

The first Dutch Dornier, X-1. (*Photograph from the Ron Dupas Collection, 1000aircraftphotos.com*)

This aircraft flew for the first time on July 3, 1937 and was proven to be successful in subsequent testing. Two months after this flight, the V3 was flown to Einswarden on the North Sea coast for further testing to evaluate how the aircraft handled the open sea. Its seaworthiness proved to be impressive. Even in rough seas, the aircraft had impressive abilities on the water, and the Dutch took over the V3 as the first Do 24K-1 service aircraft in mid-October 1937. This aircraft became Her Majesty's Flying Boat X-1. The V4 followed in February, becoming X-2.

At this point, the Dutch increased their order to ninety-six aircraft, in response to the growth of Japan as a major strategic threat to the Dutch Empire. Aware that license production would take some time to get going, the Dutch increased their direct order from Dornier to thirty aircraft. Despite this growing success, the Germans did not share the enthusiasm of the Dutch. They had by this point judged the competition and declared the BV 138 the winner, despite the issues that type was facing in its initial design stages.

The first Dornier for the Germans, the V1, finally flew on January 10, 1938. Unlike its Dutch counterparts, it was equipped with Junkers Jumo 205C engines which produced only 600 hp, a major loss compared to the Curtiss engines. Not surprisingly, the RLM's decision was not changed by this, and the V1 and V2 were allocated to serve as test beds for new equipment and to do engine cold start trials.

With the Germans unwilling to assign any productive capacity to the aircraft at all, Dornier focused on the Dutch. At this point, the Swiss factory on Lake Constance was still in use, so the aircraft were completed there, then were towed to Friedrichshafen for testing and acceptance. The first three aircraft (X-1 to 3) were delivered via Hamburg, and every aircraft thereafter was delivered through Holland. The Dutch were the first to fit a 20-mm cannon to the aircraft instead of the three machine guns it was originally fitted with, with their 20-mm gun mounted in an advanced French SAMM turret in the dorsal position. This was first fitted to X-13, and tests on this weaponry—as well as using the Do 24 in a secondary bombing role—was carried out in 1938 at De Mok seaplane station on Texel island. An indication of how well-liked the Dornier was by the Dutch was the fact that one of them (the same X-13) participated in a naval pageant near The Hague to celebrate Queen Wilhelmina's fortieth year on the throne.

Deliveries to the Dutch continued despite the outbreak of the war. The Dutch order was completed two months later, in fact, in November. The final aircraft was also the prototype of the Do 24K-2, which incorporated powerful 1,000-hp Cyclone engines that gave the aircraft higher speed. With a larger fuel capacity, it also had a longer range in the bargain. Owing to the war, this new aircraft had not even been tested in Germany, and the Dutch were the ones to do that testing into early 1940.

The Dutch had well known that native production of the Do 24 would be slow to begin, and indeed this was the case. To help with mastering monocoque construction, the work was split up. De Schelde was given the task of producing the wings at Vlissingen and Aviolanda took on the work of building the fuselages and tailplanes before handling final assembly at Papendrecht. This work was overseen by a Dornier engineer as a technical advisor, and the process did engender significant hopes for the program. The first seven aircraft were completed as Do 24K-1 aircraft, but after that, all were to be K-2 aircraft; the Dutch order increased to forty-three aircraft, which would have brought the Dutch total of Do 24s up to seventy-three in total. Despite all the difficulties, the first Dutch-completed aircraft, X-30, was finished only four months behind schedule, in June 1938. The Dutch companies apparently blamed Dornier for this delay, claiming that they simply had not received information soon enough. In any event, time was running out for the Dutch, though they did not know it yet; while Dornier was working with them, the military planners in Berlin had other ideas.

Ideas were to shift within Germany regarding the Do 24 as well. The RLM had dismissively told Dornier to concentrate on producing its Do 17 bomber design when it chose the BV 138, but the rival flying boat's lengthy teething problems stretched into years, delaying its arrival with operational units. The invasion of Norway would change everything and make the need for flying boats very keen indeed.

The initial invasion of Norway may have appeared to be a masterstroke at first, but the bold operation quickly found itself in peril as British naval strength—far in excess to anything the German *Kriegsmarine* could match—took a hand in the conflict. Specifically, the German 3rd Mountain Division under General Dietl had been isolated in Narvik by a British naval force that included the battleship *Warspite*. A naval solution to the problem was impossible, and isolation made land-based efforts futile. The solution was, naturally, to fly supplies into this

An advertisement for the Do 24 made in 1942 in an attempt to appeal to the Portuguese market. (*Photograph courtesy of the Naval Aviation and Heritage Museum*)

mountainous territory via seaplanes, and the Germans hastily deployed what aircraft they could, forming them into an *ad hoc* transport squadron. The group included three hastily-employed BV 138s, a pair of graceful Dornier Do 26 ocean-going mail planes, and the two Do 24s that had been present at Travemünde. Even with the dire need for seaplanes of any description, there was a fair chance that the Do 24s would not have been deployed in any event; the test aircraft had been flown very little and were not fully equipped. It was only thanks to the eager suggestion of a single Dornier test pilot, Adolf Mlodoch, that the Do 24 V1 was added to the mission.

The V1 had by this point been fitted with an experimental 20-mm Rheinmetall MG 204 cannon in its turret, and with the hurried loading of two machine guns, medical supplies, and ammunition, it was ready to take part in the Norwegian Campaign. The first mission was scheduled for April 12, with the single Do 24 to take part along with three BV 138s. The heavily laden BV 138s, still in the midst of teething problems, resolutely failed to take off—a problem that did not in any way bother the Do 24. The mission was temporarily scrubbed, but Mlodoch and his crew volunteered to take off on their own, with nothing for navigation other than an atlas sheet.

Amazingly, they found their way along the coast of Norway but ran into *Warspite* and her escorting warships, which promptly opened fire. The aircraft dived quickly and hid in a fjord, but by now, the crew had no idea where they were. Venturing ashore, they only encountered a scared Norwegian family who could not or would not tell them where they were. Trying again the next morning, they did another quick hop into an inlet to avoid British gunfire, and finally were able to ask their location from a shepherd. From there, they flew on to their destination. To the undoubted upset and frustration of the crew, it turned out that their ammunition was useless—the weapons meant to fire it had gone down with the German ammunition ship *Rauenfels*, which had been sunk by British ships.

This would soon be overtaken by feelings of dread, for the British launched a massive attack on the German forces that would result in a massive loss to the Germans of eight destroyers and a U-boat. The losses the German Navy suffered in the Norwegian Campaign would, in fact, permanently hobble them for the remainder of the war, but the Do 24 and its crew escaped with only minor damage from being machine gunned by the crew of a British motorboat who were engaged into trying to tow the flying boat away. The return flight, once the bullet holes were patched, was relatively calm—though the aircraft was leaking diesel by the time it arrived at Denmark.

Another flight by the V2 aircraft was cancelled, but the V1 made another flight on April 20—much more routine for the crew—bringing in two tonnes of explosives and a pair of demolition experts who were quite naturally being brought in just in the case the Germans had to abandon Narvik. Though the German position in Norway remained precarious for some time, they would ultimately hold on and the V1 and V2 aircraft would be occupied with ferrying supplies until the end of the campaign. Norway would prove the end of the V1 aircraft, though. It made an emergency landing in September and was subsequently towed into the harbour of the remote town of Vardø where it was subsequently scrapped. The V2 would follow eventually, being cannibalized for parts before the remainder of the aircraft was scrapped.

Soon thereafter, catastrophe enveloped the Dutch. Unlike World War I, German war plans did not spare their country and when the German juggernaut launched its grand campaign in the west, the conquest of the Low Countries and Denmark was on the menu in addition to the ultimate objective: France. Dutch resistance, though valiant, could not last long in the face of overwhelming odds.

The German army arrived at Papendrecht to find an assembly line, intact, of brand new German-designed aircraft that were still not in production in Germany itself. Thirteen Do 24K-2s were under construction, with a stockpile of engines on site as well. Amazingly, the Germans still seemed indifferent. Interestingly, some of the Dutch aircraft had eventful careers even after the fall of their homeland; a number of them escaped to the Pacific and would be engaged in combat by Japanese forces, with several being lost. The remainder would escape the fall of the Dutch colonial possessions in the Pacific, making it to Australia where they ended up as part of the Royal Australian Air Force—German-made aircraft that ended up serving two separate Allied nations, against a separate Axis partner. This was, to say the last, an unusual path for any aircraft to follow. More on this Pacific War service will be described in further detail later in this chapter.

Back in Occupied Holland, however, the Germans had a sudden windfall on their hands, which they decided not to use for the Luftwaffe's reconnaissance units—the *Küstenfliegergruppen*. There was one branch of German air might that was extremely eager to get their hands on these aircraft—the *Seenotdienst* (the air-sea rescue service). This service was still rather new within German organization, and had only received aircraft in the summer of 1939, despite having existed since 1935.

As of the outbreak of the war, most of the aircraft available for the task were Heinkel He 59 biplanes. German successes in the early war years stretched the seacoast that the *Seenotdienst* had to operate over, and they had very few aircraft with which to do it: perhaps thirty He 59s and a handful of Dornier Do 18s as stopgaps. More to the point, the He 59 was not the best aircraft for the task, especially given its moderate overall range and a certain amount of delicacy. The Do 18, too, had drawbacks—it had the range but the hull made accommodation and treatment of survivors difficult and all of this was exacerbated by merely adequate sea-handling qualities and lacklustre Junkers diesel engines. The commander of *Seenotflugkommando* 1, *Flügkapitan* Karl Born, wanted the Do 24s that were to be finished at Papendrecht.

The first three Do 24s completed there after the occupation were evaluated as unarmed rescue aircraft, and its 600-mile radius of action and superb, new navigation equipment made it ideal to the task. In moderate seas, or sea state 4, it apparently had an easy time of it, being described as "carefree." In sea state 6, with 4–6-metre waves, the aircraft could still manage to land with a degree of care.

In *Seenotdienst* service, the aircraft would come with a crew of six comprising a pilot, radio operator, two flight engineers who doubled as gunners, a tail gunner who doubled as a medic, and a commander who had to do triple duty, taking on the role of both observer and navigator. These Do 24K-2s entered service as the Do 24N-1, with very minor physical modifications of two hatches installed on the port side of the hull to make taking on survivors easier. Eight rest bunks were put inside for picked up servicemen, and the Wright Cyclone engines on hand were slowly used up as the formerly Dutch aircraft were finished. When these ran out, at least one aircraft used BMW 134N radials. These aircraft kept the French turret with its Hispano-Suiza cannon but used a different tail turret mounting MG 15 machine guns.

Germany was finally taking an interest in the Do 24, and the immediate result of this on Dornier's side of the equation was the penultimate version of the aircraft, the Do 24T. This carried the powerful Bramo Fafnir engines, which normally rated at 1,000 hp but could be boosted to 1,200 on take-off using water-methanol injection. The Do 24T encompassed a group of three aircraft, designated T-1 to T-3. The main differences between these versions had to do with what navigation equipment they carried and what armament accompanied it. The T-2 would for instance carry an MG 151/20 20-mm cannon in the previously used SAMM turret, but the T-3 would use an MG 151/15 15-mm weapon in an armoured HD 151/1 turret. The later T-3s would get MG 151/13 13-mm machine guns fore and aft, and also a FuG 101 radio landing altimeter.

The first production Do 24T would come out of the Aviolanda factory in April 1941, and that factory would go on to produce the majority of the remaining aircraft. Other occupied factories would contribute as well, such as Fokker's Amsterdam factory and the former CAMS seaplane factory at Sartrouville, which had previously turned out French aircraft. Interestingly, the operators of the factory were SNCAN (*Société National de Constructions Aéronautiques du Nord*) and they would go on to build Do 24s for the French after France was liberated in 1944, bringing the Do 24 under another Allied banner.

In service, the Do 24 could be found in *Seenotdienst* use in the Baltic, Black Sea, Mediterranean, and the hotly-contested Atlantic. While its duties were originally meant to be strictly those of a rescue aircraft, it took on transport and reconnaissance duties as the *Seenotdienst* itself took on an expanding role. One example of the Do 24 would even be used as a minesweeper, kitted out similarly to the BV 138MS.

In the Atlantic, the Do 24s being used were initially unarmed and painted in Red Cross colours. Both the Germans and the British were to have some difficulty here. There had been attempts to apply the same rules of war to ambulance aircraft as to land and sea ambulance operation in 1922–23, but this had not been adopted. Consequently, the Geneva Convention of 1929 had to take up the issue, passing Article 18 which was meant to protect rescue aircraft. By the time the Battle of Britain began in the summer of 1940, there was little room for niceties. The British claimed on little or no evidence that He 59 rescue aircraft were carrying out mining operations and helping get agents into Britain. In truth, though He 59s would occasionally report convoys they spotted, they also made convenient targets with some sources pointing to the simple, grim logic that with British fighter losses growing and the potential invasion of England at stake, making sure they did not have to shoot down the same German pilots twice became a piece of chilly reasoning.

The Germans protested that their aircraft were essentially hospital ships and as such ought to be immune from such attacks under the Geneva Convention. Winston Churchill icily replied: "the Germans were not in a strong position to complain, in view of all the treaties, laws of war, and solemn agreements which they had violated without compunction whenever it suited them." In truth, the British wanted to deny the Germans an advantage in pilot retrieval, and their previous behaviour made for a convenient excuse for policy. The attacks continued, with the R.A.F. even going on the offensive. By 1941, rescue aircraft trying to operate within range of British fighters in England needed their own escort, and the R.A.F. even attacked the rescue station at Ostend. For their part, the Germans would attack British aircraft and vessels engaged in rescue work as well, making rescue operations a constant source of potential danger in vast swathes of territory.

The perils of rescue efforts even without British interference is revealed more than adequately by the first loss of a Do 24. The *Seenotdienst* had already lost several He 59s, and on August 16, 1940, one was picking up survivors from a downed Heinkel He 111 when it was caught on the surface by an R.A.F. Hudson bomber and destroyed. The next day, four more He 59s and a Do 24 took off to look for survivors. They found two survivors from the He 59 and four from the Heinkel, the former on a detached float and the latter in a dinghy. The wind was at force 6, making it far too dangerous for the Heinkels to attempt a rescue. So the Do 24 attempted to set down. Unfortunately, the Do 24's pilot was making his first rough water landing and misjudged it, hitting a high wave with such force that the engines were torn off the wing. All the survivors (including the crew of the Do 24) were eventually picked up by a German motorboat, but the Germans had lost two aircraft in the attempt.

Increasing pressure from Allied fighters meant that by November, the German air-sea rescue services had been militarized with its groups now called *Seenotstaffeln*, or sea emergency squadrons. Their aircraft were given military colours and markings and were all armed. The Do 24 continued to prove its worth under these new conditions, with its wide radius of action becoming extremely helpful to German Atlantic operations. It was used to pick up survivors as far out as 248 miles (400 km) off the northwest tip of Spain. They even picked up survivors from stricken U-boats, as in the case of German submarines lost while trying to attack the Allied invasion fleet off of Normandy in June 1944. The Dorniers also rescued Allied aircrew along the way, as was the case with other German rescue efforts though this last was less out of the goodness of their hearts and more out of a desire to pick up prisoners for interrogation and intelligence gathering. By this time, over the Atlantic and North Sea, a Dornier flying alone was almost embarking on a suicide mission, as Allied fighters were always ready to pounce. The Dorniers could frequently be found picking up survivors from convoy battles on the Arctic Convoy route, and here one design problem was discovered: pilots landing in heavy seas sometimes had the tailplane break away, with many aircraft limping back into port tailless. The problem was apparently not systemic, and in any event, the fact that the aircraft still managed to float their way back pointed to the inherent durability of the design.

One unusual Atlantic incident from 1943 stands out. A Do 24 had picked up two downed Allied airmen on August 23, and while still on the water, half a dozen Boeing B-17 Flying Fortresses arrived on the scene, having been dispatched to find the same men. The Germans, in fear of the B-17s, abandoned their airplane; one of the B-17s then strafed and destroyed the Do 24, believing they had scared off another in the process. The second Do 24 ultimately picked up the flying boat's crew and the downed airmen but this revealed the dangers inherent to a flying boat caught on the surface.

One response the Germans engaged in was creating a dedicated escort squadron for its Dorniers. In the summer of 1944, the Germans created a search and escort squadron (*Such-und-Schnutzstaffel*) that consisted of Messerschmitt Me 410 twin-engine fighters based at Jever, on the German coast. Do 24s continued to operate until the end of the war in this theatre, even as certain areas became impossible in practical terms. An example of how difficult the situation had become by the late stages of the war was that in the case of one air-sea rescue unit, whenever the Do 24s went aloft, a trio of BV 138s also did to listen to communications between Allied fighters to ensure none were coming after the Dorniers.

In the Mediterranean, the Germans decided not to rely on their Italian allies for air-sea rescue. The Italian rescue aircraft were aircraft that, despite whatever excellent qualities they may have had, were particularly vulnerable by 1940, such as the previously discussed CANT Z.501 or the Savoia-Marchetti SM.66. The Do 24 fulfilled much the same role as it did elsewhere and proved very durable in warmer climes as well. One such aircraft made it back into port in July 1942 with a broken wing strut from a too-heavy landing outside the port, carrying the rescued crew of a downed Hudson bomber.

The German Do 24 squadrons were forced from base to base as the situation deteriorated, and despite being escorted in some cases by Focke-Wulf Fw 190 fighters, they remained vulnerable when caught on the ground. One solution the Germans pursued for this problem was getting the Spanish to agree to set up a neutral rescue service, though ultimately the Spanish were not willing to commit to such a large operation. The Germans ended up transferring a dozen Do 24s over to Spanish use, an action which kept the Do 24 in service far longer than one might anticipate. The last rescue carried out by a Spanish Do 24 was done on June 30, 1965, picking up a child with peritonitis from the Israeli liner *Jerusalem*. The aircraft would not finally retire until 1969.

Overall, the Do 24's situation in the Mediterranean went much the same way as the North Sea and Atlantic—combat attrition took its toll, and increasingly they

A preserved Do 24 of the Netherlands Naval Aviation Service. (*Photograph Courtesy of Michael Bajcar*)

operated over less and less territory as German territory in the theatre shrank and its operational ambitions commensurately declined, with operational groups of Do 24s taking on survivors from other groups that were driven out of the Black Sea and the Adriatic.

The Black Sea operations had been prepared well in advance of Hitler's invasion of the Soviet Union in June 1941. Two weeks before the invasion, the first German rescue aircraft had arrived in Romania. These first aircraft were He 59s, and they joined up with Romanian Savoia-Marchetti S.66 aircraft and CANT Z.501s. The first of the Do 24s did not arrive until well after the invasion had begun, arriving with *Seenotstaffel 8* in August. The early arrivals were still equipped with the Fafnir engines, which were slated to be replaced, but the first aircraft flown off to receive them was lost when it overturned on landing. This highlights the dangers of even "routine" procedures, especially those that were faced by operational flying boats on even calm waters.

The water of the Black Sea provided other challenges, too, that were not encountered by Do 24s elsewhere. As winter approached, the aircraft had to fall back to Varna in Bulgaria, since the rescue posts in Romania and further forward had frozen over. The harsh weather conditions at one point reduced *Seenotstaffel 8* to a single operational aircraft, with one of their handful of remaining Do 24s being sunk by a storm on December 30, 1941. The unit had also lost fourteen of its servicemen by the end of the year. This, too, was indicative; the campaign against the U.S.S.R. was costlier by far, even when hopes for victory remained, than anything the Germans had experienced. The experience of the rescue aircraft on the Black Sea was a proof of this in microcosm.

After the fall of Sevastopol, the seaplane base at Cape Khersones became the main base of the unit, with forward posts in the eastern half of the Black Sea. As German armies launched the catastrophic drive into the Caucasus and towards Stalingrad, the Do 24s took over reconnaissance duties in addition to their rescue operations. Perhaps the crews began to have some misgivings owing to the fact that despite fighter escort and the vast territories conquered by the Germans, Soviet fighters still rose regularly to challenge—and occasionally shoot down—their Do 24s.

As the strategic situation transitioned into peril for the German military, Do 24s were pressed into service as airlift aircraft to bring supplies to the 17th Army in the Taman peninsula as the ice began to melt, making normal airlift operations more difficult. This was a temporary assignment, but not the last of its ilk. After the failure of the offensive into the Caucasus, and the disaster of Stalingrad, the Soviets began to land hammer blow after hammer blow on the Germans. The German rescue squadron was pushed back as the Soviets advanced and faced increasing fighter opposition. By this point, the German military was as hampered by their own side as the Germans. Hitler's fanatical desire to hold every inch of territory repeatedly forbade retreats and time and again turned defeat into disaster. The Crimea, imperilled by the Red Army, was to be held at all costs and German forces were inevitably cut off and trapped in the peninsula.

The Do 24s and the rest of *Seenotstaffel 8* served to rescue downed airmen from the transport aircraft that were tasked with the futile task of providing adequate supplies. As Odessa then the Crimea were menaced by the advancing Soviets, they also became part of the frantic evacuation of personnel and what equipment could be salvaged. By mid-1944, the Crimea had fallen and there was little point to continuing rescue operations over the Black Sea. The German air-sea rescue organization in the region was disbanded, with many of the Do 24s being sent to the Adriatic. Many of these had already been borrowed from other units in the first place to make up adequate numbers. The collapse occurring in the East would be exacerbated by Romania switching sides, with the German aircraft remaining fleeing to Greece, which would be abandoned in turn.

In the Baltic, the overall situation was vaguely similar. Though they operated early on exclusively as rescue aircraft, as the region came under Soviet threat during 1944, the Do 24s found themselves increasingly pressed into service as transports and evacuation aircraft. One notable way in which Do 24s fulfilled these duties came late in the war, when they were used to evacuate children. The children had been placed in specialized camps to keep them safe from Allied bombing raids on German cities, but now they had to be hurriedly evacuated as the Soviets approached in March 1945. The aircraft took off in some cases with seventy children on board, barely able to lift off from the water. From the air, the crews could actually see the advancing Soviet tanks. One aircraft managed to take off with a staggering seventeen adults and ninety-nine children. Such things were not accomplished without tragedy. One of the Do 24s became tail heavy and crashed on take-off; of the crew and seventy-two people on board, only one woman was saved. The aircraft were still able to evacuate around two thousand people from their bases at Nest and Kamp. Elsewhere, Do 24s had evacuated 5,000 sick and wounded from a base at Pillau-Neutief.

Some Do 24s were stripped down and modified to be suicide aircraft, to be used to blow up strategic bridges to slow the Soviet advance; the end of the war and Allied fighter attacks forestalled this plan. The remaining Baltic Do 24s served until the last moments of the war, evacuating as many people as possible away from the Soviets. Even with the cessation of hostilities, the Do 24s still soldiered on. With permission from the British, they repatriated 450 wounded soldiers from Denmark on June 18, 1945. This was the last ever mission of the Luftwaffe, and it occurred in planes stripped of their swastikas, escorted by British fighter aircraft.

Outside of German hands, the Do 24 still found itself used extensively. In original Dutch hands, this involved coming into conflict with Germany's supposed partner, Japan. Before war even erupted into the wider Pacific, the Dutch aircraft were used following Japanese fishing vessels which were believed to be part of Japanese military efforts and performing reconnaissance operations to keep an eye on Japanese troop concentrations. They even took part in looking for the German raider *Admiral Scheer*. Dutch Do 24s even discovered some of the Japanese invasion fleet bound for Malaya a mere ninety minutes before hostilities commenced.

Once war came, the Dutch aircraft took on a myriad of duties. A minor note involved strafing and bombing a Japanese schooner, flying relief supplies and evacuating civilians, and even getting into a scrape with some of their opposite numbers. On December 20, Dutch Do 24s got into a dogfight with Kawanishi H6K flying boats, with one of the Dutch aircraft receiving slight damage. They would clash again with H6Ks launching attacks on Do 24 bases. The Dutch Do 24s increasingly proved capable as bombing aircraft, with three of them being part of the Dutch-led air response to the Japanese landings on British Borneo. Three Do 24s pounced on and sank the Japanese destroyer *Shinonome* on December 17.

One innovative use of the Do 24 was to lure Japanese floatplanes away from their convoys; after indicating its position to a Dutch submarine, it then successfully attacked it, sinking two ships. They also carried out bombing efforts over the Philippines, though they suffered increasing losses to Japanese fighters and were unable to alter the unfolding disaster. In all the combat use, rescue duties formed only a minor part of the Do 24's operations, in stark contrast to how the Germans had used them. Desperation soon led to further losses, as Do 24s were thrown, unescorted, into the teeth of the Japanese. The total of six Do 24s that survived three months of intense combat operations flew to Australia, with the last example still under Dutch colours in 1943.

Australia gave these battered aircraft an overhaul and intended to use them for transport and as advanced trainers. Spare parts issues had already been a major bother for the Dutch, and this only grew worse over time for the Australians. A complete unfamiliarity with German aircraft hardly helped, and though this improved over time, serviceability never really reached a level that could be described as adequate. Despite their reliability and a decent reputation, the aircraft were ultimately displaced in the transport role by Martin Mariners. By the start of 1944, they were limited to rescue duties, and they were mothballed after an accident in May where one aircraft caught fire and sank—the only accident the type suffered in Australian service. They were ignominiously scrapped before the year was out.

The Do 24 operated under other colours, as well. Two temporarily wound up in Swedish colours after being interned, and one of these was turned over after the war to the Soviet Union. Even here, under another Allied flag, the Do 24 proved useful, serving in Siberia for several years. The British also took over some of them after the end of the war. Two were used for mine-clearing duties, and according to rumour were still operated by unsupervised German crews. These were ultimately sunk. Others were evaluated by the British to test air-sea rescue equipment before being scrapped in 1946.

Of all the Allied powers, none had as much need of the Do 24 as France. The Germans had taken over French flying boats to supplement their own aircraft, and the French reversed the process. The French recovered the Do 24 production line at the CAMS factory near Sartrouville, and the decision was made to continue building them. To the French, devastated by conquest and liberation, whether the aircraft were particular effective was a secondary objective. Primarily, the manufacture of these aircraft helped get the economy ticking over again and put Frenchmen back to work. So it was that the French *Aéronavale* gained as many as forty Do 24s, which began to arrive at the end of 1944, with the last reaching French service in the summer of 1947.

The French aircraft had their gun turrets installed, but these were sometimes removed with the dorsal gunner's position used to install British ASV (Air-to-Surface Vessel) radar. The first Do 24 flights came by the end of 1945, with the aircraft being used as transports between France's African territories and Metropolitan France. Several French aircraft were lost in accidents along the way, and the same serviceability problems dogged the French that had dogged the Australians. A unique problem for the French though was that the Do 24s—and indeed the heterogeneous flying boat and seaplane units that they formed a part of—was that the growing conflict in French Indochina (which would grow into the Vietnam War with time) had first call on already precious fuel.

In French hands, the Do 24 for the first and only time took on a less than stellar reputation. Losses eventually led to a temporary grounding of the fleet in 1948, and thereafter time whittled down the number of aircraft in service. The last of France's Do 24s served briefly as training aircraft before being removed from service permanently in 1954.

The Do 24 is one of the most surprising flying boats of the 1940s for a trio of reasons. In the first place, the Do 24 proved successful at whatever role it was put to, including roles it was never primarily designed to take on, such as bombing. In service to its native Germany, the Do 24 provided excellent service as a rescue and transport aircraft that certainly proved the RLM's reticence towards the type wrong. Secondly, the aircraft served under an astonishing array of flags for an aircraft that today is primarily seen as a German aircraft. It served as extensively in Allied hands as it did in German ones. Perhaps this extensive use was not equal in numbers, but it certainly was in terms of the variety of nationalities and the vast area of the globe in which it operated. Lastly, the aircraft served far longer than anybody would have anticipated, given its rocky start, lasting for decades in a world that had passed the flying boat by. The Dornier Do 24 easily qualifies in these terms as one of the most successful flying boats of all times, and perhaps the most unexpected success of them all, given the rough circumstances of its birth.

14

Dornier Do X: First of the Giants

The Dornier Do X is one of the more recognizable flying boats from history, if only because of the mass of high-mounted engines that mark its most distinctive feature. It was also the first true titan of the flying boats, and a long-held dream. Its genesis stretches back as far as World War I, and the aircraft itself was a dream of the world to come. The Do X is also a fantastical vision of how, sometimes, a dream can escape grasp. The tale of this mammoth flying boat was one of a correct vision of the future running headlong into the technological limitations of the present, permanently limiting the result. Despite this, the resulting aircraft carved out a place in history and very accurately pointed the way that events were about to follow.

Specifications

First Flight: 1929
Powerplant: Twelve Curtiss Conqueror twelve-cylinder, liquid cooled engines, 610 hp each
Armament: None
Top Speed: 131 mph (211 kph)
Range/Service Ceiling: 1,056 miles (1,700 km), 10,498 feet (3,200 metres)
Dimensions: Length 131 feet 4 inches (40 metres), height 33 feet 7 inches (10.25 metres), wingspan 157 feet 5 inches (48 metres)
Number Built: Three

Claudius Dornier was a visionary. He foresaw the world that was to come and actively and boldly set out to make it a reality, pushing technology to the limit in the process. He gained his first aircraft experience when, in 1910, he began to serve with Zeppelin-Werke GmbH as a designer, helping to build Germany's legendary airship fleet of World War I. After the war, Dornier launched his own firm in 1920, starting with small flying boats. His first major success was the twin-engined

Dornier *Wal* (Whale). In the end, 300 of these capable aircraft would be produced, many of them in Italy owing to restrictions on German aviation design and construction mandated by the Treaty of Versailles. The Wal ended up in service as an arctic explorer under Roald Amundsen and Lincon Elsworth, and by 1927, Deutsche Luft Hansa (the precursor to the modern Lufthansa) were operating the type on Scandinavian and South Atlantic runs. The Wal's total range was around 1,350 miles, however, and carried a maximum of ten passengers. Dornier had much bigger visions.

Claudius Dornier conceived the Do X to be a transatlantic giant, and the aircraft is arguably one of the most ambitious flying boat projects ever undertaken. When the general layout of the project was decided in 1926 (a year before Lindbergh managed to fly the Atlantic), the technology to carry large amounts of passengers across the ocean by air simply did not exist. The Do X project would have to push technology to the limits, and others would try and fail in the same period. Norman Bel Geddes for instance would design a leviathan meant to carry 450 passengers, which was wildly impossible given the technology of the time. Geddes' design called for a transatlantic flying boat with a 528-foot wingspan, with twenty 1,900-hp engines. The 450 passengers would thrive on nine entire decks. This was clearly an impossible fantasy—far beyond just a dream of the future, and one that could not possibly make it past the drawing board. For comparison, a Boeing 747 in use today has a maximum wingspan of 224 feet, though it can manage to carry the passengers Geddes foresaw—albeit in rather less luxurious conditions. Unlike many of the other dreamers, Dornier would use all his talent, patience, and resilience to make sure that his vision became reality. His was a vision of an obtainable future, one that utilized existing technology rather than theory.

When he first made details of the project public in 1928, many believed that Dornier was also speaking about an equally impossible fantasy. Critics believed either that it would not be able to take off at all, or be unable to handle in the air. It was also believed that such an aircraft would have an absurdly long run for taking off and landing; there were, in short, many loud arguments against Dr. Dornier's dream.

By that time, a scandal had already attached itself to the aircraft. Dornier's company, Dornier Metallbauten GmbH, was in dire straits at the time. The project was thus secretly financed from the "black books" of the tiny German Navy, the *Reichsmarine*. The navy had plans to utilize Dornier's enormous vision as a minelayer, torpedo aircraft, or for reconnaissance. In 1927, the newspaper *Berliner Tageblatt* made this public. The ensuing scandal cost the minister of the Reichswehr his job, and Dornier had to scramble for a sponsor. Ultimately, the *Reichsverkehrsministerium* (the Reich Ministry of Transport) stepped in. They were promoting a "Transocean Program" in the wake of Lindbergh's solo crossing of the Atlantic and Dornier's design seemed ideal to create a market for air traffic from the old world to the new.

Preliminary work on the design was by this time well developed, having started as early as 1924, with Dornier and his design team mulling over several designs

A view of the Dornier Do X featuring its Jupiter Engines. (*Photograph courtesy of Dan Shumaker*)

and the number of engines the aircraft should carry. It is worth nothing here that Dornier was working on a mighty flying ship a mere six years after the end of World War I, and three years before Lindbergh's tiny Spirit of St. Louis winged its way across an ocean. The boldness of the project, considering existing technology and understanding of aviation at the time, was breathtaking. All the designs Dornier and his team considered were based around a central hull and a single monoplane wing, anticipating the form of flying boats to come. The number of engines considered in this early stage ranged from seven to twelve.

Construction of this enormous semi-cantilever monoplane was to consist of an all-metal hull made out of duralumin, with the wings constructed of a steel-reinforced duralumin framework and then covered in a heavy fabric, a fairly typical move for the time. This was then to be covered in aluminum paint. The engines were arranged in six pairs on top of the wing, and there was some debate as to whether the joining used to connect the engines formed a sort of 'auxiliary' wing that would produce more lift, though leading authorities such as *Flight* dismissed that notion. They went on to describe the hull in detail:

> The main step is placed rather farther aft than in British flying boat hulls, and is formed with fore-and-aft shallow steps which gradually merge into the forward vee of the bottom. The rear step does not, as in British practice, extend laterally out to the chines

> but is of narrower beam than the main bottom, and is fairly deep. The Germans term this form of step a "displacement step" (Verdriingungssporn), presumably because it acts by displacement rather than by dynamic pressure. From the main step to the stern post the chine members are straight and swept up at a fairly pronounced angle so as to get the tail well clear of the water. Forward of the step the main bottom becomes, as already indicated, of pronounced V-form, to terminate finally in a straight raked stem.
>
> *Flight*, 1930, p. 234

The hull had fifty-eight frames placed 2 feet 4 inches apart, with a deep keel girder running from the bow to the rear step, much like a true ship might have. This was done to gain strength; this objective was furthered by two keelsons on each side running parallel to the keel girder. When combined with that keel girder and the transverse frames, these made for a very strong hull.

In terms of layout, the Do X was noteworthy as well, and not just in terms of size. The layout was, in many ways, like that of a surface vessel. The main or lower deck was where the passengers were accommodated; below this, the hull was divided into nine compartments by eight watertight bulkheads. This is also where the fuel tanks were mounted, the number of which could theoretically be changed depending on the length of the flight route intended.

The main deck had a spacious saloon for dining or card playing, with an electric kitchen, bar, and even shower baths. The passenger deck was divided into compartments that contained divans that converted into beds. One problem here was that there was very little privacy, given that the corridor cut through all the

This photograph gives a good idea of the Do X's size. (*Photograph courtesy of Dan Shumaker*)

compartments. In practice, the flying boat would prove able to carry a maximum of 169 people on board for short trips around Lake Constance—an absolutely staggering number for the time as even the largest passenger airships had not yet carried even half that many. In regular flight, the Do X was designed to have accommodation for seventy-two people. The top deck contained the pilot's compartment meant for two with plate glass windows, and behind this was a bridge for the captain and navigators. Beyond this was an engine control room for the flight engineer and his three assistants, as well as a radio room. There was a sleeping area for the crew on the main deck, aft of the passengers.

Quite naturally given all the detailed work needed to make this titan a reality, Dornier decided that it would be useful to build some of the forms in a mock-up out of cardboard and wood, adding mock-up instruments, levers and other fittings to get a full idea of the aircraft. So it was that the Do X prototype would be preceded by a full-scale mock-up complete in every detail. Dornier found the process of building a full mock-up so useful that he decided it should be done before the construction of every Dornier aircraft thereafter.

Given the revolutionary nature of the project, the designers also sought to base as much of it in reality as possible. Experimenting with unproven ideas was avoided if possible, which Dornier admitted after the fact did handicap the original and creative nature of the design process to some extent. The benefit, however, was that modification was relatively minor overall; from tests to acceptance, alterations took only a few hundred working hours.

The layout of the aircraft was decided on in the summer of 1926, and by the end of the year, the design was finalized, and work begun. Actual construction began

Dynamic postcard view of the Do X. (*Photograph courtesy of Dan Shumaker*)

late in 1927 at Altenrhein, Switzerland. The site was chosen to get around the limitations imposed by the Treaty of Versailles after Germany's defeat in 1918. The Treaty had forbidden the Germans to make aircraft of such large size, and Dornier was not about to let a punishment clause slow him down. The construction process would take two years of work, finally finishing only on July 12, 1929.

The prototype that was finished in 1929 was not only a titan, but in many ways beyond anything that had been seen in the world before. In addition to being over 131 feet long and nearly 30 feet high, she had a total weight of 114,640 pounds, with accommodations optimistically provided for up to 100 passengers, with luxury in addition. Another interesting comparison to make to the Do X is that it had the most engines ever used to power a production airplane, the nearest competitor being Consolidated's B-36, which still had two fewer engines than the Do X. This was in addition to a crew of ten. Many had indeed questioned if such a beast could lift off, but it did so with ease. The first flight took place on July 25, 1929, from Lake Constance on the Swiss–German border where—in an irony Dornier himself undoubtedly was aware of—the first Zeppelin had lifted off in 1900.

As 1930 wore on, and the world around him sank into the Great Depression, Dornier discovered that there were some problems with the design. Tests revealed that the air-cooled engines being used were not able to deliver their 400 hp continuously, which was a significant problem. The aircraft was reaching its contracted performance benchmarks in terms of useful load, speed, and take-off, but this was being achieved by engine revolutions that were simply too high for the type of engine being fitted. Dornier was faced with the choice, as he put it at the time, of either finding engines that could reliably produce more horsepower without potentially damaging themselves or shelving the project until such engines became available, a process he felt might take years.

The difficulty lay in the nature of the engines at the time. The air-cooled engines had been chosen because they provided a savings in total weight compared to the water-cooled engines that existed then. This was done because of a mistake that was recognized only in hindsight: the team had, owing to a lack of experience, overlooked the ratio between cruising hp and full power. When heavier water-cooled engines were fitted instead, the increase in weight was compensated for by the higher cruising horsepower. Curtiss Conqueror engines were fitted that had a guaranteed 415 cruising hp, which was a substantial improvement. Unfortunately, pressed for both time and money, this increase did not come with other improvements that might have further benefitted the aircraft. The old engine mountings were modified only so much as required for the new engines, which meant that bigger-diameter propellers could not be fitted. The engine nacelle supports were also not streamlined, and in the interests of economy on-hand radiators were fitted that did work but proved non-ideal in terms of obtaining the highest possible speed.

Over the course of testing, it would become clear that this needed to be fixed, and in the second aircraft, enclosed access to the engines was reintroduced through a shaft that could also house the radiators. This was in the future, however. For the moment, it was time for the leviathan to prove not only her worth but the viability of the entire concept of a flying ship.

The test flights silenced at least some of the criticisms levelled at the concept. The record-busting 169-passenger flight was, in fact, the seventieth such flight. Interestingly, 150 of the people on board were passengers, most of them production workers and their families, as well as a few journalists. Ten more of the people aboard were aircrew, and the remainder were stowaways who just wished to be there, with or without tickets. The flight itself set a record for the number of people carried that would stand for twenty years. There are disagreements about how long the flight lasted, but the point had very definitely been made regardless.

After three months of test flights on the Bodensee, it was time for the long-distance flight trials of the Do X. Boldly, Dornier decided to conduct these in the form of Atlantic crossings, which provoked significant criticism. Dornier was certain that the boldness was justified: to his mind, there was no other way of gathering the data required and demonstrating the soundness of the concept.

The initial tests would not be smooth, which Dornier would after the fact attribute to a human factor rather than that of the machine:

> I must admit that I seriously underestimated one factor, namely, the importance of the crew becoming thoroughly accustomed to the ship. We had chosen our best people but at the beginning both officers and crew were insufficiently "*au fait*" with this new instrument; the feeling of responsibility for the safety of this large boat may also have reacted on the judgment of the officers. It thus came about and was duly observed that at the beginning of the cruise the progress of the flight was extraordinarily slow. To-day, when one considers the flight as a whole, it is easy to see how familiarity and increased trust in the ship on the part of its crew was reflected in an increased rate of progress.
>
> *Lessons of the Do. X*, pp. 761–762
> Claudius Dornier

The chosen objective for the first major test was a flight to the United States. The aircraft first took off on November 4, 1930, and it was wisely decided to eschew the North Atlantic. Given the volatility of that body of water, and the unproven nature of the aircraft and the very concept, the South Atlantic was chosen instead. Nothing was left to chance in term of the crew to be carried. An experienced command was chosen, former Navy Pilot Friedrich Christiansen, and the craft was to be piloted by Captain Horst Merz and American Clarence Schildhauer. Curtiss even sent along a representative familiar with the engines, Harvey Brewton, to ensure there was no trouble from the powerplant.

It was under these circumstances that the Do X took off from Friedrichshafen for the grand test flight. The flying boat flew on through the Netherlands, then on to Southampton. The toughness and sea qualities of the aircraft were swiftly proved after that. Winging from England to Bordeaux, it was forced down at sea in terrible weather. The aircraft successfully taxied 60 miles (96 km) through the darkness and rough water to an alternate port.

Though this was a successful demonstration of the design's seakeeping, it was the harbinger of more problems to come. Having passed through Spain and into Portugal, the Do X suffered a significant problem. A tarpaulin made contact with an exhaust pipe and this started a fire which consumed most of the port wing. This caused a significant delay of six weeks to the overall flight. The delay was primarily caused by the fact that the materials had to be shipped all the way there from the flying ship's base at Altenrhein. It took until the end of January 1931 for the aircraft to be ready to cross the Atlantic to South America, flying out of the Canary Islands. A significant time was spent doing a series of take-off and landing tests with a heavier load each time. The aircraft reached a maximum gross weight of 55 tons when the hull caved in. This, at least, is what is listed in some sources, whereas others concentrate on another version of events. While preparing for take-off on February 3 from Las Palmas, the aircraft collided with the swell which was rolling in. The boat was struck heavily, with the wings almost ripped off. It would take three more months in Las Palmas to make repairs and improve the structure. Dornier replaced Schildhauer at this stage with Flight Captain Cramer von Clausbruch, a specialist in South American flight. Whichever version of events is believed, or even if both are, the result was that the aircraft required further repairs that delayed the flight across the Atlantic until the end of May, held up not just by necessary processes but also by ill weather.

In preparation, and to do all that was possible to ensure the success of the flight, the crew were told to shed every bit of weight they could, which in practical terms meant they were not allowed to take anything on the flight other than their toothpaste and razor. This was done so that every possible pound was given over to fuel. Under these circumstances, the aircraft finally lifted off with an obliging tail wind on May 31 for the 1,400-mile (2,253-km) flight to Brazil, which was made in one single jump. It took seven hours at an average speed of 118 mph (190 kph).

The aircraft was still received with enthusiasm and was completely refitted in Brazilian finery on its way to Rio de Janeiro, where it would take on its first paying customers as everyone on board up until this point had been, essentially, spectators in one form or another. In total, the aircraft would spend a total of eight weeks ambling along the South American coast before preparing for its Caribbean voyage. The plan was to fly to the United States from Trinidad via San Juan and Cuba.

It was at this stage that the massive ship's luck finally began to improve. The huge aircraft always stayed close to land at a relatively low altitude. It reached the United States with relative ease, with frequent refuelling stops, arriving in Miami on August 22. The journey finally ended five days later in New York Harbor. The arrival of what was the largest flying machine on Earth was greeted with tremendous fanfare, with a cheering crowd and a band playing "*Deutschland über alles*" and "*Die Wacht am Rhein.*" It was a moment of triumph for Dornier;

Photograph taken during the 1931–32 American tour. (*Photograph courtesy of the Naval Aviation and Heritage Command*)

The Do X flying over Norfolk, Virginia, during her American tour. (*Photograph courtesy of the Naval Aviation and Heritage Command*)

his monumental aircraft had been received enthusiastically and the crew was welcomed by no less a personage than the American President, Herbert Hoover.

From here, however, the dark clouds of poor luck closed in once again. The world economic crisis had brought the company to the brink of ruin, and worse yet, the Curtiss Company now took a role in the proceedings. The company demanded that Dornier take formal ownership of the Conqueror engines that had been used, since they needed significant maintenance after three hundred hours of flight time. Dornier certainly could not afford the bill of 300,000 Reichsmarks.

Worse was to come. Given the collapsing of the world economy, the Reich Ministry of Transport could no longer afford to back the project. The cost of it had increased dramatically even before the economic downturn, the estimated cost of 2,370,900 Reichsmarks having ballooned to 3,549,182 before the aircraft even attempted its "maiden" flight. The RVM as a result gave the company authority to try to use the aircraft in some profitable way. Attempts to have the aircraft chartered and sold came to nothing. Dornier himself came to America to try and rescue the situation, but even creating an American branch of the company could not solve the issue. There had been discussions at one point for General Motors to take up a license contract for the aircraft, but this, too, was cancelled. With no prospects available, the only solution was to temporarily mothball the once-glorious flying boat until better prospects could be arranged.

The process of getting the Do X airborne again took eight agonizing months, in which time the aircraft served as a static tourist attraction. The RVM finally agreed with the Ministry of Finances to advance Dornier a loan—certainly not the first—to pay the running costs, and finally settled the bill with Curtiss, paying 327,199 Reichsmarks in the end. In May 1932, the enormous aircraft set off for home; coincidentally, this was close to when Amelia Earhart set off on her own solo flight of the Atlantic in a land aircraft. Much smaller than the Do X, there was in this comparison an inkling of the future course of events.

The return flight took the Do X to Newfoundland then across the North Atlantic to the Azores then back to Europe and on to Berlin through intermediate stops. It arrived there on May 24, 1932. While many sources focus on the trouble-filled east to west leg of the journey, relatively little is said of the comparatively much more successful trip back. Dornier himself attributed this to growing familiarity with the aircraft amongst the crew. Some sources do make note of the Do X running out of fuel a few miles out from the Azores and making a night-time emergency landing, wherein the chief pilot is believed to have remarked that in the dark he could not see either land or water as he set down.

This would seem comparatively minor in comparison to months upon months of troubles that plagued the aircraft on its way to North America, but it must be borne in mind that the aircraft was repaired and improved along the way, and with each stage of the journey the crew became more and more familiar with its operations and capabilities. Moreover, the Do X's test flight had demonstrated conclusively that trans-oceanic passenger service was a feasible reality, not just a possibility. It would be easy to dismiss the total journey of 740 days out of hand as being a splendid failure, but this would rather miss the point. Whatever dreams were in place of airborne passenger service across the Atlantic, the Do X was the first attempt to do this at all, let alone in a practical, commercial sense. It was done with technology less than a decade more advanced than that of World War I, and in all that time the aircraft was continually out in the open, not in a controlled hangar space. The sheer durability of the aircraft had seen it through, despite accidents that easily could have destroyed it. Despite being an unproven concept, and despite being limited by the available technology in the late 1920s, it had succeeded. The first half of the journey had taken an exorbitant amount of time but this improved and with experienced handling the return took a tiny fraction of that.

Dornier himself defended this essential point:

> The flying ship, Do.X 1a, took off from Altenrhein on the 5th November, 1930, for its great flight ... and returned to the works on the 15th November, 1932. During these 740 days the ship was continually in the open. One is entitled to assume that on such a flight, which extended over two years and during which time 65 different ports in three different continents were visited, the flying ship must have got into difficult situations and bad weather. The fact that the Do.X 1a actually only required minor overhaul work on its return to Altenrhein provides definite evidence as to the serviceability of the flying ship.
>
> *Lessons of the Do. X*, p. 763
> Claudius Dornier

Aside from Dornier's optimism, the immediate result was far less in line with what had been accomplished. Technologically, Dornier had demonstrated possibilities that in decades to come would completely revolutionize the way humanity travelled the globe, which would have profound implications for society as a whole, which are still playing out today. Economically, however, the Do X's lengthy flight had been a disaster. Dornier himself underplayed this aspect of things, insisting that the aircraft had been an experiment, not meant for regular commercial flying. While he was right in pointing to the vast amount of knowledge accrued from a practical long-distance test flight, the Do X proved unsuccessful beyond being a proof-of-concept testbed.

Some authors here dismiss the fate of the program in an off-handed manner, but the reality was more complicated. Dornier's loan with the RVM expired in late June 1932; the aircraft was passed on to the German Aviation Test Centre (DVL) and put under the official administration of the government.

Simply flying the aircraft back from Berlin to her hangar in Altenrhein was thus conceived of as a venture that could help to recoup the losses on the project. On June 23, she began what was her 233rd flight and her German tour, with viewings and promotional flights along the way, finally arriving in Zurich before returning ultimately to her original hangar on November 14.

For some months after that, the giant sat at her moorings. Ultimately, it was decided to send her on another series of European publicity flights, possibly for the same motive of recouping her cost. Unfortunately, the misfortune that had dogged the aircraft would return with a sense of finality. Her European trip was to take her along the Danube River to Istanbul, but only ten days into the journey, in spring 1933, disaster struck. Captain Horst Merz misjudged the landing at Passau and put the tail of the flying boat into the water first. The angle was much too steep and the control surfaces were ripped away.

This would take some time to prepare, and in any event, radical changes in Germany would take a hand as well. Weimar was dead, the Nazis were now the government, and the reborn RLM, replacing the RVM, decided to take the Do X out of service in October 1934. The following May, it turned up in the German Aviation Collection in Berlin, the Deutsche Luftfahrtsammlung Berlin, a new museum. The Do X became the central eye-catching exhibit in the entrance hall of the museum which formally opened in June 1936. The enormous flying boat stayed there until the war came. Plans were made to evacuate the museum's exhibits as Allied bombers began to pound Berlin in increasingly heavy air raids, but the departure was delayed since nowhere suitable could be found to house the enormous aircraft. As a result, it was destroyed by a direct hit by a British bomb in December 1943. The former Aviation Collection would be cleared up after the war, but by then the remnants of the Do X had been picked clean by people cannibalizing her aluminum framework. Today, all that remains of this pioneering aircraft is part of her tail section, the part that tore off during her unfortunate landing on the Danube.

This was not quite the end of Dornier's dream, though what followed was scarcely better. Two more examples of the Do X had been sold to the Italians in 1931–32, which became the Do X2 (dubbed *Umberto Maddalena*) and X3 (*Alessandro Guidoni*). These aircraft were slightly larger than the original aircraft and had Fiat A-22 V-12 engines mounted in new, streamlined fairings. These aircraft were considered for passenger service from Genoa to Gibraltar before this was deemed unfeasible. Ultimately, though they had been ordered for airline service, they were taken over by the government and used for prestige flights, transport, and training duties. There are even rumours that at least one of the massive craft ferried Italian soldiers to the invasion of Ethiopia in 1935, though this author has seen no substantiation of this. Both were broken up by 1937, with one of them suffering a similar accident to the original aircraft in having its tail ripped off by a poor landing.

Dornier himself used the sales to the Italians to take a shot at the Do X's critics. He commented on arguments that the aircraft's actual service ceiling was about 500 metres by noting that to be delivered to the Italians, the aircraft had to be flown over the Central Alps, and that their arrival point of Lake Constance was 400 metres above sea level to begin with. "It is therefore perhaps not inopportune," Dornier commented with what was a degree of either sarcasm or understatement, "to make known the fact that the real ceiling is somewhat higher."

There were, in essence, two visions of the Do X program. Dornier's vision was a proof of concept, a test aircraft that could prove not just the feasibility of large-scale passenger service by air across oceans, but also test the mettle of an aircraft built for that purpose. To the people backing Dornier's grand vision, there was a glittering and decidedly more earthly treasure in mind: profit. In this, they were to be sorely disappointed. If viewed purely through the lens of her difficulties and cost, the Do X could be written off as a sort of "splendid failure," a sinkhole for cash with limited usefulness despite her striking size.

Such a view would be erroneous since it neglected the revolutionary step that the Do X represented. For the first time, a large passenger aircraft had spanned oceans. To be certain, one leg of its trip had been fraught with complications, delays, and accidents; however, the return trip with longer jaunts over rougher water had gone much faster indeed. The Do X did prove itself capable of its job, which given the nature of the design and the limitations the technology of the day imposed is all the more remarkable. The Do X had blazed a path that others would follow, and it is a mistake to neglect its achievement based on time and expense. It would be even more of a mistake to compare it unfavourably to airliners that came later on the grounds of profit—the Do X went first.

The Do X was the first of the behemoth flying boats, the first of an iconic era of large passenger aircraft that created a romantic vision of flying that long survived their passing. Despite its strange design, to modern eyes, this aircraft proved what could and would come to pass. In many small ways, then, the world tied together by passenger wings we know today owes its genesis to the grand test Dr. Dornier carried out with his strange and early giant.

15

Grumman G-44 Widgeon: War and Peace

To the aviation fan, Grumman is far better known for a series of excellent and increasingly impressive fighters that would be a mainstay of the United States Navy during World War II and would do much to not only tip the tide in favour of the U.S. but keep it there. Naturally, this is not the end of Grumman's contribution and in terms of flying boats, a few Grumman products stand out. In the case of the G-44 Widgeon, it is not because of the aircraft's combat duties—though it did serve in a military role, like so many of Grumman's products—but because of the double life it led, and indeed still leads.

The Widgeon was, and is, a popular civilian craft; while it was designed to be a military aircraft and operated as such, it took on a post-war life that has ensured its enduring popularity and that it remains in use today. It even managed to find itself a niche in popular culture—in a slightly altered form, at any rate—that remains well known in the present day as well. All in all, it has had a most remarkable career.

Specifications (The G-44)

First Flight: 1940
Powerplant: Two Ranger L-440-5 air-cooled six-cylinder engines, 200 hp each
Armament: In anti-submarine duty, one 200-lb (90-kg) depth bomb.
Top Speed: 153 mph (246 kph)
Range/Service Ceiling: 920 miles (1,481 km)
Dimensions: Length 31 feet 1 inches (9.47 metres), height 11 feet 5 inches (3.48 metres), wingspan 40 feet (20.19 metres)
Number Built: 317

Very often, the arc of an aircraft's life follows a well-known pattern. It is designed for, and operated by, the military, and then is consigned to civilian life. The reverse proved to be true for the Widgeon. Originally conceived entirely for the civilian market, it found itself drawn into military service, thrown into a role it was never intended to fill.

The Grumman Corporation was, by 1940, well-established. The company had first opened its doors at the very start of 1930, founded by Leroy Randall Grumman, Jake Swirbul, and Bill Schwendler. The company started by producing a float to transform U.S. Navy biplanes into amphibians, a complicated effort with landing gear to ensure that they could take off from the land and aircraft carriers as well. According to author Rene Francillon, the way that Grumman was able to convince the navy that this new float would work was for Roy Grumman (as he was commonly known) and Jake Swirbul to ride in the back seat of one of the biplanes during catapult trials. The advanced landing gear interested the navy even more, and cemented Grumman's reputation with the navy. The company started in 1930 with twenty-three employees, and in less than a decade had ballooned to 813; in 1940, they shot up to 2,000. All of this would pale compared to wartime expansion. By 1943, Grumman had 25,000 employees; by then, they were a central producer of navy aircraft. With all this growth, Grumman maintained smooth operations, which helped to produce high-quality aircraft for both the military and civilian markets. Crossing over from one to the other would prove no special challenge for the company.

The Widgeon started life as a smaller cousin to the also-popular Grumman G-21 Goose, and the design made use of many of the Goose's design features. Most notably, the two-step hull configuration was carried over, as was the hand-operated landing gear and all-metal construction. As a newer Grumman design however, the Widgeon came off the drawing boards with Grumman's most modern features at the time, with squared-off wings and tail surfaces that will be familiar to any student of U.S. World War II naval aviation, as a similar setup was used for Grumman's F4F Wildcat or the TBF Avenger. The wing design was unique to the Widgeon, though, with the engines mounted high to keep them out of the spray.

The first flight occurred at the end of June 1940, from Grumman's plant at Bethpage, where the company maintains operations to this day. The early flights revealed a need for only a minor change, adding mass balance horns to the elevators. From the moment that was done, the Widgeon was set to enter production, and it would stay in production for fourteen years, until 1955.

Regardless of Grumman's plans for civilian use of the type, the first purchasers were the military. Designated as J4F-1, the first twenty-five Widgeons went to the Coast Guard, and started to arrive in the middle of 1941. When war came, more of Grumman's production of Widgeons and the next twenty-six Widgeons, which had been bound for Portugal and civilians, were taken on by the U.S. Army Air Force, under the designation OA-14. Until the end of the war, Grumman would produce another 121 under Navy contracts (which were designated J4F-2), and a small number of these were Lend-Leased to Britain where they were designated as the Gosling I, later being called the Widgeon I, which is where the type's historical name comes from, like many other British designations.

A Grumman Widgeon on the tarmac. (*Photograph from the Ron Dupas Collection, 1000aircraftphotos.com*)

Other Widgeons were passed on to the Portuguese and Brazilian air forces, where they stayed in service until 1968 and 1958 respectively. In the Coast Guard, the J4F-1 Widgeons were given a retrofit to allow them to carry a single depth charge beneath the right wing between the fuselage and the engine nacelle. World War II depth charges could be a lethal weapon when placed close enough, but the difficulty was getting the weapon close to an enemy submarine's hull. A single depth charge, from a small airplane, trying to hit the small target of an enemy submarine, would be a difficult prospect under the best of circumstances—let alone a maneuvering submarine offering up defensive fire. Under these circumstances, it is not surprising that the Widgeons in U.S. military service did not experience much success against marauding German U-boats. This was presuming that the pilots could find a U-boat in the vast battleground that was the American coastline. The task was difficult in the extreme, but even without sinking U-boats, the efforts of the patrol pilots were still of use. They could force a U-boat under and help direct other resources to the hunt; every spotting, every attempted attack was a small victory with a foe that relied on being unseen.

It was long thought that a Coast Guard Widgeon piloted by Chief Aviation Pilot Henry White had sunk *U-166* on August 1, 1942. The record stayed that way until an accident in 2001, when an oil exploration team stumbled upon the wreck. It was determined after investigating that the submarine had actually been sunk by a patrol craft, PC-556.

Outside of the Coast Guard, in both American and British service, the Widgeons were most often used as land-based utility transports or, in some relatively rare cases, as instrument trainers. As the war began to wind down, Grumman was even able to devote production to making civilian Widgeons again. Early 1945 would see the introduction of a new G-44A model, which had a six-seat cabin and an improved hull, a definite improvement over the standard four passengers for previous Widgeons. When Grumman had finished their batch of G-44As (a number between fifty or seventy-five, depending on sources) in 1949, production resumed immediately under license. The French *Société des Constructions Aéro-Navales* (SCAN) built another forty of them by 1952. These aircraft, known as the SCAN 30, were then, in an ironic twist of fate, sold mostly to American commercial customers.

With the war over, the various military branches of the U.S. began to phase out their Widgeons between 1946 and 1948. Five of these were sold to the Royal Thai Air Force, where they served from 1951 to 1956, with others winding up in the civilian service they were always meant for in the first place.

Though they proved—and indeed are still proving to be—popular with their owners, there was one limitation to the Widgeon in long-term service. The limited 200 hp produced by the Ranger engines, especially when using a single engine, led to early efforts to provide the type with more power. Starting in the mid-1950s, an American company called McKinnon Enterprises, based in Oregon, began to convert G-44 and G-44A model Widgeons to either 260-hp or 270-hp Lycoming six-cylinder air-cooled engines. The company combined this increase in power with better propellers: three-bladed Hartzell constant-speed models. This resulted in a significant increase in performance.

For a start, the top speed rose from 153 mph to 190 mph. Better still, the rate of climb doubled, reaching 1,750 feet per minute. McKinnon marketed these upgraded aircraft as "Super Widgeons," and up until 1970, it is thought that perhaps as many as seventy Widgeons received the upgrade. McKinnon was not the only one engaged in this process. McDermott Aviation converted Widgeons with 260-hp Continental engines, which can be easily distinguished in Widgeon sightings by its comparatively flatter cowling profile. It is unlikely that many, if any, Widgeons still in use today have not received some form of engine upgrade. The many surviving aircraft in use have all been extensively restored as well and remain popular today.

Widgeons can be seen commonly on the air show circuit, as well as normal civilian use, but the average reader may know the Widgeon best from popular television of the 1970s. The show *Fantasy Island,* which ran between 1977 and 1984, featured a SCAN 30 as the plane that ferried people to the island. The famous line "Ze plane! Ze plane!" spoken by Hervé Villechaize that became a part of popular culture referred to this one specific Widgeon. Since the show, the aircraft has had an interesting and complicated history, but most recently was sold at auction in 2016 to an anonymous buyer for $275,000 dollars. For a vintage flying boat with such a reputation and history, it was likely quite the bargain.

16

Grumman HU-16 Albatross: Adaptation, Survival, and Flying the World

It is a mistake to believe that flying boats simply died out with the end of World War II, though it is a forgivable error to make; the birth of the jet age after the war and the rise of regular trans-oceanic passenger service from land-based aircraft certainly did push flying boats out of the central role that they had previously played. Though relegated to the margins, the flying boat survived. Much like crocodiles after the age of the dinosaurs, the basic form did not change in any great measure, but it was honed. Flying boats slimmed down from their giant size and survived in a new world. One of the foremost examples of his is the HU-16 Albatross, which appeared only at the very end of the period covered by this book: in 1949. The Albatross has accomplished many feats over the decades since, and not all of them have to do with its original military service; to this day, it remains an enduring symbol of the capabilities of the flying boat.

Specifications (HU-16B)

First Flight: 1947
Powerplant: Two Wright R-1820-76 Cyclone, nine-cylinder radial engines, 1,425 hp each
Armament: None.
Top Speed: 236 mph (380 kph)
Range/Service Ceiling: 2,850 miles (4,589 km)
Dimensions: Length 62 feet 10 inches (19.16 metres), height 25 feet 10 inches (7.88 metres), wingspan 96 feet 8 inches (29.47 metres)
Number Built: 466

The Albatross' origins lay in a 1944 requirement for a twin-engine amphibian aircraft that could fulfil multiple mission types. The requirement called for a capacity of ten passengers or 5,000 lb of cargo. Other specified elements were an extended range of over 2,000 miles and it was also required that the aircraft should be capable of a range of mission types, from transport to reconnaissance to anti-submarine patrolling. To accomplish these missions, the requirement called for certain physical features, namely carrying extra fuel in the wing tip floats, and that the wing pylons should be configured to carry multiple objects, including bombs, depth charges, torpedoes, and drop tanks.

With significant experience by now building military flying boats and converting civilian ones to military use, Grumman was given the go-ahead to construct two prototypes of an aircraft that was given the designation XJR2F-1. Though Grumman got the green light in late 1944, it appears that their already heavy production priorities meant that the war had ended by the time construction on the type began. As a result, the desired role for the aircraft expanded once again; it had to now be capable of search and rescue missions for the newly-established U.S. Air Force.

The resulting product, built to carry out a multitude of roles, was a significant improvement over Grumman's past flying boat designs. While it was aerodynamically similar to Grumman's older G-73 Mallard design, the new aircraft (designated G-64) was significantly larger and most importantly came with over double the mass and horsepower. From the outset, the G-64 was meant to be a tough aircraft. The two-step hull had a deep V-section to make sure it could conquer even very rough seas. To fulfil the other half of its amphibian role, it had a very tough tricycle landing gear to make the aircraft capable of rough landings. Neither land nor sea were going to slow the Albatross down, certainly.

The first flight of the XJR2F-1 prototype happened on October 24, 1947, after which the aircraft (initially named the "Pelican" before Grumman changed it to "Albatross") and the second prototype were handed over to the U.S. Navy for official evaluations. These were carried out through late 1947 and into 1948, and the results were very favourable—so favourable in fact that not only the air force bought the Albatross, the Navy did as well. The Navy would receive their aircraft under the designation of UF-1, to fill their new utility category. The Navy had 138 aircraft manufactured between 1948 and 1954, though not all of them ended up as navy aircraft. Eleven made it to the Coast Guard with special equipment to fulfil their specific coastal missions, and eight more were sent to newly-independent Indonesia, which had emerged from brutal Japanese occupation in 1945 and almost straight into another war to throw off the Dutch colonial yoke, which had ended in December 1949.

As for the air force, they had 305 Albatrosses produced, between 1949 and 1953. These were originally ordered under a designation of OA-16A (the Navy, too, had initially gone with a different designation: PF-1A) before settling on SA-16A once deliveries started. In another similarity to the Navy, not all the aircraft the air force paid for wound up in air force service. Over fifty went to the Coast Guard, and a total of five were divided between the Portuguese and Spanish air forces. The air force also undertook interesting conversions of the type to cold-weather operations. In 1953, 154 Albatrosses were given skis for operations in snow and ice, a conversion frequently called "triphibians." Two others were sent over to the navy for operations in Antarctica, having been converted in the factory to operate in one of the most punishing environments on Earth.

As for Grumman, they had a major upgrade for the type in the works by the mid-1950s. The upgrade began to arrive in 1955 and came to commonly be known as the "B" conversion. The essential thrust of it was a new and better wing. The total wingspan came up by 16 feet 6 inches, and new outer wing panels were installed that had enlarged ailerons and fixed leading-edge camber in place of the original slots. There were other, less major improvements, including a "clean up" of antenna and aerials to improve aerodynamics, and a taller fin and rudder were added. Through to 1961, Grumman converted 242 aircraft to the "B" standard, known in the air force as the SA-16B.

Given the success of the type in U.S. service, and its versatility, it is small wonder that other countries more than happily acquired the Albatross through whatever means they could. The total list of additional non-American air arms to operate the type is extensive: Argentina, Brazil, Canada, Chile, Greece, Iceland, Italy, Malaysia, Mexico, Norway, Pakistan, Peru, the Philippines, Taiwan, Thailand, West Germany, and Venezuela. As an aside, one aircraft was modified by Japan's Shin Meiwa Industries to mount four engines, known as the UF-XS. This aircraft had a different tail, and in an unusual configuration, a General Electric turboshaft engine mounted in the fuselage, the purpose of which was to provide "bleed air" over the flaps for boundary layer control.

This technical history was indicative of the type's operational history. As was mentioned previously, there was good reason for foreign buyers to want to purchase the Albatross. The type began to see service in 1949, with the Coast Guard getting their first Albatrosses in 1951. The aircraft given to the U.S. Navy fully justified the original conditions that had birthed the machine. They served as transports, cargo planes, reconnaissance aircraft, air ambulances, and air-sea rescue aircraft. By contrast, the air force and coast guard used their aircraft specifically as air-sea rescue vehicles. Most of the air force Albatrosses were directly assigned to the Air Rescue Service. When war came again in Asia in 1950, these aircraft were on hand for operations in the Yellow Sea and would serve through the entirety of the Korean War. In practical operation, the type would often accompany Sikorsky H-19 helicopters which would accomplish the actual pickup. Most of the serving air force aircraft were further modified to carry JATO (jet assisted take-off) bottles, to improve their take-off performance and carried search radar—first under the wing and then later in a nose dome. The arrival of the SA-16B conversion solved the one deficiency that the Albatross displayed in operational use: an inability to maintain altitude with one engine when fully loaded. The B conversion reduced the type's stall speed by 10 mph, making operating on a single-engine much safer.

The Albatross retained its place as a first-rate rescue aircraft as the U.S. military began its long and tragic involvement in Vietnam. The aircraft began to operate over the Gulf of Tonkin in mid-1964, and by the end of 1965, the aircraft was credited with saving sixty downed airmen. In addition, long after its 1949 arrival in service, the Albatross proved capable of taking on yet another new role. It began to serve as and command and control platform to coordinate multi-aircraft missions. It was only pushed out of the rescue capacity by increasing numbers of (once again) helicopters, in this case the Sikorsky HH-3. But the versatile aircraft still soldiered on, finding niches as a surveillance aircraft for ice flow and oil slicks, and it also took on the role of transporting troops and supplies to support Special Forces operations.

The air force finally phased out its last Albatross in 1974, with the Navy to follow two years later. Some had been transferred to the Air National Guard, but they too were withdrawn by 1975. In the Coast Guard, the Albatross lasted still longer; the last units were not retired until 1983, and it is believed that some remained in service in other air forces until the mid-1990s.

In many cases, this might have been it, but an aircraft built to take on a variety of missions found itself being adapted quite easily to civilian use. Not all of these attempts were automatically successful, of course. The Conroy Aircraft Corporation for instance gave some Albatross Rolls-Royce Dart turboprop engines and attempted to market it as the Conroy Turbo Albatross. The salespeople were apparently unsuccessful, as only the prototype was ever made. In the event, it was Grumman itself that helped its tough amphibian gain a new lease on life. In collaboration with Resorts International, Grumman set out in the 1970s to re-acquire fifty-seven aircraft, to convert them to airline use. The effort ended up becoming almost a complete re-manufacturing of the individual aircraft, in the Grumman factory. All military equipment was removed, structural components were stripped down, repairs and replacements done throughout as needed, and most importantly the engines were rebuilt to "zero-time," essentially a complete overhaul.

This was merely the beginning. The interior was reworked to fit twenty-eight passengers, a galley, and space for a flight attendant. This was supplemented by all-new avionics and instruments, as well as new mechanical systems. The first of these upgraded and renovated Albatrosses flew in 1979, and the type was re-certified the next year as the G-111. Thirteen aircraft were ultimately converted, all but one of them for Resorts International; the last went to the Conoco Oil Corporation, for use in Malaysia. A subsidiary of Resorts International, called Chalk's International Airways, started to put the G-111 to use in 1981, and the airway that had been running since 1917 continued to operate the type until 1987. Some sources state that the aircraft remained in storage until at least 2006 and may still be there even after Chalk's itself ceased operations in 2007.

Many Albatrosses today remain in civilian use in multiple capacities, a superb legacy for Grumman. As of 2006, it was estimated that thirty Albatrosses were still plying the skies. One in particular is worthy of further mention. While it is a museum aircraft now, it has a remarkable story behind it. That aircraft led to an enlightening conversation with Mr. Reid Dennis of California. Mr. Dennis had, as a child, witnessed the old clipper aircraft taking off from the top floor of his family home and joined the U.S. Navy in 1944, though his eyesight kept him from becoming a pilot then. He rectified this twenty years later and retired at age eighty-three as a pilot in command with 9,000 hours under his belt, 1,800 of those in multi-engine seaplanes.

In the late 1980s, the Albatross finally caught his eye. At that time, several them had been restored out of the "bone yard" in Tucson, Arizona, since that was where many of the aircraft had been mothballed. Mr. Dennis was then considering recreating the old Pan American Clipper flights across the Pacific, and the range of the Albatross was very appealing, as was the fact that he already owned a Grumman Mallard, which provided some familiarity to start with a bigger flying boat. This began a complicated six-year restoration and alteration project that would dovetail into his involvement with Linda Finch's attempt to re-create Amelia Earhart's Pacific flight. Pratt & Whitney wanted a "chase plane" to accompany her and were willing to pay for oil, gas, and hotel bills. It was simply too good a deal to pass up, and the start of a thirty-stop tour of the world made possible by a Grumman Albatross.

Modifying his Albatross required "fixing" what he considered Grumman's mistakes in making the "B" model in the first place. Grumman's builders put jack pads under the wing when making the "B" models, and ended up drilling through the spar, creating a life-limited spar of 10,000 hours. For his Albatross, he picked out a hull without any saltwater corrosion, which turned out to be one of the "A" model aircraft not affected by this, but this still needed to be modified in order to add to its total range. Mr. Dennis and others involved in the process then took the wings off outboard of the engines and took the outboard panels from a "B" model and removed the 70-inch constant-chord plug, so the rest would bolt back directly to where the wings were on the "A" model.

The other thing he bore in mind was that Grumman had added eleven inches to the leading edge of the wing, giving it a droop leading edge for better control on ice, removing the wingtip slots of the "A" model. As a result, his "A" model aircraft—with their improved "B" model wing—had a wing area that was 9 per cent higher than when the HU-16A first took to the air. The total wing length was 86 feet, rather than 80 or 96. Other modifications used in the "B" model to improve handling were added in, too, creating what Mr. Dennis rightly calls a "one of a kind" Albatross. The aircraft qualified for the restricted category because of these carefully done modifications, rather than the experimental category, making it easier to be flown. He was told by at least one knowledgeable colleague that this modification was exactly what Grumman should have done in the first place, making this unique Albatross possibly the ideal one.

This Albatross was the ideal chase plane except in one respect: it had Curtiss-Wright engines, so Pratt & Whitney did not give the Albatross much publicity on the round-the-world trip. The Albatross's presence was necessary, though, since Pratt & Whitney was leery of a lone, vintage aircraft repeating Earhart's flight without assistance. The negative publicity from an accident in the vastness of the Pacific might have been terrible. The journey that Mr. Dennis and his Albatross set out on would be unique. The aircraft never once, in its long journey, got above 7,000 feet (2,134 metres), and that was to clear a mountain range before being fully loaded. Over the Pacific, it would travel mostly between 1,500 and 2,500 feet (457–762 metres)—all of this because they were so heavy with fuel, the aircraft likely could not have passed 5,000 feet. "This airplane has a thick wing and it likes dense air," he related, "so we were in most of our trip around the world—across Greece and through the Mediterranean—we were typically at 2,500–3,500 feet."

The entire process was videotaped through Mr. Dennis' willingness to hire a videographer—he stated, with a certain amount of wry humour that he was not going to fly all the way across the Pacific without one—and was further enhanced by carrying a news reporter and two photographers. There were a total of ten people including Mrs. Dennis on board, and the cameras could be aimed out of the upper hatch at the rear cabin in-flight without any wind buffeting, 3–4 inches from the edge of the airplane—a heady experience for everyone. It also was an experience unlikely to be repeated. As he put it, "You couldn't do it today, you'd have an almost impossible time getting the aviation gas at various places ... we had a couple of islands in the Pacific where we had to have gas shipped in in barrels, and Pratt & Whitney took care of that. It was a good deal ... we had to pay for our meals and that was about it."

Pratt & Whitney were not the only people enthusiastic about the flight. If you were to look carefully in some of the pictures of the Albatross, you would see a logo for the Apple Corporation saying "Apple Inside." Mr. Dennis wanted one of their then-brand new 1,400 laptops to do flight planning, but these were so backordered at the time that getting one through traditional means would have been impossible. Apple could not sell them one, but they could lend one, which did all the flight planning; Mr. Dennis put the company logos onto the plane in thanks.

The flying itself was, perhaps surprisingly given the distance, relatively simple. The Albatross performed magnificently, with no major problems aside from a hydraulic pump in Calcutta causing a delay of several days. A part of this had to do with a quirk in the repair process that had nothing to do with engineering or the realm of the mechanical:

> Probably the most frustrating part of the whole journey was that the Indians considered an airplane like ours to be foreign territory, so in order to go out and work on it each day, our mechanic had to go through customs and immigration and then out onto the field—he had to check out of the country to go out to work on the airplane. Then at the end of the day when he was finished and hadn't been able to correct the problem, he had to go back through customs and immigration and re-enter the country. I think that when the British left India, they left behind a huge inventory of rubber stamps and inkpads, and the Indians are absolutely determined to wear them all out.

After arriving at Howland Island—where Earhart originally failed to arrive in the 1930s—the flight proceeded to Kanton Island, and to Mr. Dennis this was the most interesting and fun stop on the trip. The Island used to be where the Pan American Clippers stopped to refuel on their way to Australia, in a sheltered body of water on the atoll. Naturally, to someone who had embarked on this journey in part to re-create part of aviation's golden age, this already was a remarkable experience. Part of the Republic of Kiribati today, some of the nation's citizens are sent to live on the island to keep someone else from claiming it; at the time, there was only the excellent airfield. Despite the small population, they were greeted extremely well:

> They put on a dinner for us ... they had had one other airplane land there ... about a year and a half [before] that it landed there. So there's just not traffic at all, and they don't see anybody. And they put on a banquet for us, and my wife was along and she got into a wonderful conversation with one of the women about living on the island and so forth and so on, and the men got up and did a dance ... they were the entertainment, doing native dancing.... But for a whole group of strangers, they just went all out for us.

The final leg of the trip was from Honolulu, Hawaii, to Oakland, California. The departure was delayed by a day owing to brake problems, meaning the Albatross arrived after Finch's Earhart flight, which Mr. Dennis views as a bonus. All the "hoopla" went to the first arrival, and when the Albatross came in, the people on hand were their friends and family, making for a much more meaningful arrival after the aircraft had achieved its ambitious goal. The last legs had only Mr. Dennis as pilot, the co-pilot and mechanic to save weight over long water stretches, the rest of the passengers having been sent on ahead commercially. "It was fun to have done it, and to be able to say you've gone all the way around the world and arrived back safely [with] no serious problems."

Modestly, he insists that it was not a terribly important flight, though he is proud of the video that has been seen frequently on American Public Broadcasting. Wryly, he posits that the video is run whenever there is a major event on another network, such as the Oscars or the Super Bowl. He jokes that the importance to himself was that they made it back, but they also got to see a lot of the world that people rarely got to see. "That was fun—and we got to see how wonderful people are in virtually all the places in the world you set down. People were just delighted."

After the flight, there was a further surprise in store: the director of the Hiller Aviation Museum asked if he would consider donating the Albatross to the museum as an exhibit. It has turned out to be one that draws significant, and the Albatross remains there to this day. Three or four times a year, Mr. Dennis has an open cockpit day where he goes and answers questions for the public. This reflects a passion for the Albatross that continues today. The aircraft has experienced a revival of sorts since the mid-2000s, with its capabilities ensuring that it is still very much an active aircraft today. Though this workhorse was long ago put out to pasture, those that fly it are ensuring that it's "retirement" is more adventurous and rewarding in many ways than the service it was originally intended for.

17

Hughes H-4 Hercules: Famed and Final Giant

Of all the aircraft contained in this book, the H-4 Hercules is potentially the one that is best known by the readers, at least in basic terms. Only the Catalina may rival it. It is, of course, the legendary aircraft designed by the eccentric Howard Hughes that was, at the time of its unveiling, the largest aircraft in the world, and still is a titan in every respect. In pure size, it still somewhat rivals the world's current champion for longest aircraft: the Antonov An-225 *Myria*. In fact, the Hercules' wingspan is the greater of the two, reaching a colossal 97.5 metres.

This, then, is the aircraft derided as the "Spruce Goose"—a name Hughes himself despised, and one that was never used officially. The aircraft was, indeed, made substantially of wood, and arrived too late to fulfil a strategic role for which it was eminently suited. It was a massive undertaking at the time of its construction, and ambitious in the extreme—and an example of reach exceeding grasp. The Hughes H-4 Hercules is a legend written of a famous billionaire, but in and of itself is perhaps the greatest example of just how enormous the flying boat could become.

Specifications

First Flight: 1947
Powerplant: Eight Pratt & Whitney R-4360 Wasp Major radial engines, 3,000 hp each
Armament: None
Top Speed: 235 mph (378 kph)
Range/Service Ceiling: 3,000 miles (4,800 km), 20,900 feet (6,370 metres)
Dimensions: Length 218 feet 8 inches (66.65 metres), height 79 feet 4 inches (24.18 metres), wingspan 320 feet 11 inches (97.54 metres)
Number Built: One

The Hughes H-4 Hercules is singular in many senses. Only one was ever constructed, it was the biggest aircraft of its day, and it occupies a unique place in popular culture decades after its first flight. Yet in a larger sense, it is singular because it was—perhaps more than any other aircraft in this book—the product of a single man's will. The story of the Hercules begins, thrives, and ends entirely with Howard Hughes.

Howard Hughes claimed to be the first billionaire of the United States, and his vast wealth was certainly no exaggeration. He had inherited control of his father's Hughes Tool Company in 1924 at the tender age of eighteen. The company had been made vast and wealthy on a roller cutter bit that had greatly improved the rotary drilling process on oil rigs. Hughes Senior's company became a vehicle for his son's dreams. The company became a vehicle to make two things Howard Hughes was deeply passionate about: Hollywood films and aircraft. Hughes Aircraft was formed in 1932, and within three years, Hughes and his engineering team had produced the Hughes H-1, a streamlined racer that Hughes himself piloted to the world landplane airspeed record.

When war clouds began to gather, Hughes turned his attention to producing military aircraft for the United States. His wartime projects evolved on two fronts. Initially, both were aircraft projected to use the Duramold process to avoid using strategic materials. The Duramold process involves thin layers of birch and resin construction, put together much like plywood, and it offered significant advantages over relatively scarce aluminum. Hughes began a bomber project using the process, labelled the D-2. This would never come to fruition, though a derivative would be the controversial—and very nearly lethal to Hughes—XF-11 reconnaissance aircraft program. The other track of Hughes' grand design was the H-4.

The H-4 project began when industrialist Henry Kaiser sought a solution to the loss of Allied shipping to German U-boats. In the immediate aftermath of Germany's declaration of war on the United States, submarines descended on an unprepared American East Coast, and wrought havoc. Kaiser believed the solution to this threat was to build a fleet of massive "Sky Freighters," which could carry troops and freight over the enemy threat. He described the project as "the most monumental programme in the history of aviation," but the War Department had a caveat for this grand undertaking: Kaiser could not raid talent from design teams engaged in essential war work. Kaiser initially sought help from other industrialists such as Donald W. Douglas and Glenn L. Martin, but it was Hughes who took up Kaiser's challenge. Hughes, a man who wished to set records at every turn, was the perfect man to approach with such a monumental idea. For him, building such an aircraft had little to do with patriotism and possibly nothing at all to do with profits—building it was the achievement itself, a grand accomplishment to match those Hughes had already made in his life. The War Department was ultimately persuaded to issue a development contract to Hughes and Kaiser, calling for three prototype aircraft, designated HK-1 (for Hughes-Kaiser). These were supposed to be completed within a two-year deadline, a mind-boggling fact when considering the technical challenges and the sheer scale of the project. The government would aid in development with $18 million over time, and Hughes would be technically the supervisor of the entire project—though, in practice, the man in charge was the chief engineer, Glenn E. Odekirk. Odekirk was a trusted Hughes man, though he had little experience in management of a large-scale project, and in any event, the unique technical problems of a massive flying boat were also outside of his experience. Much of the design work would be turned over to Rae Hopper, who had previously worked for Douglas and would rise in the Hughes operation over the years. The operation, in practical terms, would be chaotic.

Hopper apparently presented Hughes with sixteen different design proposals before attracting him to a flying boat with a wingspan larger than that of a modern Boeing 747. Ultimately, Odekirk, Hopper, and their team produced a design for a single-hull, eight-engine layout that would weight a colossal 400,000 lb when fully loaded and was theorized to carry 700 fully armed and equipped soldiers. The idea of turning out such a titan in such a short span was, as it turned out, extremely optimistic. After a year had gone by, construction had not even begun—the aircraft lingered in the design phase. Kaiser, who had dreamed the impossible dream that such an aircraft could be designed, constructed, and flown in less than a year, withdrew from the project. Hughes carried on, renaming the aircraft the H-4, and actual construction of the prototype began in mid-1944, a full sixteen months after the contract award. Even then, construction was extremely slow, and the war had ended long before the prototype was finished.

Interior work on the H-4 Hercules. (*Photograph courtesy of the Southern California Historical Aviation Foundation/Western Museum of Flight*)

Above: A section of the hull, detailing the complex work involved in such a massive, wooden aircraft. (*Photograph courtesy of the Southern California Historical Aviation Foundation/ Western Museum of Flight*)

Below: Work being done on one of the enormous wing sections. (*Photograph courtesy of the Southern California Historical Aviation Foundation/Western Museum of Flight*)

Emerging from initial construction. (*Photograph courtesy of the Southern California Historical Aviation Foundation/Western Museum of Flight*)

The Hughes Hercules under construction. (*Photograph courtesy of the Naval Aviation and Heritage Command*)

The reasons for the delay have been debated ever since, and many of them have focused on Hughes, namely his obsessive involvement with the project in an attempt to reach perfection, as well as an alleged mental breakdown during construction. While these may have played a significant role, a larger problem was that the design team was simply unprepared for the scale of the task Hughes threw them into and producing such a gargantuan aircraft out of wood was a time-consuming process that just took far longer than the optimistic estimates had believed.

Even though the war was ended, Hughes pressed on, even after the government cancelled the production plans. All of this was naturally a field day for the press, which dubbed the plane "Spruce Goose," which was both a misnomer since the aircraft was mostly birch and apparently infuriated Hughes. In the fall of 1947, however, the prototype Hercules was finally completed—just in time for the Senate War Investigating Committee to subpoena Hughes about the use of government funds on the H-4 project, as well as to try to hold him accountable for the failure of the XF-11. Here the murky world of corrupt politics and industrial intrigue came into play. The charge was led by Senator Owen Brewster, who both Hughes and others alleged had been bought off by Juan Trippe of Pan Am, aiming to keep commercial rivals down through political means. In his testimony to the committee, Hughes was remarkably unperturbed, despite the hostility and skepticism displayed towards him. Perhaps he was certain the evidence was on his side, or perhaps he was merely eager to test out the largest aircraft on Earth. Another reason could be he was planning a massive counteroffensive. Hughes' confrontations with Brewster were a verbal duel that did Hughes plenty of good and damaged Brewster, and Hughes continued on in trying to find men of like mind to destroy his rival. Nevertheless, Hughes certainly did seem to put his faith in the aircraft, stating during the hearings:

> … the Hercules was a monumental undertaking. It is the largest aircraft ever built. It is over five stories tall with a wingspan longer than a football field. That's more than a city block. Now, I put the sweat of my life into this thing. I have my reputation all rolled up in it and I have stated several times that if it's a failure, I'll probably leave this country and never come back. And I mean it.

This was not all there was to the hearings, of course; there was also the matter of how funds were used to secure contracts, and it was here that the Hercules story reveals some dirty laundry about how the process worked. According to Jack Anderson, a Washington columnist, Hughes understood how the game was being played behind the scenes and why he was being targeted by Brewster:

> In the manner of cornered men whose expense accounts have already been made public, Hughes admitted to misdemeanors but pled innocent to felonies. He had indeed wined and wenched government officials and military brass, sometimes to excess. It was necessary, he said; his competitors did it, and as a relative newcomer trying to buck long-entrenched interests and liaisons, he had to play the game in order to get a hearing on his proposals. He had never looked on aviation as a moneymaker,

> he insisted; he was in it because he had a passion for it. He yielded to no man in his mastery of the dark arts of making money, as the astronomical profits of his other businesses showed, but in aviation, he had lost $14 million in thirteen years.
>
> Then he got to the nub: three months before, Brewster had attempted to lobby him in behalf of Pan Am, he said, and having failed, they were both out to destroy him. Pan Am had put great pressure on him to merge Trans World with Pan Am and co-sponsor the chosen-instrument plan. Brewster himself had told him at the Mayflower Hotel that the probe would be dropped if he joined forces with Pan Am.
>
> *Confessions of a Muckraker*
> Jack Anderson

Essentially, the Hercules was the queen on a chessboard of corporate and political maneuvering, and Hughes—as part of a larger campaign—was about to make a bold move with it. During a break in the hearings, Hughes rushed back to California for what were supposed to be taxi tests for the H-4. On November 2, the giant flying boat set out on two unassuming taxi tests with the press in attendance. After the second run, many of the press disembarked, thinking the minor excitement was over, but a third taxi test began, with Hughes himself at the controls. The aircraft was supposed to reach a speed of 90 mph before slowing back down, but Hughes instead pushed her forward. Some sources believe that this was done to avoid dangerous pitching at high speed on the water, but whatever the reason, Hughes took his giant brainchild into the air. Twenty-seven people were onboard, including members of the press, and Hughes kept her at an altitude of 70 feet while going 135 mph. He took his plane for just under a mile before putting her back down. In the moment, it was a powerful argument against the idea that Hughes had taken money for planes that could not fly, though critics then and ever since have maintained that the aircraft remained in the ground effect and simply could not rise any higher. A euphoric Hughes returned to Washington with a powerful card to play: the aircraft had lifted off; therefore, he had produced what he said he would, an argument made all the stronger by the fact that he had financed the late stages of construction out of his own pocket. The government's efforts to stamp down on Howard Hughes ultimately failed.

Regardless, the aircraft never flew again as Hughes lost interest in it, and the concept itself was thoroughly unnecessary in any event. Yet Hughes, in his eccentric way, insisted that the aircraft be maintained in flying condition in his own hangar until he died in 1976. Four years later, the H-4 was purchased by the California Aero Club and put on display next to the liner *Queen Mary*, one of very few museum exhibits that could make the Hercules look small in comparison. For a time, the Hercules was even a Disney attraction, as the company purchased both in 1988, but after disappointing profits, the company sold the aircraft on to Evergreen Aviation Museum in 1995, where it has resided on display ever since.

The Hercules was, and is, the largest flying boat ever completed. It also remains one of the most instantly recognizable and well-known aircraft in the history of

The H-4 on her test flight. (*Photograph from the Ron Dupas Collection, 1000aircraftphotos.com*)

aviation. Even people who have never seen the aircraft, who could not identify it from a photograph, still know the name "Spruce Goose." The name has taken on connotations of being superfluous or a failure, and in some ways is a corollary to the idea of a "white elephant"—whatever its capabilities, something that is rare or unlikely, even if impressive. This sort of cultural cachet is rare for any single object, let alone an aircraft. Which makes it all the more ironic that Hughes himself would be quite upset that the term "Spruce Goose" came to mean an airborne white elephant that is remembered more than the aircraft itself. History is sometimes unkind to the legacies people try to leave behind.

There is also still great controversy over the aircraft in certain circles, with many claiming that it never flew at all—that it merely took advantage of the ground effect much like a dedicated ground effect vehicle (or ekranoplane in better-known Russian parlance). This debate is ongoing and is unlikely to stop any time soon. In much the same way that palaeontologists debate stridently back and forth over whether the Tyrannosaurus Rex was a hunter or just a scavenger, it has engendered a back-and-forth that is by itself fascinating to witness in action.

In the end, this is all completely as it ought to be. The largest flying boat in history certainly should create continuing discussion if only because it keeps the aircraft, and indeed the era, alive in some small way. The Hercules was mighty in conception and execution—it is perhaps almost inevitable that its legacy should remain in much the same way.

18

Kawanishi H6K: Eyes of the Empire

Perhaps more than any other combatant nation during World War II, Japan possessed a tremendous need for maritime aviation. The very nature of the empire Japan planned to, and violently did, construct would require maritime patrol. The Japanese envisioned what they came to euphemistically call the Greater East Asia Co-Prosperity Sphere, a vast empire dominated from Tokyo that would at its furthest extent cover nearly a quarter of the Earth's surface. Most of that vast area was water, and the imperium Japan would dominate also included thousands of islands and incredible amounts of coastline. To defend and patrol this territory, as well as to carry out reconnaissance in the vastness of the Pacific Ocean, Japan had a pressing need for seaplanes and flying boats.

The Kawanishi Aircraft Corporation, formed in 1920 in Hyōgo Prefecture, stood more than ready to provide, and would equip the Japanese military with two large flying boats during the war. The first was the Kawanishi H6K, officially known as the Type 97 Large Flying Boat. The Allied powers that would encounter the aircraft would know her as "Mavis."

Specifications

First Flight: 1936

Powerplant: Four Mitsubishi Kinsei 43 or 46 fourteen-cylinder radial engines, 1,000 hp each

Armament: Four 7.7-mm (0.303-inch) Type 92 machine guns, one in the nose, one in the spine, and two in the waist blister, one 20-mm Type 99 cannon in the tail turret, and either two 800-kg (1,764-lb) torpedoes or 1,000 kg (2,205 lb) of bombs

Top Speed: 211 mph (331 kph)

Range/Service Ceiling: 4,112 miles (6,580 km), 31,520 feet (9,610 metres)

Dimensions: Length 84 feet 3 inches (25.63 metres), height 20 feet 6 inches (6.27 metres), wingspan 131 feet 2 inches (40 metres)

Number Built: 215

The Japanese were relatively recent arrivals into the arena of large flying boats, with their first experience coming from a previous Kawanishi design, the three-engined biplane known as the H3K, or the Navy Type 90-11 flying boat. This early aircraft was itself adapted from a British Short Brothers design known as the K.F.1 that was created for the Japanese Navy. The Japanese paid careful attention to initial tests before using it as a template for the H3K. These aircraft were built by Kawanishi with the supervision of a British technical team.

This process allowed the Japanese to rapidly acquire technical and construction experience in large flying boats that they had not possessed before, and by the mid-1930s, they were more than ready to create their own first-class designs to rival anything else then being produced. Here it is also important to pause and mention that these facts have been used by less-than-stellar sources to make an argument for Japanese technical and technology inferiority to "the West," which in the past was often made on racial grounds, but in any event is an incomplete reading of facts divorced from context. It is always critical to remember a larger context in addition to specific facts when evaluating history, and in this regard, it is important to remember that Japan's military needs were evolving rapidly in scale and variety in the early and mid-1930s, which necessitated rapid expansion in fields such as large flying boats that previously had not been a requirement. Similar processes, in different ways, played out in various other air forces in the decade as war clouds began to gather and the aircraft of the early 1930s were made obsolete at an increasingly rapid rate as major improvements in engines and airframe design were made.

In any event, by 1933, what had been cutting-edge technology in 1930 was now rapidly falling behind Japan's needs and the technical curve. As a result, the Japanese had a need for a more capable design, and Kawanishi was given a specification to submit two different proposals, one with three engines and the other with four. These were to be designated the Type G and R, respectively, though neither submitted design was initially found to be satisfactory. As a result, in 1934, the Imperial Navy issued a revised and more demanding specification that called for a cruising speed of 137 mph and an approximate range of 2,795 miles (4,500 km). For comparison, the cruising speed being called for was very nearly the H3K's maximum speed—an indicator of how rapidly the change was occurring.

These increased demands did not happen in isolation. The Japanese had noted the performance of the new Sikorsky S-42 passenger flying boat, and fully realized that where civilian aircraft were leading the way, military aircraft could follow. Kawanishi began work on what would be termed the Type S, under the direction of Yoshio Hashiguchi and Shizuo Kikuhara. Both these men had rapidly picked up experience working with the Short Brothers establishment in Britain, and as a result, they imagined an ambitious leap from the H3K to an aircraft that could handle reconnaissance, bombing, and transport duties. The design was a slender one, with a graceful two-step hull under a high parasol wing. The wing was to be strutted and braced beneath its undersurface outboards of the midspan, and inside of this the four engines would be mounted, four 840-hp Najakima Hikara 2 radial engines. The tail, mounted high on the rear fuselage, was a monoplane tailplane with twin fins and rudders. The normal crew was planned as nine individuals, and the H6K1 prototype first flew on July 14, 1936.

Early tests showed a need for some improvements, and the hull was modified to improve water handling, but the aerodynamic qualities were more than satisfactory. There was, however, one respect in which the prototype failed to live up to expectations: the engines were found to be underpowered, and so three of the first four prototypes were given the more powerful Mitsubishi Kinsei 43 radial engine, each developing 1,000 hp. This aircraft was accepted into service as the Navy Type 97 Flying Boat Model 1.

The aircraft was ordered into production at the same time, and over time, a total of 215 would be built in different versions. The initial production model was labelled the H6K2, similar to the final prototypes aside from minor equipment changes. Armament was to consist of three 7.7-mm (0.303-inch) machine guns, placed in trainable mounts in the bow, a power-operated dorsal turret, and a non-powered tail turret. The aircraft could also carry 2,205 lb (1,000 kg) of bombs, and a sign of the prominence and capability of the design was that two examples were to be specifically completed as VIP transports known as the H6K3, generally similar in configuration. Future upgrades to the type would mainly alter the weaponry configuration and the powerplant, though in every other way, it remained virtually the same aircraft.

One interesting use to which the H6K2s were put was as a pressure on the U.S.S.R. In January 1939, tensions between the two empires were high, and they would eventually erupt in a brief border war in the Khalkhin-Gol region that

A view of the graceful H6K. (*Photograph from the Van A. Swindelle Collection, 1000aircraftphotos.com*)

would result in a sharp defeat for the Japanese. However, earlier in the year, the Japanese were negotiating with the Soviets about fishing rights in the Sea of Okhotsk and used four of the new flying boats to try to exert pressure on Soviet officials by projecting Japanese strength in the region. Six of them were subsequently sent to the Marshall Islands to start to develop open-sea strategies, as well as undertaking long-range photo reconnaissance missions of what would, soon enough, become military targets.

The main production variant was the H6K4, which in the main had a heavier defensive armament, but also increased fuel capacity. Weaponry was increased to four 7.7-mm machine guns in the bow, two side-blisters and an open dorsal position, as well as a 20-mm cannon in the tail. From August 1941, this variant received Kinsei 43 engines, developing 1,070 hp each. The only improvement on this was the H6K5, which deleted the bow gun position entirely in favour of a single 7.7-mm machine gun to the rear of the flight deck with uprated Kinsei 51 or 53 engines.

The aircraft was also not only intended for military use, but for a civilian one as well—to bind together Japan's far-flung territories and enable larger-scale Pacific travel. In 1939, two H6K2s were converted to unarmed prototypes for Greater Japan Air Lines, which resulted in production of an unarmed H6K2-L, equipped to carry eighteen passengers. Eighteen aircraft were produced in total for this purpose, two of them being slightly different converted H6K4s, followed by twenty more H6K4-L unarmed transports for the navy. These last were not terribly different aside from the fact that they came from the H6K4 and had Kinsei 46 engines.

The early operational service of the H6K came in the Sino-Japanese War, but a far more extensive role awaited it in the vastness of the Pacific Theatre. Initially, the aircraft was to be deployed as a bomber, but as 1942 progressed, rapid improvement in the Allied fighters that were arrayed against the aircraft that, by now, had been given the name "Mavis" by her opponents (the unarmed transports were named "Tillie"), meant the type's withdrawal from the role. Increasingly, the type would be deployed to combat zones where interception by fighters was less likely and it would serve mainly as a reconnaissance transport throughout the remainder of the war.

In the early stages of the war, none of these outcomes were clear, and the H6K was swiftly put to work as a bomber. The Japanese Navy had sixty-six of the aircraft on hand, divided among four squadrons, and they quickly had an effect. Six of them attacked a Dutch seaplane tender, the *Heron*, at year's end of 1941, then a few days later, as 1942 began, they started to carry out bombing missions against Rabaul. The type continued to carry out night bombing missions against the Dutch while also scouting for the aircraft carrier U.S.S. *Lexington*, which ultimately was unable to reinforce the Dutch. The H6K would also go on to serve in bombing missions over the Philippines.

By summer, the aircraft was carrying out bombing raids against Australia, but a similar problem plagued it to the Italian Piaggio P.108 bomber—there were simply never enough aircraft available to be effective. Regardless of its effectiveness—and some authors posit it was superior in many regards to the PBY Catalina—it never had the impact it might have. The Catalina was produced in numbers fifteen times that of the H6K, and this said nothing of ever-growing swarms of deadly fighters. When it did encounter the Catalina, the H6K could be lethal. In one incident, an aggressively flown H6K ran into a Catalina over the Solomon Islands and shot it down without much trouble.

The Allies would see "Mavis" again in the skies over and around Guadalcanal, where it was again pressed into service as a bomber. At least two aircraft were lost at Tulagi when aircraft from the U.S.S. *Wasp* attacked the base there. The aircraft was even deployed as far away as Kiska Island, but here too it suffered—in this case, three aircraft destroyed on August 7 by naval gunfire rather than fighters, with a fourth destroyed later that day as the U.S. Navy carried out diversionary bombardments as troops were landed. Before that day, there had been a total of at least six aircraft in the area, carrying out offensive actions including the last one the Japanese in the region undertook, an attack on the seaplane tender (formerly a destroyer) U.S.S. *Gillis* on July 20. What may have been the remaining two aircraft in the region fell to P-38 Lightning fighters on August 9, becoming the first combat kills for the P-38s.

Due to these vulnerable numbers in the face of growing opposition, and it being supplanted by its sister the H8K, the H6K found itself increasingly relegated to secondary duties but soldiered on until the end of the war, unable to effect the outcome at any point in Japan's favour. Apparently, it did take over anti-submarine duties, but without much in the way of notable success. Slow attrition reduced the type's numbers still further, including one incident in May 1945, where an H6K was shot down by a Coronado—one of the last instances in history of an already rare thing: two flying boats engaging in direct combat with each other. Even after the war had ended, "Mavis" still found an unexpected, if temporary, niche: one of the aircraft was restored to flying condition by the Indonesian nationalists and put to use in their campaign to attempt to liberate themselves from the Dutch.

It is perhaps likely that had there been more of this excellent flying boat available, it would have made more of an impact. As it was, it proved an important bomber and scout for the Japanese, limited primarily by a small number of available units in any place at one time, and by fighter opposition that could prove lethal. This may have been true of any bomber, but in the case of the H6K, being badly outnumbered at any given time certainly did not help. Nevertheless, the Japanese went from no real conception of how to build a large flying boat and by analyzing foreign aircraft were able to leap forward with one of their own that was a better aircraft all around—and one that served the Japanese until the end of the war.

19

Kawanishi H8K: Japan's Heavy Flying Boat

Kawanishi's Type 97, the H6K or "Mavis," had been designed, flown, and built before Japan's full commitment to a wide-scale Pacific war became clear. In combat conditions, a new flying boat was called for, one that would be more robust in an atmosphere that was increasingly hostile to Japanese military aviation. As luck would have it, work on the replacement for the H6K had already begun soon after the type first flew. The result of this need, and Kawanishi's efforts, was the H8K, known to the Japanese military as the Type 2 Flying Boat. To the Allies, she would be "Emily," and she represented what is perhaps the apex of Japanese military flying boats.

Specifications

First Flight: 1941
Powerplant: Four Mitsubishi Kasei 22 fourteen-cylinder radial engines, 1,850 hp each
Armament: Five 20-mm Type 99 cannon, one in the bow, dorsal and tail turrets, and one each in two waist blisters, five 7.7-mm (0.303-inch) Type 92 machine guns in fuselage hatches, two 800-kg (1,764-lb) torpedoes or 2,000 kg (4,410 lb) of bombs or depth charges
Top Speed: 290 mph (465 kph)
Range/Service Ceiling: 4,440 miles (7,150 km), 28,740 feet (8,760 metres)
Dimensions: Length 92 feet 4 inches (28.15 metres), height 30 feet (9.15 metres), wingspan 124 feet 8 inches (38 metres)
Number Built: 167

The H8K was designed to fix the shortcomings of Kawanishi's previous design, the H6K2, just then entering service—namely, increasing its range and making it a more capable attacker and a tougher defender. This need was perceived as early as 1938 when the Imperial Japanese Navy issued a development contract

Above: Preserved Chinese Be-6 on display at Datangshan, China. (*Photograph courtesy of John Thomson*)

Below: Side view of the same Beriev. (*Photograph from the Chris Pinn collection, 1000aircraftphotos.com*)

Below: Exterior view of the Boeing 314 replica at Foynes. (*Photograph courtesy of the Foynes Flying Boat Museum*)

Left: Interior view of the crew space in the Foynes replica. (*Photograph courtesy of the Foynes Flying Boat Museum*)

Below: Another view of the crew compartment. (*Photograph courtesy of the Foynes Flying Boat Museum*)

Below left: The cockpit of the Boeing 314 replica. (*Photograph courtesy of the Foynes Flying Boat Museum*)

Below right: A shot of some of the passenger space. Note the bottle of chilled champagne! (*Photograph courtesy of the Foynes Flying Boat museum*)

Above: Photograph taken from the process of rebuilding a Vedette, showing the fine details of hull construction. (*Photograph courtesy of the Royal Aviation Museum of Western Canada*)

Right: View of a PBY looking forward. (*Photograph courtesy of Michael Bajcar*)

Above: A PBY-5A in flight. (*Photograph courtesy of Michael Bajcar*)

Below: PBY-6A in Danish colours. (*Photograph courtesy of Michael Bajcar*)

Above left: A PB2Y in retirement at Pensacola, Florida. (*Photograph courtesy of Michael Baldock*)

Above right: A different view of the same aircraft. (*Photograph courtesy of Michael Baldock*)

Below left: This rather interesting aircraft is the Do 24ATT, a much modernized design that grew out of a charity project and was headed—and is flown—by Dornier's grandson. (*Photograph from the Philo Lund Collection, 1000aircraftphotos.com*)

Below right: A modern Widgeon looking serene on the water. (*Photograph courtesy of Lars Kambech*)

Above left: A civilian Albatross at an airport. (*Photograph courtesy of Dan Shumaker*)

Above right: One of the Chalk's Aviation Albatrosses, which lingered on in civilian airline use. (*Photograph courtesy of Dan Shumaker*)

Above: An airborne Albatross in 2008. (*Photograph courtesy of Dan Shumaker*)

Below: A view of the same Albatross snugly on the water. (*Photograph courtesy of Dan Shumaker*)

Above: Reid Dennis' specialized Albatross in flight. (*Photograph courtesy of Reid Dennis*)

Below: Reid Dennis with his round-the-world aircraft. (*Photograph courtesy of Reid Dennis*)

Above: The Albatross at her current home. (*Photograph courtesy of Reid Dennis*)

Below: The route followed by Reid Dennis on the epic flight around the world. (*Photograph courtesy of Reid Dennis*)

Above: A civilian Widgeon. (*Photograph courtesy of Michael Bajcar*)

Below: A beautifully painted Widgeon seen in 2010. (*Photograph courtesy of Dan Shumaker*)

Above: A preserved H8K in Japan in the present era. (*Photograph taken by Max Smith*)

Below: The modernized cockpit of *Hawaii Mars*. (*Photograph courtesy of Greg Howard*)

Above left: Hawaii Mars as she appears today. *Philippine Mars* appears in the background, still in the water in this shot. (*Photograph courtesy of John Olafson*)

Above right: A 2014 shot of one of the Seabees powered by a General Motors LS-7 V-8 engine. (*Photograph courtesy of Dan Shumaker*)

Below: Rear view of a modern Seabee. (*Photograph courtesy of Paul Cuny*)

A twin-engined solution to the Seabee's original power problems. (*Photograph courtesy of Paul Cuny*)

Above: Sitting Pretty: Paul Cuny's Seabee on the water. (*Photograph courtesy of Paul Cuny*)

Below: Take-off run. (*Photograph courtesy of Paul Cuny*)

A gathering of Seabees. (*Photograph courtesy of Paul Cuny*)

Above: The Trigull: A Seabee derivative. (*Photograph taken by John Kimberley, provided courtesy of Steinar Saevdal*)

Below: A close-up of the single preserved aircraft. (*Photograph courtesy of Fred Nicolau*)

Above left: Side view of the preserved S.55. (*Photograph courtesy of Fred Nicolau*)

Above right: A Sandringham comes home to London. (*Photograph from the Ferenc Varga Collection, 1000aircraftphotos.com*)

Left: A museum-preserved Sunderland today. (*Photograph courtesy of Michael Bajcar*)

Below: Replica S-38 in flight in modern times. (*Photograph courtesy of Michael Bajcar*)

The preserved Southampton hull today. (*Photograph courtesy of Michael Bajcar*)

Above: A preserved Walrus with her wings folded. (*Photograph courtesy of Michael Bajcar*)

Below: A preserved Walrus from the Royal Australian Air Force. (*Photograph courtesy of Rob Fox Photography via RAAF Museum*)

Above: The mighty *Hawaii Mars* in flight. (*Photograph courtesy of Heath Moffatt, the original photographer*)

Below: The Mars demonstrating her firefighting capability. (*Photograph courtesy of Heath Moffatt, the original photographer*)

for the replacement. The Japanese estimated that it would take three years for the new aircraft to fly, which was a very accurate assessment. Though it was a direct successor the H6K, the H8K was not particularly similar except in being a four-engined flying boat. The hull was designed to eschew the slender, streamlined one of the H6K in favour of a deeper, more conventional one. Behind it rose a high, single fin tail. The wing was entirely new, a high-set cantilever design that tapered in both chord and thickness.

Interestingly, the H8K was meant to move on the land, albeit a bit awkwardly, with small wheels mounted under the pontoons that themselves were installed at the two-thirds marker of the wings. Power for the three ordered prototypes and the early production aircraft would be provided by four Mitsubishi Kasei 11 engines. Inside the aircraft, there was accommodation for a crew of ten, but beyond that, the true purpose of the deeper, more conventional hull became clear when the designers turned their attention to offense and defense.

The aircraft was also built to have a lethal punch. The initial design called for five 20-mm cannons, located in blisters on the port and starboard side, as well as in nose, dorsal, and tail turrets. This was supplemented by a trio of 7.7-mm (0.303-inch) machine guns in side hatches and a ventral position. The aircraft was given extensive armour protection, with the fuel tanks inside the hull being partially self-sealing. A lack of self-sealing fuel tanks was a frequent vulnerability in other Japanese aircraft, and one that made other Japanese bomber aircraft particularly at risk for fire. The notion of preventing fire was taken a step further by the H8K's designers, since they also incorporated a carbon dioxide fire extinguishing system within the hull as well.

All of this reflected a significant ambition on the part of the Japanese, who had specified an aircraft with capabilities equal to that of a Short Sunderland. It also reflected Japan's rapid growth of knowledge and confidence regarding large flying boats, but the H8K program was not destined for an easy start. When the first prototypes emerged from the works for testing, it was discovered that the aircraft was dangerously unstable on the water. The solution to this was to increase the depth of the hull by 1 foot 9¾ inches (0.55 metres), which produced an immediate improvement. The second and third prototypes made additional improvements, with other minor hull improvements and a taller vertical fin. Ultimately, the H8K would not equal the H6K's water performance no matter what was changed, but the characteristics in the air were more than enough to order the type into production late in 1941.

The first production version was the H8K1, which was the same as the second and third prototypes, and a total of sixteen of this initial mark were produced. The main version was the H8K2, however, which accounted for 112 aircraft. The H8K2 was equipped with new Mitsubishi MK4Q Kasei 22 engines and a revised tail unit. There was also more armament added, as well as anti-submarine radar, suddenly making the H8K one of Japan's most lethal anti-submarine weapons.

One interesting development of the type was a transport version that was a "spin off" from the first prototype. This particular aircraft received the new

An H8K2 Emily out of the water. (*Photograph from the Bill McBride Collection, 1000aircraftphotos.com*)

A stranded H8K next to a demolished facility, late summer 1945. (*Photograph courtesy of the Naval History and Heritage Command*)

engines that the H8K2 were but was converted over to a passenger aircraft that could carry between twenty-nine and sixty-four passengers depending on what role it was carrying out. This was designated H8K1-L, which was later made into a production variant that came with a much lighter armament of one 20-mm cannon and a single 13-mm (0.5-inch) machine gun. Thirty-six of this version were built, and it was named the Type 2 Transport Flying-Boat *Seikū* (meaning "Clear Sky").

Other developments of the aircraft did not go very far but are worth mention here. The H8K3 was created by taking two production aircraft to be used as development aircraft and making significant modifications. Chief among these was making the wingtip floats retractable, with a similar process for the dorsal turret. These were in turn later tested with Mitsubishi MK4T-B Kasei 25B engines, which rated at 1,825 hp. These aircraft became known as the H8K4, but neither of these two versions went into production.

The aircraft came into service in 1942, and its first mission called for it to be used as a platform for a daring raid, which was proof of just how far flying boat technology had advanced. After their initial devastating surprise attack on Pearl Harbor in Hawaii, the Japanese military had made plans to keep up the pressure on this distant target. Dubbed K-Operation, it was an outgrowth of Japanese submarine doctrine, which saw a use for submarine-launched aircraft. By the beginning of the war, several Japanese submarines had been built and launched to be, in essence, miniature aircraft carriers—surfacing and launching seaplanes such as the Yokosuka E14Y1 for patrol and attack purposes. By and large, these small air operations would achieve relatively little, but for K-Operation, a larger idea was to be used. Rather than launching the seaplanes, Japanese submarines of the Sixth Fleet would serve as refuelling stations for the H8Ks at a remote atoll, and the aircraft would then fly on to attack Hawaii.

Considerable thought was put into how to carry out further raids. Japanese planning began to focus on the Marshall Islands as a launching point, with refuelling at the French Frigate Shoals, Washington, or Necker Islands. Other schemes called for take-off from the Gilbert Islands at Makin Atoll, with refuelling to occur at Christmas Island, but, ultimately, the Marshall Islands plan was selected, with Wotje Atoll becoming the official launch point. French Frigate Shoals was an ideal refuelling stop for the Japanese, as the atoll was both remote and uninhabited. It was also in easy range of Pearl Harbor.

The Sixth Fleet had a significantly complicated operation ahead of them. Two submarines, *I-15* and *I-19*, were to be the refuelling ships, with their seaplanes removed and their hangar space converted to gasoline storage with refuelling equipment. They could carry 10 tons of aviation fuel each. A third submarine, *I-26*, was to accompany them and act as a picket vessel as well as an alternate refuelling ship. *I-15* and *I-19* were to shell any American observation posts they discovered, then enter the lagoon to await the arrival of the Emily aircraft. Two more fleet submarines would take part as well. *I-9* was the flotilla's flagship and was stationed approximately 700 miles southwest of Oahu in order to broadcast a navigational signal for the aircraft. *I-23* was to take up station roughly 10 miles south of Pearl Harbor to act as a rescue vessel if a plane were forced down, as well as to monitor the weather. Lastly, two small coastal submarines were located 300 miles northwest of Wotje Atoll to help guide returning raiders to their base.

At the time, there were only two operational H8Ks, assigned to the 24th Air Flotilla. The two aircraft and their crews were put through extensive training for the operation, and on February 15, 1942, the aircraft took off from Yokosuka and departed Japan after having been rushed into service just for this particular raid. They flew a course first to Saipan in the Marianas, then on to the major Japanese base at Truk in the Carolinas, then to Jaluit in the Marshall Islands before the final hop to Wotje. The strike was planned for March 1, to coincide with a full moon to give the night-time raid the maximum visibility—a necessity for take-off on a long water run with potentially hidden hazards.

At this point, the clockwork nature of the raid began to fail. Outside events began to take a hand against Japanese planning. For a start, the Americans became alerted that something involving Japanese submarines was in the offing, as the Naval Intelligence Group in Pearl Harbor under Commander Joseph J. Rochefort detected and decrypted radio transmissions from Japanese submarines in the area of French Frigate Shoals. The Americans remained unaware of just what that action would entail, but a further blow was to follow. The Japanese were heavily reliant on weather updates from the area around Pearl Harbor, and two factors combined to remove this major advantage. The Japanese had been relying on U.S. daily weather reports being broadcast from Midway, Johnston Atoll, and from the Hawaiian Islands themselves. On March 1, the U.S. military changed the code for these reports, depriving the Japanese of this source of information. Thereafter, keeping track of the weather on the path to Pearl Harbor was dependent on I-23. The submarine, however, failed to report, and disappeared without a trace. On February 24, I-23 transmitted her last report from the Hawaii area, then nothing was heard from her again. The most common explanation advanced for her loss is a diving accident, though it has never been fully explained.

The next delay was caused by Japanese planes spotting an American task force, including the aircraft carrier *Lexington*. This high-priority target and the rest of the taskforce were reported approaching Rabaul on New Britain Island, and naval headquarters at Truk diverted all submarines and surface vessels in the area to intercept the Americans. The Americans would ultimately abort the attack on Rabaul, but two days were spent searching for the ships without success, and this delayed the planned start date from the 1st to the 3rd.

In the early morning, everything was prepared. Plane No. 1 was under the control of Lieutenant Toshio Hashizume, selected as flight commander. Plane No. 2 was under Ensign Tomiro, and the H8Ks were airborne by 3:25 a.m. I-9's radio transmissions kept the planes on course, and by 2 p.m., they were passing over "Point M"—the position southwest of Oahu. At 6:30 p.m., they had spotted French Frigate Shoals and began a slow reconnaissance before landing and anchoring astern of the submarines.

By sunset, refuelling was complete, despite a moderate swell and unfavourable winds, and each plane had taken on 3,000 gallons of fuel. By 9:38 a.m., they were airborne and *en route* to Pearl Harbor, despite Plane No. 1 suffering a minor hull puncture on take-off. Arriving over the Hawaiian Islands, the Japanese headed south between Kauai and Niihau Islands before heading towards the western tip of Oahu—unaware that the Americans had radar on the island.

They prepared for their bombing run, aimed at Ten-Ten Dock—a series of three dry docks that could accommodate large vessels. The weather had so far cooperated, but suddenly swung against the Japanese, increasingly obscuring Pearl Harbor. With some confusion, the Japanese dropped their bombs, aiming as best they could on location assumptions based on supposed sightings of Ford Island and dead reckoning. Honolulu records report that explosions were heard, and it appears that four of Plane No. 1's bombs hit the uninhabited slopes of Mount Tantalus, only damaging a thicket of trees. Plane No. 2's bombs fell harmlessly into the ocean.

The Japanese made their escape, aided by the thick weather that hid them from P-40 Warhawks scrambled to intercept them, as well as PBY Catalinas attempting to find them as they retreated. Plane No. 1 flew directly back to Jaluit Atoll for repairs, with No. 2 going to Wotje. The Japanese reported a battleship in dry dock under repair, and a carrier and cruiser at anchor. Official Japanese records stated that there was extensive damage done by the raid, a victory for Imperial arms—very far from the truth of the almost farcical raid. The pilots themselves reported they could not gauge whether any damage had been done or not. The raid was so ineffective that local Hawaiian islanders assumed American planes had mistakenly dropped the bombs on their return to base themselves, and for a time, the U.S. Navy and Army blamed each for this supposed accidental action. In fact, experts believed no Japanese planes had the range to carry out the attack at all—it would not be until the bomb fragments were examined thereafter that the truth would become known. The Emily was so new that the Americans had little idea about its capabilities.

A second K-Operation raid was planned by the Japanese prior to the Midway Operation to judge what the U.S. carrier strength at Pearl Harbor was, since they were certain that the *Yorktown* had been sunk along with the *Lexington* in the Battle of the Coral Sea a few weeks before. This was not the case, but the Japanese were not to find this out. The submarines assigned to reconnoitre French Frigate Shoals, *I-121*, *I-122*, and *I-123*, found that the atoll was now being watched closely by planes and warships, and the raid was cancelled. Had Admiral Yamamoto been able to go through with the second reconnaissance mission, the Battle of Midway might have gone significantly differently for the Japanese. As it was, the massive radio traffic related to the second K-Operation was decrypted by Rochefort's group at Pearl Harbor, meaning that Midway was identified as the target of the upcoming major fleet action, not further south as had been predicted. The cancellation of a second overflight by the H8K had consequences for the Japanese of titanic proportions as a result.

Somewhat ironically, the U.S. believed that the Japanese had copied the plan from an American work of fiction. Then-Lieutenant W. J. Holmes was writing at the time under the penname of Alec Hudson, and he had written a story entitled "Rendezvous" to be published in two parts in the August 1941 *Saturday Evening Post*. The story detailed a long-range bombing raid by American flying boats on a mythical Japanese base—using a fictional Moab Atoll where they would be refuelled by three submarines. After the war, Rear-Admiral Edwin T. Layton examined Japanese records and concluded that the Japanese had been inspired by the story to plan the K-Operation raids consequently. While this is possible given that fiction has frequently served as inspiration for later fact, given Japan's emphasis on operations combining submarines and aircraft, it could also be highly probable that the operation was derived rather more naturally.

The H8K was becoming an increasingly important piece of Japan's maritime strategy. Part of the preliminaries for the Battle of Midway involved the Japanese trying to find out as much as they could about the disposition of American forces on and around Midway Atoll. A single Emily was sent out a mere three days after the failure of the second raid on Pearl Harbor. Tough or not, a lone flying boat over an American base was vulnerable, and the Emily was shot down by American fighters. The result of this was that in addition to not gaining any real useable intelligence from Pearl Harbor, the Japanese failed to pick up important information from Midway, too. Instead it would be a PBY Catalina that spotted the Japanese fleet as it steamed towards battle and disaster.

In some cases, it was not even combat attrition that was the enemy of the H8K, but the simple geography of operations in the vast Pacific. Such a fate befell the Emiej seaplane base on the Jalwog atoll. The base itself was not directly attacked—it was merely bypassed as the Allied juggernaut began grinding its way across Japan's once-vast "Co-Prosperity Sphere." Nevertheless, the aircraft was a respected opponent throughout the war. Japan's land-based bombers proved repeatedly fragile and vulnerable, but the H8K earned the respect of the Allied pilots who went up against it. It was tough and well-armed, a rugged aircraft that had armour that could withstand significant punishment. Owing to that and its defensive armament, many Allied pilots considered it the most difficult target of any Japanese aircraft. Some authors have gone further still and posited that its range, speed, and capability made it the best all-around flying boat design of World War II. At the very least, it would certainly be a contender for that title.

As Japan's situation became desperate, these valuable flying boats were earmarked not for concentration or more defensively-minded operations, but to be shepherds for kamikaze operations. Five flying boats (some sources list two or six aircraft) from the 801st Naval Air Corps were called up to be part of Operation Tan. The purpose of Tan when it was launched on March 11, 1945, with the H8Ks leading twenty-four Yokosuka P1Y kamikaze bombers of the Azusa Special Attack Unit, was to attempt to attack the U.S. Task Force 58 at Ulithi Atoll in the Caroline Islands. Bad weather delayed the launch of the operation, and, in any event, only eleven aircraft reached their destination. The

An Emily destroyed on the ground in late November 1943, at Butaritari Island, Makin Atoll. (*Photograph courtesy of the Naval History and Heritage Command*)

kamikazes plunged down towards their targets, but ultimately only managed to damage the aircraft carrier U.S.S. *Randolph*. The two H8K2 flying boats, their grim task completed, flew back to their base.

As the war moved into its final months, even the H8K became vulnerable in areas it once would have flown in safety. One such transport H8K was flying from Ambon in Java to Japan about a week after the first Operation Tan when it was attacked by a PB4Y-1 Liberator of the U.S. Navy. The Liberator did its best, raking the H8K with fire before being forced to break off the engagement through lack of fuel. The damaged flying boat, with thirty-three passengers on board, had to make a forced-landing on the mudflats of a river estuary on the China coast. Chinese soldiers attacked the aircraft and overwhelmed the defenders, and this caused a major loss for Japan because one of the passengers was Vice-Admiral Seigo Yamagata, who committed *harakiri*, or ritual suicide, to avoid falling into enemy hands.

In the end, with fuel stocks badly depleted and with little chance of replenishment, the H8Ks became even more vulnerable. Large flying boats required a lot of fuel, and with emergency fighter defence of Japan a priority, the aircraft were increasingly caught on the ground. In the closing weeks of the war, twenty-five H8K flying boats were destroyed at their moorings. In many cases, their destroyers were another, far smaller flying boat—“Black Cat” PBY Catalinas, mauling whatever remaining targets they could find on Japanese-held Pacific islands.

Ultimately, this was the end of the H8K flying boat, an almost sitting duck for Allied aircraft when once it had been a powerful opponent—a fitting metaphor for Japan’s military might. Only one H8K remains today, out of a total of four aircraft that were still in existence when the war ended. This last aircraft was taken to the United States for evaluation, and was returned to Japan in 1979, and it spent years at the Museum of Maritime Science in Tokyo before arriving at its current location, Kanoya Air Base in Kagoshima. Other than this aircraft, the only legacy of the H8K in today’s era is to tourists. Some wrecks of the aircraft remain popular diving spots today. This was not the legacy the Japanese military would have wanted for such an aircraft, but the aircraft is now a symbol of remembrance, recalling the destruction and tragedy of the Pacific War.

Latécoère 300: To Carry the Mail

In the history of flying boats, France deserves considerable recognition for crafting and utilizing both innovative and numerous designs. The French realized the potential of flying boats to span the globe, and perhaps more importantly to span their own vast empire. The French had proven to be one of the most enthusiastic nations to pursue aviation technology in the first half of the twentieth century, and in the 1930s, France operated a host of aviation companies. One of these was Latécoère, a company that is still active today. The company had a strong affinity for flying boats in the 1930s and would design a remarkable range—covered here and in the next two chapters with examples chosen for various purposes. The Latécoère 300 was one of those planes made to span an empire—specifically, a mail plane.

Specifications: (Latécoère 302 Military Version)

First Flight: 1931
Powerplant: Four Hispano-Suiza 12Ydrs2 twelve-cylinder engines, 930 hp each (on the original *Croix du Sud*, these were Hispano-Suiza 12NBr engines, 650 hp each, which were also mounted on the 301)
Armament: Three 7.5-mm (0.3-inch) Darne machine guns, one in the bow, two in beam windows, plus up to four 75-kg (165-lb) bombs
Top Speed: 149 mph (240 kph)
Range/Service Ceiling: 2,050 miles (3,300 km), 16,400 feet (5,000 metres)
Dimensions: Length 85 feet 9½ inches (26.16 metres), height 26 feet 2⊠ inches (7.98 metres), wingspan 144 feet 4¼ inches (44.01 metres)
Number Built: Seven

As France's capability for worldwide air travel developed, there was a commensurate interest in using flying boats to help bind together France's imperial territories by air. As with many other such projects, the impetus came from the idea of sending mail across the vastness of the ocean. In the 1920s and 1930s, as may already be crystal clear, the only aircraft capable of doing this with regularity were flying boats.

The Latécoère 300 began life as a response to the French Air Ministry putting out a specification in 1928 for an aircraft that could transport a ton of mail across the South Atlantic. The design would be capable of carrying 2,204 pounds of cargo to a potential maximum distance of 2,982 miles (there is some disagreement amongst sources on this total). Latécoère was, as discussed in the chapter on the Blériot 5190, one of a trio of competitors for the same position. The reason for the French desire to move into this field was the simple fact that they were beginning to face stiff competition for the lucrative mail trade. As late as 1934, the French were ferrying their air mail by ship—a problem that the specification had been ordered to fix—while the German Lufthansa was using catapult-launched aircraft to deliver the mail more quickly, thus securing a major commercial advantage.

The design would ultimately beat out its competitors not necessarily on its merits. Either the Latécoère project enjoyed a charmed life or its competitors were cursed—the government would renege on contracts to both of the competing aircraft, the Blériot 5190, and an updated version of the Couzinet 70 land plane. This was not a merit-based process: the government simply reneged on the contracts in both cases without any formal explanation. If this seems an unusual way to proceed in the procuring of aircraft to secure air mail, it must be borne in mind that this is symptomatic of what could be called the doldrums of French aviation in the 1930s and 1940s. Though French designers and engineers had not lost any of their excellence, they were undermined by inefficiency and bureaucratic infighting.

Even relating to the air mail service, the contract withdrawals were only a part of what hampered the French. Incompetence and corruption attacked the very root of success. The prime mover in creating France's air mail lines between Europe and South America was Marcel Boillox-LaFont, who had essentially organized *Aéropostale*'s success under his direction and with the financial support of the government. This not only was suddenly withdrawn, but then *Aéropostale* was nationalized and made part of a national air carrier under the direct control of the French Air Ministry.

Such infighting and politics would undermine the French aviation industry in critical ways that would last until the Fall of France, a fact that, while tragic for France, should significantly undermine the mythology that the French failed in the air owing to inferior aircraft. Inefficiency and production issues would do more than anything there, regardless of the quality of French aircraft and the bravery of their pilots and crews.

But to return to the point, this infighting left Latécoère in something akin to splendid isolation regarding mail plane contracts—they were the only ones, after all, to whom the French government ever delivered contracted payment for further aircraft. The Latécoère design team were also quite capable, and the design that emerged was a basically sound one.

A Latécoère 300 looking sleek on take-off. (*Photograph courtesy of the San Diego Air and Space Museum*)

The aircraft featured that peculiar French predilection in the 1930s for matching pusher and puller engines. In this case, the high-wing monoplane mounted four engines in two nacelles, with two facing forward and two facing backwards in the same nacelles. Each engine had a fixed pitch, three-bladed metal propeller. Interestingly, the trailing edge of the aircraft's center section was recessed to allow the aft propellers to stay clear of the aircraft itself. Unlike the Blériot 5190, it eschewed the superstructure and built a more traditional cockpit into the hull. The aircraft was in the main a long, thin hull, and was designed to take-off with a maximum weight of 22½ tons, double its empty weight. The construction of the aircraft was all-metal, with the then-typical fabric coverings on the wings and tail surfaces. The parasol wing had a large overall surface area and was attached with several struts to the low floats. Overall, the aircraft in many ways resembled some of the company's smaller designs, specifically the Latécoère 27 and 38.

Inside, the aircraft did not scrimp on crew accommodations. The crew of four would be happily ensconced within the hull owing to the luxury sleeping and dining accommodations—a fairly rare feature for this type of aircraft at that time, and a far cry from the conditions enjoyed not too many years before from those flying aircraft such as the Supermarine Southampton, seen later in this work.

The aircraft's cruising speed in the air was very slow, only 99 mph (159 kph), but the design more than made up for this in efficiency. Not only could she carry

A Latécoère 300 pre-war. (*Photograph from the Nico Braas Collection, 1000aircraftphotos.com*)

the volume of mail required, being able to carry 2,204 pounds (1,000 kg) of it, she could take on 23,000 pounds (10,432 kg) in fuel. This certainly more than made up for a slow speed, and it could indeed outdo its Blériot competitor in terms of range and load capacity.

The first prototype of the aircraft would ultimately be named *Croix du Sud*, or "Southern Cross." The aircraft would make its first flight in 1931. Bad luck struck hard in December of that year, however, when the aircraft sunk in the Étang de Berre near Marseilles during taxiing trials. The aircraft apparently rose unbidden into the air at too steep an angle, stalled, and broke into two parts. The aircraft was raised and salvaged, given a full rebuild and a new registration and re-flew in October 1932. This is when it officially received its name. It arrived in service in December 1933, and it did so in style. The aircraft was given to *Capitaine du Corvette* Bonnot for a non-stop flight from France to Senegal. The aircraft took off on the last day of 1933 from Berre, flying successfully to St. Louis in Senegal in just over twenty-three hours—a total distance of 2,286 miles (3,679 km). On January 4, 1934, it arrived in Brazil, completing the South Atlantic mail run. It would then go on to make six more successful runs.

Croix du Sud held sway over this route until December 1936, when it was lost at sea. This was a particularly heavy blow to the French, since the aircraft was piloted by the famed French aviator Jean Mermoz. Mermoz had turned back shortly after his initial take-off to get a quick repair for a troublesome engine, an oil leak having fouled the electrical system. Concerned that the mail would be late,

Mermoz lingered only long enough for the oil to be cleaned up, refusing to wait for a new aircraft to be sent out for his use. Four hours later, a message arrived saying that further mechanical difficulties were occurring. The voice on the radio said "Let's cut the starboard rear engine," and this was cut off abruptly with a violent sound, and no trace of Mermoz, his crew of four others, or the *Croix du Sud* was ever found.

Despite this tragedy, Latécoère would then deliver a total of three production aircraft to Air France for regular service. The French Navy, more than capable of understanding the use of such an aircraft, took on another three. The French authorities both in the Air Ministry and the Navy were impressed with the aircraft's long range. The first three aircraft for the mail service would be designated as Latécoère 301, with the remaining aircraft for the military being designated as the Latécoère 302, which emerged as military reconnaissance aircraft for the *Aéronavale*.

These would be aircraft that incorporated improvements from the original aircraft, which had actually been made to *Croix du Sud* before her loss. There was an increase in the wing dihedral and also in the tail's vertical area. The first trio of 301s were named *Orion*, *Eridan*, and *Nadir*. The first flight of one of these aircraft came in early September 1935. Their names were changed before their entry into service in early 1936, becoming *Ville de Buenos Aires*, *Ville de Rio de Janeiro*, and *Ville de Santiago du Chile*. *Orion/Ville de Buenos Aires* would prove an early loss while flying between Natal and Dakar on February 10, 1936. *Ville*

Postcard of *Croix-du-Sud* by *Editeur* Louis Petit. (*Public domain image via Wikimedia Commons*)

de Rio de Janeiro would be stored in a hangar at Dakar when the war began and was ultimately cannibalized to keep the other 301/302s airborne.

The Late 302 military version carried a total crew of eight, double that of its commercial counterpart. The aircraft also had a different enclosure for the cockpit which reached to the extreme nose. They were, naturally, also given armament. They were also given the names *Guilbaud*, *Cavellier du Cuverville*, and *Mouneyres*. The military version of the aircraft first flew on February 22, 1936. The armament would change from its initial setup to actual service. Initially, they came with a retractable gun turret in each wing positioned on the outboard side of the engine nacelle. These were removed, leaving the standard armament listed in the specifications. The aircraft were delivered to *Escadrille* E4 of the French Navy at Berre in late 1936. When war came, these aircraft were based in Senegal, and one of the civilian 301s, *Ville de Santiago du Chile*, would be modified to join them as *de l'Orza*. They would survive the Fall of France and briefly serve with the Vichy Regime's forces, being retired in December 1941. It was not obsolescence or inability that ultimately retired them, but the fact that new spare parts were simply not available. According to some sources, the last aircraft was kept in the air as long as it was by cannibalizing the others for what few parts remained.

To those unfamiliar with French flying boats, and French aviation in the 1930s, it may be surprising to discover that the Latécoère 300 is a well-remembered aircraft in France overall. Much of this has to do with French pride in its pre-war aviation, but also has much to do with the story of Mermoz and the glory days of famous aviators.

21

Latécoère 521: France's Bold Atlantic Vision

French design often took interesting turns in the 1930s. Both on land and sea, the French seemed particularly willing to experiment with the unusual in an attempt to find what would work best. Many of the bomber aircraft that would come to stock France's air force, the *Armée de l'Air*, are examples of this seemingly wide-reaching design philosophy. On the sea, this proved equally true. The Latécoère 521 is an unusual sort of flying boat, in some ways looking like something more out of science fiction from the time. It was instead a very concrete fact and was one of the early giants—a realization of the dream of transporting large numbers of people vast distances by air, across the globe. Much like the ocean liners France was building at the time, foremost among them the astonishingly capable and beautiful *Normandie*, it was also meant to carry out its duties in luxury.

While only the barest handful ever saw even partial construction, and the program was marred by setbacks and invasion, the Latécoère 521 was still a noble attempt at the realization of the grand dream of flying boats, and an interesting example to study.

Specifications

First Flight: 1935
Powerplant: Six Hispano-Suiza 12Ydrs twelve-cylinder piston engines, 860 hp each
Armament: None
Top Speed: 162 mph (261 kph)
Range/Service Ceiling: 2,548 miles (4,100 km), 20,669 feet (6,300 metres)
Dimensions: Length 103 feet 9 inches (31.62 metres), height 29 feet 9 inches (9.07 metres), wingspan 161 feet 9 inches (49.3 metres)
Number Built: One

The Latécoère 521 was the logical "next step" from the 300. Where the 300 aircraft had been designed with the South Atlantic routes in mind—binding together France's colonial possessions in Africa—the 521 was an ambitious French contender for the North Atlantic route. The 521 as she was designed was a giant, nearly as large as the Dornier Do X had been just a few years before—up to this point, the Do X had also been the standard for attempts at a transatlantic airliner. So the Latécoère 521 was from the very conception a shot at one of aviation's highest crowns. It was also, perhaps obviously given this description, the largest aircraft built in France up until that point. The final aircraft could carry between thirty and seventy passengers, depending on how she was configured, carrying a total weight of 83,627 pounds, an impressive size for her day. Much like the Dornier Do X she was attempting to follow, however, the 521 program would be marred by troubles. The prototype was damaged on its first attempt at a transoceanic flight, and though it was repaired, it would take until August 1938 for it to make its maiden Atlantic flight.

The design was in some ways a logical outgrowth of the earlier Latécoère 300, and the design team was led by Engineer Marcel Moine. The hull, for instance, was also a central one with two stub wings. Reflecting the times, the design was almost all-metal, and of the aircraft's total empty weight of 17 tons, fully 10 tons of it was described as being vedal and duralumin—with the hull consisting entirely of these materials. There were two decks inside the hull, the main deck and the upper deck in what sources at the time described as the "superstructure"—yet another comparison made at the time between flying boats and ships. There was a two-step bottom to the hull, and overall it was shaped much like an inverted "T," with the superstructure narrower than the hull bottom. Stressed skin was employed throughout the hull, which was divided into seven watertight compartments.

The wings were also of a standard Latécoère model, with a semi-thick section constant over the span of the wing and built in three sections. The centre section was metal, with the outer two being fabric-covered. On either side, the wings were braced by four inclined and faired vee-struts. The wing was thick enough for direct access by the mechanics to the engines from the hull. The stub wings carried the fittings for the wing struts, and also were designed to be very resilient towards local shocks on the water. The three watertight compartments that comprised the fuel tanks and could carry 2,906 gallons (11,000 litres) of fuel each. There were also two feed tanks in the wings, and the aircraft in total could carry 6,155 gallons (23,300 litres) of fuel. The tail had metal structure with fabric covering, what was still considered a normal construction for a monoplane at the time. The rudder and elevator were statically balanced and fitted with tabs.

Inside, the layout of the main deck had the marine gear in the bow, followed by the compartments for the wireless operator and the navigator. Beyond that was a salon for twenty passengers, which in turn was followed by six cabins that each contained two berths and a washstand. Another cabin lay aft of this that could accommodate a further twenty-two passengers. From here, a traveller could either

A Latécoère 521. (*Photograph from the Nico Braas Collection, 1000aircraftphotos.com*)

head up a companionway to the upper deck or head further aft into the kitchen and bar, followed by the baggage compartment.

In the upper deck, there was a position for the commanding officer in the nose, with the pilots positioned behind this and slightly above, seated side by side with dual controls. Aft of them came positions for the three mechanics the aircraft was meant to carry in flight, easily positioned to access the aircraft's six engines. The remainder of the upper deck held a third cabin for eighteen passengers and another kitchen and bar, plus another lavatory and baggage hold.

The design was originally meant for the Mediterranean service, to carry so many passengers, but would along the way be looked upon as a transatlantic airliner, in which configuration it was to carry eight crewmembers and twenty-six passengers. In the difference between the two totals of passengers carried lays an important reminder of the relationship between carried weight and overall range—more weight required more power to lift the aircraft, which increased fuel consumption and brought down range. To get passengers in even small numbers across oceans, larger aircraft were required with four or more engines, which in turn is what made the flying boat concept work in the 1930s. They were large enough to carry the necessary equipment the necessary distance, which is what in turn required long take-off runs. This was the era in which flying boats were becoming larger and larger to service a growing passenger trade, a process ultimately terminally interrupted by the outbreak of war.

In terms of the aircraft's powerplant, the 521 was originally conceived as having four 1,200-hp Hispano-Suiza engines that had been developed from 1,500-hp engines made specifically for the Schneider Trophy, which at the time was a very prominent showcase for "cutting edge" aircraft engineering and design. The aircraft was going to carry four or them, but in the event, they were not ready in time and the design was modified to carry six less powerful Hispano-Suiza engines. The engines were fitted in an unusual configuration, with four forward-facing "tractor" engines and two rearward facing "pusher" ones. This was an innovative way of fitting two more engines without a massive redesign of the wing.

The redesign process for six engines delayed the overall project, but what emerged into testing proved more powerful than anticipated, with the original design being believed capable of lifting 37 tons, proving more than adequate to lifting 40 tons. In addition, the initial tests found that a top speed could be achieved that was 5 kph faster than what had originally been predicted. The aircraft also proved capable of lifting off in between twenty-nine and forty-three seconds, with either a weight of 22 or 35 tons, respectively. This latter fact shows rather well the major challenges posed by increased weight on flying boats. The test pilots were named Crespy and Gonord, and almost like taking a ship out to sea for the first time, these men were overseen by one Captain Bonnet, who was representing the French Air Ministry.

The main problem for the design proved to be the protracted design process, ultimately lasting for five years, by which point, the design was already considered technically obsolete before it even took to the air. At the time, however, there was really only one aircraft to compare it to, the immense Dornier Do X, examined previously in this work. One source put it thus:

> The power necessary in the Do.X had to be divided into 12 groups, the engines available at the time scarcely exceeding 500 horsepower. Dr. Dornier's "flying ship" has always operated under this handicap. The wing structure, once it had been designed to furnish 24 supporting points to the struts carrying them in tandem,

A Latécoère 521. (*Photograph courtesy of Dan Shumaker*)

would have been difficult to adapt to the installation of a smaller—even though more powerful—number of groups.

Mounting the engine[s] on top of the wings constituted another handicap. Fitted into the wing, with distant control, as in the recent Do.18, or in front of the leading edge, if the diameter is small enough (Twin Wasp in the Martin 130) is **far preferable**.

Lastly, in comparing the two, we must not lose sight of the fact that the Do.X took to the air in 1929, and the Latécoère 521, in 1935.

In the Do.X the useful load represented 36 to 43 percent of the gross weight as against 50 percent in the Latécoère 521. The latter, which weighs 10 tons (22,046 pounds) less than the Do.X, carries—with a total of 5,300 horsepower instead of 7,500 horsepower—a weight of 9 tons (19,842 pounds) instead of 6 tons (13,228 pounds), for a distance of 1,200km (745.6 miles), and at a speed of 220 km/h (136.7 mi./hr.) as against 170km/h (105.6 mi./hr.). For a distance of 3,000km (1,864 miles), it carries a weight of 3 to 4 tons (6,614 to 8,818 pounds), while the Do.X could scarcely carry enough fuel for such a flight.

Aircraft Circular No. 202
National Advisory Committee for Aeronautics, pp. 6-7
[Bolding is in the original.]

To pull together what was at the time one of the largest aircraft in history, the sub-assemblies were built at Monaudran, Toulouse, and then taken by road to Biscarosse for final construction. Biscarosse had been designated as France's "hydro-base *transatlantique*." The 521 was meant to help the French compete for the Atlantic aviation market with the emerging American and British large flying boats. The aircraft, when finally completed, was named *Lieutenant de vaisseau Paris*, in memory of a famed French aviator who had held fifteen international records in 1930–1931.

The official inaugural flight came in January 1935. The flight took place at Etang de Biscarosse, near Bordeaux. Building on this, at the end of the year, a more impressive demonstration flight was planned. This flight was designed to commemorate three centuries of French presence—and rule—in the western hemisphere. The aircraft would fly to Pensacola, Florida. The flight began in December, and the aircraft winged its way without major incident through Dakar in Senegal and Natal in Brazil and then on to Martinique in the French West Indies, before the final jaunt to Florida. Here, the aircraft attracted significant press attention from the United States, but the journey did not end on a positive note. Shortly after its triumphant landing, the flying boat proved vulnerable to the wrath of nature. It was struck by a hurricane, flipped over onto its back, and to all practical purposes was almost wrecked. The remains of the aircraft were shipped back to France and ultimately repaired, but this further delay meant that it was not until August 1938 that the aircraft made its first trip to New York. Air France purchased another 521, though it would never serve in that capacity—the gathering storm of World War II would overwhelm these efforts.

The 521 prototype, having been completely rebuilt, was proven to be rather durable—the fact that a hurricane could damage but not destroy it may well have attested to that. As it stood, however, the 521 sought to prove itself on its merits. Back in action, it set a distance record for seaplanes in November by covering 3,603 miles (5,800 km) in thirty-four hours and thirty-seven minutes. The next month, it set a flurry of other records for seaplanes in terms of speed-to-load and load-to-altitude.

Based on this, the Ministry of Aviation decided to order another aircraft and improve it. This one took stock of the advances in aviation made since the 521 was conceived. The nose was redesigned to be more aerodynamic, removing the more angular and unusual appearance originally sported by the 521 in favour of something more familiar to modern onlookers. More powerful engines were also fitted, resulting in an aircraft designated Latécoère 522, though in most respects, it was merely a modification. This aircraft flew for the first time in April 1939 and was named *Ville de Saint-Pierre*. This was the basis for a civil airliner version of which three were apparently ordered, though none appear to have been built given the outbreak of war.

The original 521 had first been boldly conceived as an aircraft that could fly from France to New York in twenty hours. In the event, this conception did not become a reality. It did complete three lengthy survey flights of the Atlantic between 1935 and 1939, but only called on New York once more, in late August 1939. War was imminent, with the German invasion of Poland just days away. On August 27, the *Lieutenant de Vaissau Paris* was abruptly recalled to France, ending the French dream of creating its own version of a passenger service across the Atlantic. As with so many other dreams, World War II proved a calamitous end. The original aircraft would be seen along with the *Ville du Saint Pierre* in Bermuda before they were pressed into service, but having seen the world, the *Lieutenant de Vaissau Paris* would meet a sad end. She was brought into military service when the war began, being assigned to *Escadrille* E6 based in Morocco. After the armistice, she was dispatched to Berre, her final resting place. She would ultimately be dynamited by the retreating Germans to keep her from falling into Allied hands in August 1944. *Ville du Saint Pierre* met precisely the same fate, when the Germans dynamited the hangar alongside the Étang de Berre. Both were likely operated beforehand by the *Ministre des Colonies de Vichy* before meeting their end.

The French Navy had clearly understood the nature of the boat's capabilities, and put in an order for three armed, navalized versions of the aircraft for long-range maritime reconnaissance, which would ultimately be dubbed the Latécoère 523. The military version of the aircraft came with a total of five Darne machine guns, each of 7.5-mm (0.29-inch) calibre. Four of these were located in lateral positions, with the fifth in a dorsal turret. The aircraft could also carry a decent bombload, topping out at 6,834 pounds (3,100 kg). The aircraft proved excellent for maritime patrols and, given its range and bombload, was apparently well-suited to anti-submarine patrolling. It could stay aloft for a total of twenty hours. The

Latécoère 522, *Ville de Saint Pierre*. (*Photograph from the Nico Braas Collection, 1000aircraftphotos.com*)

Another view of the same aircraft. (*Photograph from the Nico Braas Collection, 1000aircraftphotos.com*)

crews of the massive aircraft also appreciated the spacious accommodations. The engines proved to be somewhat unreliable in service, and the aircraft had some limitations in addition to this. The aircraft had a low maximum speed, and its cruising altitude was very low—a fact that would make the aircraft vulnerable to enemy aircraft as well as anti-aircraft fire. These facts limited the number of missions the aircraft could carry out.

Originally, all three were assigned to *Escadrille* E6 based at Lanvéoc-Poulmic, and they suffered various fates. One, named *Algol*, was lost just after the war began. On September 18, 1939, the aircraft suffered a fuel failure and engaged in an emergency landing off Ouessant. An attempt was made to tow it to safety, but the torpedo boat *Le Boulonnais* accidentally collided with the flying boat. The damage was great enough that the aircraft had to be sunk by naval gunfire. The other two aircraft were not destined to survive the Fall of France. After this incident, the 521 and 522 were temporarily put into service, though both would be returned to civilian service after the armistice. Some accounts hold that the other two aircraft were mothballed by November 1941, but others hold that one of the remaining aircraft were destroyed to keep them out of German hands. This was supposedly the fate of the second aircraft, *Aldebaran*, which apparently ended up immobilized and was scuttled to keep it from the Germans on June 18, 1940. The third boat, *Altair*, apparently lasted the longest. During the Battle of France, it ended up being sent to the flying boat base at Biscarosse in mid-June1940, as catastrophe unfolded in France, before being sent on to Morocco the next day. It

A Latécoère 523. (*Photograph from the Nico Braas Collection, 1000aircraftphotos.com*)

was subsequently put into service with *Escadrille* E4, and was eventually laid up for lack of replacement parts and was scrapped sometime in 1942.

The military versions of the aircraft were too few to make a major impact on the course of the war. Indeed, there were also simply too few of the civil version of the aircraft to make a lasting impact; even if there were, the onset of the war denied the aircraft the chance to prove its worth in any meaningful way. This unique design was an ambitious attempt to project French aviation prowess onto the world stage, and in this it failed through no fault of its own. Circumstances in history can frequently overcome even the best laid plans, and this is certainly the case with much of France's aviation efforts in the 1930s and 1940s. It would not be the last time that the French tried to send their giants across the Atlantic—soon enough, another six-engined Latécoère would find itself in a similar position, and it would suffer even worse misfortunes.

22

Latécoère 631: Unlucky Giant

There was a belief in some quarters that the reign of the flying boat could go on indefinitely. That they could persist as the liners of the air, dominating air travel routes through the 1940s and even into the 1950s. Had the war not occurred, the titan flying boats may have had some extension of their lease on life, but even without the acceleration of events caused by worldwide conflict, the writing was on the wall. The vast increase in technology and capability for land-based aircraft that was already occurring was greatly boosted by the necessities of war, and the post-war world was not one in which the flying boats could compete as they had before.

In the case of the Latécoère 631, that evolutionary decay was part of a triple tragedy. This massive, graceful-looking aircraft was designed to continue the role that its predecessors had so amply filled, yet it was an aircraft racing against time. Then came the war, and the Fall of France, a second layer of tragedy to afflict the program, to say nothing of the greater tragedy that was Nazi occupation and Vichy collaboration. There was yet a third factor that would doom the Latécoère 631. While it might at first glance seem more mundane than such grandiose things as global war and politics or the entire evolutionary sweep of aircraft design, it was no less final. The problem for the aircraft, at its very core, was accidents. Nevertheless, whatever became of the program, the result was still the same: France created the largest passenger flying boat to ever see service—it is perhaps only fitting that one of the last great flying boats would also be one of the most gigantic ever made.

Specifications

First Flight: 1942
Powerplant: Six Wright R-2600-A5B Cyclone fourteen-cylinder radial engines, 1,600 hp each
Armament: None
Top Speed: 245 mph (394 kph)
Range/Service Ceiling: 3,750 miles (6,035 km), 13,123 feet (4,000 metres)

Dimensions: Length 142 feet 6⅝ inches (43.46 metres), height 33 feet 1½ inches (10.1 metres), wingspan 188 feet 1¼ inches (57.43 metres)
Number Built: Eleven

France's last titan owed its genesis, like so many other French aircraft in this book, to the pre-war years. The French Directorate responsible for Civil Aviation issued a specification in 1938 (some sources say 1936) for an airliner that could carry up to forty passengers (the prototypes built would exceed that by a few), with twenty carried in a sleeper configuration, to a range of 3,700 miles (6,000 km). Latécoère was one of the three competitors for this position, the others being the newly-formed SNCASE (their design, which had started at Lioré-et-Olivier, became the Sud-Est SE.200) and Potez-CAMS (the Potez-CAMS 160). Interestingly, all three designs were to be six-engined flying boats, because the specification specifically required six engines, namely the Gnôme et Rhône P.18.

None of the aircraft was ever competitively evaluated against the other since the outbreak of war slowed development of all of them. Development came to a complete halt with the Fall of France, and what little work done under Vichy was again halted by the German takeover of the rest of France in 1942. After that, work only proceeded with the say-so of the Germans, who wanted to develop any long-range capacity for themselves. Between these two events, assembly of the 631 prototype took place at a hangar in Marignane, oddly enough nearby to its erstwhile SNCASE rival. The aircraft that developed was typically laid out for a large passenger flying boat of the period, but had a unique dihedral twin fin tail, and seems almost to have been stretched out.

The internal accoutrements of the 631 were equally impressive to the vast and relatively conventional exterior. There was a large kitchen and bathroom aft of the entrance, and if a passenger were moving forward from that entrance, they would find eight sleeper cabins that came with leather seats and were enclosed by wooden panelling. The windows were small in comparison to those on contemporary American and British passenger aircraft, but the high wing of the aircraft meant that passengers had an entirely unobstructed view through them. Further along was the aircraft's restaurant and bar, where there was a ladder that led up to the flight deck. The restaurant did have the minor drawback of vibrating significantly when in flight, owing to its proximity to the engines. In an example of how the passage of time changes ideas from excellent to foolhardy, the interior of the fuselage had been sprayed with asbestos to reduce noise. Beyond the vibrating restaurant, an observer would find the luggage compartment and the crew toilet, and after that, they would find a pair of eight-seat and four-seat cabins. At the very front of the fuselage, there was a single pair of seats below a large window, allowing yet another clear view.

The aircraft carried a total crew of nine. In addition to no fewer than three pilots, there were two navigators, a pair of flight mechanics, and two radio operators. The spaces dedicated to these crewmen were also well worth remarking upon. In the bow, there was a mooring compartment that allowed a crew member to walk out to a pontoon via a hatchway that was long and curved, which could be swept upwards and rearwards. Between the pilots' seats, there was a sort of metal capstan with metal wheels on it, which gave the impression the French wished—that it was a call to the past days of sailing vessels. This imagery was furthered by a mast placed on the elongated nose, which by itself was a full 23 feet long.

Getting the 631 ready ran afoul of the rapidly changing war situation. British advisers had been sent across for the purpose of getting the giant ready, but when France began to collapse, the advisors had to be hastily withdrawn—with Chief Designer Harry Smith and Chief Engineer Percy Allison catching one of the last boats to leave Le Havre. Work on the aircraft continued under the Vichy Regime, and the aircraft was flown to Lake Marignane in November 1942. It did not remain in French hands for long, however. The Germans were by this point in need of any aircraft they could get their hands on, and the first aircraft was confiscated for evaluation as a transport aircraft. It would ultimately be destroyed in April 1944 by de Havilland Mosquito aircraft, on Lake Constance.

This piece of bad news may have been offset somewhat by the fact that the French provisional government had decided that the 631 would be the chosen aircraft for France's needs after the war. The competing designs, interesting in their own right, were consigned to the shadows. Whatever might happen, Latécoère would alone reap the benefit—if there was any to be had. The post-war future would prove unkind to their massive design.

A Latécoère 631. (*Photograph from the Nico Braas Collection, 1000aircraftphotos.com*)

In the meantime, the second aircraft had a story that was more interesting still. It was completed in 1943, but before even leaving the factory, it took part in the war in an unusual way. Despite its size, the aircraft was dismantled and hidden to enable the French resistance to blow up the factory to deny it giving aid to the Germans. After the liberation of Toulouse in August 1944, the aircraft was able to emerge from hiding. The factory was rebuilt, and the massive aircraft's parts were retrieved and assembled. The fuselage and wings were transported to Lake Biscarosse, and after three months of refitting, the aircraft was able to fly for the first time at the beginning of March 1945. It received Wright engines of significantly higher horsepower than the original Hispano-Suiza engines it had been given. Much equipment had to be revised to achieve this, which worried some of the people involved in its building. There was, after all, little time to test and evaluate all the changes. Nevertheless, the Air Minister Charles Tillon decided the type should go into service on overseas flights. For France, this was imperative as a matter of prestige and prospective economics—and for Latécoère, it would help put to bed accusations that the company had engaged in collaboration with the hated Germans during the war.

As was traditional for large French flying boats, the aircraft was given an official name. In this case, it was named after the fighter ace Lionel de Marmier by the new Minister de l'Air Charles Tillon, formerly part of the French Resistance. The aircraft was flown to Dakar in a total journey of 3,760 miles (6,051 km) before ultimately making display flights to Paris and South America. Even these display flights revealed what in retrospect appears to be an ominous warning: one of the landings involved hitting a block of concrete and ripping a 20-foot (6-metre) hole in the hull.

Soon after, the third aircraft was completed. It too received the name of a famous aviator, in this case *Henri Guillaumet*. Guillaumet had also formerly been a director of Air France, which made the name of the aircraft all the more appropriate when it began service on the transatlantic route to the French West Indies in July 1945. More aircraft were coming, and after years of chaos, war, and occupation, it looked as if France would finally get her chance to carry out her long-standing ambitious plans to conquer the Atlantic passenger routes.

When the aircraft arrived at Hythe in 1947, the striking nature of the aircraft was put vividly on display, described by authors such as Leslie Dawson. Everything about the aircraft seemed elongated and graceful. The fuselage looked like it went on forever, intersected by wings that seemed to match. The tail rose thin and graceful behind, finishing an image that overall looked like something out of a work of fiction. The aircraft was only slightly taller than the Short Empire boats that were nearby, but it dwarfed them in wingspan and had nearly double the length. The Short Empires were serviceable aircraft, workhorses of British air travel, but the 631 moored alongside looked like a thoroughbred.

In truth, both aircraft were doomed, though the Empire boats would shortly make their slow exit from a long and successful career, the 631 was not destined to end well. Rather, it would end in a flurry of accidents. Aside from the publicity

Interior of the 631's cockpit. (*Photograph from the Nico Braas Collection, 1000aircraftphotos.com*)

visit to England, the 631s were meant to fly on a route from Biscarrosse to Forte de France in Martinique, via Mauritania, as well as to South America. Even early on, there proved to be fatal problem. The first came on October 31, 1945, when the second aircraft (F-BANT) was on the way from Brazil to Uruguay, the propeller of the number three engine tore off mid-flight, and damaged number two engine next to it. This caused a propeller blade to slice a nearly 10-foot (3-metre) hole in the cabin, killing two of the passengers and starting a fire. The aircraft managed to land in the Laguna de Rocha in Uruguay, and was subsequently repaired, but it was only the beginning of the accidents that would plague the type. This accident, coming on the heels of the hull-ripping incident, created a healthy mistrust of the aircraft. Despite this, Air France purchased four of the completed aircraft, designed to carry forty-six passengers at a maximum.

On February 21, 1948, another 631 (F-BDRD) was returning to Biscarrosse when it ran into a heavy winter storm. The pilot apparently descended to try to get away from the weather, and the aircraft hit the sea off St. Marcouf, France, killing all nineteen on board. Worse was to come just a few months later for the aircraft (F-BDRC) named *Lionel de Marnier*. On August 1, the aircraft was due to arrive at Port-Étienne in French West Africa after departing Fort de France. On board were forty passengers and twelve crew members. A mayday was received, and there were confused reports about other signals, but that was all—and a major rescue effort was mounted, which would turn up some wreckage that showed evidence of fire. The rescue effort had been an international one, with the French

Air Force and Navy both taking part, with help from the Portuguese. Eight days after the aircraft disappeared, the search was called off. This second accident was enough for Air France, which withdrew the 631 from service.

A contemporary magazine described the accident in this manner:

> There now appears to be little hope that the Latécoère flying boat which vanished on a flight across the South Atlantic can still be afloat, and once again the aviation world, it is to be feared, is left to mourn the loss of many lives in mysterious circumstances.
>
> The fact that the aircraft involved was a flying boat, and a large one at that, gave good cause for hoping that it might have made a safe descent, and that thus the passengers and crew might be rescued. In a fairly recent case a Boeing flying boat came down in the North Atlantic in a very rough sea, but in spite of all this the occupants were taken off safely. Reports indicated that the weather was fairly good in the South Atlantic at the time when the Latécoère, still flying, sent out its message to report all well.
>
> There is some difficulty in reconciling the reports of faint distress signals received days later with still more recent reports of finding wreckage believed to have been from the flying boat.... Several explanations are possible, and it may be that fire broke out while the boat was still airborne, that the pilot managed to alight, that the fire was got under control but that parts of the radio equipment was put out of action, thus preventing the sending of the distress signals until a later time. This, of course, is conjecture but appears to fit in with the known facts.
>
> *Flight*, August 12, 1948, p. 170

Whatever the cause, the result remained unalterable, and the Latécoère 631's days were numbered. The remaining aircraft were passed on to other carriers, and the type's bad luck continued. At the time, all the remaining 631s had come to be operated by the *Société d'Exploitation du Matériel Aéronautique Français* (SEMAF), which was flying one of them (F-WANU) to try and determine what had caused the previous catastrophe. SEMAF wanted to use them for transporting cotton in Africa, but their dream was also not to be. On March 28, 1950, the plane was conducting a test flight out of Biscarosse when severe vibrations of one of the engine's gear boxes caused the aileron control couplings to fail. This aircraft, too, fell out of the sky, killing all twelve of the crew on board. The crash took SEMAF with it.

What little remained of the once-ambitious 631 program had by now either been lost or put into storage—aside from one last flying aircraft. This last Latécoère 631 started shipping cotton in Africa between Chad and Cameroon and had spent several years lingering in this service under a carrier known as France-Hydro, which had taken over SEMAF's old role. The aircraft could apparently haul 3,300 tons of cotton with each trip. On September 10, 1955, the aircraft was heading back to their old base at Biscarosse for maintenance when it flew into a tropical storm. The extreme forces, probably windshear, caused one of the wings to break

A 631 on its take-off run. (*Photograph courtesy of Dan Shumaker*)

away from the aircraft, and once again, all sixteen people on board, passengers and crew, were killed. This was the final straw for the program. The remaining aircraft, which had been stored for conversion to cargo-carrying purposes, were summarily scrapped.

It was an ignoble end and it remains to assess just what there is to say about the program that birthed this six-engined titan. The original pre-war plan for the aircraft was ambitious enough, but when coupled to the fact that it was hurriedly reassembled after the Liberation of France, the ambition behind the type perhaps took a step too far. France had little choice but to try to start generating revenue from passenger travel, and even less choice regarding aircraft. There were simply no other planes available, either through bombing raids or accidents, and Latécoère had certainly come through before. This time, it was not to be. It is doubtful whether the accidents that followed were the fault of the designers, and in any event, it is unlikely blame can ever be affixed if indeed there is something to blame. If anything, the rushed changes and abbreviated testing that followed could be theorized to have been an error. Perhaps it was coincidence that the type seemed almost cursed, but regardless of why the accidents happened, the result was to firmly scotch France's plans to conquer the Atlantic with their graceful flying boats. France had never quite been able to pull it off, despite valiant and often fatal efforts, and the 631 was the last try to restart the golden age of the flying boat by the French.

23

Loire 130: Eyes of the French Navy

The idea of aircraft carried on naval ships was, by the 1930s, no longer a novelty; it was a commonplace reality. The first experiments had begun as far back as World War I, and the post-war years had seen their development continue apace. The first aircraft carriers would set sail for Japan and Great Britain in the early 1930s, but the ideas ranged much further than that. The idea of capital warships carrying spotter aircraft had developed, too, and by the 1930s, cruisers and battleships of every description could be seen sporting aircraft on launch ramps—aircraft meant to scout ahead and direct the fire of the great naval guns.

In this effort, the French Navy was no laggard. The vast French fleet needed eyes in the sky just as much as their counterparts, and the Loire 130 served ably in this regard.

Specifications

First Flight: 1934
Powerplant: One Hispano-Suiza 12Xirs twelve-cylinder Vee engine, 720 hp
Armament: Two 7.7-mm (0.303-inch) Darne machine guns, two 75-kg (165-lb) bombs
Top Speed: 137 mph (221 kph)
Range/Service Ceiling: Seven-and-a-half hours' endurance, 19,865 feet (6,056 metres)
Dimensions: Length 37 feet ⅞ inch (11.30 metres), height 12 feet 7½ inches (3.85 metres), wingspan 52 feet 7⅞ inches (16 metres)
Number Built: 125

The Loire 130 began life as a replacement for France's older reconnaissance units, specifically stemming from a French requirement in the mid-1930s for a new reconnaissance seaplane meant for service on French battleships and cruisers. At the time, there was a view in most navies that despite the emergence of aircraft carriers as a part of naval strategy, there was a significant place for shipborne reconnaissance that could double as gunnery spotting. This role would ultimately be taken over by radar, and very few aircraft designed to be ship-mounted ever carried out gunnery spotting in any way.

In any event, at the time, France's specification was hotly contested, with a total of six proposals submitted before the Loire 130 was chosen. Production was to begin in 1937, by which time the amount of the order was already on the rise from what France had originally posited its needs to be. The design itself was in some ways very similar to other aircraft being built at the time, but there were some unusual elements.

The arrangement for the pilot was a little bit unusual, located in an open cockpit set slightly to port above the main cabin. In that main cabin, there were two more crewmembers who found themselves taking on dual roles: one as an observer and navigator, the other as a radio operator and gunner. The total weight of the aircraft, when it was fully loaded, could reach 7,716 lb (3,500 kg), which was actually above the rated weight of France's naval catapults; as a result, the aircraft was limited on ships to a total weight of 7,187 lb (3,260 kg).

The first prototype of the aircraft took to the air for the first time on November 19, 1934. The initial testing of the aircraft revealed that it had issues with directional instability, as well as cooling problems with the engine. The former problem was eventually solved by making the auxiliary fins larger, and the latter by a complete redesign of the radiator system on the engine. Once these issues were solved, the French government placed an order for a total of forty-five aircraft. Forty of these were Loire 130M aircraft, which stood for *Metropole*—these aircraft were meant for service in and around France itself. The other five were 130C aircraft, or *Colonial* flying boats. These latter aircraft featured a larger radiator to deal with the tropical heat, and also came with structural strengthening to fulfil the French Navy's desire for them to carry out shallow dive-bombing missions. To do this, the 130C aircraft had an added OPL38 bombsight. All of this increased weight and drag, bringing the top speed down by 12 mph (just over 19 kph).

The aircraft proved very durable in actual service, and in terms of its capabilities, it has been compared to the Supermarine Walrus, which features later in this book. If the aircraft was flown at 93 mph (149.6 kph), it could stay in the air for seven and a half hours, a very useful patrol time. Moreover, in addition to the crew, the aircraft could carry an additional four passengers when it was used as a liaison and communications aircraft.

The order would ultimately be increased, as well. By 1936, a further ten aircraft would be ordered, and more would be added in the next two years: twenty in 1937 and nineteen in 1938. The last of these three increases included an order not just for the navy but also the French Air Force, which wanted a dozen 130Cs. In naval terms, what the steady delivery of these aircraft meant was that by the time war broke out, most of the major warships of the French fleet were equipped with the aircraft, though the order was not finished by the time hostilities started. The aircraft equipped not just major capital ships such as the *Dunkerque* and the *Strasbourg*, but also four cruiser squadrons and the seaplane carrier *Commandant Teste*. Further afield, the type equipped an *Armée de l'Air* unit in French Indochina,

A Loire 130 sitting in front of either the *Dunkerque* or the *Strasbourg*. (*Photograph from the Nico Braas Collection, 1000aircraftphotos.com*)

A catapult-mounted Loire 130 on the light cruiser *Georges Leyguess*, New York City, 1939.

as well as units based at Dakar, Tripoli, and Lebanon, and even in the West Indies at Fort de France at Martinique, the capital of the regional department.

When mounted on French capital ships, the aircraft were typically stored in a hangar with wings folded. If two aircraft were able to fit in the hangar, they would be placed inside one in front of the other. The end of the hangar was closed with a metal "curtain" that slid upwards, with maintenance workshops directly below the hangar, and to starboard, a magazine for the aircraft's bombs, as was the case in the *Dunkerque* and the *Strasbourg*. When the time came for action, the aircraft were rolled out of the hangar on their launching trolleys on rails that ran from the hangar to an elevator on the deck. The aircraft was then pushed onto the elevator and its wings extended, then it proceeded to launch. When it returned, it was winched aboard by a crane. It was theorized that battleships could carry anywhere from three to five of the aircraft.

The Loire 130 served a unique purpose in the French Aeronavale: standardization. Before its arrival, there were no less than eight reconnaissance types in service, ranging from models of the CAMS 37 that had been in service since the latter stages of the 1920s and was painfully slow, the similar but still slow CAMS 55, the Gourdou-Leseurre GL810, 812, and 832 that were also increasingly antiquated, the Potez 452 and Levasseur PL14, and fifteen biplane floatplanes. The Loire 130 was not terribly faster than all of these, but it was much more of a multirole aircraft and operating one type instead of at least eight would undoubtedly simplify maintenance and repair to no end. It is worth noting that the Loire 130 had replaced most of these by 1940, with the notable exception of the Potez 452—coincidentally, another flying boat—which lingered on in France's Asian possessions until 1944.

After the Fall of France, one of Loire 130s joined the exodus of French servicemen, aircraft, and even ships attempting to join the English and fight on. This single Loire 130 was under the control of Georges Blaize and Raoul Gatien, both of whom had decided that surrender to the Nazis was not an option. Their aircraft, mounted on the battleship *Richelieu*, took off on a routine flight on October 15, 1940, and the pair diverted to Malta. Their aircraft, strangely enough, wound up as part of R.A.F. 228 Squadron based at Kalafrana Bay, where it was used for clandestine operations. Thus it was that sitting among powerful four-engined Sunderlands, there was a single little redoubtable French flying boat, joined by a Latécoère 298 floatplane that had also made its escape to Malta.

Other aircraft served Vichy loyally. When the British fleet sailed to attack Dakar, it was a Loire 130 that detected them approaching the port after the first air raid. In this, it was fulfilling the role that became its standard in November 1942: coastal reconnaissance. It took part in such operations all through France's colonial possessions in the Mediterranean and to all accounts did its job well, though with France's parlous state, it could never achieve any real success.

Its role in France's furthest-flung possessions is perhaps the most interesting, since the aircraft not only gave stellar service in wartime but continued afterwards as well. The aircraft had also proved itself in the brief and sadly forgotten

A Loire 130 in German hands. (*Photograph from the Nico Braas Collection, 1000aircraftphotos.com*)

Rear view of another German-use Loire 130. (*Photograph from the Nico Braas Collection, 1000aircraftphotos.com*)

Franco-Thai War. The Japanese sought to egg the Thais on towards reclaiming territory that was a part of French Cambodia and Thailand's (then known as Siam). Marshal Phibun used a series of border incidents to try and generate a swift conflict to retake what he considered occupied Thai territories. The French were significantly outmatched in terms of materiel, especially in the air. The Loire 130 was on hand from its bases in French Indochina and it was put to work almost immediately. One particular 130 shot down two enemy aircraft. The first was an old Vought O2U Corsair that was downed by the flying boat's gunners. The second came on December 12, 1940, when the same Loire knocked down a significantly superior Curtiss Hawk fighter. On land, despite Thai air superiority, the situation bogged down after initial successes for Thailand.

The aircraft was a part of one of France's relatively few naval victories during the war years, at the Battle of Ko Chang. Given France's overall weakness, it must have looked as if the Thais could easily achieve by sea what it could not on land. They had a powerful force in the area, built around a pair of Japanese-built coast defence vessels, the *Ayuthia* and the *Chonburi*, which were armed with four 8-inch guns. Accompanying them were two other ships with a pair of 6-inch guns, a destroyer, five submarines, and a mixed force of torpedo boats and sloops. The French had the light cruiser *Lamotte-Picquet* with 6.1-inch guns, three sloops with 5.5-inch guns, and the small sloop *Marne* that had four 3.9-inch guns. The French were significantly outgunned.

The solution was boldness. This force put to sea on January 17, 1941 to surprise a Thai force of enemy warships in an archipelago of small islands on the border. A crucial part in this was played by a Loire 130, which located the Thai warships first while the French were still shrouded in fog. In the ensuing battle, both the *Ayuthia* and the *Chonburi* were so badly mauled that they never entered service again, and three torpedo boats were lost against no French losses. The embarrassed Japanese ultimately brokered a ceasefire, and the little Loire 130 had certainly done its work well.

The Loire 130 was still flying with the French in the Far East until 1951. It represented the bulk of the early air support for France's military efforts to secure her colonies, centred on the *Divisions Navales d'Assaut*, or *dinassaut*. At first, aside from a few leftover Sea Otter aircraft, the Loire 130 was all the air support the French soldiers could count on, until the arrival of aircraft carriers began, and aircraft purchased from the British and Americans started to make their presence felt in 1951. Once those aircraft were in place, the by-now elderly Loire 130s could be taken out of service and eventually scrapped. None of the aircraft survive today.

Despite its relatively small overall deployment, the Loire 130 is a revealing aircraft in several ways. First, it emphasizes the importance that many nations put on catapult-launched aircraft before aircraft carriers became strategically central to the idea of aviation's power at sea. This was a concept that appealed to many navies in the period, often concentrating on the idea of gunnery spotting—a task rapidly over taken by radar. Second, it reveals France's hurried (or perhaps harried is the better word) attempts to modernize its aerial forces and simplify their supply situation. Third, it highlights a forgotten corner of World War II that is well-worth further study in detail. In all of these facets, the Loire 130 proved to be quite the little gem, though it could do nothing to slow the march of forces France could not possibly contain: first, the German Wehrmacht, and second, the rise of anti-colonialism, which the Loire 130 could only help delay. In the long run, though the aircraft helped the French hold "their" territory in Asia for the moment, there was no force on Earth that could stop people from demanding freedom and independence from the yolk of European empire.

24

Martin JRM Mars: Last of the Giants

For this chapter, it is necessary to start with something of a personal aside. Those of you who have read this author's first book *Rare Birds: Forgotten Aircraft of the Second World War*, will know the Martin Mars well—this marks its second appearance. There are a few reasons for this, the first of which being that it is something of a sentimental favourite. The Martin Mars was and is an impressive aircraft, one of the most capable aircraft of the 1940s. Though other flying boats are still in active use, the continued use of the Mars stands out. The last of the Martin Mars aircraft is, at the time of this writing in late 2017, still ready for service, over seventy years after it first took to the skies. If that remarkable and lengthy career is a suitable second reason, the third is that the Mars has succeeded at whatever mission it has been called to perform. No aircraft so unique, so tough, and, above all, such a survivor could be excluded from this work. The Martin Mars was the product of a doctrine unique to the United States, which had already been withdrawn by the time the aircraft first took to the air. Its entire existence has in some ways been a paradox, an aircraft that has kept on finding unexpected roles, and continued to survive as truly the last of the dinosaurs—the last, and perhaps greatest, of the titan flying boats.

Specifications

Note: Specifications are for the final production example, the JRM-3, as the type was continually upgraded.

First Flight: 1942
Powerplant: Four Pratt & Whitney R-4360-5 Twin Wasp twenty-eight-cylinder, air-cooled engines, 3,000 hp each
Armament: None
Top Speed: 238 mph (383 kph)
Range/Service Ceiling: 6,750 miles (10,863 km), 14,600 feet (4,450 metres)

Dimensions: Length 120 feet 3 inches (36.66 metres), height 38 feet 5 inches (11.71 metres), wingspan 200 feet (60.96 metres)
Number Built: Seven

The United States had pursued the concept of large flying boats both for combat and for transport duties, foreseeing a role in both for any upcoming Pacific conflict. Sources sometimes disagree over whether or not the Mars was meant for the Sky Dreadnought concept or the Sky Freighter one—though it theoretically could have easily fulfilled either (indeed, it is entirely possible it was intended for first one, then another as they were abandoned in turn). These concepts would both be overtaken by events and the service of other aircraft in any event, but in the mid-1930s, both seemed a major path forward for large, four-engined flying boats. The specific impetus for the Mars came as early as 1935, when the U.S. Navy first took interest in pursuing such large aircraft.

Glenn Martin had apparently great faith in the ability of the prototype he wished to build as an unstoppable aircraft. He apparently envisioned—and proposed—an aircraft that could fend off anything in the sky and still deliver a payload of 10,000 lb (4,536 kg) of bombs far away from American shores. This is a startling image: the idea of a massive flying boat bomber tough enough and prickly enough to survive any opposition to drop more tonnage than would in reality be carried by either a B-17 Flying Fortress or a B-24 Liberator. In fact, this weight of bombs would only be practically reached by the B-29 Superfortress. His presentation garnered enough interest for the navy to order a prototype to be designated XPB2M-1.

The prototype Mars: XPB2M-1. (*Photograph from the U.S. Navy National Museum of Naval Aviation*)

Work had begun in 1937 on the Martin Model 170, using knowledge gained from the Mariner program. In many respects, the Mariner proved highly influential on the program. Despite the vast size difference, the XPB2M-1 project borrowed in terms of structural design, aerodynamics, and hull performance. In the vast hull under the high wing, munitions were to be stored in two hull compartments just below the wings, with bombs to be released by sliding racks. The major problem for Martin had nothing to do with the design, but with actually building the aircraft. By that time, the company was engaged in contracts for the B-26 bomber for the U.S., as well as overseas orders for the Baltimore and Maryland bombers. As a result, the construction of the new giant did not take begin until well into 1940, whereupon it was christened "Mars."

Initially, things did not go well when it was finally completed. During initial taxi trials in early November 1941, the number three engine lost a propeller blade and a fire ensued. The wing and engine nacelle were badly damaged, along with damage to the hull where the propeller blade struck when it broke off. Repairs took six months, delaying the XPB2M-1's first flight until July 2, 1942. It was the second largest aircraft in the world at the time by a nose, and the largest flying boat by a significant margin. Unfortunately, by the time it flew, the navy's interest in the very concept had drained away. It was cheaper and more efficient to purchase and build larger numbers of twin-engined machines, which fit in with the increasing pace of rearmament—a decision that the outbreak of war confirmed and added urgency to.

A new danger had arisen in the interim, however: the threat of the U-boats to Allied shipping. The losses of ships created a significant belief in large scale flying boats as a solution, a concept that spawned the Hughes H-4 Hercules (in

The prototype on the ground, giving a good sense of scale, 1942. (*Photograph from the U.S. Navy National Museum of Naval Aviation*)

fact, before approaching Howard Hughes, Henry Kaiser had approached Martin about license-building the Mars in vast numbers, which Martin refused—Kaiser then went to Hughes, and the rest is history). Martin was directed to strip out the combat equipment already installed—no defensive armament was ever fitted—and modify it as a transport. This "new" aircraft finished its factory testing in mid-1943 as the XPB2M-1R and was handed over to the navy. By this time, it looked like the aircraft was too late yet again. The U-boats were on the retreat and the production of ships had long since outstripped the abilities of the Axis to sink them. The idea of manufacturing large amounts of transport aircraft was dropped, and it looked like there would only ever be one Mars.

The prototype entered service with transport squadron VR-2, operating out of Alameda, California. Here the aircraft rapidly proved its worth. It ran cargo out from California to Hawaii, regularly carrying 10 tons (9,072 kg) on each flight. The aircraft was affectionately known as the "Old Lady," and it would serve as a trainer (to its younger sisters) before being withdrawn from service in 1945, to be scrapped later. This might have been all there was to say, but the course of the war had produced some concerns about future operations. Namely, the U.S. was, by mid-1944, pondering what an invasion of Japan might require in terms of logistical support. It is easy to see the thinking in retrospect. While today almost any reader of history knows that the Manhattan Project was moving towards success and terrible deployment in 1945, the project was known to only a handful of people outside the project itself. It was so secret, in fact, that Vice-President Harry S. Truman did not learn of the project until he assumed the presidency after Franklin D. Roosevelt had died. As far as the navy was concerned in 1944, an invasion and final defeat of Japan would have to be done the old-fashioned way: with a long, bloody campaign.

In this paradigm, they saw the need for a small number of large airborne transports, to augment the transport capacities of the Naval Air Transportation Service (NATS) over the vast distances of the Pacific. Under these circumstances, a giant flying boat remained an ideal aircraft. In June 1944, the navy decided that, based on the performance of Martin's XPB2M-1R prototype, they should authorize Martin to construct twenty giant flying boats that would in practice work out to be a major improvement over the original prototype. Though the wing and engines from the prototype were retained (specifically the R-3350 engines), the rest of the aircraft was majorly redone. The hull itself took on an extra 6 feet of length in the front, with the aft fuselage shortened by 3 feet. The aircraft also took on a new tail structure with a single large fin and rudder. Internally, many of the bulkheads between compartments that had marked the first prototype were removed, optimizing the total cargo space available, with a hoist installed for quicker loading and unloading.

The new aircraft was dubbed the JRM-1, and while Martin was working on the navy's order, it also optimistically began to design a civilian version for post-war service, since, by early 1945, when design work was well underway, it was clear that the end of the war was approaching. This would have been even clearer when the first JRM-1, dubbed *Hawaii Mars*, was delivered to the navy in July 1945. The

Philippine Mars on its take-off run. (*Photograph courtesy of Dan Shumaker*)

first *Hawaii Mars* did not last, however, being destroyed in an accident a mere two weeks later at Chesapeake Bay in a landing accident.

Despite this, Martin had high hopes for the aircraft. A company advertisement put it this way:

> At some far-flung naval base, special equipment is needed ... quickly. Big events are in the making; and the war can't wait while plodding freighters cross sub-infested seas. This is a job for the 72-ton Martin Mars, world's largest flying boat. Our Navy's answer to the cry of "more supplies ... *faster*," the Martin Mars can carry 20 tons of cargo to the *farthest spot on earth* in 5 days or less. Now in regular service with the Navy, the Mars is the most efficient airplane yet built ... per pound of material used, per horsepower and per gallon of fuel. Twenty more of these giant ships, each 82 tons, are now being built for the U.S. Navy.
>
> Into the Mars went hard-won Martin knowledge gleaned from the construction of the original trans-Pacific Clippers ... the giant Russian clipper ... and the Navy's long range patrol bombers. From the Mars have come further important findings which will lend added speed, safety and comfort to tomorrow's greater Martin airliners. The Martin Mars is doing more than help win a war ... she's blazing the trail to a new and brighter tomorrow!

"About the Mighty Mars," Glenn L. Martin Company
Life Magazine
June 19, 1944, p. 116

Clearly, optimism was in the air at Martin. The same advertisement went on to posit that that aircraft could not only carry the equivalent of a sixteen-room mansion, but that in the future even this mighty aircraft would be surpassed by airliners of up to 250 tons. At least in its advertisements, Martin seemed to assume that there was no practical upper limit to how big these aircraft could get. Having an aircraft with the practical power of the Mars would certainly have encouraged such opinions.

Four more examples of the Mars were completed by the end of 1945, but the defeat of Japan had meant a drastic curtailing of the order to a total of six aircraft. No civilian interest seemed forthcoming either, so the future of the Martin Mars looked particularly grim. Nevertheless, the company continued with its deliveries to the navy, each taking on a name in turn: *Philippine Mars*, *Marianas Mars*, *Marshall Mars*, and *Hawaii Mars II*. The sixth and final aircraft, *Caroline Mars*, received an upgraded set of engines, R-4360-4 models, and had longer-cord cowlings. In the end, all the extant Mars aircraft would receive the new engines, bringing them up to a final designation of JRM-3. The main advantage of the upgrade was that the two inner engines had fully reversible propellers, meaning water handling became so exceptional that the aircraft could successfully back up. It also meant that the take-off weight increased by 16,000 lb, but even here caused further gain by allowing another 10,000 lb of useful load. All the aircraft then active were retrofitted to become JRM-3s.

All five of the aircraft were assigned to the same squadron their elder sister had been, VR-2. Their primary duty was also the same, hauling cargo from California to Hawaii. There were interesting departures along the way, though. *Caroline Mars* was responsible for two successful missions that can only be described as feats. In 1949, she carried a total load of 68,282 lb (30,972 kg) from Baltimore to Cleveland on Lake Erie—double the aircraft's usual maximum load. The next year, she hauled 144 Marines from San Diego to Honolulu, and the year before, *Marshall Mars* had demonstrated this was nowhere near the upper limit of soldiers the type could carry by lifting 301 of them (plus the crew of seven) from San Diego to Alameda. It is worth bearing in mind that merely twenty years before, the Dornier Do X had staggered the world by lifting 169 people—this was indicative of significant progress, and indeed prowess, for flying boat design. As it was, the aircraft would not long survive its feat. In 1950, she was lost when an engine caught fire. Forced to make a sea landing, the crew had no access to working fire equipment, and while they safely escaped, the aircraft burnt and sank.

This was the only blemish on the type's safety record in naval service. Already, the type was establishing its claim to truly legendary durability. They served as hospital transports during the Korean War, ferrying the wounded to Japan with apparent ease, but once the war was over, the type faced an immediate crisis. The navy no longer saw any need for the type, and beached all four remaining aircraft in 1956, as the navy was purchasing Convair R3Ys. In 1959, all of them were sold to a scrapyard for a total price tag of $23,650.

One of the Mars aircraft demonstrating remarkable water handling despite their size. (*Photograph courtesy of the Naval History and Heritage Command*)

Four of the mighty Mars aircraft together in one shot. (*Photograph courtesy of the Naval History and Heritage Command*)

Fate spared them this ignominious end. A Canadian pilot named Dan McIvor had for some time been considering how best to employ aircraft to put out forest fires. This was not done out of a notion of conservation, but of preserving future stocks for lumber companies. For this role, he envisioned large flying boats as being perfect, but by 1959, there simply were none being produced anywhere. By chance, he was informed about the four Mars aircraft awaiting their fate, and all four were bought out of waiting oblivion by a consortium of lumber companies in British Columbia. The aircraft were registered under the corporate name of Forest Industries Flying Tankers. In addition to the aircraft, McIvor had cannily bought the remaining stockpile of parts for the aircraft, and an additional thirty-five R-3350-24WA engines. These were less powerful than the engines on the JRM-3s, and payload was reduced by around 10,000 lb (4,536 kg), but they were significantly easier to maintain over time.

Each aircraft was restored to flying condition, and each in turn flew off to Victoria, British Columbia, when ready. There they were modified at Fairey Aviation of Canada to aerial fire-bombers. All military equipment was removed and 6,200-gallon (50,100-lb) water tanks were added in place of some of the fuel tanks. Retractable scoops were installed in the hull's planing surface, meaning the aircraft could refill their tanks by simply skimming across a lake without taking the time to land and take-off again. The first of the modified water bombers, *Marianas Mars*, took to her new role beginning in 1960. She did not last long, unfortunately, when the pilot cartwheeled the aircraft into a forest in June 1961, killing four. *Caroline Mars* followed in 1962, and it took a typhoon to destroy her—while ashore for maintenance, the aircraft took the brunt of typhoon Freda, and was damaged beyond repair. Undeterred, *Philippine Mars* and *Hawaii Mars II* took up their role in 1963 and 1964.

The last two Martin Mars aircraft carried out their work in tandem without any major mishap for decades. For forty years, the aircraft dropped massive amounts of water on forest fires, and it was only in 2006 that FIFT decided to stop using the two. They were put up for sale, and again their career might have ended, but they were purchased by Coulson Forest Products. From 2007, *Hawaii Mars II* began to fight fires again, as far away as the type's old haunt, California. *Philippine Mars* went into a sort of semi-retirement, ready but not flying. There have been plans to retire her to the National Naval Air Museum in Florida in her original colours, but these plans are on hold as of mid-2016.

Thus, the last flying aircraft, *Hawaii Mars II*, continues on. According to the Coulson group, today she can drop 7,200 U.S. gallons (27,276 litres) of water over an area of 4 acres in a single drop. The time to recharge those massive tanks is apparently around thirty seconds, and she can also carry 600 U.S. gallons (2,270 litres) of foam concentrate to allow the load drop to gel. Along the way, she has also been used to train Chinese firefighting pilots.

The British Columbian government announced in 2013 they would stop using the aircraft for firefighting owing to its age—despite extensive upgrading and modernizing—but in 2015, amid public outcry at a new round of forest fires, the last Mars went back to work. Though the company apparently seeks to sell the aircraft, she remains at the ready. As of 2017, she has not been used in the current fire season, despite continuing public pressure from some British Columbian citizens to do so. Part of the reason is that until late August 2017, the type is to be under maintenance, and the province claims the aircraft is limited in where it can pick up water, a fact Coulson disputes.

A recent comparison held that the Mars could drop 2,200 gallons in three-and-a-half-second drops, compared to other planes that are only capable of dropping 400 per second, for two seconds. The province claims that this volume is actually a problem—firefighters have stop work when the Mars makes a drop, thus supposedly giving a fire a chance to escape containment. Coulson and the province dispute costs as well, and so the future of the last remaining aircraft is, at the time of this writing, once again in doubt.

In all fairness, it is a shame that it is so. After such a lengthy career, one must hope that either some future use for the aircraft be found, or that it is guaranteed a dignified retirement as an exhibit and monument to its achievement after decades of service. This goes for *Philippine Mars* as well, a pair of aircraft that offer a living historical reminder of not just the past, but the present as well. One would presume that after a career spanning from 1945 until 2017, the aircraft would well deserve a certain amount of respect. Of course, the Martin Mars spent all that time earning respect from everyone who operated it, and in every role that it took on. The aircraft began its life as an attempt at a Sky Dreadnought, then as an attempt at a Sky Freighter, then became a heavy transport and medical aircraft, and finally has spent decades dropping an enormous tonnage of water on forest fires. The career of the Martin Mars has been exceptional at every turn, and while it does not hold the title of the largest flying boat ever, this author believes that out of all the aircraft in this book, it has in a sense attained the title of the most successful. It was never produced in the highest numbers, nor did it roam the globe or create an image of a golden age, but it is the only survivor of that age. Of all the four-engined titans, only the Mars still flies. That an aircraft built so long ago still has the potential to serve in 2017 is astonishing, and the Martin Mars easily earns its place in any historical work on aviation.

25

Martin M.130: Competitor for the Golden Age Crown

The Martin M.130 is another one of those aircraft that, much like Hughes' enormous Hercules, was rarely known by its actual name. Unlike the Hercules, the difference between the popular conception of the aircraft and the reality worked out positively—Martin certainly did not dislike the reputation as Hughes disliked his. Martin officially knew the large passenger flying boats as the Martin Ocean Transports. The public, however, came to know them as the China Clippers, and this would become a term given to all the giant flying boats being used by Pan American Airlines.

Aircraft like the M.130 were the symbols of the golden age of flying boats, enduring images that suffuse our understanding even today. The full, complete story of such aircraft is no less interesting than the vision that has surrounded them ever since.

Specifications

First Flight: 1934
Powerplant: Four Pratt & Whitney R-1830-S2A5G Twin Wasp fourteen-cylinder radial engines, 830 hp
Armament: None
Top Speed: 180 mph (290 kph)
Range/Service Ceiling: 3,200 miles (5,150 km), 10,000 feet (3,048 metres)
Dimensions: Length 90 feet 10½ inches (27.7 metres), height 24 feet 7 inches (7.5 metres), wingspan 130 feet (39.7 metres)
Number Built: Three

Glenn Martin had begun his aviation career with kites, but by the early 1930s, he was a major name in aviation. The impetus to create the aircraft that would become known merely as the "China Clipper" came once again from the ambitious head of Pan Am, Juan Trippe. Trippe wanted aircraft that could span the Pacific with reliability on passenger routes, and ultimately this would benefit both Martin and Sikorsky.

Martin's team would rise to the occasion with a design that was more advanced than the Sikorsky aircraft then in service, according to some sources, and was certainly designed to meet Pan Am's always-ambitious plans. In fact, the aircraft was the first flying boat to truly have the range to cross the Atlantic, and the earliest such conception, with the initial design stages dating back as far as 1931. The construction of the flying boat was to be all-metal, with a streamlined form, built of a riveted aluminum alloy with a roof of corrugated duralumin.

These basics would have to undergo significant change. As has been related in earlier chapters, the British were determined to slow down Pan American's attempts to conquer the Atlantic with aircraft. As a result, Juan Trippe's airline changed the specifications of the project. They had already approached Sikorsky and Martin both to produce aircraft for the North and South Atlantic, and now told Sikorsky to concentrate on the Atlantic, and Martin the Pacific. The Pacific route facing Martin would have been daunting to any engineer of the day. It had been surveyed by Charles Lindbergh and would require an aircraft that could cover a total distance of 8,200 miles (13,197 km)—a route that started in San Francisco and ran through the Philippines, with a stop in Hong Kong added later on as planning advanced, stopping in Hawaii and also at Wake and Guam. One of the more demanding sections of this was the 2,400-mile (3,862-km) leg between California and Hawaii. In the early 1930s, this was still a feat at the cutting edge of aviation design, and Martin's engineers realized they would need a combination of advanced aerodynamics and the most powerful engines they could install.

The struts and braces of previous flying boats had to go, and the two-step hull was streamlined significantly. Strut-braced wing floats, still common features on most flying boats at the time, would also have to go. They were replaced by airfoil-shaped sponsons, which had the added bonus of giving the aircraft additional lift. The wing also had to be as efficient as possible in order to meet these extensive requirements. The Twin Wasp engines were to be encased tightly that blended in an unbroken line into the nacelles. The hull had to be improved as well, with the design formally incorporating an upper section made of corrugated Alclad to strengthen it. In addition, the shape of the hull enabled an upper space for a flight deck for the seven-person crew, leaving a great deal of space in the lower deck for passengers. The new hull was rated to hold forty-six people for day trips, and eighteen in sleeper berths for the long-haul flights. Some sources denote that given the aircraft's actual fuel load, it could only carry nine or ten passengers in the latter configuration.

The interior of the control cabin was arranged in a somewhat unusual manner, despite its height. While the pilots and radio operator were situated normally, the flight engineer's station was within the wing superstructure itself. On the lower deck, there were three passenger cabins that each had eight seats that could be converted into six sleeping berths in something of a quick-change act. There was the necessary galley and almost as necessary lounge space, and the aircraft also had dressing rooms with wash basins that could be folded back when not in use.

Side view of a Martin M.130. (*Photograph from the* David *Horn Collection, 1000aircraftphotos.com*)

Martin's engineers certainly must have been happy with what they had wrought. The practical aircraft was to be equipped with Pratt & Whitney engines, and these enabled the aircraft to have a cruising speed of 163 mph (262 kph), while lifting 23 tons of aircraft, accoutrements, and human beings. All of this could be done on just 60 per cent of the engines' total available power. The final aircraft was ready to fly by 1934, and it represented a major advance over previous flying boat designs and was indicative of where development would proceed in the future. While its speed, maximum altitude, and capacity were similar to flying boats available in the years immediately prior to its first flight, such as the Sikorsky S-40, the real difference was in range. While the S-40 had a total range of 875 miles (1,408 km), the M.130 would have a range of 3,200 miles (5,150 km), this several-fold increase coming with only a few years of development between the two aircraft. The aircraft picked up an additional benefit along the way. Its powerplant and aerodynamics allowed it to come with 50 per cent more lifting capacity than contemporary landplanes, in addition to outranging them significantly.

The M.130 took to the air for the first time on December 30, 1934, the first of three aircraft to be ordered by Pan American. The aircraft proved mostly satisfactory in its tests, and the first two aircraft were delivered to Pan American in the course of 1935—*China Clipper* and *Hawaiian Clipper.* This latter aircraft would have its name shortened to *Hawaii Clipper* later on, and the two would be joined by *Philippine Clipper* in early 1936.

After the first flight of the aircraft, *Popular Mechanics* had this to say about the aircraft:

> It will be "wings over the Orient" soon for the *China Clipper*, luxury liner destined for the transpacific passenger trade of Pan-American Airways. Latest addition to the

> fleet that is preparing for regular scheduled flights across the ocean, the *China Clipper* is the largest aircraft built in America. From tip to tip its wings measure 130 feet, and its gross weight is 51,000 pounds. Of the sesquiwing type, this flying boat is powered by four motors developing 3,200 horsepower, and cruises at 157 miles an hour over a 4,000-mile radius. On its maiden flight Capt. Edwin C. Musick and a crew of four flew the *China Clipper* with thirty-eight passengers aboard from Baltimore where it was built in the Glenn L. Martin plant, to Washington and return in little more than an hour. The great ship is fully equipped for the comfort of travelers on long hops across the Pacific, and during the night flights the passengers sleep in commodious upper and lower berths.
>
> *Popular Mechanics* Magazine
> January 1935, p. 33

Pan American had prepared extensively for what they were certain would be their conquest of the Pacific. The aircraft that the public would just come to call "China Clippers" were to inherit excellent, brand-new facilities just for them. At the express order of Juan Trippe, there were stations constructed for them at Guam, Midway, and Wake Island that had radio and navigation aids to guide the aircraft in, refuelling facilities to fill their thirsty engines, and luxury hotels built to house the passengers and crews between flights.

All that remained was to prove the aircraft in service. *China Clipper* would go first, and was ferried out to Pan American's Alameda, California, base of operations. The first journey was to carry mail only and was to be captained by Edward Musick. With all the mail loaded on board, the aircraft took off from San Francisco on November 22, 1935. It completed the route without serious issue, arriving at a brand-new seaplane hub at Manila after a total flight time of just under sixty hours that covered a journey of over 8,000 miles (12,875 km). The total time of the flight was six and a half days, a third of what a ship would be required even by sleek ocean liners.

With all three aircraft arriving in service, Pan American could start cargo operations by March 1936, with passenger service following in November. This inaugurated the first truly transpacific passenger air travel in history. The new route to Hong Kong was ready to be flown in April 1937, and thereafter, Pan American had a regular service operating between San Francisco and Hong Kong. They operated the service weekly, and a round trip would take between thirteen and fourteen days.

Despite all these impressive figures and feats, Martin found itself making a loss with the aircraft. The problem arose from the per-unit cost. These were advanced aircraft, and they came with a price tag of $417,000 each. This was compared to a cost of $242,000 for a Sikorsky S-42 or $78,000 for a Douglas DC-2. Had Martin sold more units, this would not have proven to be a long-term issue, but since only three were ever ordered, the aircraft proved to be a loss: Martin simply could not recoup the design and construction costs generated by the program. In the final analysis, only Pan American could possibly make money with the aircraft.

Distant shot of an M.130 in service, arriving at the Pan American floating dock in Manila Bay, 1936. (*Photograph courtesy of the Naval History and Heritage Command*)

This was unknown to the public and likely would not have mattered in any event. This was a fascinating aircraft that could after all reliably carry human beings across the vastness of the Pacific in a fraction of the time it had taken ships. It was the coming of a new age that would fundamentally change how humans traveled, with attendant social and cultural effects that continue to evolve today. The natural result of this was a cultural space for the "China Clippers" in the public's mind. The biggest immediate result of this was that the aircraft had a film named after them.

The movie *China Clipper* arrived on the silver screen in 1936. Directed by Ray Enright and written by Frank Wead, the movie's stars are not exactly household names today, aside from one of them. The film starred Pat O'Brien, Beverley Roberts, Henry B. Walthall (this would be the last of his many roles stretching back to 1909, as he died shortly before the film's release), Ross Alexander, and Humphrey Bogart. The film was in fact a thinly veiled biographical film of Juan Trippe, and as such, it rather unsurprisingly received a lot of cooperation from Pan American. Newsreel and aerial footage were used to tell the story of the attempt to establish an airline and related aircraft that could reach China. Veteran and stunt pilots were drafted in to ensure that the flight footage made for the film was as realistic as possible, and the overall result was well received by the general public and critics alike. The film was a rare moment where popular culture was depicting the growth of technology as it happened, provoking a great deal of fascination.

Unfortunately, the real-life aircraft did not continue to have a similar level of success. Tragedy began to stalk the China Clippers. In July 1938, *Hawaii Clipper* vanished without a trace on a regularly scheduled flight between Guam and Manila. All was well for just under three and a half hours, with the aircraft reporting clouds and moderately rough air. After that, there was nothing, and the aircraft took the lives of nine crew members and ten passengers with it. Its location and the cause of its loss both remain unknown with any degree of certainty to this day. At the time, this was the worst aviation disaster in the Pacific, though it would not remain that way for terribly long.

When the Japanese attacked the United States, both aircraft were soon to be pressed into service with the U.S. Navy. *Philippine Clipper* certainly had an unexpectedly violent start to its war, and a close encounter in the bargain. The aircraft had just returned to Wake Island after a routine flight to Guam. Just over two hours earlier, they had received the message that the war had begun, and the aircraft needed to return to Wake to take up patrol duties. Soon enough, the Japanese air force came for Pan American's Wake Island facility. *Philippine Clipper* was still on the ground, and the aircraft was too big to stay unnoticed. A Japanese fighter swooped down and strafed the aircraft from nose to tail while it sat at its dock, and while Pan Am's staff could only seek cover and look on in fear and frustration. The raid lasted a mere five minutes but killed nine of Pam Am's employees—and the base was a ruin.

The Japanese would be back, and the only way out was *Philippine Clipper*, which had been holed ninety-six times by machine-gun bullets. Nevertheless, the aircraft was still made ready to fly, and all the surviving staff were loaded aboard for a doubly dangerous flight on December 8, 1941. In addition to any lurking Japanese aircraft, the aircraft was badly overloaded. The crew and staff aboard must have had a very nervous time of it as the aircraft twice tried and failed to become airborne. Finally, to an undoubted sense of relief throughout the aircraft, she finally made it into the air and began a three-day flight to Midway, bringing with it some of the earliest first-hand accounts of war in the Pacific.

After this harrowing incident, both aircraft were placed into service with the Navy with the slightly different designation M130. Both aircraft continued on in this service, but neither would survive the war. *Philippine Clipper* would be lost first. The aircraft crashed in the north of California on January 21, 1943. The weather was poor, and the aircraft crashed into a mountain. The crew of nine and ten passengers were all killed on impact, including Rear-Admiral Robert H. English, then the commander of the American submarine fleet in the Pacific. The cause was eventually determined to be pilot error, owing to the pilot not fixing his exact position before descending to a low altitude in awful weather. *China Clipper* survived longer, lasting until January 8, 1945. The aircraft was flying to the Belgian Congo from Miami and was arriving at Port of Spain in Trinidad and Tobago. The aircraft had missed its first approach to land and came down too low on the second and hit the water too hard and the hull broke in two and swiftly sank. Twenty-three of the passengers and crew were killed in the crash, though seven people survived.

This was the end of the M.130 program, and the end of an aircraft that had fuelled the imagination of the public. The Martin M.130 was an aircraft that inaugurated an era of aviation travel that has only expanded since the aircraft first took to the air in the 1930s. Though there only ever a few of these aircraft, and they were all claimed by accidents, the legacy of this graceful flying boat remains intact even now. The photographs, footage, and even the popular Hollywood film of the M.130 survives, and the China Clippers are unlikely to be truly or totally forgotten in the foreseeable future. What began as a bold venture in pushing the envelope of aviation design set the pace for everything that would come with it, and secure Pan Am's place in the history books.

There was one final partial legacy to the aircraft worth mentioning. Martin did try to develop a successor aircraft to the M.130, known as the M.156. It was designed to serve Pan Am's growing need for a larger aircraft to take over the increasing amounts of passenger trade on their Pacific routes. It was similar to the M.130, though it could carry more passengers through a combination of a longer wingspan and increased fuel capacity. In addition, there were other minor changes such as flaps being added and new stabilizers in the tail. The aircraft also took on more powerful engines, in this case, Wright Cyclone G2 radials that developed 1,000 hp. The sole example of this aircraft was rejected by Pan Am in favour of the Boeing 314, and it was purchased instead by the Soviet government. They put it into service in 1940, intending to mass produce it—a plan that was permanently interrupted by the German invasion. It was utilized by the Soviet airline Aeroflot until 1944, when it was scrapped.

26

Martin PBM Mariner: Combat Flying Boat

While Martin may be best remembered for its giants such as the Mars or the M.130, the company also built dedicated combat flying boats. Whereas the Mars was intended for a combat doctrine that never materialized, the PBM Mariner was designed from the outset to be a combat aircraft, meant to patrol the shores of the United States in tandem with the PBY Catalina. The Mariner was meant to be a hunter, not merely a passive observer, and the aircraft would play its part in the titanic Battle of the Atlantic that would come home to the coast of the United States almost from the moment that the U.S. entered World War II.

The Mariner would make its bones in the thousands of incidents that made up that fight, and indeed its combat service. It would survive into the Cold War as well, proving to be a resilient and useful combat aircraft, in service to both the United States and other nations.

Specifications: (PBM-1)

First Flight: 1939
Powerplant: Two Wright R-2600-6 fourteen-cylinder radial engines, 1,600 hp each
Armament: Eight 12.7-mm (0.50-inch) M2 Browning machine guns, two each in the nose, dorsal and tail turrets and one in two amidships blisters, two 2,213-lb (1,005-kg) Mk 13 torpedoes, 4,000 lb (1,800 kg) of bombs or depth charges
Top Speed: 205 mph (330 kph)
Range/Service Ceiling: 3,000 miles (4,800 km), 19,800 feet (6,040 metres)
Dimensions: Length 79 feet 10 inches (23.50 metres), height 27 feet 6 inches (5.33 metres), wingspan 118 feet (36 metres)
Number Built: 1,366

The Martin PBM Mariner was one of the most successful combat flying boats of its day, and certainly one of the most advanced designs of the time. The factors that created the design had nothing to do with advancing the technology or even fulfilling a need; instead, desperation led to the construction of an aircraft, since Martin was a company in some trouble.

The M.130 program, despite its capabilities, had proven to be a financial disappointment to the company, with the program staying in the red and accumulating precisely zero sales for the aircraft past the initial three for Pan Am. Consequently, Martin turned to a hopefully more lucrative market—that of combat flying boats. They must have done this with a certain amount of foreboding since this field was currently being dominated in the United States by Consolidated. Not seeing much chance of succeeding in the twin-engine market, Martin instead tried to set the hook for the Navy with a four-engined flying boat proposal they termed the Model 160.

This was not just a long shot. The Bureau of Air had just contracted two prototypes from Consolidated and Sikorsky, and Martin hoped they could shoehorn themselves into the competition and wrangle a contract. The downside of this bold move was that they would have to start by throwing good money after "bad"—since they had not been contracted for the prototype, to get into the competition, they would have to fund the prototype themselves. This presented a conundrum: they could not afford to do it.

The way out was to build a quarter-scale flying demonstrator of the larger flying boat they intended to make. This project did not get very far along on the drawing boards before the Bureau of Air chose not to consider another four-engined flying boat design. To not waste the effort already invested into the project, Martin decided to revise the program. As a result it was in early 1937 that they proposed their Model 162, which they then boldly claimed would outperform Consolidated's Catalina in speed, range, and potential payload. Predictably, Consolidated's President was very displeased about this sudden development, threatening the Navy with political consequences if they were denied a production contract. As president of a company already providing large orders to the navy, Reuben Fleet had enough pull to ensure a compromise. Martin would produce a prototype designated XPBM-1, but any future production plans would have to rely on it passing significant testing. Martin started to race as quickly towards a prototype as they could, knowing that development time would still run eighteen months. They knew full well Consolidated might use that time to produce a successor design to the Catalina and snatch even this frail straw from Martin's grasp (Consolidated tried to do exactly that with the XP4Y).

These circumstances are worth summary at this point. In short, Martin had thrown itself into one crowded field to shore up their financial position and tried to finesse that stage, and when that did not work, they hastily converted a four-engined design process into a two-engined design process. This new process ran them headlong into a powerful, well-established rival and now they had to rush to complete their hastily changed program ahead of that rival. None of these sound like the ingredients of a successful aircraft program. A reader might well be excused for thinking they sounded like the ingredients for a sort of industrial farce, with Buster Keaton featuring as chairman of the board. That it resulted in a superb aircraft and a major commercial success seems unthinkable—and yet it happened.

Martin saved time by constructing a three-eighths scale model dubbed the M160, which became the M162A and flew before the year was out. This small demonstrator worked. Martin received a contract for twenty-one aircraft in December 1937 to be designated PBM-1. Then, in yet another unexpected move, Martin continued to work on the demonstrator even though it had already achieved its goal. This was a wise move, since the extended study program yielded significant information that the company applied to the design of the final prototype, the XPBM-1.

The design that finally emerged was state of the art for flying boats in the late 1930s, and a significant leap forward over the PBY Catalina of their rival. The design was crafted with aerodynamic efficiency in mind at all points, and the most visible place for this was in the wing. Not only was it high mounted, but it was in a gull configuration. What this meant was that the engines were always clear of spray, so there was no need for strutting or pylons. The hull was fairly conventional, but the tail curved up sharply from the hull to a high twin-fin empennage. This was designed to provide the best possible stability and also make single-engined flight easier, anticipating mechanical faults and combat damage.

This tail unit required some tweaking during initial testing, when it was found that there was a tail flutter, and this was solved by adding dihedral to the horizontal stabilizers that matched the angle of the inner wings. This not only solved the problem but gave the aircraft a distinctive look. Further efforts at aerodynamic streamlining were visible in ensuring the munitions could all be carried in enclosed bays in the nacelles, and even the floats could fold up into the wings. The end result of this was that while the aircraft was only slightly faster than the Catalina, it could go a third further carrying twice the ordnance. The Catalina would prove a lethal opponent when in its element, and the XPBM-1 demonstrated even more potential. This was not exactly hurt by the fact that the aircraft was armed to the teeth for an aircraft of its size. It came with five 12.7-mm (0.5-inch) machine guns, mounted in powered nose and dorsal turrets, two waist positions and one tail position, with a 7.62-mm (0.3-inch) machine gun firing downward in the aft fuselage.

Perhaps as a result of this performance and potential, the Navy was more than happy to receive its PBM-1s. In fact, it expanded the order. With war on the horizon, the Navy knew that it needed to grow its air arm quickly, and the result for Martin was an order for another 379 aircraft. Martin's response was to start to provide these in an improved version of the aircraft, the PBM-3 (the XPBM-2 was only ever built in prototype form, and was an experimental aircraft meant to be launched from ship-based catapults and with a longer range). The PBM-3 was a little bit longer than its predecessor, coming in at 2 feet 8 inches longer. It also had more powerful engines: Wright R-2600-12s with 1,700 hp each. These engines came with bigger nacelles, which in turn meant an increased armaments load. All this meant a major increase in weight, a total of 11,000 lb (4,990 kg),

A PBM-1 in formation with PBM-3s. (*Photograph via the Naval History and Heritage Command*)

A PBM-3 at rest. (*Photograph courtesy of Dan Shumaker*)

A dramatic take-off for a Mariner. (*Photograph from the Eugene W. Penick Collection, 1000aircraftphotos.com*)

which would lead to complaints that the aircraft was underpowered on take-off in certain conditions.

The moment the war broke out, the Navy increased its order to 677, and the first examples started to arrive in service in the spring of 1942. The type would remain in production for two years and would come in several major variants as the type's capabilities led to a proliferation in adaptations. One aircraft had been used to test the installation of APS-15 search radar, and this would ultimately find fruition in 274 examples of the PBM-3C, which had a radome (initially, they were empty, and were filled in whenever radar units became available) and also had more efficient four-bladed propellers, and three more 12.7-mm machine guns added to the bow, dorsal and nose positions. The Navy also invested in a transport version of the aircraft, dubbed PBM-3R. This version had its armament removed and floor strengthened, and forty-nine of these were built. The British were very pleased to receive some of these aircraft as well, taking on thirty-two aircraft as the Mariner G.R.1, giving the aircraft its common name. These British aircraft entered service in mid-1943, but twenty ended up being returned, and twelve wound up in Australian service.

As 1943 progressed, the emphasis of production shifted to anti-submarine aircraft, namely the PBM-3S. What was desired for this version of the aircraft was a 25 per cent increase in patrol range, and to do this, the armour was stripped down, and the powered turrets removed, with some of these aircraft subsequently winding up in Coast Guard service, where it was mostly used for search and rescue. Total production of this version was ninety-three, and it started to arrive in late 1943.

The design did switch direction thereafter, adding back the powered turrets and the armour, but also adding self-sealing fuel tanks and installing more powerful

R-2600-22 engines of 1,900 hp. This resulted in a run of 259 aircraft designated PBM-3D, starting in October 1943 and arriving in service by mid-1944. This was a step towards fixing the power problem that had been known since late 1941. In fact, there had already been a plan in place to upgrade the Mariner with R-3350 engines that would be called the PBM-4, but all of these engines were requisitioned for the B-29 Superfortress program. To get around this, two PBM-3s were modified with Pratt & Whitney R-2800-34 engines early in 1944, which developed 2,100 hp. These engines brought about a major improvement to take-off and climbing, with a slight increase in speed—and a consequential, if minor, decrease in range. These became the PBM-5, which went into production in mid-1944, and proved to be the main version of the aircraft, with 592 being built by war's end, with another 137 built afterwards until 1947.

Indeed, the aircraft's production continued well after the war, proliferating into still more versions. From late 1944 until the end of 1945, a specialized, unarmed Coast Guard version was built: the PBM-5G, of which forty-one were built. The final production variant was the PBM-5A, an amphibious version of the "standard" PBM-5, which was built until March 1949, representing the last thirty-four aircraft. This may be recitation of types and numbers, but it is indicative of the sheer success of Martin's design, a stellar result from the company's roll of the dice. The engineers had done very well.

In actual service, they began their careers by performing Neutrality Patrols that, on the outbreak of war, turned into combat patrols. Though never as numerous or as frequently seen as the PBY Catalina, the Mariners proved to have significant teeth in terms of attacking German U-boats, accounting for ten of them during the war. The Mariner had the armament and durability to go head to head with the U-boats, with the aircraft far more durable in this role—though also less numerous—than the PBY Catalina. In the Atlantic, the Mariner was mainly used as a patrol aircraft, but in the Pacific, it would really come into its own.

There, the Mariner went essentially wherever American air power did. Much like in the Atlantic, the aircraft was used for forward patrols and to all appearances was just as potent a ship-killer in one ocean as the other. It also carried out bombing attacks and took part in American amphibious assaults, taking on the amphibious roles that the Catalina just was not durable enough to carry out. The Mariners were based entirely with seaplane tenders in the Pacific, creating floating bases near to amphibious forces. In this manner, the Mariner took part in every major campaign in the Pacific in the war's closing years, and it was a Mariner that spotted the Japanese Fleet as the U.S. was invading Saipan, leading to the so-called "Marianas Turkey Shoot," and one of Japan's greatest defeats.

In "Dumbo" open-ocean rescue missions, the Mariner also performed a vital duty. The missions were named for the popular Disney character at the time, and the name originally came to mean large bomber aircraft such as the B-17 Flying Fortress or Avro Lancaster fitted with a droppable lifeboat. When carrying these boats, the aircraft looked very ungainly—like a flying elephant. The name became synonymous during the war for any aircraft carrying out a rescue at sea. The aircraft was durable enough for even heavier seas, and rescued hundreds of airmen and seamen during the war, ranging from sailors of downed ships to soldiers from amphibious assault to aircrews who baled out as part of attacks on Japan's home islands. They also carried out reconnaissance duties, and black-painted Mariners called "Nightmares" carried out attacks in the darkness just like the Catalina did—everywhere the PBY went, it seemed, the Mariner was determined to follow and strive to outdo its rival. It was Martin that would have the ultimate triumph on that front, for when the war ended, the Catalinas were rapidly retired, with the Mariner chosen to soldier on instead.

The Mariner served on into the Korean War as well. When the war broke out, there were only six squadrons of Mariners still in service, three of them meant for the Pacific and based at San Diego. Most of the remaining aircraft were PBM-5S, a modification of the PBM-5 model for ASW work. It had sonar buoy equipment, a magnetic anomaly detector, and electronic countermeasures. There were slight changes to the defensive armament, namely the removal of the top deck turret, and the offensive armament consisted of bombs, depth charges, or a Mk 24 torpedo. By the war's end, this had evolved into the PBM-5S2, which came with APS-31 radar in a teardrop radome with weight reduction through removing some armour plate, the MAD equipment, and radar bombing equipment. These last aircraft could carry the Mk 34 homing torpedo, making it more dangerous than it already had been.

Supported by seaplane tenders, the Mariners once again went to war. The first use of the type was providing anti-submarine protection for the convoy ferrying the 1st Cavalry Division from Japan to Inchon on July 15, 1950. The aircraft began to carry out more aggressive patrols thereafter, searching for surface and submarine targets as well as carrying out mining and reconnaissance duties, and even being used as gunnery spotters. When China entered the war, Mariners provided patrols to guard against an invasion of Formosa (Taiwan), and they also took on mine spotting duties, finding minefields to be cleared and shooting out single or drifting mines. This was not without its risks, since the most common kind of mine, a Russian-made Mk V, had an explosive plume of 500 feet (152 metres), and low-flying Mariners could be heavily rocked by the concussion from the explosion if they were too close, at best.

As the war progressed, three more squadrons of Mariners joined the fight from the U.S. Naval Reserve, and all of them rotated back and forth to the United States regularly, always keeping at least two squadrons in the theatre. The aircraft did suffer losses, but they almost exclusively came through accidents, and once the Wonsan invasion had occurred, their duties became more routine, with thirteen-hour patrols becoming normal.

In May 1952, this routine was suddenly shattered when one of the Mariners was attacked by Chinese MiG-15s, and the aircraft more than proved itself even against jet opponents. Despite being hit by cannon fire, the Mariner returned to base with no injuries. Crew members would be killed in other MiG attacks, but the aircraft losses continued to be from weather and accidents, not enemy

A PBM-5 being pulled aboard U.S.S. *Curtiss* during the Korean War, likely 1950.

action. MiGs remained a potential threat until the end of the war, but thereafter, the Mariner continued to play its role in surveillance and passive electronic monitoring as part of the Cold War. This war could suddenly become hot, with at least three incidents of attacks by MiG-15s even after the Korean armistice had been signed. In part, these aircraft survived these jet attacks by pressing low to the water, where it was dangerous for jets to follow—pilot and crew skill did much of the rest. Still, when push came to shove, the Mariner proved more than able to shrug off MiG cannon shots.

In the Atlantic, Mariner squadrons were deployed to try to best meet the threat of Soviet submarines, based at Norfolk, Bermuda, Trinidad, and the Panama Canal Zone. Some even operated from Cuba in early 1952 before being replaced by Martin's newest flying boat, the P5M Marlin. This was the beginning of the end for the Mariner, though for the moment, they still had a role to play. They took part in the NATO exercise Operation Mainbrace in 1952, which in addition to 80,000 men also included 1,000 aircraft. One strange consequence of this was that the Mariner crews tried to ship back Shetland Ponies—which they were delighted with—for children in the United States in what was called the "Pony Express." It was found that one of the ponies could be fit in the aircraft nicely, but when the planes returned to Norfolk, it transpired that they had to wait several weeks to be cleared—at a price—and for years afterwards, it was apparently Navy lore that you could tell one of the Mariners that had brought a pony back by the smell.

Mariners were slowly replaced by Marlins but lingered in Atlantic service until 1956. They continued in naval service as advanced trainers until 1958, the same year the Coast Guard retired its Mariners. The very last flight of a Mariner in a naval capacity was by a Uruguayan aircraft in 1964. The aircraft had served also with Argentina and the Netherlands.

The Mariner has never achieved the enduring fame of its rival, the PBY Catalina, and in terms of their rivalry, perhaps this more vibrant legacy is Consolidated having the last laugh. Yet the Mariner's story is unique from its rival—that of an aircraft that, given the circumstances of its birth, should by all rights have never succeeded as it did. Yet succeed it did, and somehow in a frenzy, Martin's engineers created a masterpiece. The tough, enduring aircraft they created would serve over two oceans and through two decades of turbulent times. Today, only one complete Mariner remains, at the National Air and Space Museum in Washington, D.C. The scale test aircraft survives, too, and is on display at the Baltimore Museum of Industry. Though little physically remains of the aircraft, its proud history certainly remains.

27

Republic RC-3 Seabee: Flying "Fan Favourite"

Heraldry is an ancient art that has helped define the image and beliefs of noble houses throughout history. When it comes to the sea, heraldry not only took up the creatures of the deep as its own, it created all new ones. Generally, these were created precisely as one might expect, but there were chimeras as well. A chimera is a term taken from a monster of Greek myth to include any combination of parts from more than one animal. In creating heraldic creatures of the deep, heraldry would create its own chimeras, one of them the sea-bee, a bee with the tail of a fish. The symbol would find a home in the U.S. Navy, becoming the description for a member of the United States Naval Construction Forces (N.C.F.). It would also become the name for an unusual little flying boat.

The Republic RC-3 Seabee was the product of a dream. In this case, the dream of its creator, and it would follow an unusual path from birth to service. The Seabee would find itself in strange roles and far-flung places despite its diminutive size and is one of the classic-era flying boats that remains popular until the present day, and undoubtedly well into the future.

Specifications

First Flight: 1945
Powerplant: One Franklin 6A8-215-B8F (or B9F) six-cylinder horizontally opposed engine, 215 hp
Armament: None
Top Speed: 148 mph (238 kph)
Range/Service Ceiling: 520 miles (836 km), 12,000 feet (3,657 metres)
Dimensions: Length 27 feet 10 inches (8.48 metres), height 10 feet 1 inch (3.07 metres), wingspan 37 feet 8 inches (11.48 metres)
Number Built: 1,060

The Republic Seabee began life as an engineer's dream, and in many ways, this continues on today—for a long time, the aircraft held the record for the most-produced civil amphibian. It all started as one man's dream. Percival Spencer, known as "Spence" to his friends and fans to this day (he had adopted the name out of a dislike of the name Percival), was an engineer descended from an engineer. His father, Christopher Miner Spencer, had been the inventor of the Spencer Repeating Rifle, a weapon that had given the Union forces a distinct advantage during the American Civil War (it is frequently remarked upon at the gulf in time between father and son—"Spence" always had to point out that his father was sixty-three when his third son was born).

The Seabee's designer was interested in engineering and design from a very young age, a process encouraged by his father. In the years before World War I, the elder Spencer helped his son along in his early glider work, and the son would pay the father back by taking him on flights, with the father even working on a helicopter design shortly before his death in 1922. By 1916, Spence was part of the aviation industry, working for multiple companies including Sikorsky. By 1937, he founded his own company, the Spencer-Larsen Aircraft Corporation, operating out of Long Island. Their first amphibian, the SL-12C, had some difficulties—Spencer had only been lightly involved in its design—because of its ambitious design features. The company did not go much further as far as Spencer was concerned, as it changed hands and Spencer himself left in 1940.

Spencer then began to work on his ideal amphibian, an effort that culminated in an aircraft known as the Spencer Air Car No. 1. The arrival of World War II unfortunately put restrictions on civilian flying, and Spencer had to put his idea in storage. This lasted until 1943, when he sold his design patent to Republic Aviation Corporation. Spencer became design consultant when Republic decided to produce a variant of his Air Car, since the company was looking forward to post-war civilian production. He was also the test and demonstration pilot for the program between 1943 and 1945, as well as other Republic efforts—he would personally fly many P-47 Thunderbolts, even having a very close call in one. Yet he never strayed too far from his amphibian beginnings and would work on his Air Cars until the 1980s.

Construction of the aircraft was all-metal, distinguishing it from Spencer's original wood and fabric design. The result of the switch was a much more durable airframe. The floats were built on a single strut, and the landing gear arrangement of the original SL-12C was retained, though the main wheels retracted into a flush position against the hull. The upswept hull aft of the engine blended perfectly into the tail structure, and the extensive streamlining overall was carried forward by trying to partially bury the overhead engine. This RC-1 prototype was designed for the Franklin 6A-6, which developed 175 hp.

The first prototype emerged in November 1944, with Spencer himself making the first flight. After that, the aircraft was flown to a convention in Missouri to debut it to the public, where it was a smash hit. Republic planned to sell the aircraft for $3,500, and they received a staggering flurry of orders owing to major interest—the company received 1,972 deposits at just this first convention. The Seabee was even demonstrated for the U.S. military, which gave the company

The trim-looking Seabee prototype. (*Photograph courtesy of Dan Shumaker*)

the right to use the name "Seabee" in civilian usage in 1945. The military had another gift for Republic: a healthy order for the Air Force for the aircraft, to be designated OA-15. These were never delivered, as the military cut the contract upon the conclusion of the war. But for a time, all looked rosy for Republic's post-war plans.

Republic moved rapidly towards a production version. The designation RC-2 had already been allocated to theoretical commercial version of their XF-12 Rainbow, so the production version would be known as the RC-3. Republic's construction methods centred around a philosophy of having as few parts in the aircraft as necessary, and this attitude led to a unique building technique wherein there were only three ribs and two spars used to construct each wing panel, a method they had not used before. Moreover, to give the wing more strength, Republic's engineers installed small bumps running chord-wise along each wing panel, about 4 inches apart. This strengthening meant the wing needed fewer ribs in each wing, saving time, parts, and weight. A new Franklin engine with 40 hp more at its disposal was also chosen, the first of innumerable engine changes that production Seabees would experience during their lives. Republic felt confident enough in the post-war market to acquire the company that was making Franklin engines. The final design for the RC-3 used several automobile components to keep the cost down, and the entire airplane had a total of 450 parts. It had some parallels to a car internally, too, with seating for four and interior fittings much like those of a contemporary automobile. This had another practical benefit: construction of the aircraft took only about 1,000-man hours.

Unlike the automobile, Republic found the mass marketplace they had anticipated for their product rapidly evaporating. The first RC-3 production model made its first flight on December 1, 1945, with Spencer again at the helm, and production had begun in full by mid-1946. This was not matched by the explosion of post-war buying Republic had been anticipating. Moreover, despite their emphasis on simplicity, production costs began to rise, and inflation also took a hand, bringing the price of the aircraft up to $6,000 by year's end. A year later, the production line was suspended, awaiting further sales, and in October 1947, Republic announced the permanent termination of all production. A total 1,060 Seabees had been sold, and the last of these was delivered in 1948.

Republic may well have considered the Seabee an overall failure owing to lower than expected sales, but in every other sense, Spencer's light amphibian was a remarkable success. In a way, the Seabee has become very much like a classic car—whatever it did in actual sales, it has achieved a place in the hearts of the people using it, and a cherished one at that. In the short term, the Seabee was enormously popular with its owners, doing well on lakes and on coastal regions around the world. The aircraft proved very capable in the bush areas of North America, where it both ferried passengers and supplies, but it was also eminently capable of moving from land to water operations. It is said that, as of 2006, almost a quarter of the original fleet of Seabees was still operational, and it seems unlikely that this percentage has decreased that much in a little over a decade since.

The main issue for owners has proven to be power, and they have pursued several options and installations to solve this. One interesting solution was that pursued by the United Consultant Corporation, which in 1960 started to upgrade the aircraft to the UC-1 Twin Bee, which removed the original pusher engine and installed two tractor engines, specifically Lycoming engines of either the O-360-A1a (180 hp) or the IO-360-B1D (200 hp). This did necessitate some changes to the aircraft structure, most importantly extending the hull after body by 3 feet and 4 inches (1.01 metres) to adjust for the change in the centre of gravity, as well as extending the wings by 3 feet. The company had converted at least twenty-three aircraft by 1987, and this had significant benefits to both cruise and top speed, an increase in the total range, and even an increase in lifting capacity, all while providing more cabin space.

Nor was this the only major revision of the Seabee that was pursued long after production had ceased. Spencer himself, along with his son-in-law, Charles Herbst, started to work on a more modern design based off the RC-3. This ended up being taken over by the Trident Aircraft Corporation, headed by David Hazelwood and C. S. Newton. The Canadian-based company ended up producing the Trident TR-1 Trigull, which shared the Seabee's basic layout but was essentially a new aircraft with tricycle landing gear, a swept fin and rudder assembly, and retractable floats. The aircraft design also aimed to increase engine power through a variety of planned means, and the company flew two prototypes in 1976, along with a third used for static tests. The company went under in 1980, taking their ambitious plans for a successor to the Seabee with it—though there remains a chance that it might be revived someday.

In working on this chapter about the Seabee, the author was blessed by access to first-hand accounts from Seabee owners, owing to the aircraft's large and apparently thriving community. Foremost among these accounts came from Stephen C. Mestler, who first laid eyes on the Seabee as a child watching the television show *Jungle Jim*, which occasionally featured the aircraft. From this childhood moment, a fascination grew that one suspects is similar for many aviation enthusiasts. He was further inspired by his father, an American Airlines mechanic (and later flight engineer), and the inspiration of his father along with an ever-growing love of aircraft led to his purchase of a Seabee named *Ol' Marty B* after he obtained his seaplane rating in 1974. Today, Mr. Mestler operates the International Republic Seabee website, created originally by the late Mr. John Hooper in the 1990s. Hooper was originally a Seabee salesman, and created the website when the internet was just beginning. Mr. Mestler has kept up and changed the website significantly since then, focusing on providing all the essential facts, news, and information for Seabee owners, and to help newcomers decide whether they would want to own or could handle owning one of these unique flying boats.

By his account, the Seabee's longevity is in many ways down to those that love the aircraft. As he put it:

> The Seabee owners, as a group, realized that the Seabee was something special and a few little tweaks here and there would make it a "perfect" seaplane. Many of the unsung heroes are the engineers and owners that have made the Seabee a reliable, safe and bulletproof airplane that it should have been coming off the Republic assembly line. Updated engines, wing modifications, use of space age materials and a network of Seabee lovers has made the Seabee just that. These men should be applauded and I know that every Seabee owner flying today thanks them.

For those interested in a flying boat experience, Mr. Mestler describes the Seabee as a "healthy challenge," and in his case, it was a love affair from the start. It is an aircraft that, in his words, is "the best of all three worlds"—perfectly at home on land, in the air, and on the water (and the Seabee does very well on the water). In modern use, the aircraft is very stable on the water and gives plenty of warning if the pilot has made a mistake in handling it. The Seabee also has reverse thrust, making docking and water work easy. Above all, the durability of the aircraft, in terms of both hull and airframe, make it able to withstand adverse conditions. Being a flying boat rather than a seaplane means it has a lower center of gravity—this changes conditions for the pilot. "Consider the dreaded downwind turn," Mestler says, "most floatplanes must make the turn at idle power or not at all.

The Seabee can make the turn with ease and has no tendency to flip over once the turn is started. Floatplanes don't have that luxury."

There are challenges in maintaining and handling a vintage aircraft, though the Seabee comes with unique challenges. Mr. Mestler uses the words of Rick Durdan to describe it, saying the Seabee is the "maintenance of a boat and an airplane ... squared!" It is not, he makes sure to mention, an aircraft for beginners. Waterproofing and engine maintenance are the most prominent issues, but he also points out that it is easy to forget to put the hull plugs in, and that many accidents have been caused by trying to land on the water with the wheels down, causing the aircraft to flip over. This event is thankfully seldom lethal, but it is a major expense to get the aircraft back into the air again thereafter. Mr. Mestler's personal experience points out some interesting facts:

> There are limits on airspeed for the gear and flaps (117 mph and 100 mph respectively).... Sandy beaches give us a thrill now and then. If you don't keep the power up when pulling up on a beach you will most likely get stuck. That's when you get the required shovel out and start digging. If the Seabee is moving it should keep moving especially on sandy or soft beaches. Tides and river currents are another thing all together. You must be aware of low tide to prevent an eight-hour sit waiting for high tide again. Crosswind takeoffs and landings can be a challenge on runways but can be handled with experience. On the water with the large tail surface in the back the Seabee always wants to point into the wind and that's not always where you want to go. A trick is to open the bow door and use it as a sail to counteract that large rudder in the back. This doesn't always work if the wind is over about 20 knots. Another limitation is the main gear mechanism. With the gear [either in] up or down it is very strong and will handle almost anything *but*, when the gear is in transit the linkage is susceptible to breaking with even a moderate load applied to it. If one hits the beach or a rock with the gear in motion there is a good chance that the linkage will break. It is designed to do that so that other larger parts of the gear system will not be damaged.

The author was also able to speak to Paul Cuny, whose experience with flying boats started with working as a gas boy for Catalinas in the 1960s, which became a thirty-year career as a commercial pilot, flying Boeings. He also flew on his days off, and he wanted something challenging for a sportsman, pilot, and explorer; the solution was the Seabee, which could do all he wanted in safety. He was drawn to the aircraft's utility, buying a Seabee in 1988 from another owner that had upgraded the aircraft with a 270-hp Lycoming engine, which Mr. Cuny then upgraded again with a 340-hp supercharged Lycoming (also replaced was the traditional reversing two-blade propeller to a three-bladed one to improve manoeuvring on the water).

The usefulness of the aircraft makes it "real dependable ... you could call it a jeep or a motorboat. It has the ability to both go anywhere and do things that other types of flying airplanes can't do, they're a little more fragile." He also enjoys how it can simply roll itself out of the water with the landing gear down to push up a dock. Mr. Cuny has further enjoyed the network of owners, which has aided with finding parts as well as sharing advice. He has also seen over a dozen Seabees brought together at a single air show, as well as other occasions where multiple Seabees have gathered—in every way, Seabee owners are a community that flocks together.

Mr. Cuny also knew Spencer, and he related that Spencer test-flew almost every single Seabee from the factory. Mr. Cuny related that though Spencer was not the exclusive designer of the Seabee, they were in many ways still descendants of his designs, and he left a mark on the tail numbers of every aircraft he flew to denote what needed to be adjusted or what he liked, and according to him, he flew at least 70 per cent of the aircraft. He was, in his later years, embraced by the community as the father of the Seabee, which he accepted with humility and eagerly engaged with the people who had gathered because of his efforts. He was able to interview the man in person, hearing about how he got his start in flying by having his un-powered early efforts pulled along by his father in a motorboat. Spencer and his partner, Dale Anderson, lived in California and operated their own company to try to perfect the Air Car, and he emphasized the lifetime Spencer spent working on fulfilling his dreams for an amphibious aircraft. Most of his history is at the Bradley Museum in Connecticut, which is where Spencer's archives reside—though a lot apparently requires curation.

Mr. Cuny also emphasized the role Richard Sanders played in the growth of the community. He started the Seabee Club for the nominal fee of $10 a year and helped Seabee owners find out where they were, allowing a connection between all the differently-engined Seabee owners; in these early decades, the newsletters and bulletins sustained the community before John Hooper brought it to the internet. The conversation really denoted a sense of continuity, that despite the brief production life of the aircraft, there has been no disruption in its very vibrant usage life ever since.

A handful of quotes from the conversation between Mr. Cuny and this author well serve to describe, from a practical user of the aircraft, where it came from and what its benefits are:

> It has a great ability to fly places and do things other planes cannot, and that makes the Seabee very useful as far as being able to travel and go places that you feel comfortable taking an airplane like this ... it is a pickup truck of the air. Now, it is not fast, it is not fuel efficient, it is not real pretty, but it does what it is supposed to do ... it is an honest airplane, there is not any real tricks to it other than it is a little bit difficult to get it on the ground and to its parking spot in a strong wind.

> This airplane was designed with the pilot in mind. It is almost like a glass greenhouse. When you look at an airplane, normally the wing is either right below the pilot or right above [them] in the small airplane world. This airplane has the engine in the back which affords the cockpit to be placed way forward of the wing ... so you are

> actually sitting out with a windshield in front of you that is very rounded … so the passengers can look up and down relatively easy from the backseat for observation, and the two pilots … have a totally unobstructed view.… It is just absolutely picturesque to have that much visibility, you feel really, really nice.

> They basically made a canoe and put a cabin on it, so the design of the boat is independent of the cockpit, so when you look at the design of many airplanes it is basically a cockpit with the rest of the airplane designed around it … well what they did on the Seabee was they thought "well, you know, we'll make a really nice boat and then we'll put a cabin on the front of it … and wow, we need a wing on there, so we'll stick the wing behind the cabin and then we'll stick the motor back there" so that is how Spencer came up with this design … he wanted a boat first, he wanted the occupant of the boat out of the weather, then the motor behind so that #1 it would not be hit by the water, #2 it would not be in the front to chew up anybody as he went up to the dock, and that the final thing is that by having it behind him, he had that much more visibility.

> It looks like a pollywog … and he [Spencer] did a really strong hull, and then when these engineers made it out of aluminum they made it even stronger … so you could actually de-rivet the cabin in the area where the engine is and turn it into a lake boat, and that has been done. People have taken Seabees when they have become too far gone … have taken the cockpit off and turned them into motorboats.

The Seabee allows Mr. Cuny to go so many places because it freed him from being landlocked, and it takes the pilot from a sterile environment to a natural environment, going from the formal world of flying into the world of sportsmanship, and you can even fish directly out of the aircraft's front door. Mr. Cuny has flown the aircraft from Texas to Hudson Bay, heading into areas that only First Peoples know well. The aircraft is, in its continuing use, summed up by time (very accurately) as "adventurous." The Seabee is also continuing onwards, with an Ontario group taking an engine used for a Corvette to be mounted in a Seabee with a composite propeller. This means that the aircraft continues to be modernized, and this has recently been approved by the Federal Aviation Administration, meaning that after flying in Canada, a new version is still coming to its home country.

When asked what he would say to someone looking to perhaps purchase a Seabee, part of his answer was to ensure the aircraft was modernized, but above all that it needed to be well taken care of. As he put it: "… get the airplane that has the most horsepower, and an approved engine or this new Corvette [engine]. Do not buy a Franklin one. And buy one that has been flown by its owner that loved it, that pampered it, that took care of it. Then make it your own … but look at its bones, look at how it has been taken care of." It is a complex aircraft, not terribly fast, and needs to be taken care of, but he recommends it to someone willing to take on its challenges, since the rewards are apparently decidedly worth it.

In speaking to the Seabee's owners, what stands out to this author is not the aircraft itself, but rather the remarkable sense of community that has grown around it. What has been described is a community that organizes, helps each other out in any situation they can, and share their knowledge freely—even with outsiders seeking to write a chapter in a book about the aircraft they love so dearly. Many of the members of the community have spent their lives around the Seabee and seem to know every last detail of the aircraft and its history. In the final analysis, though the aircraft itself is remarkable, it is matched by the people that love it, and who will undoubtedly keep it flying long into the future. The Seabee's story, from start to finish, is about the personalities of people who love aviation, and the aircraft remains a labour of love, as it was when Spencer designed her so many decades ago.

28

Saunders-Roe (Saro) A.36 Lerwick: Desperation and Failure

"Saro" is an abbreviation for the collaborative work for the Saunders-Roe company, the British firm that perhaps can be said to be the most dedicated to the idea of the flying boat over the course of many decades. Saunders-Roe Limited had produced flying boats since the 1920s, generally only single examples with a few exceptions. One of the exceptions was the Saro London, which had entered both civilian and military service. It was out of a desire to produce a replacement that Saunders-Roe embarked on the project that would become the A.36 Lerwick.

Not all flying boats are created equal, and Saunders-Roe were about to produce what can most charitably be described as a lemon. The A.36 was meant to supplement the mighty Sunderland, explored in a later chapter, but what was created instead was an accident-prone aircraft that failed to live up to expectations. The story is an important one to tell, amid graceful giants and widely-popular aircraft, since even possessing all the right ingredients for a great aircraft does not automatically result in success. The A.36, the Lerwick, was a dangerous failure for a company that believed in the dream of the flying boat until long after the great age for such craft had faded.

Specifications

First Flight: 1938
Powerplant: Two Bristol Hercules II radial engines, 1,375 hp each
Armament: One 7.7-mm (0.303-inch) Vickers K gun in a bow turret, six 7.7-mm (0.303-inch) M1919 Browning machine guns, two in a dorsal turret, four in a tail turret, 2,000 lb (900 kg) of bombs
Top Speed: 214 mph (345 kph)
Range/Service Ceiling: 1,540 miles (2,479 km), 14,000 feet (4,270 metres)
Dimensions: Length 63 feet 7½ inches (19.40 metres), height 20 feet (6.10 metres), wingspan 80 feet 10 inches (24.64 metres)
Number Built: Twenty-one

The mid- and late 1930s saw a rapid period of rearmament in Britain. The threat of war was, to a certain extent, obvious. A major need was a revitalized R.A.F. to meet the ever-growing threat of the German Luftwaffe. Consequently, the R.A.F. was expanded greatly, and a result of this was that many new designs were ordered—many of them directly off the drawing board. While this approach meant that new designs could be rapidly put into production, it did have its drawbacks. Chief among them was the fact that if a design proved to have difficulties, it would already be well along the process of development and production—imperfect or not.

The Lerwick was to be part of this programme, ordered under Specification R.1/36, which called for a monoplane flying boat to replace the R.A.F.'s older, similar aircraft like the Saro London and Supermarine Stranraer biplanes. Four companies were given the opportunity to submit designs when the specification was issued at the beginning of March 1936: Blackburn, Saro, Short Brothers, and Supermarine. The R.A.F. wanted a twin-engined flying boat, with a total weight of 25,000 lb, carrying a crew of six. The R.A.F. also wanted an offensive load capacity of 2,000 lb with defensive armament carried in three power-operated turrets. The proposals were received very quickly, and the Air Ministry tender conference judged the entrants by June.

Blackburn's entry was immediately separated out owing to a revolutionary design—unfortunately powered by the Rolls-Royce Vulture engine—and would require much more extensive testing to judge its merits, something the R.A.F. did not have time for in the immediate expansion period. The R.A.F. initially favoured the Supermarine design, also Vulture-powered, though it had the notable drawback of being significantly more expensive. This left the Saro and Short Brothers entrants "tied," as it were, in the second rank. Ultimately, despite being ordered off the drawing board, Supermarine ran into a core difficulty with developing their project. Deeply committed to the development of the Spitfire program, which would prove increasingly important as the capabilities of the Messerschmitt Bf 109 became apparent, the company had little time or resources to spare to carry forward their flying boat design.

So with Blackburn's design too revolutionary to develop quickly and Supermarine too heavily committed elsewhere, the competition boiled down to Saro and Short Brothers. In the interim, Saro had made modifications to their original drawings, chiefly authored by Saro's chief designer Harry Knowler. The original idea had featured a shallow hull with a gull wing, which Knowler revised by deepening the hull and substituting high-mounted cantilever wings with both increased span and area. Knowler also made a definite improvement to the offensive layout, scrapping the idea of underwing mountings for bombs with two small bomb bays made in the underside of the engine nacelles.

It became clear that it would be at least two years until Supermarine was able to devote any considerable resources towards the construction of their design, and as a result, Saro was awarded a production contract for their revised design in November 1936. Though only ten aircraft were ordered, twenty-six serial numbers were issued, indicating the R.A.F.'s determination that rapid expansion be a priority as needed. The per-unit price was predicted as being £54,750, and within a month, the number requested had been increased to sixteen to twenty aircraft.

Promisingly, the aircraft—now given the designation S.36—was to be powered by the engines that were at the time the most powerful in the world: a pair of Bristol Hercules HE.1M sleeve valve engines, rated at 1,290 hp at take-off and 1,375 hp at 4,000 feet. The Hercules had just become available, freeing Saro from the necessity of using the flawed Vulture. This choice of powerplant changed other facets of the design as a result, first and foremost allowing a higher gross weight of 28,500 lb with a maximum overload of 33,200 lb with a range of 1,540 miles. The new engines received 13-foot 6-inch-diameter de Havilland constant-speed propellers, which in turn meant that the hull needed to be deepened further, and this provided accommodation for a crew of nine, a decided increase from the six originally specified.

The production hull was designed as a single-step design, though the taper aft of the step appeared like a second, vertical step under the tail plane. The aircraft was all-metal, with the then-standard fabric-covered control surfaces. The wing was a high-cantilever design, with a parallel-chord centre section holding the engines and the tapering outer wings having cantilever shock-absorbing V-struts. The tail was a cantilever tailplane with a single fin and rudder—and all control surfaces had trim tabs. The floats changed after the initial example of the S.36, going from stepless to single step. The fuel tanks were arranged in each wing in two groups of three, with a further three overload tanks mounted inside the hull. The total fuel capacity was 780 gallons, and with the overload tanks, this could rise as high as 1,440 gallons. A heavy complement of weaponry was installed, starting in the bow with a single 7.7-mm (0.303-inch) Vickers K gun in an FN 7 turret, then a pair of 7.7-mm (0.303-inch) Brownings in a retractable dorsal turret, and a heavy four-gun Browning installation in the tail's FN 4A turret. The aircraft could also carry four depth charges in the engine nacelles, or a total of 2,000 lb of bombs. The S.36 also could carry smoke floats, carried in small hatches, one on each side of the hull under the wing roots.

The cockpit featured the pilot and co-pilot flying in tandem and had a space for the engineer. In practice, it would provide extra functionality. The bomb-aimer's aperture was in the extreme bow underside, and the field of vision was found to be very limited in practical terms, and in actual service, sighting—at least at low level—was done from the co-pilot's position. Though the total crew could be nine, it was believed that in practical use that a crew of nine would be entirely too cramped, and in practice, the crew remained six or seven. In full, besides the pilot and co-pilot, the aircraft could have an engineer, air-gunner/observer, three fitter/air-gunners, and two other gunners.

Saro bet quite a bit on the success of the Hercules engines, and as a result, the aircraft had a very high wing loading of 33.5 lb per square foot. The predicted top speed was thought to be 230 mph, with enough thrust provided by the engines to keep take-offs to a reasonable distance on the water. Off the drawing board, in practical reality, the S.36 would never achieve this, and soon after it took to the air, other problems would become very clear.

The production order came in April 1937, calling for a total of ten S.36 aircraft to be built, laying aside the decision of the previous December. Then in June, the order was expanded to twenty-one aircraft, with the first three aircraft (labelled L7248–L7250) to serve as prototypes. By October 1938, Saro had completed the first aircraft at Cowes, and it was launched on the last day of the month. L7248 would be the first to fly the next month, taken into the air by test pilot Frank Courtney. Problems became apparent even from this first flight. The prototype demonstrated hydrodynamic instability best described as "severe," with overbalanced elevators. In the air, it was found to be unstable in the roll and yaw under normal cruising conditions. By now, the aircraft had been dubbed "Lerwick," and it was in significant trouble—hands-off flight was deemed to be impossible, a problem that modifications would never manage to successfully rectify, a definite sign of the future.

Porpoising became a problem in early tests, an alarming problem that Saro had thought eliminated. In testing models of the aircraft, the problem had been ironed out with the assistance of the Royal Aircraft Establishment at Farnborough by moving the hull's step aft, a modification built into the first Lerwick. L7248 unfortunately began to porpoise in her tests, a bouncing sort of movement that occurred at high speeds and attitudes.

By the beginning of 1939, the first two Lerwick prototypes were under heavy testing by Saro, confirming all the problems that had been diagnosed in the first aircraft. In early March, L7248 was handed over for testing. In less than two weeks, it was handed back over to Saro for modifications, as the faults had all been confirmed. Saro made extensive changes to try to redress the issues, primarily attempting to fix the in-air stability problem. Saro tried to do this by installing an extended-chord rudder and two auxiliary tailplane fins. While the first aircraft was being modified, the second aircraft took its place in trials. L7249 arrived for trials on June 13, and disaster would strike September 1.

Before even making it into the air, the aircraft was being launched from the Felixstowe swing-launcher. The camera-gun hatch, located in the extreme nose, was not properly secured. As a result, the Lerwick filled with water before it could be reattached to the hoisting slings—and the Lerwick sank. Though it was raised, it was only ever used for static tests thereafter.

In a sense, this may have been a bit of an omen for the entire project. Saro was simultaneously having repeated headaches trying to modify the Lerwick to be stable in the air. The first modifications did not correct the problem, and nine total tail configurations would be tried until one was found to be satisfactory. This entailed a larger fin and an enlarged rudder, and it became standard on the type as it improved lateral and directional control—at least in part.

By January 1940, with the war underway and soon to turn dire for Britain, the original prototype was still under modification to try and solve the type's control

Side view of a Saro Lerwick. (*Photograph courtesy of Dan Shumaker*)

issues. L7248 was modified again at Cowes to have twin oval fins and rudders that were scaled up from one of Saro's smaller experimental flying boats, the A.37 Shrimp research aircraft. When placed on the Lerwick, it entailed a tailplane set 15 inches higher than in the original version, with a slightly revised upper rear hull. Yet again, the arrangement was unsatisfactory, and it failed to improve handling significantly and was discarded. In the final configuration adopted as standard on almost all Lerwicks, the leading edge of the fin was built out and the rudder was fitted with an auxiliary top plate. This brought the flight characteristics up to an acceptable level, though the Lerwick would never be an easy to fly aircraft. At the least, it would have reasonably adequate directional control and a reduced tendency to roll.

The poor overall flight characteristics remained, however, with the Lerwick's performance never living up to expectations. In late June 1940, the disposable load of Lerwicks was officially limited to 8,300 lb on all the authorized examples. Now, with the flight problems at least partially solved, more problems emerged.

After everything, the hydrodynamic problems persisted. The problems at R.A.E. Farnborough grew severe enough that Short Brothers were called in for advice. Extensive alterations were made, with the hull steps moved aft various distances and the planning bottoms made deeper. An attempt proposed by the Short Brothers personnel to attach a Short Sunderland-type afterbody and raising the tailplane proved unsatisfactory, but it was indicative of the type's issues that grafting on part of another aircraft's design was not just proposed but failed.

Step depth alterations, along with the idea of trying a scaled down Sunderland hull bottom were tried or proposed without success. Between Farnborough and Cowes, multiple attempts were made to fix the problem, involving changing the hull bottoms, step positions, and depth. Ultimately, the set of modifications deemed marginally acceptable were adopted. These consisted of a deeper step placed slightly aft of its original position, with a slightly lowered planing bottom. This reduced porpoising at high speeds, but the type was always to be prone to it occurring.

Even with all this solved, in air performance lagged behind expectations. A top speed of 230 mph had been expected, but in tests, the type managed 214 mph, while the specification had wanted 235 mph. The reasonable take-off distance that had also been required turned out to be problematic. When L7251 was tested for this in the summer of 1939, it was found that it took forty-one seconds for the aircraft to become airborne at its normal loaded weight. When given an overload of 31,500 lb, it took a full minute. To achieve even this lacklustre performance, the Hercules engines had to work very hard and as a result developed overheating issues. It became essential to shed weight, and the first suggestion to remove the Lerwick's rear turret was wisely vetoed since this would remove its primary defensive weaponry when it was expected to be deployed in areas where it would face significant enemy air activity. To avoid making the Lerwick a sitting duck, other measures had to be tried but there was only so much that could be done. Dropping weight was a primary reason a final crew of six was settled on, and some moveable parts for the dorsal turret were removed—and on operations, whatever could be left behind was. This included anchor chains. In the end, all the attempts to shed weight led to a total drop of just 100 lb, which did precious little to improve the dismal take-off performance.

At this point, it might strike a reader as unusual that the Lerwick even made it to an operational status given all the type's issues. In the end, necessity emerged to save the type just as it had prompted its design and production in the first place. The R.A.F.'s Coastal Command was consistently starved of aircraft. Given the desperate need for patrol aircraft as the war evolved, the type was ordered in quantity, temporarily rescuing the faltering production program. In the summer of 1939, four Lerwicks were allocated to No. 240 Squadron at Invergordon. At the same time, the other completed examples of the Lerwick were sent to the R.A.F. seaplane base at Calshot, pending a decision on the future of the program.

Events did not improve for the Lerwick at this point. By year's end, Air Vice-Marshal Sholto Douglas wrote to the Air Chief Marshal Sir W. R. Freeman arguing that the Lerwick program should be scrapped and Saunders-Roe put to building the Short Sunderland. His views were based on the numerous complaints from R.A.F. officers about flying the aircraft. He viewed take-off as dangerous, the aircraft as a difficult and unpleasant beast in the air, and that its range was inadequate. Even as he wrote this, production of further Lerwicks had been cancelled in late October, but on November 1, this was countermanded because the Lerwick was viewed as better than nothing and converting the Cowes production line over to Sunderlands would result in months of lost production. The immediate decision was that five more Lerwicks were to be completed, with the last two stored at Cowes. Further hulls were also to be manufactured at a pace that did not interfere with the production of the Supermarine Walrus, a contract for which was then being negotiated.

In February 1940, the order of Lerwicks was increased to twenty-one. The first four of these got Hercules HE.1M engines, and it was intended that the next eight would get Hercules II engines, and the nine thereafter the Hercules IV. This was modified in May, and L2752–L2760 got the Hercules II, and L7261–L7268 got the Hercules IV owing to the scarcity of the latter type.

While this was going on, a final attempt was made to try and improve the aircraft's numerous performance issues. L7254 was chosen for these changes, which were being made to try and improve on the type's abysmal take-off performance. The wing incidence was increased from 3.5 degrees to 5.5, and it was given new propellers that came in at 14 feet 6 inches long, with new spinners. This modification brought the normally loaded take-off time down to thirty-one seconds, and improved flying qualities. The controls became more effective with less roll and yaw problems. There was a drawback to this improvement: water performance became poor. A compromise had to be reached, an in the end, the original propellers were refitted but the wing incidence was retained. This compromise was deemed, in effect, "good enough," and with great caution, the Lerwick was deemed useful and started to enter service.

The Lerwick would mainly end up serving in the Hebrides and the Shetlands, with the Lerwicks being tested at Calshot handed over to No. 209 Squadron at Oban, to replace their elderly Stranraers, perhaps more of a lateral move than an improvement given everything that afflicted the Lerwick.

This was in part because service life did not improve the Lerwick's personality to any considerable degree. In fact, new problems arose. In early 1940, it was discovered that the Lerwick's bomb bay doors had the tendency to open in flight owing to hydraulic leakage. As a result, a pilot-operated locking device had to be installed. Excessive spray occurring at high-speed take-offs was also found to be sucked into the discharge chutes and the openings between the rotating ring and cupola frame—and this was causing excessive corrosion around the rear turret. Despite adding flexible rubber masking plates, this problem too was never fully solved.

The litany still did not end there. By September, another serious deficiency had come to light. The Lerwick was, as it turned out, nearly impossible to keep in the air on a single engine. With only one engine running, the Lerwick was unable to maintain height or to keep up directional control against the torque of the single engine, working at full capacity. A series of rudder trim-tab alterations followed, another need that did not particularly help the Lerwick's service career. To add a further cherry to the cake, the centre of gravity proved to be frequently at the aft of the range, making weight reductions and distributions a tricky task. Beyond this, the floats on the last Lerwicks (those with the Hercules IV) had to be modified at the bow to create increased incidence, and buoyancy was improved by 15 per cent and bilging facilities were improved.

To round out the "minor" issues the Lerwick had, deflector devices of various designs had to be fitted to correct a pitch-down in attitude when the rear turret was rotated from aft to beam. By mid-1941, engine mountings had to be changed, too, since they were causing excessive pitching vibrations when taking off or landing in rough seas.

Just prior to this, a more serious problem emerged. During routine inspection, it was discovered that the wings of L7248 had in some way failed. Buckling was found in the upper surface wing skinning along the chord, compression failures caused by an upward deflection of the wing. This was somewhat mysterious, given that L7248 was a test aircraft and was suffering a failure that was not being seen on service Lerwicks, which rightly might be expected to see more damage in the rougher atmosphere of routine use. Best guesses had to be applied as to what had caused the damage. Either it had been caused by a very heavy water landing, or maybe during side-slips during stalling tests that had been done shortly before, or more probably during "falling-leaf" tests. This latter was when a pilot performed a wings-level stall, from which point the aircraft can fall into a spin and from there descend much like the eponymous falling leaf.

The falling-leaf tests were undertaken with a certain amount of trepidation given the aircraft's already less-than-sterling reputation. Until it was done in testing, nobody had been bold enough—or foolish enough—to deliberately stall an aircraft that already possessed so many potential consequences even in normal flight. When a clean stall was performed with the power off, the aircraft did not go into a spin but was still severe—and when the test was repeated with the power on and flaps lowered, the Lerwick went completely out of control. When these tests were repeated in 1941, the same results were noted. In an emergency, the Lerwick was not an aircraft a crew would desire to be in.

Opinion on the Lerwick was only to get worse with the passage of time. After the crash of aircraft L7265, an enquiry report was fairly damning. It stated that the Lerwick was "unstable in all three planes and pilots must be prepared to re-trim the aircraft at any time, particularly during the approach and landing." A simple translation of this would be that the aircraft could suddenly turn on a pilot at any moment, even during routine flight, but with a special tendency to be a dangerous problem when taking off and landing. Understandably, pilots and crew did not think well of the aircraft, and accidents mounted with the passage of time. The Lerwick's problems could never be fully solved, despite attempting to finesse how the aircraft was handled and the litany of attempts to refine the overall design.

The first service Lerwicks had begun deployment at the end of 1939, with the first patrol being flown from Oban on Christmas Day. These early Lerwicks required frequent maintenance, and by early February, all ten that had been deployed were grounded for modifications again after the throttle lever had collapsed on one of them, thankfully while still water bound. Soon after, they were allowed out again, and L7253 went out on her first patrol. The patrol was almost immediately abandoned owing to poor weather, but on her approach, the aircraft hit the water hard, collapsing the starboard float and causing the aircraft to turn over and rapidly sink, with four of her crew drowning before rescue boats arrived. At this point, the Lerwick had yet to sight a single hostile vessel of any sort.

It would take until March for the Lerwick to provide any return whatsoever on the effort, time, and lives being put into it—with L7256 dropping a bomb at a submerged U-boat, though without any positive effect. By late May, No. 209 squadron was fully equipped with Lerwicks, having made their final flight with the Stranraer in late April. Given their growing familiarity with the Lerwick, it is entirely possible they were saddened to see the old biplane go—though the Stranraer's own reputation had not precisely been sterling to begin with. As their service life began, various Lerwicks were rotated out of service for the modifications to the wing, as new examples arriving had already been updated. For a term, it seemed that the type might at least "break even," with serviceability reported at 81 per cent in May—but this dropped to 40 per cent by June as engine failures mounted.

Both the aircraft and the squadron using it would be grounded time and again, sometimes in fits and starts, as modifications were adapted as part of the endless effort to rectify the type's faults. Having been temporarily grounded owing to the scattering and updating of their aircraft, 209 Squadron resumed operations in early January 1941, and lost three aircraft, none of them to enemy action. One was lost, thankfully, without accompanying loss of life, when a gale blew up and a poorly-built float collapsed. Another crashed when trying to take-off, with the aircraft never reaching flight speed; the hull was holed by an obstacle and the aircraft sank in two minutes, with the loss of two of its crew. A third Lerwick disappeared into a clear sky in late February and no trace was found of it. A fourth was lost in another gale when the front turret and rear entrance hatches had not been fastened shut, and the craft simply filled with water and sank.

No. 209 Squadron had been moved around frequently as the pressures of the war and other factors required them, but were eventually sent to Lough Erne, as yet another Lerwick was lost. Detached from the squadron and operating from Pembroke Dock, the aircraft was testing an experimental blind-flying apparatus, and was unable to reach a safe landing site, landing in 8-foot seas. She was immediately thrown upwards, and an engine tore off at the bulkhead, with the propeller slicing through the hull. Remarkably, though the aircraft sank immediately because of this, no lives were lost in what must have been a shocking incident to the crew.

Having accomplished nothing but trouble for the squadron, Catalina aircraft began to replace it in 209's arsenal in late April, with the Lerwicks being sent elsewhere, probably to the relief of the aircrews. Most of the Lerwicks were sent on to another unit, No. 4(C)OTU, a Coastal Command Operational Training Unit based at Stanraer by the end of May. This transfer did not improve the luck of the aircrews assigned the Lerwick, as two more accidents occurred. The first was the worst yet. On October 14, example L7268's port engine failed in flight, with the aircraft diving into the sea. Tragically, extra crew members were being carried without the written permission required to do so on a Lerwick, with the result that nine people were killed and three injured. A second Lerwick "merely" sank at its moorings, hardly an auspicious start for a squadron taking part in training duties.

At this point, nobody was in any doubt as to whether the Lerwick would become a viable part of R.A.F. strategy—it was in service merely until other, better aircraft could be brought into service. For a time, a handful operated with No. 422 (Canadian) Squadron at Lough Erne, in the summer of 1942. These aircraft were on loan from their coastal command squadron and were meant as a stop-gap until Sunderlands were to arrive. All the Lerwicks were withdrawn by September, but in that short period, one still managed to be lost. On September 10, one aircraft hit the water and bounced in moderate winds, skidding violently in a motion that severed the entire tail section. The accident was put down to pilot inexperience, and a certain finicky nature of the exactor control system.

As the end neared, the very first Lerwick (L7248) was lost in late October. While on a routine calibration test, the starboard engine likely at least partially failed, and the wing was seen to dip before the aircraft slammed into the side of a hill, killing all seven on board and being totally destroyed. The report on the crash noted that the aircraft had never been able to successfully fly on one engine, and this was in a sense a tragic "full circle" for the Lerwick to follow. Despite all the modifications and efforts to fix the aircraft from the very start, its problems were never solved, and the aircraft took a terrible toll on its own aircrews for absolutely no success in return.

The end was ignominious, with most of the aircraft sent to Scottish Aviation starting in October 1942. Most of the surviving aircraft ended up there, though at least one was simply abandoned at Pembroke Dock. Only one aircraft escaped the rapid disposal of the type, and that was L7254. This aircraft survived for a time simply because it had been involved in mooring tests—on the conclusion of these, it was handed over to the Maritime Training School before arriving, at the end of March 1943, at No. 63 Maintenance Unit at Wig Bay. A total of twenty-one Lerwicks had been built, all of which had been built and deployed between March 1939 and March 1941 amid constant tinkering—and all had been withdrawn by December 1942 and subsequently scrapped during 1943.

The short, disastrous career of the Lerwick may at first glance seem to be something that does not quite fit in a litany of capable aircraft of various descriptions. While achieving precisely nothing, the Lerwick was a costly failure in terms of time, money, and human life at a time that Britain could ill afford all those things. Yet the story of the Lerwick illustrates very well the pitfalls inherent in aviation design. The company behind the Lerwick were very experienced at designing successful flying boats, and indeed would go on to create innovative designs even in a world that no longer had a comfortable "fit" for the dreams they made real. Yet despite all this, initial errors created unsolvable conundrums that would plague the aircraft. The designers pinned their hopes on the most powerful available engines, which, in the event, simply could not give the airframe the performance it depended on.

Often times, even a design that faced initial flaws could be salvaged but fixing one problem with the Lerwick seemed to exacerbate others, or even cause entirely new ones. The design was an endless headache both in the air and on land, highlighting the unique challenges inherent to building a flying boat, an aircraft that also must have excellent water-handling qualities in order to truly be successful.

In the end, the Lerwick is indicative of Britain's desperate need for aircraft of all types in the early war years, and that the demands of wide-ranging operations covering not just Britain itself but also the Atlantic and the North Sea—to say nothing about British overseas commitments—kept every possible aircraft employed. The Lerwick was a product of a desperate need for expansion in a time of crisis. It was also a design that never quite worked. It is important to remember the failures in aviation history, not only for what they reveal about the aircraft themselves, but also what they reveal about the times that forged them.

29

Saunders-Roe Princess: The Last, Graceful Throw of the Dice

After the failure of the Lerwick, Saunders-Roe did not give up on creating flying boats, and ultimately crafted the idea for what would be their final completed sea-giant. Between the Lerwick and the Princess, there would be one more aircraft (discussed in the next chapter) that attempted to insert the flying boat into the post-war world, but the Princess was a far grander attempt, though ultimately just as doomed. The Saunders-Roe Princess was a vision of what the future should look like that never came to fruition, but what the company did create was the largest all-metal flying boat to ever take to the air.

This book has frequently spoken of the dream of flying boats, and indeed it was that in reality—a combination of true potential and a romantic vision that endures still. The Princess was an aircraft too late for her world, a giant that looked like what a bygone age had envisioned the future to look like. The aircraft was enormous, beautiful, and, sadly, doomed by the passage of time.

Specifications

First Flight: 1952
Powerplant: Four Bristol Coupled-Proteus 610 coupled turboprop engines, 2,500 hp each, and two Bristol Proteus 600 turboprop engines, 2,500 hp
Armament: None
Top Speed: 380 mph (611 kph)
Range/Service Ceiling: 5,720 miles (9,205 km), 39,000 feet (11,887 metres)
Dimensions: Length 148 feet (45 metres), height 55 feet 9 inches (16.99 metres), wingspan 219 feet 6 inches (66.90 metres)
Number Built: Three (only one ever flying)

Saunders-Roe was one of the last companies to still be pursuing large-scale flying boat development. Despite the arrival of the jet engine in growing use by the end of World War II, despite bigger and more capable land aircraft that operated from an ever-larger number of land-based airstrips and then airports, the company continued to develop water-based projects. While the SR.A/1 program adapted somewhat to the jet age, the aircraft that became the Princess was something else entirely.

A gas-turbine powerplant was a new idea that could be used, and this offered some tantalizing possibilities to a company at the beginning of the jet age, when it was still uncertain what path aviation was guaranteed to take. The gas-turbine powerplant had a better power to weight ratio, offering the potential for an even larger passenger flying boat than had been seen before in Britain. In 1944, the company produced a study in broad strokes for an aircraft with a total weight of 187,000 lb (84,822 kg). This initial conception was taken over very shortly by Harry Knowler and Arthur Gouge, and radical changes were made. Incorporating the gas-turbine powerplant meant that the design could be scaled up impressively, and provision was made for a relatively new innovation: a pressurized hull. This innovation would revolutionize passenger air travel, allowing aircraft to travel above the weather in increasing comfort. The first aircraft to enter commercial service with pressurization had only entered service in 1938 as the Boeing 307, and only came into extensive use in 1943 with the arrival of the enormously successful Lockheed Constellation.

By the summer of 1945, the enlarged study had been given an official designation: SR.45. The initial design was for an aircraft with a 220-foot (67-metre) wingspan that would bear six Armstrong-Siddeley Cobra engines. A two-deck, 146-foot (44.5-metre) hull was drafted with a theorized range of 3,300 miles (5,311 km) that could rise to a maximum height of 39,000 feet (11,887 metres). The company took this initial design to the British Ministry of Supply, and Minister George Strauss was apparently quite enthusiastic about this new development. The Ministry of Supply felt that the SR.45 concept could be important to British aviation's post-war future, though Britain's main commercial airline, B.O.A.C., was not as enthusiastic. Nevertheless, an order was placed for three aircraft for a total of £2.8 million in May 1946.

There was a great deal of confusion about who should oversee the project, with authority switching back and forth before the Director-General of Technical Development (Air) at the Ministry of Supply finally decided that B.O.A.C.—as the operator—should deal directly with Saunders-Roe. This was likely the best choice, but it revealed the first signs that the project might be less promising than it first appeared. B.O.A.C. was less enthusiastic about the design, though all other parties presumed it would be used on the transatlantic routes. This may not have been helped by the fact that practical development of the project was prolonged owing to all the innovations being built into the aircraft.

Revisions to the design put an emphasis on using the Rolls-Royce Tweed engine, and a wing design incorporating them had been well developed when things hit a snag: Rolls-Royce announced that the engine would not go into production, and this caused a cascade of different engines being considered and then rejected—a total of five before a final choice was made: the Bristol Proteus. This was a risky choice; the propeller-turbine Proteus project was underdeveloped, though it had significant potential. The company was extremely confident in their choice, and as a result, in January 1948, the press was invited to view the aircraft's initial construction, and the announcement of the Proteus was officially made. The aircraft was, it was said, to carry ten engines in total. Eight of them were to be in coupled pairs, with two single engines at the outside edges of the bank of engines.

Taking on the Proteus required a redesign of the wing, since it was a reverse-flow engine that drew air in near the rear. Large ducts and inlets also had to be included as well, and like falling dominoes, other features had to change. The tailfin grew larger, with the tailplane itself mounted higher up. The fuselage had to change as well, with the previously hemispherical nose being altered so the cockpit was further forward than it had been. Beyond these heavy changes, Saunders-Roe was being bold in the extreme in terms of the innovations they were building into the design, essentially developing them into a practical reality as the aircraft was designed and built. Beyond hull pressurization, they chose to include air conditioning and power-operated irreversible flying controls.

The SR.45 was the cutting edge of technology as a result, and extremely ambitious in execution. Adding the pressurization and air conditioning required a labyrinth of internal pipes and other features, with the pressure provided by a compressor driven by each inboard power installation. The Boulton-Paul concern contributed to creating the power-control system, even though Saunders-Roe had already worked on more rudimentary versions of such an installation. The aircraft was simply too big to be successfully controlled without something of the sort, and Saunders-Roe was leaving nothing to chance. What ended up being installed was extremely complex, but was thoroughly tested on a rig in 1949, and then further tested in a Short Sunderland as the company continued to improve on it. Amazingly, this was not the end of the company's attempts to innovate in the

The Princess in flight. (*Photograph from the Ron Dupas Collection, 1000aircraftphotos.com*)

aircraft. They planned to reduce the size and weight of the power unit by changing the positioning of the units and adding aerodynamically-balanced surfaces. "Fly-by-wire" was even considered briefly, an extremely advanced concept for the time. The company remained outwardly confident in the outcome, declaring in January 1948 that the first flight would take place late the next year; the company also announced that the aircraft finally had a name: Princess.

As late as March 1949, the company still insisted that all was on schedule, but the engine development began to prove problematic. The first coupled Proteus installation was not successfully placed into the aircraft until February 1951. The start-date for flight trials was pushed to an unspecified time in 1951–52. Meanwhile, the Cowes operation had to expand rapidly to accommodate all of the development and also the building of the aircraft. This alone required extensive planning since the three prototypes were so large that it would take almost all the space in the company's Columbine hangar just to house them as they were built. Even the apron and slipway had to be enlarged and reinforced to successfully launch the new giants.

To alleviate the space issue, the first prototype Princess—still without its engines, outer wings, or fins—was moved onto the apron. As the hulls themselves were finished, internal details were also finalized. The aircraft had a "double bubble" cross section, with the waist of this forming the division between the two decks. The bottom of the planing hull was—perhaps surprisingly, given everything else about the aircraft—rather normal for a large flying boat, which was unpressurized and had several watertight compartments.

The flight deck incorporated a place in the extreme bow for the captain and first officer, with seats behind them for two flight engineers. While some aircraft might be able to have only one engineer, the complex and advanced nature of the Princess undoubtedly required two. There were also spaces for navigator and radio room operator. Behind these operational spaces were the restroom for the crew and one of the aircraft's galleys. The lower deck had two large holds that could accommodate a total cargo weight of 18,000 lb (8,165 kg). The passenger arrangements were a little bit more complicated, as several were discussed and rejected. The one most favoured, which was developed in conjunction with B.O.A.C., called for the accommodation of 105 passengers in two cabins. In addition, there would also be a cocktail bar, powder rooms and toilets, and a planned passenger galley with a large dining room. This would have been a rather more comfortable ride than most passengers would have been used to since the aircraft's systems also included heating and air-conditioning.

None of the passenger quarters would ever be installed, come the actual event. B.O.A.C. was certainly not growing more confident as the project dragged on, and it was concerned that public acknowledgement of its involvement in interior design would be interpreted as a firm commitment to buy the aircraft. There is something inherently demoralizing in how much effort the designers continued to go to for an aircraft that would never see any furnishings, such as labouring over making sure that the portholes were both big enough to afford an adequate view, but also with building in a failsafe in case of cracking or breakage.

A beautiful view of the Princess. (*Photograph courtesy of Dan Shumaker*)

This attention to advanced, rich detail continued in the all-important wing, which was built in five sections. The centre section bridged the hull and extended as far as the inboard nacelle, with the inner wings reaching as far as the outboard engine installation. The centre section had a parallel chord with the inner wings slightly tapered and the leading edges on the outer wings swept back. All the required engine structures made designing and constructing the wing a very difficult task. The wing also came with de-icing equipment powered by hot air drawn in by tail pipe cooling shrouds. The same air for the heated cabin came from here. Given the complex, interconnected systems that made up most of the aircraft, the tail was also surprising. It was as conventional as the bottom of the hull, with a rudder split into three sections with the elevators split in two. The tailplane had a 12-degree dihedral, and at the fillet of the dorsal fin there was a ram orifice to feed the tail de-icer.

The advanced Proteus engines proved to be a significant problem to develop. The final version developed for the Princess, the Proteus 3, would ultimately fulfil the promise of the program, but the engines fitted would be badly underpowered. The aircraft had to wait so long for their engines that two of them were put inside of cocoons in order to keep them from the weather while they sat outside the hangar. The prolonged development process for the entire project also meant that the price tag for development had ballooned. The cost for the engines had increased from the initial estimates of £407,000 when the program was first planned in 1946 to £4,920,000 by 1951. The overall cost of the project had long since outstripped the £2.8 million to reach a total of £10.8 million. For Saunders-Roe, with B.O.A.C. more and more skittish as time went by, this was a dangerous position to be in. There was also an element of mystery to all of this, since Bristol was also preparing to use the Proteus for their upcoming Brabazon aircraft and there were questions about why the process had become so expensive, which Bristol apparently had no satisfactory answer for. In summation, the prices were spiralling, the main customer was possibly slipping away and certainly was showing no enthusiasm for the aircraft, and the development process had taken far longer than anybody had anticipated. None of this boded well at all for the aircraft.

Though for a moment, there was something positive. The three aircraft had been given their registrations, and the first of these, G-ALUN, had finally been completed in August 1952 (the other two aircraft were G-ALUO and G-ALUP), On August 21, it was lowered into the water before midnight, and fuel taken on for its first flight the next day. There was significant public interest in the aircraft, and crowds began to gather once the aircraft was moved past the harbour breakwater. The big moment was preceded by engine and taxi tests, and a 2-mile stretch of water was cleared for the take-off, though it was expected that the Princess would be able to do it in less than 1,000 yards. On board were eleven people for the maiden flight, and it came off without any serious issue, and the same could be said for subsequent tests.

Unfortunately, the aircraft had already been doomed for two years, though Saunders-Roe did not know it yet. B.O.A.C. and the British government had decided not to pursue commercial flying boats in 1950, with B.O.A.C. focusing its interest on the de Havilland Comet. None of this was terribly clear publically, since B.O.A.C. and the Ministry of Supply vacillated on the Princess, and certainly did in their announcements. To save money, it was made public in February 1951 that the third Princess would be scrapped to stem the hemorrhage of cost overruns. This announcement was not an official one, and in any event, the Ministry of Supply made a contradictory decision within a month, saying that all three examples would be handed over to the R.A.F. for its use. B.O.A.C.'s interest was fading, but the R.A.F. apparently saw at least some use for the aircraft, and it was theorized that the Princess could transport 200 soldiers.

Then B.O.A.C. seemed to reverse again. Saunders-Roe had organized a subsidiary company, Princess Air Transport Company Limited, to see if they could generate interest elsewhere for the aircraft. The position of general manager in the company was given to a B.O.A.C. man, H. W. Alger. Whether this reflected an attempt to generate a connection to B.O.A.C. or reflected one already there is somewhat unclear, but in any event, B.O.A.C. ended up making some tentative noises about using the Princess for a marine development flight. This frail branch was snapped by the disappointment of the Proteus 2, and with the Proteus 3 still an uncertainty, there was no suitable powerplant immediately available for the aircraft.

To the undoubted frustration of Saunders-Roe, B.O.A.C.'s private decisions—tilting once again against the Princess—did not reflect public pronouncements.

Inwardly, the airline had decided that the concept of flying boats was itself obsolete for passenger travel. Outwardly, B.O.A.C. expressed itself more than satisfied with the Princess when it took to the air, saying it was "tremendously interested" in the aircraft. This statement was made in October 1952, and B.O.A.C.'s chairman, Sir Miles Thomas, stated that the company was in favour of the idea of using the Bristol BE.25 propeller-turbine, later called the Orion, to reinvigorate the prospects of the Princess. Almost inevitably, by the time Thomas said this, the development team at Cowes had already committed to the Proteus 3 engine, since this required the least amount of change to the aircraft already developed and on hand.

The problem was that even installing the Proteus 3 required a lengthy testing problem that would take the Princess into the mid-1950s, which was a heavy counterweight to the aircraft's performance. On the water, the Princess was found to be satisfactory, which was matched by a more than adequate performance in the air. The only note made against the Princess in the air was that the simulated feel characteristics and control to surface ratios required modification. Even when flying on asymmetric power, the Princess was stable in the air. Perhaps surprisingly for an aircraft of such size, it proved to have good stall characteristics, and provided good warning.

It would sadly not be enough to save the aircraft. The Ministry of Supply ordered all work halted in March 1952, and G-ALUO and G-ALUP were both placed back into cocoons, and the aircraft were beached thereafter at Calshot Spit. Further development of the Proteus 3 was given low priority, even though G-ALUN continued to fly. Her last public appearance was at the SBAC show in September 1953. The aircraft sported a striking livery in blue, white, and yellow, looking every inch the successful aircraft. Looks were, as ever with the Princess, deceiving. The next month, the Ministry invited independent operators to bid on the aircraft to be rid of them. One interesting bid was made by Aquila Airways, under the auspices of its chairman Eoin C. Mekie, to purchase all three for over £1 million per aircraft. Perhaps with a mind to making up some of the cost of the aircraft, this offer was rejected, and no other substantial offers were forthcoming. As a result, the program was mothballed in its entirety in June 1954. G-ALUN had made forty-seven flights by this point, a total of almost ninety-seven hours in the air. She, too, was cocooned without her engines at Cowes.

Out of perhaps a genuine belief in the aircraft, or out of more practical concerns about making back some of the cost of the aircraft, a plethora of vague schemes were floated even into the 1960s to find some practical application of the cocooned aircraft. The government and Saunders-Roe made several detailed examinations to try and find something for the aircraft, and even B.O.A.C. took part, searching for suitable sites from which the aircraft could operate and trying to find destinations it could fly to. Everywhere seemed to be considered. Perhaps the aircraft could fly much like the older flying boats had on the imperial routes, heading to Cape Town in South Africa. Perhaps it could fly the route to New York,

An unusual shot of a cocooned Princess. (*Photograph courtesy of Brian Green via Doug Green*)

likely landing at La Guardia's still-extant flying boat terminal. Pacific destinations were discussed ranging from Wellington in New Zealand, to Vancouver in Canada, and to San Francisco in the United States. Jamaica, too, was floated as a possible destination for the Princess. Nothing would come of any of this.

Nor would anything come of an even more fascinating discussion. Rumours arose in 1955 that the United States Navy might purchase the aircraft. The huge aircraft would make ideal flying test beds for nuclear reactors. The image is astonishing to consider, like something out of science fiction of a decade before—an advanced, huge flying boat kept aloft by the power of the atom. These rumours had some truth behind them, and in June 1958, representatives of the company went to the United States to pursue the possibility. Sadly, for advocates of the Princess, nothing came of these talks, either.

This did not end the attempts to find use for the aircraft, though they seem somewhat feeble in retrospect. In late 1958, Air Vice-Marshal D. C. T. Bennett met with a South African businessman named B. G. Halpin who made a bid to purchase all three aircraft. The idea was to re-equip the aircraft with Rolls-Royce Tyne 11 engines to give the Princess the power it lacked. The Ministry let the offer languish until 1960, not giving any decision at all; this lack of a decision ironically created a decision, namely the abandonment of the concept. Saunders-Roe themselves had made their own attempt even before this to find some niche for the aircraft by studying how to modify it to be a landplane, also with the Tyne engines. There was no real impetus behind these efforts, and the company flailed about conceptualizing it as either a commercial aircraft or a military transport with no enthusiasm for a land-based Princess extant at all.

Halpin remained as a champion of the aircraft long after most everyone had given up hope. He formed his own company, British Princess Flying-Boats Limited, in November 1960. He approached the government once again about buying all three aircraft—so long as the British government would guarantee operating rights for him for at least one aircraft on a high-density air route. Halpin had ideas about linking Southampton to Baltimore, Chicago, and Detroit. This last is yet another striking image to this author, for whom Detroit is a very familiar sight. With the Tyne engines, Halpin hoped to be in operation by 1962. This was perhaps the last solid chance for the Princess, and the British government scotched it by refusing to give a guarantee to Halpin. After two attempts to purchase the aircraft from the British government, with negative results each time, Halpin can certainly be forgiven for abandoning the Princess after this last display of uncooperativeness from the government.

Even into 1962, the fate of the aircraft remained uncertain. The Ministry of Aviation announced the sale of G-ALUN to the Wider Company in Florida for an undisclosed five-figure sum. This turned out to be a house of cards and simply collapsed. The War Office tried once more time in 1963 to find some interest. On behalf of the Ministry of Supply, he asked for tenders from any remaining interested parties after having already driven off the most likely of these. In a typical manner for the Princess, the War Office asked for all offers to be put in by December 12 but had only made the announcement in November. The only tentative interest was shown by Aero Spacelines, which had made a study for NASA on the idea of using the Princess to carry components of the Saturn V rocket. This, too, was yet another striking image—the idea of a flying boat, by this point long passed by the jet age—carrying pieces of the space age. The image became even more striking since the study considered the possibility of producing a twinned aircraft with a new centre wing section.

For a few shining moments, things swung into action again. Eoin Mekie emerged again, in January 1964, and purchased the aircraft—getting them for the fire-sale price of £30,000. The idea was that he would provide Aero Spacelines with the pieces needed for Saturn V transport, and in July 1965, G-ALUO and G-ALUP were finally brought out of the cocoons they had languished in for twelve years and were partially dismantled for shipping to the United States. The cocooning process had kept out most of the corrosion, but in the summer of 1964, the contract governing inspection between Westland and the Ministry of Air for inspection had lapsed and was not renewed. By the time Mekie was able to look over his purchases, deterioration had begun on both aircraft. Both aircraft would only move to Southampton, where they would be scrapped in the latter stages of 1965.

This left only G-ALUN. She was de-cocooned for Aero Spacelines, but this also fell through since the exact same deterioration began after she was removed from her protective casing. On April 12, 1967, G-ALUN too was towed to the scrapyard, ending the dream of the SR.45 Princess. Even this process was not straightforward. Her wings and tailplane were stripped away, and part of the hull

A 1962 shot of the Princess lingering at Cowes, next to the SR/A.1. (*Photograph courtesy of Dan Shumaker*)

was used as part of the actual premises of the breaker's yard, with the upper deck housing an office and the lower deck a workshop. This, too, was destroyed when the yard expanded. Some of the portholes ended up as windows on a yacht, but the Princess had come to an inglorious end.

There is much blame to go around in the story of the Saunders-Roe SR.45 Princess. Elongated development, perennial power problems, the changing of the eras, and the delays and failings of the British government all played their role. For an aircraft that only even spent less than 100 hours in the air, the Princess program lasted for an astonishingly long time while somehow accomplishing almost nothing. It would be simple to say that the aircraft was just passed over by events, but there was so much more to it than that. An aircraft designed at the end of the era of flying boats nevertheless had so many chances to find a niche all the way into the space age. Many flying boats have survived into the present day, of course, but there is something unique to the Princess—it would have been the only large passenger flying boat to have made that jump into the future. In the final analysis, its failure to do so owes as much to the follies and failures of British bureaucracy as it does to anything about the aircraft itself. It was in part owing to these delays—these failures to act or foolish decisions—that doomed "might have been" to becoming "never was."

30

Saunders-Roe SR.A/1: Jet-Powered Finale

Saunders-Roe did not give up on the idea of creating militarily viable flying boats at the end of World War II, and in the SR.A/1—it was never officially given a designated name—came a bold, if ultimately unsuccessful attempt to solve a problem that was generated by Britain's situation in the Pacific, and would ultimately be overtaken by the passage of time. The SR.A/1 was one of the rarest sort of flying boat: a jet-powered one. Meant for a war that was swiftly turning in the favour of Great Britain and her allies, the SR.A/1 would be plagued by accidents nearly as much as it would be by circumstances. Ultimately, these were to prove the type's undoing.

It remains a unique aircraft in the annals of flight, even if it never took hold like Saunders-Roe might have hoped. The Saunders-Roe SR.A/1 was a fascinating and unique attempt to project the flying boat into the jet age, and is no less interesting because it failed to do so.

Specifications

First Flight: 1947
Powerplant: Two Metropolitan-Vickers Beryl MVB.2 turbojets, 3,850 lbf
Armament: Four 20-mm Hispano Mk 5 cannon, two 1,000-lb (455-kg) bombs or rockets
Top Speed: 512 mph (824 kph)
Range/Service Ceiling: One hour forty-eight minutes, 48,000 feet (14,600 metres)
Dimensions: Length 50 feet (15.24 metres), height 16 feet 9 inches (5.11 metres), wingspan 46 feet (14.02 metres)
Number Built: Three

The Saunders-Roe SR.A/1 looks like something that a reader might have seen in an issue of *Amazing Stories*. The aircraft in many ways resembles something out of the past's conception of science fiction, a sleek vision of where the flying boat might have gone had their era continued onwards. It was to be the first jet-powered flying boat in history, one of very few aircraft to bear such a description. The aircraft was the brainchild of Henry Knowler's design team, planned at Cowes on the Isle of Wight. Initial work on the type was carried out as early as 1943, while D. M. Smith of Metropolitan-Vickers began secret work on an engine to power it. It was designed to meet British Air Ministry specification E.6/44 issued in May 1944, which called for a high-speed fighter aircraft to be operated from coastal waters in the Pacific theatre. While still fighting the war against the Japanese, the British faced a dilemma like that which had produced Japan's own flying boat plans: airfields in the vastness of the pacific were relatively few and far between—flying boats and other seaplanes could patrol the wartime skies, and then protect and span imperial territories thereafter. The initial design was originally submitted in December 1944 as the Saro S.44 but had taken on its proper designation by the end of the war.

The design that Knowler's team arrived at looked outwardly conventional but was in truth bold in conception. The aircraft incorporated a pair of Metropolitan-Vickers (Metrovick) Beryl turbojet engines entirely within the hull, mounted side by side. They were placed just below and behind the cockpit, using an air intake at the nose to feed their fire. The air intake could be extended like a snout to keep out spray when necessary. At the other end, there were separate jet-pipes behind the wing, angled outwards at almost 5 degrees to clear the rear parts of the hull and tail surfaces. Given the still-revolutionary nature of jet engines, the hull and wings had to be designed to serve both the speeds required to fly while still being able to handle upon the water. The standard floats of most previous flying boats would not do, and on this new design, the stabilising floats were mounted at the two-thirds' span of the wing and not only retracted inwards after take-off but rotated 90 degrees so the curved upper surface was outermost when they were fully retracted. The hull itself was built out of thirty-four frames and with an additional seven half-frames in the centre section. The internal structure of the hull was shaped around the two engines, and the wing spar was bolted to the hull form at the fourteenth frame.

The streamlined hull and all these features combined to create an aircraft that was superior by far to anything similar that the Japanese had. The flying boat hull form, applied to a jet, was far more efficient than adding seaplane floats to a standard design, such as the Nakajima A6M2-N "Rufe" (a seaplane version of the Mitsubishi Zero) or the Kawanishi N1K1 "Rex." This was without even considering the vast increase in speed that the jet engines would bring.

Inside the hull, the pilot's compartment was built as a single unit underneath a transparent Perspex canopy and fitted with a still very new piece of equipment: the Martin-Baker ejection seat. It was in fact the first production aircraft to be fitted with this unit. The projected armament for the craft was to be four 20-mm Hispano cannon. The aircraft's fuel capacity could also be increased by an impressive 60 per cent by adding flush-fitting slipper tanks beneath the inboard wing panels. The flush-fit ensured that even added fuel tanks would not harm performance, and they could be jettisoned in combat or an emergency.

View of the SR/A.1. (*Photograph courtesy of Jeremy Hughes*)

There was some excitement about the design in the wider community. *Flight* magazine enthused:

> There is no doubt that the Saunders-Roe twin-jet single-seater fighter flying boa is one of the most interesting and unusual designs ever to take to the air. On close inspection one becomes more and more intrigued as the various details of equipment and construction are revealed. In particular, however, the overall impression gained is one of uniqueness, so different in shape, layout and conception is the SR.A/1 from all other fighters and aircraft of any other class. One feels impelled to liken the aircraft to a submarine and to pursue the comparison through the various major units. The hull is a floating powerhouse.
>
> *Flight*, July 28, 1948, p. 123

The article went on to posit that a chief advantage to the flying boat in Far Eastern operations would be that it could hide in many small rivers and would be easily camouflaged there. Moreover, they noted that such an airstrip could not be bombed out of use like a conventional airfield. They also were viewed to be a savings in terms of aircraft—any emergency landing owing to running out of fuel or becoming lost in the far-flung islands of the Pacific would likely result in the loss of an expensive jet fighter. A flying boat was much more likely to survive such an eventuality.

The British government ordered three prototypes, numbered TG263, TG267, and TG271. The first of the now formally designated SR.A/1 aircraft took flight for the first time on July 15, 1947, with Geoffrey Tyson at the controls. In this initial aircraft, the turbojets were limited to a total thrust of 3,250 lb (1,474 kg); in subsequent aircraft, this would become 3,500 lb (1,588 kg) when its MBV 2 engines were mounted. In the third prototype, this was increased still more with Metrovick F.2/4A Beryl Mk I engines that produced 3,850 lb (1,746 kg) of thrust. A new, reinforced canopy was also installed in 1948, along with a streamlined "bullet" fairing, added where the tailplane met the fin to improve the airflow. What all this meant was that in testing the new aircraft, it shattered records by flying 70 mph (113 kph) faster than the seaplane records of the day.

Tyson demonstrated the aircraft's superb take-off speed, getting her airborne in eleven seconds. He was noted by observers for his confidence with the aircraft, though observers also considered the aircraft rather surprisingly quiet. While the aircraft was not initially meant to be testing on the open sea, the Chief Engineer of Metrovick's Gas Turbine Department, D. M. Smith, sprayed the intake of a Beryl engine and it was found to make only a slight reduction in the engine's performance and a minor accumulation of salt on the compressor blading. The extending intake was meant to cure this problem, but in any event a fresh water spraying down was recommended as a "just in case" solution.

For a while, it seemed like the concept might go somewhere. While it was the first jet-flying boat and the first jet-powered flying boat fighter, it was not alone. The United States was working on the Convair XF2Y/F-7 Sea Dart, which would first fly in 1953. Convair's aircraft oddly enough came from completely different thinking. While the first wave of American jet aircraft fit quite well on carriers, it was believed in some circles that the upcoming jets would be too large for the carriers that existed at the time. The size increase of aircraft carriers as the decades passed was not even conceived of at the time, and in any event, a sea-based aircraft might be a vastly cheaper alternative. The U.S. Navy responded on two tracks. One of them was experimenting with VTOL aircraft that resulted in profoundly strange aircraft like the Convair XFY-1 "Pogo" among others. The potentially more promising track was a more conventional waterborne fighter. Ultimately, the American approach was aware of Saro's attempts but wanted a much higher-performance fighter, resulting in a delta-winged, turbojet powered aircraft that first would fly in 1953. It ended up mirroring the Saro program in terms of accidents, but what ultimately kept Convair's jet from service was improvements to carriers that ironically were borrowed from the British: angled flight decks and automatic landing signals. This was further matched by the funding and building of vastly larger supercarriers, and the Sea Dart was doomed. By that time, Convair had good reason to wonder if they had not been cursed by history to follow Saro's lead.

At first, all seemed well for Saro's design. After initial testing was completed, the completed aircraft were put through a program of demonstration flights for the military and the type was shown at the SBAC Show at Farnborough in September

Take-off run of the SR/A.1. (*Photograph from the Jacques Trempe Collection, 1000aircraftphotos.com*)

1947. The aircraft had an impressive speed, matching the Hawker Sea Hawk then under development for the Royal Navy. Geoffrey Tyson also demonstrated the type to be more than capable of aerobatics, and the type was felt to have good handling. Saro had in fact put a good deal of thought into the aircraft's water handling. The aircraft came with an automatic nose pick up hook, located on the keel below the waterline, and the aircraft was supposed to be taxied between markers that would help it automatically lock on a mooring cable. There was another hook at the tail to make for easy towing, and both could be detached from the cockpit by the pilot. The aircraft taxied well and its control in cross-winds, aided by the aircraft's water rudder, was found to be good. This was all very promising from Saro's point of view—it surely must have seemed that they had a winner on their hands. There was even some belief that it would attract foreign interest, with the Scandinavian countries noted especially by *Flight* magazine as likely to be interested in an aircraft that could suit their rocky coastline, or the Dutch at some point in the future with their widespread and scattered colonial empire.

The third prototype was put to work with high speed tests, and it managed to read 498 mph (801 kph) at 20,000 feet (6,096 metres), and in a dive, it was even more impressive. In a dive on August 12, 1949, the aircraft achieved Mach 0.82. The performance of the aircraft was indeed spectacular for a seaplane, but the trouble was that by 1947, the need that had called it into being had ceased to exist. Japan was defeated, and land-based jet aircraft were becoming more and more capable. Interest in the aircraft evaporated over time, and Saro were unable to restart it. Testing—and attempts to sell their jet flying boat—continued into 1950, and the company thought it saw a ray of hope in the outbreak of the

Korean War. Surely another war in the Pacific would do the trick. Saro even had an answer to the argument that the aircraft carrier was the superior choice. They said that the flying boat could still be a valuable escort craft in the Pacific, and that their boat could escort still-vulnerable carriers and other ships. There were two other major limitations. First, the cockpit offered very poor visibility outside the aircraft, and the Beryl engine had ceased to be produced since Metrovick had pulled out entirely of jet engine development, meaning that even if the aircraft proceeded, the engines it depended on would be available only in limited supplies. To Saro's undoubted disappointment, the Air Ministry cancelled all further work in December 1950. For a time, the prototype was put in storage, gathering dust.

Saro made a last-ditch effort to attract customers by taking the SR.A/1 prototype out of storage and taking it to the Festival of Britain in June 1951. The company further tried to sweeten the pot, as it were, by promoting an even more advanced jet flying boat. This was a swept-wing aircraft with a forward-placed cockpit and Armstrong Siddeley Sapphire engine, called the P122. This, too, did not go anywhere, and the ambitious idea to create a future for the jet-powered flying boat fighter was doomed, but along the way, nails still had to be placed in its coffin. A reader may recall that there were three aircraft made, but by the time of its cancellation, there was only one.

The first loss occurred in 1947, when the second prototype was being tested. While in the air at Felixstowe, something went wrong during aerial manoeuvring and the aircraft crashed into the sea, killing the pilot. The second loss nearly claimed the R.A.F.'s finest test pilot, Eric "Winkle" Brown. When trying to land the aircraft on August 12, 1949, he struck a submerged log and the aircraft began to sink in the Solent, at Cowes. He was knocked unconscious in the crash and would have drowned were it not for the intervention of Geoffrey Tyson, who pulled him from the cockpit.

In the end, only the original prototype aircraft survived long enough to be cancelled. It is preserved to this day at the Solent Sky aviation museum in Southampton. The program that had created the SR.A/1 was revolutionary in conception, but it was a creation made for a dying time—the age of the flying boat was passing. That is not to say that the aircraft was not a well-designed machine, as by all evidence it was, and capable enough. It was not anything owing to the design itself, nor the accidents two out of three aircraft suffered, that would ultimately doom the aircraft, but just the passage of time. It was an aircraft built for yesterday's war, and it was simply outpaced by events and developments. It nevertheless remains a fascinating look at what might have happened under other circumstances if different decisions had been made. It also forever holds the record for being the first jet flying boat, and the first such aircraft to be built as a fighter. While it is perhaps a footnote today, the aircraft was the first of its kind and one of the only—and still remains a harbinger of the jet age that was even then being born.

31

Savoia-Marchetti S.55 / S.66: Strange Fascist Symbol

Italy was one of the nations that was an enthusiast early participant in aviation, and one of the foremost companies to arise from Italy's dedication to flight was Savoia-Marchetti. Originally founded in 1915 as the *Società Idrovolanti Alta Italia*, or SIAI, the company had produced its first flying boat by 1917. It was, in fact, the company's first aircraft. After World War I, the company was renamed *Società Anonima Costruzioni Aeronautiche Savoia*, after its founder, Umberto Savoia. In 1922, its fortunes began to increase rapidly after the arrival of engineer Alessandro Marchetti, and within two years, the new form of the company had produced a decidedly successful flying boat. The S.55 was an unusual design for a flying boat, featuring a double hull and high mounted engines, but it was superb to its purpose, and in the nascent fascist state, there was great use to put such an aircraft to.

The S.55 and its enlarged version, the S.66, would linger on through the 1940s, a symbol of fascist might and accomplishment, but in the end also a symbol of the systemic weakness of that totalitarian ideology.

Specifications: S.55X (Except First Flight and Number Built)

First Flight: 1926
Powerplant: Two Isotta-Fraschini Asso 750V, 880 hp each
Armament: Four 7.7-mm (0.303-inch) machine guns, one torpedo or 4,409 lb (2,000 kg) of bombs
Top Speed: 173 mph (279 kph)
Range/Service Ceiling: 2,200 miles (3,500 km), 16,405 feet (5,000 metres)
Dimensions: Length 55 feet (16.75 metres), height 16 feet 5 inches (5 metres), wingspan 74 feet 9 inches (24 metres)
Number Built: Approximately 243 S.55, twenty-four S.66

Fascism has always relied on both spectacle and the propagandistic projection of strength—even where none really exists—to further its ends. Fascist Italy in the 1920s was certainly no exception to this rule, and the Savoia-Marchetti S.55 was used from the outset to service these aims. Its successes could be used to try to distract attention from Italian weaknesses, and to make the regime of Benito Mussolini look far better than it was. This was a heady era for Italian aviation before the strains of war would reveal the very evident limitations in Italian strategic air power.

For the moment, there were glories to be had. Alessandro Marchetti designed an aircraft for the *Società Idrovolanti Alta Italia* (Savoia) in response to an Italian government request for proposals. The idea was to create a flying boat patrol bomber, a concept which in the 1920s was rapidly gaining momentum with maritime powers. The idea behind the S.55 was that it could be used in multiple marine combat roles, from bombing to becoming a torpedo aircraft to even being an airborne minelayer. At a time when biplanes still ruled the skies, Marchetti's vision swung to the innovative, and the result was a striking aircraft that still looks unusual today and was a revolutionary vision for the time.

Marchetti started by eliminating the idea of a central fuselage altogether, a staple of aviation design. Instead, he separated the crew and cargo compartments into two 30-foot pontoons. Each of the pontoons was a fully-enclosed boat. Across the two boats went the wing, thickening in the centre to contain the flight deck—though it was remarkably thick overall. Above the flight deck were the twin engines, mounted in a pusher-puller formation. The cockpit was originally an open design and would only become enclosed later on. Each hull supported an uncovered, or open-work, rear boom structure that in turn carried the twin fin and triple rudder tail assembly.

The weapons load was to be suspended beneath the centre section, and in the rear of each hull was a Scarff ring mounting for a machine gun. Over 200 such military aircraft would eventually be built, being dubbed the S.55M.

Adding to the overall strangeness of the design, Marchetti's vision was to be constructed entirely of wood; this was common for the smaller flying boats of the time, but even by the mid- and late 1920s, it was becoming unusual for larger aircraft.

The prototype, by now one of the period's most unusual designs, first flew in August 1924 using two 400-hp Lorraine-Dietrich engines license built by Isotta-Fraschini. An indication of just how well Marchetti had done his work is provided by the fact that, in short order, the aircraft set fourteen separate world records for speed, payload, distance, and altitude in its class. The Italian state could hardly fail to recognize the potential they had on their hands to project an image of a modern, powerful Italy.

The year 1927 saw one of the more famed S.55 exploits, where Francesco de Pinedo and Carlo del Prete flew one of the first series of S.55s, which they dubbed *Santa Maria*, in an epic 27,230-mile flight around the Atlantic Ocean. The next year, Stefano Cagno and Umberto Maddalena would utilize one of the aircraft to search for the crashed dirigible of Arctic explorer Umberto Nobile and his expedition.

The greatest exploits of the type, however, came under direct Fascist control. Then a favourite of Mussolini, General Italo Balbo—the commander of Italy's

Front-on view of an S.55. (*Photograph from the Ron Dupas Collection, 1000aircraftphotos.com*)

Regia Aeronautica—engineered mass demonstration flights using the S.55. Balbo himself was a legend in Italy, a gallant World War I soldier who had become a prominent fascist and one of the leaders of Mussolini's coup that had launched him into power. He was also something of a contradiction, a high-ranking Blackshirt—essentially the same as Hitler's Brownshirts: political soldiers used for organized violence against opponents of fascism—yet was also pro-Jewish and increasingly anti-German with time. Whatever his own politics, Balbo saw quite clearly that an alliance with Germany would ultimately prove a catastrophe for Italy, though he would not be there to see it. In the chaotic opening phases of Italy's war, Balbo was shot down when trying to land by friendly fire. There have been conspiracy theories ever since that Mussolini had him eliminated to remove a popular potential rival, but the evidence for this is at best conjectural. Early on, however, Balbo only wanted to promote the Italian air force, and both learnt to fly and began to organize his mass demonstration flights with the help of renowned aviator Francesco de Pinedo and leading seaplane advocate Stefano Cagna.

Balbo led from the front in this effort, starting with a 4,300-mile (6,920-km) flight around Italian bases in the Aegean and Libya in May 1927, flying in an S.55—the aircraft that would become synonymous with him. There were practical purposes in addition to the headlines: the flights tested the operational skills of *Regia Aeronautica* personnel and could and did help generate foreign orders for Italian aircraft, specifically the S.55. At the end of the same month, Balbo led a massive formation of ten S.55s and fifty-one Savoia-Marchetti S.59bis on a 1,750-mile (2,816-km) circuit around the Western Mediterranean. It was a curious flight, with each of its six stages geared to not exceed three or four hours' flying time and having to land in bays at each stop that were large enough to hold the

A formation of Balbo's S.55X aircraft on the ground. (*Photograph courtesy of Dan Shumaker*)

entire formation. By the end of the trip, the aircraft were all taking off together—certainly succeeding in Balbo's efforts to impart experience. The formation arrived over Marseilles, the last stop, in such a tight precision formation that it apparently provoked spontaneous applause.

The Italians followed this up with a similar flight in the Eastern Mediterranean in 1929; this flight included thirty-two S.55s as well three other aircraft that covered 3,300 miles (5,310km) through Greece, Turkey, Bulgaria, the Soviet Union, and Romania. Even in Odessa, where fascism encountered its mortal communist enemy, the Italian achievement was rewarded with a triumphal arch. From these initial triumphs, Balbo plotted even greater achievements using just the S.55, which had proven its reliability.

The first of these was launched in December 1930, with Balbo leading a flight of fourteen S.55s from the Italian base at Orbetello, just north of Rome in Tuscany, and taking them on a 6,462-mile (10,399-km) flight all the way to Rio de Janeiro in Brazil. By this time, Balbo had fallen out with de Pinedo and appointed Umberto Maddalena in his stead. The attempt nearly started badly, with his fourteen aircraft (two were spares) running into violent storms near the Balearic Islands, which damaged the aircraft and caused a delay for repairs before they set off for West Africa on December 21. The aircraft worked along the African coast in stages before reaching their transatlantic take-off point at Boloma in Portuguese Guinea. The departure was chosen for when the temperature would be lowest, early in the morning of January 6, 1931. Everything possible was done to lighten the water-soaked wooden hulls for the long-distance 1,865-mile journey (3,001-km) flight to Port Natal in Brazil. Balbo led the first flight into the air with no incident, but an aircraft in the second flight crashed into the sea and caught fire, resulting in a fatality. Almost immediately after that, another aircraft crashed and burnt, killing all four aboard. The two-spare aircraft were rotated into the flight, and the journey continued. Two more seaplanes would force-land along the way but were retrieved by Italian warships stationed along the flight route and towed to the island of Fernando de Noronta, where one would successfully be repaired to rejoin the flight. After eighteen arduous hours in the air, they arrived in Port Natal.

Balbo took eleven of the aircraft on to Bahia, then brought them to their ultimate destination, arriving in Rio de Janeiro with precise timing to coincide with the appearance of the eight supporting warships. It was a spectacular success that overshadowed the loss of the two aircraft and the casualties they caused. The airmen returned in a seaward journey, with the aircraft left behind for the Brazilians to use.

To celebrate the tenth anniversary of the force, Balbo arranged an ever-grander display. In 1933, he launched a group of twenty-five S.55s on a demonstration flight going even further—a grand tour to culminate at the Chicago World's Fair. The effort was preceded by two years of intense training before twenty-four S.55

Aircraft from the same flight in the air. (*Photograph courtesy of Dan Shumaker*)

aircraft (along with a spare aircraft) took off. For a start, these would be upgraded S.55X aircraft, fitted with the uprated Asso 750 engines. The flight was to venture across the North Atlantic from Londonderry, Northern Ireland, and the *Regia Aeronautica* stationed mechanics and meteorologists there to try to best ensure success. In addition, six meteorological trawlers were positioned along the ocean route, each equipped with a wireless set to communicate with the flight.

The aircraft departed Orbetello on July 1, 1933, flying in eight arrowheads over the Alps, crossing Switzerland and Germany before arriving and landing on Amsterdam's Zuidersee in the Netherlands. Here, tragedy struck again, with an aircraft capsizing and drowning a crewman—the spare aircraft once again being rotated in to take its place. The next day, they flew onto Londonderry, escorted in by British aircraft that had, in previous years, become famous for distance flights: Supermarine Southampton flying boats of the R.A.F.'s No. 201 Squadron.

Bad weather held them for several days before they could fly on to Reykjavík, Iceland, whereupon dropping temperatures and further bad weather kept them in place for a further six days. It undoubtedly gave the fliers time to dwell on the next daunting leg of their journey to Cartwright, in Labrador, then part of the Dominion of Newfoundland. Conditions on the journey when they did take-off were likely not encouraging. The crews ran into rainy skies and notorious Greenland fogs, with moisture leaking into their cockpits. According to Balbo's own recollection, the fog was so thick at points they could not see past their own wingtips and descended as low as 300 feet (91 metres) to evade it. Despite all of this, there were no stragglers or serious mechanical problems. Balbo kept the formation together with regular wireless roll calls and achieved what was at the time a major feat. It was a testament to the S.55 that, in a period where single aircraft crossing the Atlantic was still major news, an entire formation could do it.

All twenty-five arrived at their destination, having passed through New Brunswick and Montreal on their way. They arrived in Chicago on July 15 to a thrilled welcome, where the mayor declared it "Balbo Day"; even the Sioux honoured Balbo by awarding him a feathered headdress and calling him "Chief Flying Eagle." Later on, to honour the aviators, Mussolini would send an ancient Roman Column from Ostia to Chicago's Lakefront Trail, where it still stands today as an object of some controversy as the Balbo Monument.

Here it is worth taking an aside from aviation in general. To the modern eye, this thrilled welcome of fascism may seem naïve at best, but it must be remembered that in the complicated political world of the 1920s and 1930s, fascism was seen by many as a viable solution to economic and political woes and a stalwart foe of communism. The innate violence and prejudice that forms a core of fascist belief in the past (and present) was overlooked by some, and in any event, the passage of time has revealed the nature of the ideology more fully. Citizens today, if they have even a passing knowledge of history, are aware of the true nature of the beast. At the time, however, the worst was all yet to come. Moreover, the memory was complicated by the event. The Chicago World's Fair was more properly called the Century of Progress Exhibition, and as such was meant to be a positive display of the growth of humanity and of improving relations between the United States and Italy. Hotly debated over the decades, even today, the Balbo Monument is a reminder to some of an optimistic past and the glory days of Chicago—not a piece of fascist braggadocio.

The essential point here is the complexity of memory and how single events and objects can be viewed different ways by different people. It is also testament to how seductive and innocuous fascism can appear to be, both then and today. Yet in the larger sense, history's complexities ensure that even discussing a specific aircraft's achievements can touch on vast, complicated subjects. History rarely manages to be simple.

However, in the immediate aftermath of the flight, all was euphoria. After four days of being lavishly entertained, the aviators flew on to a ticker tape parade in New York City. Balbo lunched with President Roosevelt and was awarded the Distinguished Flying Cross for his achievement.

The crews then flew back from New York and then on to the Azores, where a single plane was lost when it capsized, killing the pilot. Their return to Rome after the 12,045-mile (19,384-km) trip was played for all the propaganda value it was worth. Truth is a concept that fascism only has a passing acquaintance with when it suits its purposes, but in this case, there was more than enough truth to be used to create a bombastic and spectacular story. The celebration that was put on by Romans for their returning airmen was compared to that of Constantine welcoming back the Roman Legions—serving to tie justifiable pride in a national feat to Mussolini's goal of comparing Fascist Italy to the Roman Empire, claiming legitimacy from the mantle. Balbo was made the first ever Marshal of the *Regia Aeronautica*, but his triumph was not to last. Mussolini would, out of a sense of paranoia common to totalitarians, banish Balbo to Africa— "promoting" him to be governor-general of Italy's Libyan colony. His legacy in aviation was secure, however; even after his death, British pilots would refer to large formations of German bombers over England by his name.

After these massively popular and famed flights, the S.55 settled into more prosaic but also more useful service as a passenger aircraft. It was operated by Italian airlines with accommodations for eight to ten passengers, depending on the configuration of the S.55 involved. These commercial aircraft were in service between 1926 and 1937 in this capacity in air routes all over the Mediterranean, operated by airlines such as *Aero Espresso*, *Ala Littoria*, and *Società Aerea Mediterranea*. Over time, the type was improved to gain range. The final evolution was the S.55X, which came into regular service in 1933. All the versions used Isotta-Fraschini Asso engines, but these were upgraded over time. Whereas the initial production S.55s had come with the twelve-cylinder type 500 engine, rated at 500 hp, the S.55X received an eighteen-cylinder successor that rated 750 hp. The total range for the S.55X was 2,400 miles, which was over double the range of the initially prototype.

In an unusual development, the S.55 also evolved into its own successor, rather than being pushed aside by another type. Except for the engines and tail surfaces, the S.66 was almost precisely the same aircraft. The difference came in that it had three engines, twelve-cylinder Fiat A.24Rs, rated at 750 hp. This version also came into service in 1933. In everything save engine configuration and tail surfaces, they were essentially the same aircraft. Interestingly, the wings were divided into fifty-four watertight compartments, so the aircraft would still have a certain amount of buoyancy even if the hulls were damaged. The three-engine arrangement did enable them to become slightly larger, and it could now carry between fourteen to eighteen passengers. In actual passenger operations, the S.66 was marked by efforts to ensure safety and to maintain the same ease of use that the S.55 had demonstrated. To this end, the various parts of the machine could be easily replaced at a repair facility. A hull could be replaced in a day, and wing units, the tail assembly, or engine nacelles could all be replaced in a matter of hours. These aircraft also flew throughout the Mediterranean from Gibraltar to Haifa with numerous Italian air carriers. In essence, wherever Italian airlines went, the S.55 and the S.66 went also.

The S.55 also found itself flying under Soviet colours. The Soviet Union already had a history of acquiring many foreign aircraft, including those from Italian firms, and already had a relationship with Savoia-Marchetti, having imported and sometimes reverse-engineered earlier flying boats since the early 1920s. The S.55 had proved itself in Russian eyes, too, having flown a trans-Siberian flight of 6,065 miles (22,530 km). The Soviets purchased the passenger version of the S.55 in 1932, acquiring a total of five aircraft, and they used them for air communications along their vast Pacific Ocean coast during the 1930s. At least two were also delivered to the United States, with a third being built under license by the American Aeronautical Corporation.

By 1939, a handful of S.55s were still on-hand with the military in 1939, but they were by then hopelessly obsolete and did not see significant wartime service, symptomatic of one of Italy's core failings: despite all the ostensible achievements of Italy's formation flights, Italian air power remained ultimately hollow. There were too few aircraft to make a critical difference, production of replacements was entirely too slow, and many of the types Italy entered the war with were endlessly outclassed by their Allied counterparts. So much for Mussolini's airborne glory. There are reports, however, of a handful of the remaining S.66 aircraft serving in wartime. Sixteen were still in airline service in 1939, and there are reports that, in 1940, a handful of these were being used as air-sea rescue aircraft, with 613ª *Squadriglia Soccorso* and based at Cagliari-Elmas on Sardinia.

One interesting aside about the S.55's development path is that it evolved into a third aircraft. Marchetti mated the wooden outer wings of the S.55 to a steel tube fuselage and fixed-landing gear, creating the S.73 trimotor airliner. Owing to the use of S.55 parts, development of this airliner took a mere four months.

The story of the last remaining S.55 in the world is a tumultuous one that is still in the process of being told. Here the author is indebted to the assistance of Fred Nicolau for helping to piece the current situation together. The surviving aircraft is De Barros' *Jahú*, which remained in Brazil. De Barros himself had been born in 1900

An unusual view of an S-66: this crashed one shows off the main difference in powerplant. (*Photograph courtesy of Phillip Hayes*)

in Sao Paulo State, specifically in Jahú (now known as Jau). After the transatlantic flight in 1927, and a few short flights to Sao Paulo, he never flew his S.55 again. After his death in 1947, the fate of the S.55 was in doubt until the Santos Dumont Foundation was created in 1955 in order for a new home to be found for it.

This was merely the beginning of the aircraft's story of survival. The *Jahú* remained out of the public eye, and likely forgotten by most people outside the Santos Dumont Foundation, until the Museu da Aeronáutica at Ibirapuera Park in Sao Paulo City opened in 1960. The situation remained relatively stable until 1999, when the museum was evicted by the city. The aircraft went to the local Military Police hangar—the state police in the region. Later, it was transferred to the Helipark Company, a service company for helicopters. It remained in their installations for refurbishment, done at the company's own expense. Later still, the Italian Air Force contributed funds to repair the tail section, and the aircraft once again remained out of public viewing until 2007 when it was sent to a newly-opened museum known as Museu Asas de um Sonho, later to become the TAM Museum, in Sao Carlos. The museum was the creation of the president of TAM airlines, then Brazil's largest such organization. When TAM merged with LAN airlines in 2015, however, the museum was shuttered, with vague whisperings of a reopening in Sao Paulo. Stories since then have spoken of selling off the collection, with talk of reopening the museum diminishing. Once again,

Jahú is no longer visible for public display and the world's last Savoia-Marchetti S.55 faces an uncertain future.

In the history of an aircraft laced with stories, there is one more that should rightly be told, of a S.55 that can almost be called a lost treasure ship. The S.55 was, as previously stated, purchased by the Soviets and used for important official duties in some cases. So, on June 26, 1935, an S.55 took off from the town of Alexandrovsk-Sakhalinsky with twelve people on board, and 2 million roubles in cash. The money had been collected from a local tractor repair shop and was on the way to the regional capital at Khabarovsk. An hour and fifteen minutes into the flight, communication was lost, and the aircraft vanished from history for decades.

Search parties failed to locate the aircraft, and the case was quickly classified—two of the men on board had been agents of the NKVD, Stalin's secret police and the chief instrument of his terror. The incident descended into legend, with local rumours speaking of sabotage by an unknown third party trying to steal the money. So, matters might have stayed were it not for the Russian Search Movement, a non-governmental organization dedicating to finding Russians lost in accidents. Wreckage from an airplane was reported in 2006, and the RSM dispatched investigators who had to cross over 2,000 miles (3,218 km) of taiga forest, whereupon they found the remains of two men and one woman from the crashed aircraft, laying where they fell when the wooden hulls came apart, surrounded by scattered personal items and parts of their seats and seat belts. The investigators were able to reconstruct the likely last moments of the doomed flight. The aircraft encountered low-lying fog soon after taking off from Sakhalin Island, and the crew descended to a low altitude to try to escape it, probably to use the Amur River as a guide. As a consequence, the aircraft slammed into the side of a hill, likely killing everyone onboard instantly. The roubles, however, went unrecovered—treasure hunters had looted the wreckage, and the roubles are unlikely to be recovered. Hopefully, the same cannot be said for the remaining lost passengers.

In the final analysis, the S.55/S.66 certainly claim the title of the most unusual design in this volume, beating out even the BV 138 for sheer strangeness to modern eyes. There is more to it than that, naturally; the Savoia-Marchetti flying boats demonstrate the process involved in aviation design in the late 1920s and early 1930s. They were record breakers at the time in their class, and made distance journeys in unheard of numbers. While all of this was meant to glorify a violent, totalitarian state, it was also part of the larger dream of aviation at the time: that it really could encircle the globe. Thankfully for posterity, it was this dream and not the fascist one that ended up coming true. The S.55 and S.66 found their true purpose as civilian passenger aircraft and rescue machines, not as propaganda tools. The Balbo flights may well be what the type is most famous for, aside from its catamaran design, but the substance of their service lives point to something more prosaic but altogether more positive.

32

Short S.23 Empire: Spanning the Empire

Short Brothers was in many ways the high note of British flying boat development, and certainly produced some of the most successful flying boats ever to fly across the vast territory of the British Empire. The company itself was founded in 1908, and still exists today as a subsidiary of Bombardier Aerospace—over a century of existence, and certainly a well-established name in the history of aviation. The company's apex might well be said to be the 1930s and 1940s—the heyday of its production of flying boats, for which it was particularly noted.

One of the finest examples of this would be the Short Empire, an aircraft that debuted in the mid-1930s and carried on until after the end of World War II. The Empire was aptly named, for it traversed the vast reaches of the British Empire from Egypt to India and even to Australia, carrying regular passengers for Britain's Imperial Airways among other airlines. The aircraft flew further afield still, all the way to Bermuda and New York City. Rare indeed are the flying boats that are this successful, let alone established regular air routes to and from every continent. The Short Empire was emblematic of the Great Britain it served, and an enduring reminder of the age of the flying boat.

Specifications

First Flight: 1936
Powerplant: Four Bristol Pegasus radial engines, 920 hp
Armament: None
Top Speed: 200 mph (322 kph)
Range/Service Ceiling: 760 miles (1,223 km), 20,000 feet (6,100 metres)
Dimensions: Length 88 feet (26.82 metres), height 31 feet 9¾ inches (9.70 metres), wingspan 114 feet (34.75 metres)
Number Built: Forty-two

By the mid-1930s, British Imperial Airways was eager to take advantage of the newest technology in aviation to push forward air services around the British Empire, including the sending of mail overseas. The first British commercial flying boat route had been established as early as 1923, and Imperial Airways was the result of amalgamating several companies to create a state-owned airline that could carry the flag anywhere.

By 1931, they were able to ship mail from Australia to Britain in a mere sixteen days, half the time of sea travel. Imperial Airways and Qantas ultimately partnered to establish regular travel and mail services between Australia and England. The joint venture, Qantas Empire Airways, planned a ten-day service between Rose Bay in New South Wales and Southampton that soon was so successful that the volume of mail exceeded the volume of available space on aircraft.

The solution was a new aircraft, and in 1933, the two airlines asked the Short Brothers to design a new large flying boat for the job. Imperial Airways and Qantas both undertook to purchase aircraft. The result would be the S.23 Empire flying boat, known popularly as the C-Class. The design that Short Brothers produced was very modern for the time, a streamlined and all-metal aircraft.

The design was for a high cantilevered wing that came with four Pegasus XC in-line engines. The chief engineer was Arthur Gouge, who designed the aircraft to carry from between sixteen to twenty-four passengers and 3,306 pounds (1,500 kg) of freight. The aircraft could also provide sleeping berths for a total of nineteen plus the five crew, but on the longer runs, they were meant to only carry seventeen passengers to fit 1½ tons of mail and baggage. The large fuselage held two decks, with the mail loaded into a large hold in the upper deck that was located behind the crew, which was then sent into compartments on the lower deck. The deep streamlined hull meant that the interior could be much larger and more spacious than in previous vessels, and it incorporated as many modern features as possible. That space was mainly taken out by two large passenger cabins, divided by class. There were also lavatories, separated for women and men, a large kitchen and a promenade cabin. There was also a small but well-stocked wine cellar, a feature that undoubtedly livened many a long flight.

Above this was the crew cabin, which contained the pilot and co-pilot as well as the flight engineer, radio operator, and navigator. There were also two stewards to ensure that every passengers' need was seen to, and their job also included cooking the on-board meals. To air travelers today used to being given a tiny packet of peanuts or pretzels, the menus they prepared must seem staggering. *Pâté de foie gras* was a regular item, as was ox tongue and York ham, roast fillet of lamb, and poached *écosse*. There were also salads for those who wanted something lighter, and for dessert a passenger could have Peach Melba, figs, or *crêpes* Suzette.

A still relatively new choice in aviation design was mounting the engines into the wing itself, reducing drag from the usual choice of previous flying boats, which was to mount them above the lower of two wings. Another useful installation was the use of the newest Gouge wing flaps, which meant that despite being significantly larger than the biplanes they were replacing, the new Empire boats had a shorter take-off and landing distance.

The initial prototype took to the air for the first time on July 4, 1936 and was considered a complete success. Short Brothers had done their work well and

An Empire at rest. (*Photograph courtesy of Dan Shumaker*)

had produced a flying boat that was capable of a major transformation of how air travel worked all over the British Empire in terms of speed, comfort, and reliability. By January of the next year, the aircraft were entering service in the Mediterranean, and by mid-year, they were regularly flying between England and South Africa, and were linking Britain's holdings in the western hemisphere by flying from Bermuda to New York. By December, the aircraft were completing the route between England and Australia, having previously linked India and Australia. The first aircraft to arrive in Australia was *Centaurus*, commanded by Captain J. W. Burgess. The very arrival of the aircraft proved the practicality of the route, and *Centaurus* was to fly on to New Zealand thereafter in advance of beginning a regular route there as well. Beyond proving the boat and the route, the arrival of *Centaurus* was a promotional coup, and it also had corollary effects for promoting the purchase of British designs.

Centaurus had covered 13,048 miles (21,000 km) in eighteen days, and upon its arrival, it was the largest and most advanced aircraft ever seen in Australia. Even moored, the aircraft drew tourists and generated daily newspaper articles before flying on to New Zealand, and then heading back to England after three weeks, completing a round trip of 34,361 miles (55,300 km). The massive journey came with no hiccups and made the Australians even more eager to receive their own boats, the first of which was *Coolangatta*, which arrived at the end of March 1938.

In actual operation, there were downsides. The technology was far superior to what had been designed previously, but when the aircraft were designed, there was no such thing as a pressurized cabin, which meant that the aircraft could not climb over the weather. On the long-range flights, this meant that the

Side view of an Empire (or C-Class) flying boat. (*Photograph from the Fred Kullas Collection, 1000aircraftphotos.com*)

aircraft would have to plow through sandstorms, monsoons, or through bumpy air created by the tropical heat. This was not aided by the fact that the boats were slow and rather noisy, and this in turn was not improved by the total of twenty-nine landings and take-offs the aircraft would make on the long-haul flight to Australia.

In part because of this, several aircraft would be lost in the relatively short span of time that Empire boats were able to fly along that route before the outbreak of war. Despite these losses and a few close scrapes, there was a total of only six passenger fatalities. In most cases, passengers were offloaded and put onto trains to carry on their journey—or sometimes bullock carts. A bigger problem for the airway was to repair downed aircraft. An aircraft brought down in a remote area of the Empire could be very far indeed from spare parts or skilled repair crews. In one case, when *Corsair* hit some rocks when trying to take-off for the Congo from Lake Victoria in March 1939, it took nineteen months to get the aircraft back to Hythe in England.

Empire boats were not meant just for Africa and the Far East but were meant to project British commercial power over the Atlantic. The first such flight was for surveying purposes, running from Hythe to Newfoundland in early July 1937. Sir Alan Cobham had pioneered another revolutionary idea that aided these boas over the Atlantic: in-flight refuelling. With that advantage in hand, *Cabot* first flew the mail on a flight of thirteen hours from Poole to Botwood in Newfoundland in September 1939, before flying on to New York. The first regular service flight had begun a month earlier, though Empire boats had been flying a regular twice weekly service between New York and Bermuda since 1937. The direct route between New York and London had still been conquered by the Boeing 314, but for a time there was a significant British presence on the air routes of the Atlantic. These routes were meant for *Cabot* and *Cambria*, which could fly the Atlantic from Ireland to Newfoundland with increased fuel loads and reduced overall accommodation. Unfortunately, the Empires only began to fly from Southampton to New York in August 1939. These boats, *Cabot* and *Caribou*, managed this with the still novel use of mid-air refuelling, being resupplied by Handley-Page Harrow bombers converted to flying tankers stationed in Ireland and Newfoundland.

The outbreak of war brought all of that to an abrupt end, with the British having to shut down Imperial Airways' North Atlantic routes, with some of the boats being passed on to the Royal Air Force for war service. In early 1940, Imperial Airways was merged with British Airways into the British Overseas Airways Corporation, which inherited twenty-one of these aircraft, and would continue to operate them for another six years. In B.O.A.C.'s service, the aircraft were used to keep open the imperial lifelines, particularly to South Africa, India, and Australia. These aircraft were moved from Hythe to a wartime base at Poole, converted to carry twenty-nine day passengers and as much cargo as possible. With the entry of Italy into the war, the route had to change to what was termed the "Horseshoe Route," running from Britain to South Africa, then up to Cairo to link back to the older eastern portion of the route to Sydney and Auckland. With the fall of Singapore, the route terminated in Calcutta.

Two Empire boats were lost in R.A.F. service, *Clio* and the pioneering *Cabot*. Both of these were taking part in the Battle of Norway in May 1940 and were shot down by the Luftwaffe. Two more aircraft would be lost to wartime accidents. On the Australian side, five of the Empire boats were used by the RAAF: *Centaurus*, *Calypso*, *Coogee*, *Coolangatta*, and *Clifton*. All but the last two would be lost in wartime service. Accidents would claim the others as they carried out transport and coastal patrol duties, except for *Centaurus*, which was destroyed in a Japanese air raid in early March 1942. Destroyed alongside her on the same occasion was the still-civilian *Corinna*. Two more Empires were lost to possible or confirmed enemy action while still wearing their civilian colours. *Corio*, still in service with Imperial Airways, was shot down by the Japanese in late January 1942, and it is believed that a similar fate befell *Circe*, serving under Qantas, less than a month later.

The war was harsh on the Empire boats, but the post-war would prove even harder. Given their heavy engagement—and significant losses—it is perhaps fitting that the first flying boat to land at newly-liberated Singapore would be an Empire, *Coriolanus*, on October 8, 1945. *Coriolanus* would in fact be the last of the Empires to serve. As the world rapidly outpaced them and the type began to be withdrawn from service, *Coriolanus* inaugurated a new air route from Sydney, Australia, to Fiji, which it would fly until 1947. She would also be the last of the Empire boats to exist, being broken up in Rose Bay in 1948.

In their service life, the Empire boats were updated continuously, taking on a variety of marks and new designations with each generation. All told, production came to forty-two aircraft across eleven different variants. Four were marks of the S.23, which accounted for thirty-one of the aircraft. These Mk I, Mk II ("Bermuda"), and Mk III ("Atlantic") aircraft—two each of the latter pair—mostly just came with significantly more powerful versions of the Pegasus engine, reaching 920 hp. The last S.23 was the S.23M, which came with a pair of Boulton-Paul gun turrets and anti-submarine radar, two Mk I aircraft being converted for this purpose. After this came the various marks of the S.30, which were re-equipped with Bristol Perseus engines that were more efficient. The airframe was strengthened as well, and performance in terms of range was comparable to the original S.23 aircraft. There were five versions of the S.30 with minor changes, accounting for nine aircraft in total. Two of these Mk III aircraft would also be converted for military use as the S.30M. The last development was to be the S.33, constructed in essentially the same way as the S.30, but using Bristol Pegasus XI engines. Two were finished and delivered, with a third being scrapped before completion.

A last aside worth mentioning about the Empire boats is the most unusual way in which they were used in a single example, a unique attempt to solve a range issue. Imperial Airways always wanted to extend the range of the Empire type. In 1937, R. H. Mayo, the technical general manager of the airline, came up with the idea of piggybacking a smaller flying boat on top of a modified S.23. This came to be called the Short/Mayo Composite. The idea was based around the knowledge that an aircraft could carry more weight in the air than it could take-off with in terms of payload and fuel. Thus, the modified S.23, known as S.21 Maia, would use its power to lift the S.20 Mercury aircraft up to altitude, where it would release the aircraft on its back and return to base while Mercury carried on across the Atlantic.

To give a sense of just how powerful Maia was, she was lifting an aircraft that weighed 20,500 lb (9,299 kg) when fully loaded for composite work. The air-launching gave the aircraft a theoretical range of 3,900 miles (6,276 km). The first attempt at this sort of work was undertaken in January 1938, with attendant success. As a result, on July 20, the composite made its first transatlantic flight, which was followed in October by a flight from Dundee in Scotland to Cape Town. Only the one composite was ever built, eventually being superseded by better technology. The war ultimately put an end to it, with Maia destroyed by German aircraft in 1941, and Mercury broken up for her aluminum. Strangely, this weird little off-shoot had a lasting impact on the Space Age. When NASA needed to transport the space shuttle into the air for test flights, a NASA engineer named John Kiker remembered the Short Mayo composite, with a Boeing 747 standing in for the Short Empire.

The Empire flying boats were, whatever model they came in, some of Britain's most successful passenger aircraft. At a time when even large airlines such as Pan Am would take on only a handful of examples of their large flying boats, it

The Short/Mayo Composite. (*Photograph courtesy of Dan Shumaker*)

is worth noting the heavy number of these four-engined passenger aircraft that served Britain, Australia, and New Zealand. At one point, seeing one would have been as regular a sight as many passenger aircraft today—albeit with numbers that still could not compare to air traffic today in terms of scale. The Empire boats were Britain's main method of making passenger travel that spanned the globe, and for a time, they were potent symbols of the size of the Empire they were named for. While no physical trace of these aircraft remains today, their legacy across the world remains intact as the main jewel in Britain's contribution to the golden age of flying boat passenger travel.

33

Short Sunderland: Britain's Sea Hunter

While the Short Empire traversed the British Empire, the Short Sunderland could be said to have defended it. This was perhaps a natural outgrowth of an aircraft that was, in part, based on the S.23 Empire that had preceded it. What emerged from this process of evolution and re-engineering, however, was a very different bird altogether. The Sunderland would be a scourge upon Britain's enemies, and could probably be called the most successful large combat flying boat of all time.

The Sunderland was enormously capable, and this was amply demonstrated not only by the type's wartime service, but also the fact that it survived well into the post-war world. In civilian use as the Sandringham, the type served as late as the 1970s—a tough survivor in a world far different than the one it had been born into.

Specifications: Sunderland III

First Flight: 1937
Powerplant: Four Bristol Pegasus XVIII nine-cylinder radial engines, 1,065 hp
Armament: Sixteen 7.7-mm (0.303-inch) Browning machine guns, two 12.7-mm (0.50-inch) M2 Browning machine guns, various ordnances in bombs, depth charges, and mines
Top Speed: 210 mph (336 kph)
Range/Service Ceiling: 1,780 miles (2,848 km), 16,000 feet (4,880 metres)
Dimensions: Length 85 feet 4 inches (26 metres), height 32 feet 10½ inches (10 metres), wingspan 112 feet 9½ inches (34.39 metres)
Number Built: 777

The most potent flying boat in the British inventory has often had its origins attributed to the Short Empire boats. While their technical advancement and proven ability undoubtedly influenced future designs, there was no direct path between the two aircraft. The capabilities of long range, four-engined flying boats that the Empire boats proved did generate much knowledge that could be used for successor aircraft. As early as 1933, the British had issued a specification looking towards the future, R.2/33. The specification called for the development of the next generation aircraft to carry out various duties over long distances, which could also potentially carry out maritime reconnaissance missions. A maximum limit was placed on the engines, so the new aircraft could only carry a total of four. The specification was issued early enough that either a biplane or a monoplane design could be considered, which demonstrates a lack of a direct line in and of itself between the Empires and the Sunderlands.

Short was already working in the early stages on a military flying boat but put its emphasis on designing the S.23. The knowledge and advancement that went into that aircraft would be put into the company's military project. By October 1934, the company had decided on the general configuration of the aircraft. The aircraft might superficially have resembled the S.23, but the internally-designated S.25 was a much-improved aerodynamic design that from the outset was meant for combat. The hull was deeper than that of the Empire boats, but in general terms, the construction was similar. Where it differed was in the fact that the engines might appear oddly placed to an observer. This was because the centre of gravity was considered to be too far back on the Empire boats, and rather than be faced with the headache of designing a new wing, the company swept the wing back instead. The exterior of the aircraft was flush-riveted to give it every advantage in terms of aerodynamics, and the hull construction was extremely robust. Interestingly, though tough in the air, the Sunderland's hull was not built for heavy seas, and an aircraft wishing to land had to find calmer coastal waters first. While Sunderlands would take part in search-and-rescue operations, they would not themselves usually be able to pick up survivors. One last feature of the hull was its single step, designed to help "unstick" the aircraft from the water with a minimum of effort.

Inside, the aircraft was designed for a crew of seven (this would increase in wartime to eleven), and the first model to see service, the Mk I, was to be powered with four Bristol Pegasus XXII engines. The fuel for these was in ten self-sealing fuel tanks located in the wings. The aircraft also came with a nose and tail turret (two 7.7-mm (0.303-inch) machine guns in the nose turret, four more in the tail turret) along with two more guns (also 7.7-mm (0.303-inch) guns) in hatches on the upper aft fuselage. The aircraft was meant to carry a heavy offensive load, and in any event, in practical use, the armament of the aircraft would scale up quite a bit. If the crew were pleased by the defences and capabilities of the aircraft, they would also be pleased by the fact that the passenger-carrying ancestry had carried through. Internally, the aircraft had two decks, the lower of which had six bunks for the crew to take turns sleeping, along with a galley with stove, a porcelain flushing toilet like that found on a yacht, and there was even space in the capacious hull for a small machine repair shop.

The Air Ministry received the proposal for the aircraft that would encompass all this in late 1934, and the Air Ministry authorized the construction of a prototype

A Sunderland looking powerful on her take-off run. (*Photograph courtesy of Dan Shumaker*)

alongside a competing aircraft, the Saro A.33. In the event, the A.33 prototype was lost owing to structural collapse during high-speed taxi tests, leaving the Short design in splendid isolation (the A.33's unusual wing is worth mention here. Though a four-engined design, the high wing featured no central connection to the hull, stringing all four along an unbroken span, braced to the sponsons. This unique feature did not hold up in testing). The first Sunderland prototype flew on April 21, 1938, with John Parker at the controls. This and the other test flights were successful, and after turret tests and testing of the auto-pilot, it was turned over for operational evaluations. These, too, were successful and the prototype became a service aircraft. It was lost in 1942 when it crashed while escorting a convoy and its depth charges exploded.

The R.A.F. committed early on to twenty-one aircraft, with the Sunderland becoming Britain's first four-engined military flying boat, with the first produced examples going to 210 Squadron at Pembroke Dock and 230 Squadron in Singapore. The British well realized the formidable nature of the aircraft on their hands. The Sunderlands could stay in the air for ten hours, bringing a payload of 2,000 lb (907 kg) to any fight and defending themselves with eight guns. A related bonus was the fact that, when war came, the Sunderlands were the only aircraft that could patrol out far from their bases to defend convoys and other shipping. When war came, there were more Sunderlands on hand, but far from enough. Still, from the very beginning, this aircraft would make its mark.

Britain declared war on September 3, and by the 8th, Sunderland flying boats had carried out their first attack on German U-boats, albeit without success. The trouble was that the bombs the Sunderland had been equipped with early on were either 250-lb (113-kg) or 500-lb (227-kg) weapons, and the specialized naval bombs the British had ordered off the drawing board performed poorly in reality. Depth charges were not yet available, though they held the potential to change the game when they did. As it was, the first "kill" by a Sunderland of a U-boat did not occur until January 30, 1940. A Sunderland pursued U-55, damaged by naval gunfire, and harassed it to the point that the captain scuttled her. The first full kill would come under Australian hands, when an RAAF-operated Sunderland destroyed a U-boat in July.

In these early days, Luftwaffe aircraft were a potent danger, and by the Fall of France, a more present one. In these early encounters, the Sunderland was more successful. Unlike many large flying boats, even when caught alone by enemy aircraft, Short's masterpiece proved more than capable of defending itself. Part of this was down to the structural integrity of the craft itself, but it also carried a heavy armament that was arranged in such a way as to ensure the aircraft had no blind spots, especially when near the surface of the water. As time progressed, the Sunderland only became a pricklier customer for German pilots and aircrew. In one encounter in April 1940, six Junkers Ju 88 bombers—superb aircraft in their own right—tried to shoot down a Sunderland. The Germans' weapons outranged those of the British, and with icy nerve, the rear gunner of this particular Sunderland held his fire until the Germans closed to point-blank range before opening up, his four gun barrels firing right into the nose of the enemy. That doomed Ju 88 crashed into the sea and a second got away with only a light mauling and trailing smoke. The remaining aircraft withdrew. The exact same aircrew would repeat their performance, this time against Bf 109 fighters, while on a mission to locate the battlecruiser *Scharnhorst*. Attacked by four fighters, the Sunderland's crew shot one down and damaged all the other ones, since the low-flying Sunderland left so few avenues for attack.

The British eventually produced ninety Mk I Sunderlands, and in the early years of the war, they went wherever the British needed, from participating in the Norwegian campaign to carrying important personages on various missions. Over time, they began to take on ASV radar, making them more capable still. This reflected Britain's military situation. Even in retreat and peril, the Sunderland proved more and more necessary. When retreating, it was capable of great feats, such as evacuating the Kings of Yugoslavia and Greece with their families, even carrying eighty-seven passengers and somehow not sinking. But where Britain needed to strike back, it was becoming critical: the U-boats were once again doing great damage to Britain's lifeline, and the presence of flying boats with the convoys served three purposes. First, the Sunderlands might well sink a U-boat. Second, even if they only damaged the submarine, that could leave it crippled on the surface, easy prey for the surface escorts the Sunderland's crew would whistle up. Third, the mere presence of a Sunderland could deter attack. Even if a German submarine was almost certain his anti-aircraft gunners could deal with air attack, the risk of damage was usually far too great. The U-boat captains ordinarily preferred to dive back under the waves, where they were significantly slower. Thus even just having a Sunderland spot a U-boat could save a merchant ship.

By the end of 1941, the Mk II Sunderland was coming into service. In addition to having Pegasus XVIII engines with superchargers that developed 1,065 hp, the aircraft had updated ASV radar and a new armament. This consisted of a new tail turret that had double the ammunition of the previous model, as well as a new dorsal turret in later examples. Only forty-three of this model were produced before it was rapidly replaced by the Mk III aircraft, which first flew in December 1941. The Mk III proved to be the mainstay of the type, with 386 were made (sources disagree on the numbers, with the total perhaps as high as 407). They had a redesigned hull for better aerodynamic performance and were slightly heavier and thus slightly slower than their predecessors. This was made up for by the addition of, over time, more ammunition for the gunners and the supplying of Browning 12.7-mm (0.50-inch) machine guns on the sides to replace guns removed from the Mk II. These aircraft also came with an updated radar unit, as the Germans had adapted to the Sunderland's old equipment. Most important of all, the Mk III aircraft started to be equipped with depth charges, suddenly becoming a much more lethal opponent for the U-boats. The storage method for these depth charges meant more ordnance could be carried, and the aircraft also began to take on light anti-personnel bombs meant to suppress the anti-aircraft crewmen of U-boats.

The Sunderlands may have been a lethal opponent, but German submarines continued to evolve to survive in the ever-harsher waters of the Atlantic. It is important to remember that the defensive armament of a U-boat consisted of heavy anti-aircraft batteries, weapons that could be extremely dangerous to any aircraft, and they outranged the Sunderland's own guns. Nevertheless, by 1943, it seemed like the U-boats were on the defensive and that victory over their menace might be just past the horizon. However, as far as the Allied aircraft were concerned, the U-boats were about to strike back. To combat the rising numbers of hostile aircraft, anti-aircraft armaments on U-boats began to increase. Not only were these improved, long-range boats a renewed menace to convoys, they started mounting increasingly heavy anti-aircraft armaments of 20-mm and 37-mm weapons in various configurations, a lethal punch against aircraft. Sunderland losses to U-boats began to rise.

The British response was to just give the Sunderland more punch of its own. Four additional 7.7-mm (0.303-inch) machine guns were added onto the newest Mk III Sunderlands rolling off the assembly lines, giving these aircraft a total of twelve guns. This new Sunderland is reputed to have been called "Stachelschewin" by the Germans, meaning "Porcupine" (the name is often attributed generally to the Sunderland, and it is difficult to say with certainty when the term came into use, or indeed if it ever was used regularly). It was not just the U-boats that felt the increased sting of the Flying Porcupines, but the Luftwaffe as well, which already had significant reason to dislike tangling with Sunderlands. One memorable incident came in June 1943, when eight Junkers Ju 88s of KG 40 tried to jump a Sunderland of 461 Squadron over the Bay of Biscay. The ensuing battle lasted for over an hour, and three of the Ju 88s were shot down. The Sunderland had a crew member killed, lost an engine, and limped home to a forced-landing on a beach in Cornwall on three engines.

The Mk III Sunderlands remained in production until the end of 1943, and in that time frame, they also began to be used more regularly as transport aircraft as the U-boat threat began to recede. B.O.A.C. made use of several examples that had been converted for long-range passenger travel from mid-1943 onwards. This would have long-term effects that nobody at the time likely intended or had any conception of.

In the meantime, the fourth Sunderland variant was about to become different enough to be classified as an entirely new aircraft. The R.A.F. had issued a new specification, R.8/42, to replace or enhance the Sunderland. Among other things, the aircraft was to have better engines and an even heavier defensive armament. Short stretched the forward hull by about 3 feet, added a new planing bottom, a thicker-skinned wing, and the Bristol Hercules engine (developing 1,720 hp each). Another critical difference was the armament, which was upgraded to six Browning machine guns in the nose and tail turrets and the dorsal positions, with two 20-mm Hispano cannon in a dorsal turret and two fixed 7.7-mm (0.303-inch) machine guns. Initial tests of this aircraft found that the more powerful engines caused a certain amount of aerodynamic instability, and the tail had to be redesigned to suit this. In time, the Sunderland Mk IV became known as the Short Solent, and in the event, out of the thirty aircraft ordered, only eight aircraft, plus two prototypes, were ever completed. This was mainly since the first Solent/Mk IV did not fly until April 1945, by which time, it was unnecessary.

The final variant was the Mk V, which made it to production before the Mk IV did. The main issue for the Mk V was solving the developing power problem in the aircraft. The weight of the Sunderland had steadily been increasing owing to the equipment mounted, and to achieve full performance, engines routinely had to be run at combat capacity, which inevitably created a strain and reduced engine life. The solution to the problem came from Australian Sunderland crews, who suggested installing American Twin Wasp engines, and in early 1944, a pair of Mk III Sunderlands were taken off the production line to be equipped with the Twin Wasps. The engines were paired with new constant-speed fully feathering propellers and solved the power issues without any appreciable decrease in range. The Twin Wasps also made the aircraft even more durable: it could stay aloft with two engines knocked out on the same wing. Switching to Twin Wasps made sense, and the first production example arrived in February 1945. The last Mk III Sunderlands had been receiving newer Mk VI C ASV radar, and this became standard on the Mk V. By this time, the Sunderland was in some ways an aircraft without a purpose. There were very few U-boats left for it to seek, and only 155 Mk V aircraft were built, with thirty-three Mk IIIs converted over.

With the war coming to an end, it looked as if the Sunderland's career was over, but this doughty bulldog was not going to surrender to history without a fight. Many aircraft were withdrawn from service or scrapped, true, but the R.A.F.'s post-war needs would keep the Sunderland employed (there are persistent stories that brand-new Sunderlands were rolled off the production lines to fulfil contracts, then promptly sunk. This author has not been able to find more than anecdotal evidence of this, though there may have been discussion about disposing of obsolete aircraft in this manner). In Europe, the Sunderland was in a world of prepared airfields—in the Far East, there was far less infrastructure for an aircraft to rely on. The same theories that helped produce the SR.A/1 certainly applied to this tough heavyweight. As a result, it remained in service in the Far East much later under several colours, the last of which was the Royal New Zealand Air Force, which only retired its last Sunderland in 1967. Sunderlands would serve in the Korean War under British colours, where they flew daily ten- to fourteen-hour patrols until late 1954. The last of the R.A.F.'s Sunderlands were retired in 1959, and the French carried on using their Sunderlands until 1960. Even in Europe, the end of World War II did not mean the end of the Sunderland's useful role. The type had its last European "hurrah" during the Berlin Airlift, with Sunderland aircraft flying supplies to isolated Berlin and landing on Havel Lake until ice prevented their further usage.

Meanwhile, far and away from combat, the Sunderland had taken on a second life as the Sandringham. B.O.A.C. had been operating Sunderlands as passenger aircraft since 1943 with bench seating, and these aircraft came to be called the Sandringham. After VE-Day, these aircraft had their camouflage painted over and became true passenger aircraft. B.O.A.C. was eager to reopen the Empire flying boat routes they had been forced to abandon by the outbreak of war, and the Sandringham was really the only available option if they wished to do this quickly. The S.25V Sandringham had all of its military equipment stripped out and was usually powered by the same Twin Wasp engines with which it had been originally equipped. The difference was that the aircraft had the same powerplant but significantly less weight, and thus a higher cruising speed and service ceiling. These aircraft were redesigned to carry twenty-two passengers on day routes and sixteen in sleeper configurations.

B.O.A.C. took on nine of these aircraft, and five of a thirty-seven-seat version were sold to Scandinavian airlines. Short Seafords/Mk IVs became the Short S.45 Solent, being almost identical to the Sandringham except they could carry a maximum of forty-four passengers. B.O.A.C. bought twelve of these, which served until 1950 when land-based aircraft replaced them. The Sandringhams lasted significantly longer than that, however. Many were passed on to other airlines and served as late as the early 1980s, an astounding piece of longevity.

A now-preserved Sunderland flew for the last time in 1996, operated by the Fantasy of Flight museum; it was reported to be kept in flyable condition until that museum was closed in 2014. Many other Sunderlands have been preserved, and there are plans to raise some discovered wrecks for restoration. There are

A conversion to a Sandringham that looks rather the worse for wear. (*Photograph courtesy of Michael Bajcar*)

The finished product. (*Photograph courtesy of Michael Bajcar*)

also considerable written materials on the Sunderland and its descendants that can cover far more than a short chapter ever can; there are also the invaluable contributions by those who flew the aircraft and their descendants. All of these things keep the legacy of the Sunderland alive and well. While an aviation enthusiast is unlikely to see one flying again, though all of those reading this will undoubtedly hope to see that one day, the legacy is easily one of the most well-preserved of any aircraft in this book. It is also indicative of the durability of the fascination of these large flying boats that such substantial knowledge and enthusiasm for more information remains out there. The Sunderland lives on, with the survivors still drawing visitors and reminding people of the prowess of Britain's wartime flying boats.

34

Sikorsky S-38: Small Beginnings

In the annals of aviation history, the name Igor Sikorsky stands very tall indeed. One of aviation's early innovators, Sikorsky would continue making important contributions to the history of aviation for the rest of his life, almost all of them to the ultimate benefit of his adopted homeland, the United States. Sikorsky had fled his native Russia after the Bolshevik Revolution in 1917, finding refuge in a new land and enriching it as immigrants and refugees always have done. Immigration can be said to be the lifeblood of nations, a force that pumps in new ideas and ways of knowing, new tastes and sights and sounds. This is a fact very easy to forget when foolish and uninformed voices rise to say that immigrants and refugees are a negative factor—history proves the willfully ignorant very wrong indeed on this point. Igor Sikorsky was, and is, one small proof of the value of immigration and the acceptance of refugees.

The Sikorsky S-38 was by no means the first of Sikorsky's innumerable contributions to aviation in his adopted land, but it is certainly one of the better remembered ones. The graceful craft first took to the air in the late 1920s but has lingered on ever since both in memory and in fact. The S-38 would fly in many skies, and sometimes in ways never predicted by her designer, and it was a very successful civilian flying boat in her time.

Specifications: For S-38B

First Flight: 1928
Powerplant: Two Pratt & Whitney R-1340 Wasp nine-cylinder radial engines, 400 hp each
Armament: None
Top Speed: 120 mph (192 kph)
Range/Service Ceiling: 750 miles (1,200 km), 16,000 feet (4,878 metres)
Dimensions: Length 40 feet 3 inches (12.27 metres), height 13 feet 10 inches (4.22 metres), wingspan 71 feet 8 inches (21.85 metres)
Number Built: 101 (some sources state 120)

Igor Sikorsky had encountered relatively little success with his commercial aviation designs before the S-38 was first imagined. The last of them had only ever received six constructed examples, this being the S-36, but it had shown some promise and the decision was made to improve on it. The design was essentially scaled up 30 per cent, and every effort was made to maintain the same proportions of the previous aircraft. To do this, the engines were suspended from the upper wing on some of the aircraft's extensive strutting, and the wing floats of the S-36 were lowered. The hull itself remained proportional but was re-contoured and constructed of a wooden framework and skinned in duralumin. The aircraft would unfortunately forever be slow because of the masses of strutting and exposed wiring that created aerodynamic drag. In addition to just a mass of struts and braces, there was also exposed control wires, fixed landing gear, fat wings, and a large tail structure.

The hull was an elegant piece of construction, but the heavy strutting and high wing led the aircraft to be described famously as "a collection of parts, flying in formation." Despite this derisive nickname, Sikorsky was quite literally betting everything on the aircraft. He had already purchased the engines, propellers, and materials to build ten aircraft—he was taking a risk on the rising air-mindedness of the American populace that might, if he failed, carry away his entire company.

As designed, the S-38 could carry a total of between ten and twelve people, two of them crew, in civilian service. While it may not have been the far larger and more regular passenger flight experience of later, grand flying boats, the S-38 immediately attracted attention. The aircraft was ordered by the New York, Rio & Buenos Aires Line (NYRBA) in South America. The founder of NYRBA, the former World War I flying ace Ralph O'Neill, ensured that he purchased the very first S-38 off the line. This was rapidly followed by orders for Pan American for Caribbean service, and Western Air Express to Catalina Island. A trio of boats were also ordered by the U.S. Army (XC-6) and Navy (PS-2), and a single example became a luxury transport for John H. Whitney, publisher of the *New York Herald Tribune*. Sikorsky's gambit had paid off. He sold the aircraft he had risked his company on within two weeks, and after that business rapidly increased to the point where Sikorsky had to expand his operations to keep up with demand. This included moving to a new factory in Connecticut in early 1929, building a new airport and using the waters of the Long Island Sound to test the aircraft as they were completed.

These customers, with the addition of Northwest Airways and Curtiss Flying Service, also lapped up the main production variant, the S-38B. Over 100 of these were sold, and they were not terribly different from the original S-38. The main difference was the addition of more powerful Wasp engines and a greater fuel capacity to go along with it. This also ended up in military service with the Navy as the PS-3. The largest customer, owing to its primary position, in passenger aviation, was Pan Am—which had over thirty examples of the S-38 in service in the early 1930s. The S-38's service to Pan Am had big results for Sikorsky. Namely, it convinced Juan Trippe to order Sikorsky's larger passenger transports that followed, the four-engined S-40 and S-42. The diminutive S-38, aside from

A Sikorsky S-38C looking rather sleek. (*Photograph courtesy of Dan Shumaker*)

any other immediate accomplishments, thus had a very important in Sikorsky's future. The aircraft was important to Pan Am's future, too. The company had only started to fly in 1927, and a year later, Juan Trippe—with help from friends—managed to win two international routes to carry U.S. mail. The S-38s were to be used on these routes, and it was this aircraft's success in the moment that provided the foundation of Pan Am's future growth.

Juan Trippe wanted to make a splash with his S-38s, to use an appropriate metaphor. They enlisted no less a personage than Charles Lindbergh to make the first S-38 flight for the airline, making the first airmail flight to Panama before touring the Caribbean on a demonstration flight.

Over the next twenty years, Pan Am would rake in $50 million in profits just by carrying the mail. Small wonder Trippe was willing to make use of Sikorsky designs in the future!

There was one last production version to be considered, the S-38C. It did not differ terribly much from its predecessors, except in that it carried two more passengers and had a lower fuel capacity. Only around ten of this version was produced, coming into service in 1929 for shorter-haul passenger routes. The S-38C spent much of its service life in an idyllic setting, with many of the aircraft working for Inter-Island Airways, flying between the islands of Hawaii. The remaining aircraft served over the Great Lakes as part of Colonial Western Airways.

These commercial examples of the S-38 would serve on into the 1940s in some cases. The military aircraft did not last quite as long, but there were some interesting features worth mentioning. The Navy armed their PS-2s and PS-3s, mounting a gun position in the nose and tail with a single gun each. They then

Side view of another S-38. (*Photograph coutesy of Dan Shumaker*)

removed these and reclassified the aircraft as a transport and redesignated them RS-2 and RS-3. One of these even served the U.S. Marine Corps, serving both at the Marine base at Quantico and even operating as far afield as Nicaragua.

The S-38 did more than just ferry passengers for years and help cement an aviation titan—as if more were required to qualify it as a success—it became a vehicle for exploration and excitement that reflected the growing prevalence of private aviation. It was not a cheap aircraft, costing $50,000 in 1928. But the relatively wealthy took to it with extreme alacrity. The explorers Ora and Marin Johnson used the aircraft and their cameras to explore the splendours of Africa. The photographs and films they captured from the S-38 introduced many people, particularly Americans, to Africa in great numbers by showing them not just the continent but the majestic Mount Kilimanjaro.

Despite its size, the aircraft was no slouch in terms of accoutrements. In many ways, it can be called a forerunner of modern private jets, with the interior built with comfort in mind. Sikorsky's builders would make an aircraft with a custom interior, which could feature large chairs or comfortable couches. It is easy enough to slip into imagining a world of the rich and famous flying in their luxurious Sikorsky aircraft and rolling up on whatever beach they might want to. There is a romance to the image, certainly, and while the S-38 was not the first aircraft to take on this role and certainly not the last, a role in the popularizing of aviation can be attributed to it.

The aircraft simply suited the needs of the time for private owners, and it became as much of a status symbol as a car—though of considerably more utility and expense. Journalist Alan Farnham wrote of the S-38:

> So many private owners used their S-38s to commute to work that Manhattan's East River was sometimes congested with tycoons "yachting" in from Long Island. They could alight in water off the foot of Wall Street, then go straight to work.
>
> In 1935, Hib Johnson undertook an epic adventure in his S-38, flying it from his corporate headquarters in Racine, Wis., to the forests of Brazil–15,500 miles–in search of carnauba palms, which provided the wax used in Johnson's Wax. At a time when (by modern standards) few airports existed in the U.S. and virtually none existed in the undeveloped world, an amphibian was the only type of aircraft capable of making such a trip. As a Pan Am engineer once quipped, the S-38 carried "its own airport on its bottom."
>
> "The Aviator's Air Yacht," Online
> Farnham

Part of the secret to this success was that the S-38 not only was elegant, but relatively easy to fly. Years later, one of the pilots of the S-38 at the time, Vem Carstens, recalled flying the S-38 fondly:

> Certainly taking off from the water always caused problems, because the spray whipped up by the slipstream of the propellers was thrown into the cockpit windows. Visibility was nil until the amphibian rose onto the hull step. After that, taking off was simple. Even with a strong cross wind, touching down on the water turned out to be easy, as the hull had been particularly well designed.
>
> Moving either on the water or the land wasn't a problem. The landing speed of 50mph made it possible to use runways less than 500 yards long ... the way the S-38 took off gave the impression that it could lift any load. As for its flying qualities, they gave no cause for criticism.
>
> Nicolau, p. 79

Despite its success and despite its popularity with those who flew it, the S-38 did not survive with time. Scrapping and accidents slowly accounted for all the aircraft produced, and today, the only traces of it come in replica form. This was to change in 1994, when the son of Hib Johnson, Sam Johnson, decided to retrace his father's flight accompanied by his own sons—and all that would do for a flight that would link three generations of the family would be to make a working, replica S-38. Working with master craftsmen and utilizing archival Sikorsky materials, in a job that took three years and cost an estimated \$1.7 million in today's money, Johnson made his flight in 1998; after his death in 2004, there are plans to put the aircraft on display at the SC Johnson headquarters.

Another replica was built by real estate developer Tom Schrade, costing him \$1.2 million. This aircraft has been seen by probably more people than anybody since

A pair of U.S. Military S-38s, likely the unarmed versions. *iPhotograph from the Captain Robert E. Selff Collection, 1000aircraftphotos.com*)

the aircraft first moved into service, since it featured in the movie *The Aviator*. In the film, about the life of Howard Hughes, the famed aviator, eccentric, and mogul uses an S-38 as a luxury transport and it features as part of his romancing of Katherine Hepburn. This reflects reality in at least some regard, since Hughes did indeed own an S-38. According to Schrade, though he was paid for his flying in the movie, he gladly would have done it for free, just for the sheer joy of flying an aircraft he loved.

A last replica has been built by Walter Treadwell, a fine aviation builder who worked from scratch just out of idle interest in the aircraft using modern materials and construction methods to craft a scale replica of this vanished legend.

These replicas keep the S-38 alive today, and interest new generations of airshow attendants and aviation enthusiasts in this long-vanished era of aviation. Today, a venture like the S-38 might not seem much of a risk, but for Igor Sikorsky, it was possibly a matter of life and death for his company. The story of the S-38 more than adequately demonstrates the important convergence of two factors in history: skill and opportunity. The S-38 was a well-designed aircraft, even if by today's standards it might be said to have the best aerodynamic performance, to say the least. But it must be remembered that this was an era before wide-spread wind tunnel testing, before the importance of streamlining was properly understood by aviation designers. Sikorsky and his builders created an aircraft that excellently balanced stability with luxury. This excellent work took full advantage of the time in which it occurred. Aviation had transformed in just over twenty years from an experimental revolution into a popular pastime that had captured the imagination of the world. Flying had become reliable enough, and accessible enough, to allow people to fulfil their dreams for travel. The S-38 perfectly juxtaposed craft and luck, and as a result, it remains a small but crucial piece of aviation history.

35

Sikorsky VS-44: Sikorsky's Attempt at the Golden Age

The Sikorsky VS-44 was separated from the S-38 by less than a decade and is ample demonstration of how quickly an aviation company can grow and how far its capabilities can reach in a relatively short amount of time. Whereas the S-38 was a light civilian aircraft, the VS-44 was built for the then-lucrative trans-oceanic passenger trade. The story of the VS-44 is one of the intense corporate competition for this trade and of the great standard of luxury that these airborne wonders once sported.

The VS-44 rounds out the story of the great passenger flying boats of the golden age, and while it might be less well-known than the Boeing 314, it still provided an important part of aviation history and continues to inspire visitors today. The story of the VS-44 is one of dedication, tragedy, and survival against the odds—a story certainly of interest to any aviation enthusiast, to say nothing of a fan of flying boats.

Specifications

First Flight: 1937
Powerplant: Four Pratt & Whitney Twin Wasp R-1830-S1C3-G fourteen-cylinder radial engines, 1,200 hp each
Armament: None
Top Speed: Cruise speed 210 mph (337 kph)
Range/Service Ceiling: 3,800 miles (6,116 km), 17,500 feet (5,334 metres)
Dimensions: Length 79 feet 3 inches (24.15 metres), height 27 feet 7¼ inches (8.41 metres), wingspan 124 feet (37.79 metres)
Number Built: Four

Sikorsky had already experienced significant success in the large flying boat market with the S-42, which itself was a vast improvement on the already pioneering S-40. The S-42 had featured an all-metal structure with four Pratt &

Whitney Hornet engines that had developed 188 mph (302.5 kph) at top speed with a range of 1,200 miles (1,930 km). This was already impressive and a major stepping stone in the development of the United States' already burgeoning capabilities for trans-oceanic travel.

By 1940, Sikorsky had merged with Chance Vought (thus the VS designation) and needed a new aircraft. Pan Am's clippers had taken over the role that the S-42 used to occupy with newer aircraft, and a replacement was considered to reclaim this dominant position. Thankfully for these efforts, Sikorsky had an idea on the books from years before. A project that had been known as the S-44 had been kicking around since 1935, when the U.S. Navy had been considering "Flying Dreadnought" aircraft. Sikorsky and Consolidated were both invited to submit designs, a process to that Martin would be invited three years later.

The trouble for Sikorsky was cash. The other flying boats had been expensive enough, but the per-unit cost the new four-engined design Sikorsky was considering was over $300,000 per aircraft—an enormous sum at the time. This would just be to construct the aircraft and did not consider the cost of developing it. Thankfully, the Navy only wanted single prototypes to start with, and any building thereafter would only come after an extensive competitive testing process. Sikorsky got a contract for a prototype in June 1935 that was designated the XPBS-1. The boat that Sikorsky and his engineers turned to was to be significantly more advanced than anything they had previously built. Gone would be the high wing with its struts and engines mounted between the wing and the fuselage, in favour of an all-metal high-wing monoplane.

Sikorsky had been heading in this direction with his previous S-42 flying boat, which had become known as the "Flying Clipper" or the "Pan Am Clipper." The S-44 project removed all strutting except on the pylons and had a deep two-step hull that curved upwards to raise the tail clear of the spray. Blending the wing into the hull was far more important, and this tapering, fully cantilevered wing came with fully-articulated trailing flaps. Originally, the aircraft was to come with Pratt & Whitney R-1830-68 engines that developed 1,050 hp, which would give it a top speed of 227 mph (365 kph). As with many aircraft that are constructed close to the cutting edge of technology, the engineering and construction process was somewhat prolonged. It took a total of two years to build the XPBS-1, which flew for the first time on August 13, 1937.

Early testing revealed that while the aircraft was likely very well within the specifications for flight range, there were some issues in the air. The aircraft was found to have some stability problems, and these were traced to the wings. The response was to add some dihedral angling to the horizontal stabilizers. With this taken in hand, the aircraft was handed over to the Navy for evaluation in October. It would be joined by its Consolidated competitor, the XPB2Y-1, in mid-1938—the future Coronado. Immediately after that, the two aircraft began to engage in competitive testing against each other. For a moment, it must have looked to Sikorsky that his aircraft had triumphed. The Navy formally accepted the aircraft in January 1939, but then the Bureau of Air announced that they were going with the Coronado instead, with the aircraft announced as having won on a points basis.

This provoked an immediate crisis for the program, despite the aircraft itself doing well enough. The original prototype did enter limited naval service, being handed over to Patrol Wing Five, based at Norfolk in Virginia. Here it was used evaluate long-range bomber operations. It would survive until just after the declaration of war but would meet a sudden end. Assigned to transport squadron VF-2 out of Alameda, California, the prototype was used to run freight to and from Hawaii. On June 30, 1942, it was returning from Pearl Harbor on a routine flight and struck a log in San Francisco bay, rapidly sinking. One member of the flight crew, Lieutenant Thomas Roscoe, was killed. There were only minor injuries besides this, which was fortunate for the United States' war effort because among the crew and passengers was Admiral Chester Nimitz, the Commander of the Pacific Fleet.

This was, if anything, a secondary concern for Sikorsky at the time. There were very few prospects for a large four-engined flying boat in 1939—the market was well filled, with relatively few potential buyers to begin with. The program was likely on the way to being formally cancelled and was saved only by the arrival on the scene of American Export Airlines. AEA was a newly formed venture with a bold goal in mind: to break Pan American's hold on the Atlantic Ocean. For this, they needed a new, impressive flying boat that could compete with the Boeing 314—and Sikorsky seemed an ideal choice.

When the merged Vought-Sikorsky company was approached by AEA in December 1939 to create a commercial version of the S-44 project, the company was likely quite enthusiastic. AEA wanted a total of three aircraft, pending approval of AEA's transatlantic route by the U.S. government. Once this was achieved, the company set to work on what was now being designated as the VS-44A. AEA eagerly exercised its option to purchase three aircraft, bringing a total of $2.1 million into the company. Work began immediately on the new version of the aircraft, which was to accommodate thirty-two passengers on day flights, with the aircraft able to fly sixteen passengers in sleeper berths on overnight flights. Importantly for AEA, the company's new purchase would have luxury comparable to its Pan American rival, and most important of all would come with a 3,100-mile (4,989-km) range, which meant it could fly the Atlantic even when fully loaded.

Sikorsky's engineers had built in some interesting equipment to ensure that these new passenger aircraft could also provide some significant scientific data while on the New York–Lisbon run. The instrument required the cooperation of the U.S. Weather Bureau, the Navy, and the eventual operator. The aircraft used a radio sonde system to send regular weather conditions to the Weather Bureau, the first time such updates had been available. The Weather Bureau provided the equipment and the Navy provided the land bases to receive the information via radio. AEA was to provide the operators for the equipment, which could measure temperature, humidity, and the height of these weather features. Unlike sonde balloons sent over land, which could be recovered by having silk parachutes attached, there was a price to these regular sea-based sets of data. Namely, that it cost $40 every time one was sent up—since when the balloon deflated, the equipment simply sank into the ocean.

The first of the new aircraft would make its maiden flight on January 17, 1942 and was named *Excalibur*. The ambitious plan to challenge Pan Am on its home territory had to be modified, however: the United States was at war, and the vast infrastructure of the nation was being fully geared towards defeating the Axis powers. If AEA wanted to operate commercially, it needed to get approval a second time. As a result, AEA contracted with the Naval Air Transportation Service to provide wartime flights over the Atlantic.

Excalibur was soon joined by her two sisters: *Excambian* arrived in May 1942 and *Exeter* followed the next month. The aircraft flew a route between New York City that terminated in Foynes, Ireland, with an intermediate stop at Botswood in Newfoundland. They were only briefly commercial aircraft—total war demanded much, and it certainly demanded all the heavy transport capacity that could be laid on. The giant passenger flying boats were extremely useful in this regard, and since there was only ever a handful of these aircraft, nearly all of them were requisitioned. The VS-44s were no exception, and all three were swiftly pulled into naval service under the designation JRS2-1. The three served together only briefly before tragedy struck. Much like the original prototype, *Excalibur* would come to a sudden end. In October 1943, *Excalibur* was undertaking a routine take-off when some kind of pilot error occurred, and the aircraft crashed back down into the waters at Botswood, killing eleven people.

This tragedy was an outlier, and by and large, the aircraft flew well under their military colours, and did so until late in 1944. By that time, the progress of the war was such that the military could begin to draw down some of their expenditures, and as a result, the aircraft were returned to AEA and repainted in gleaming white civilian colours and they kept flying their freight and passenger routes on military contracts. The war was coming to an end, and perhaps AEA looked forward to once again pursuing its Atlantic dreams. Sadly, this was not to be.

AEA's assets had been acquired by American Airlines, which had very definite plans for its post-war operations—which involved the total dissolution of any sea-based flights once the war came to an end. AEA's last flight with its VS-44s would come in October 1945, and the aircraft were put up for sale. The aircraft had a good reputation, but their post-war life became something like that of used cars. The aircraft began to pass through a series of owners, all of them trying to employ the aircraft in cargo flights or as charter aircraft.

Exeter ended up with a company called Tampico Airlines, based in South America. In carrying out these duties, the aircraft took on a record flight from Lima, Peru, to New York City. It would not prove to be a glorious career for an aircraft meant to steal the skies from Pan Am. It did better than *Exeter*, however, which would be lost in what is believed to be an episode of skullduggery. The aircraft was put in use by a charter operation for Skyways International, having

The Sikorsky VS-44 serving in Avalon Airways colours. (*Photograph from the David Horn Collection, 1000aircraftphotos.com*)

The VS-44 airborne for American Export Airlines. (*Photograph from the Ray Crupi Collection, 1000aircraftphotos.com*)

previously been based in Uruguay. Supposedly, this charter was meant to carry weapons to Paraguayan rebels. On the return flight on August 15, 1947, the aircraft came in for a night landing at Montevideo and crashed, killing four out of the five crew members, though the two passengers survived.

Excambian soldiered on, only to find itself impounded for nonpayment of fees in Baltimore. Ultimately, she was sold off for a mere $500. This was by now the 1950s, and her new owners believed they could turn her into a flying trading post, operating up and down the Amazon River. This was an unusual idea for any aircraft, and particularly for a flying boat of this size. Perhaps not surprisingly, the venture went bust eventually and *Excambian* was left to rot as a derelict at Ancou in Peru. Here the aircraft might simply have wasted away and become mere dust in the pages of history, but it was luckier than many aircraft—it was purchased in 1957 by two of the owners of Avalon Air Transport, Walter von Kleinsmid and Dick Probert. The men felt the VS-44 would be perfect for the tourist trade, even if their choice would require significant tender loving care before the aircraft could be put to that use.

She was ferried all the way to Long Beach, California. There, the aircraft not only was restored but significantly modified, and rebuilt for service with forty-seven passengers. It was placed in service with AAT on a run from Long Beach to Catalina Island, both in California, and was called *Mother Goose* given that it was a bigger sister to the other Grumman Goose aircraft the company had. She flew during the summers to meet travel demands, then spent its winters being maintained, a calm life for such an aircraft. Here the aircraft truly revealed the capabilities of Sikorsky's original design, since it flew a total of 8,172 flights and carried 211,246 passengers in complete safety. It may well have been an idyllic lifestyle for any aircraft, and likely the best possible service life available to a large flying boat in the jet age. Gentle hops in warm weather on calm waters continued until 1967, when the aircraft was sold again to Antilles Airboats and Charles Blair, the husband of actress Maureen O'Hara.

The aircraft was flown to St. Croix in the U.S. Virgin Islands to start Caribbean flights as a passenger ferry. It was in this role only until January 10, 1969. A take-off run was aborted, and the aircraft struck some submerged objects. Like its sisters, the aircraft began to sink—but was more fortunate. It sank in only 4 feet of water, and thus could be drained and towed ashore. Unfortunately, the owners decided that restoring the aircraft to flying condition was simply too expensive a proposition. They abandoned the aircraft for a second time, leaving it to rot on the beach in 1972. It lingered there for six years, even apparently being used as a hot dog stand.

Excambian's luck continued to hold, because it was donated in 1976 to the Naval Aviation Museum in Florida. It had to endure for a little longer, since it sat outside until 1983 before restoration efforts began. The effort to restore it was undertaken in an era where this was no longer just a passenger airplane of significant size, but by luck, *Excambian* had outlived all its counterparts to become unique. *Excambian* was the last of the grand passenger flying boats by the 1980s, all of its competitors having long since disappeared. It was the last of a vanished era, and it was loaned to the New England Air Museum permanently to undergo restoration.

This process would ultimately consume more than 300,000 hours of painstaking effort. The start of the process involved going home; with the last VS-44 coming back to a Sikorsky facility, in Bridgeport, Connecticut. From here, *Excambian* arrived at Sikorsky Memorial Airport, also in Connecticut, on April 6, 1983. It took some time to plan the restoration, and in the event, it was carried out by volunteers. Many of these volunteers were current or former Sikorsky employees, and quite a few had worked on the VS-44 when it was first built. Not only had the aircraft returned home, but some of the hands who had lovingly built it in the first place now took their turn restoring its grandeur.

The restoration coordinator was Harry Hleva, a thirty-six-year veteran of Sikorsky who was then retired. Hleva had been one of the original builders of the VS-44 and spoke with great pride of the efforts of the team he called "first rate," working in excellent collaboration and pride to save an aircraft that was in dire straits when they began work. The project ultimately required the replacement of 37 per cent of the aircraft's structure, and 97 per cent of the skin. Oxidation had been very unkind to *Excambian*. Nevertheless, the process was pursued by these dedicated hands, all of it carried out less than 300 feet from where the aircraft had been born decades before. *Excambian* can now be seen, resplendently painted in its original AEA colours, at the New England Air Museum.

The story of the VS-44 is one that not only covers the decades but is full of the unexpected. An aircraft built as a competitor to giants such as Pan American ended up outliving all its competitors. The process required a lot of luck and willing operators, and it still claimed two out of three of the giants. But with all its luck, the last vestiges of the "golden age" of passenger flying boats may well have simply rotted away on a beach regardless, though it lasted long enough to become a valuable and fascinating historical artifact. The aircraft is restored now, but it is well worth noting how this came to happen. The volunteers who restored this aircraft did work that should be as well regarded by history as that of the engineers and pilots who designed and flew it. Restoration efforts around the globe continue to rebuild the legacy of historical aviation. Sometimes it stays on the ground, other times their work takes to the skies, yet all of it requires vast amounts of effort, passion, and dedication—to say nothing of skill and perseverance. Their work has fascinated generations ever since. That the VS-44 can still be appreciated today, that it can fascinate new generations, is entirely down to these people.

36

Supermarine Southampton: The Old Guard

In the 1920s, the Supermarine Southampton was a pioneer. Like the Canadian Vickers Vedette, by the beginning of the 1930s, it had already become a dinosaur. The pace of change never ceased, but the Southampton has a unique place in the history of flying boats that is well worth exploration. It was a durable, well-liked aircraft that had a long service career in an era where new aircraft were rapidly rising to replace the old. Along the way, the Southampton would be the platform from which the British Empire "showed the flag," and the Southampton would become famous for long-distance, trailblazing flights that would pave the way for other aircraft. In a final testament to its success, its service life of eleven years was the longest of any R.A.F. flying boat bar one: the legendary Sunderland.

Specifications: Data for Southampton II

First Flight: 1925
Powerplant: Two Napier Lion VA inline W-block engines, 500 hp each
Armament: Three 7.7-mm (0.303-inch) Lewis machine guns, up to 1,100 lb (498 kg) of bombs
Top Speed: 95 mph (153 kph)
Range/Service Ceiling: 544 miles (876 km), 5,950 feet (1,814 metres)
Dimensions: Length 49 feet 8½ inches (15.15 metres), height 20 feet 5 inches (6.2 metres), wingspan 75 feet (22.86 metres)
Number Built: Eighty-three

To say that the Southampton was fortuitous for the Royal Air Force would be a significant understatement. In the mid-1920s, the R.A.F.'s stock of flying boats were of World War I vintage, and aging rapidly. They were in desperate need of a replacement when they were approached by Supermarine about a military version of an already developed aircraft, the Supermarine Swan designed by R. J.

Mitchell, who would later go on to design the most famous British aircraft of all: the Supermarine Spitfire.

The Swan had been designed and flown in 1924 as an experimental aircraft, part of a development program to replace the Felixstowe F.5, which had come into service in 1918. What emerged as the Southampton was a much more capable design. The aircraft was designed with a two-step, circular section hull of a sort known as a "Linton Hull" in the 1920s. This was a significantly more flexible hull, and the steps were built onto it as a separate structure. Significant freeboard was included in the hull design in order to keep the open cockpits and the propellers well clear of any spray while on the water. All the fuel was to be carried under the wings, and as a result the hull could be traversed in its entire length by the crew, who could even put up hammocks. This was to say nothing of the radio installation and cooking equipment added to make the aircraft entirely self-contained. When it came time to describe the aircraft's combat design, one observer for the National Advisory Committee for Aeronautics stated:

> The whole seaplane has been designed with a view to eliminate "blind spots," i.e., areas blanketing the gunners' view and field of fire. As a result the "Southampton" is well able to defend itself, and the manner in which the usual "blind spot" behind the tail has been avoided, is extremely interesting. To begin with, the tail has been designed as a semicantilever, the supporting struts projecting but a very short way out from the tail root. Secondly, the cockpits for the aft guns are placed as far out as possible laterally, and staggered in relation to one another, so that from one or other of the two cockpits there is no blind area beyond a distance of 50 feet from the tail.

The tail section was adjustable and had triple fins and rudders. The aircraft was designed, essentially, to be both combat capable and durable. The latter was demonstrated ably by the fact that it could remain in the air even on a single engine—still a relative rarity at the time. The wings were designed to use as few struts as possible, with a W-arrangement of the centre interplane wing struts leaving the centre section across the lower wing clean. Initially, the Southampton was to be entirely made of wood, but as time passed, an all-metal hull would be substituted, and later in the aircraft's production run, metal wings would be added as well. A total crew of five would not only man the aircraft, but in many ways live in it.

The entire design process for the Southampton, owing to the development work already done on the Swan, took only seven and a half months, and the aircraft was accepted with almost no changes. It was at the time the most advanced flying boat of its type in the world. Its water handling was excellent, and apparently the early tests went very well:

> This seaplane was found to provide one of those somewhat rare instances in which a seaplane is absolutely "right" straight away. No modifications of any kind were

> found to be necessary, and the seaplane was delivered by air to the Experimental Air Station.... The seaplane then went through its type tests "without a hitch," with the result that the trials were completed in record time. The "Southampton" was then adopted as the standard twin-engine reconnaissance seaplane of the R.A.F., and by now a large number of Southamptons have been delivered, while many more are still on order.

This was demonstrated quite handily in September 1925. Four Southamptons made a 10,000-mile (16,000-km) cruise around the Irish Sea, much of it in bad weather, which the Southamptons handled with ease. The aircraft that emerged into service in 1925 was specifically meant to operate from fixed bases, with the first examples deployed at Calshot with 480 Coastal Reconnaissance Flight. These first aircraft were Southampton "I" models, the all-wooden variety, and they were quickly put into significant operational tests, not only flying around the British Isles but entering training with the Royal Navy. With these satisfactorily completed, further flights were undertaken to the Mediterranean and Persian Gulf, and despite frequently poor weather these were all completed without mishap.

These flights laid the groundwork for a grander effort to "show the flag" that revolved around four new Southampton aircraft built for what was termed the

A pair of Supermarine Southamptons in flight. (*Public domain image, originally taken by the Royal Air Force*)

Far East Flight. There were more practical effects than just this, namely opening air routes to the Far East and to see how capable air crews—and flying boats—were operating away from fixed bases and in varying climactic conditions. The aircraft were to fly in stages from England all the way to the great imperial base at Singapore, a major feat for the time. Under the command of Grp Capt. Cave-Browne-Cave, the aircraft took off from Plymouth on October 17, 1927, flying over France and then on to Alexandretta in southern Turkey, arriving on November 3 without incident despite periodic bad weather.

The next leg of the journey took the aircraft away from open waters and over mountainous terrain to Baghdad, and though these aircraft were more advanced than the original Southampton Is, they still carried the original engine layout and found that the service ceiling of the aircraft was lower than anticipated; as a result, the engines battled against the downdraft coming off the mountains and gained height agonizingly slowly, and burned preciously calculated fuel in so doing. Headwinds, rain, and dust storms all contributed as well, making this leg far more hazardous and difficult. After nearly nine hours of these conditions, the flight commander decided to bring them down on the Euphrates River, as they were dangerously short of fuel, and they alighted only 60 miles short of their destination.

Refuelling took place the next day from R.A.F. emergency stores ferried by inflatable dinghies kept aboard, and from there, the aircraft took off over the desert to reach Iran. Iran and Britain had difficult relations in this period and would continue in this manner for decades to come; Iran was reluctant to admit flights over its territory, something that would frustrate British commercial aviation ambitions for years. As a result, when the aircraft landed at Bushire, the crews were told they were quarantined, and had to spend two nights sleeping on the aircraft, making a total of three nights on the water, including the one night spent floating on the Euphrates. Despite this quarantine, local visitors were fascinated with seeing the aircraft, and the crews spent hours entertaining them.

From Iran, the aircraft winged their way to the R.A.F. base in Karachi, India—the last time the crew would find themselves at a completed British base for a year. The aircraft were inspected and found to be in excellent condition, so on December 15, they set off for Singapore. The flight created much excitement owing to the fact that nothing of its kind had ever happened before. Despite difficult flying conditions, the aircraft arrived in Singapore precisely on time, at the Seletar base then under construction. The conditions were rough, since the mangrove and rubber trees had only just been cleared and the buildings were all huts and matting. Despite this, morale remained high as the crews of the Southamptons understood that they were pioneers in the frontiers of the Empire.

After checks and maintenance, the aircraft departed for another major task: a circumnavigation of Australia. Before this, however, a strange incident occurred that highlighted the unique problems of flying boats—especially so far isolated. As the aircraft were taxiing on the Java Sea, one began to signal that it was taking on water fast and was in danger of sinking. The problem was found in the rear of the aircraft. A crewman was found sitting on the lavatory, holding on with both hands, trying to prevent the ocean from washing up into the hull. The broken toilet was bolted shut and the flight proceeded. The aircraft arrived over Broome on June 1, 1928.

They began to travel anti-clockwise around the continent, flying from Albany across the Great Australian Bight. This 850-mile stretch of deserted coast offered only one real landing spot to refuel, a small spot called Israelite Bay that had little in the way of facilities and no boats to ferry out fuel. Luckily, two farmers had manhandled fuel drums to the end of the jetty, and these were painstakingly ferried out on the durable dinghies—800 gallons of petrol in all.

After their arrival in Melbourne, things became more difficult. The aircraft had to cross 300 miles of open water with no reference points, then find their petrol tins on one of the thousands of possible sites that formed the Gulf of Carpentaria and Arnhem Land. All of this was to be done on the only existing map available: a rough sketch done by a missionary. A boat was sent ahead, which was found in short order despite hostile weather conditions—the flight's luck continued to hold. From there, they returned to Singapore. At this point, one of the aircraft was sent back for inspection, becoming a major attraction; it afterwards returned to service in Singapore until 1931.

A fourth Southampton was assembled from parts to bring the flight up to strength, and they were tasked again with managing a huge achievement, flying from the Philippines to Hong Kong, which had never been done before. Emergency landings would be impossible thanks to monsoons, and when one aircraft's engine began to fail, it had to turn back. This aircraft later caught up with the flight after a worrisome incident in which it missed a navigational marker and was feared lost, but were ultimately escorted into Hong Kong harbour by a biplane from H.M.S. *Hermes*.

The Far East Flight would ultimately return to Singapore—after further adventures along the way for one aircraft in French Indochina, today Vietnam—on December 11, 1928, having covered 27,000 miles over fourteen months and keeping mostly to their timetable. The flight would be disbanded in 1929 to become No. 205 Squadron, the first permanent R.A.F. presence in the Far East.

It is a small wonder, given the sensational nature of the Far East Flight's time in and around Australia that the developing Australian air forces would end up purchasing the Southampton for their own use, part of a small but growing defence establishment some commentators treated with great pride.

Writing about the flight decades later in 1970, Grp Capt. G. E. Livcock reflected on how different the world of their achievement had been:

> I was struck not so much by the advances aviation has made in the past half-century, but by the enormous gulf that divides "flying" in those days from the present day. It is laughable for instance to record that our average speed over the ground for the whole Far East Flight was 70kt–80mph, the greatest height we achieved was 5500ft and we had to land for fuel 27 times between England and Singapore. It may be more

> efficient to be dragged through the air in a tin box at ten times that speed and height, but it is not nearly so much fun.

In the end, Grp Capt. Livcock summed up the achievement with understandable pride: "We had broken no 'records,' but had scored a good many 'firsts,' e.g. the first R.A.F. flight to Singapore and Australia, etc. I am confident that, had we been asked, we could have turned round and flown back to England."

The Southampton improved in its long service life of over a decade. Aside from the early production models, the R.A.F.'s principle version was the Mk II, which introduced an anodised duralumin hull that lowered the weight of the aircraft by 540 lb (245 kg) and eliminated water absorption, saving more weight over time. This version also carried upgraded Napier VA engines. The Mk II also had increased petrol and oil capacities, and had improvements in the living conditions for the crew, though it was undoubtedly as cramped as the Mk I. There were a handful of Mk III aircraft, which were all-metal, including the wings. There was also a one-off variant, a three-engined version called the Southampton Mk X.

In service, the Southampton would equip Nos. 201, 203, 204, 205, and 210 Squadrons, and be used around the world from the British Isles to Iraq and Singapore, encompassing in its day a large portion of the British Empire. The last aircraft would not be phased out of service until 1935, by which point revolutionary new aircraft had taken to the air and aviation technology was on the far side of a massive forward leap.

Depending on the source consulted, between seventy-eight and eighty-three Southamptons were built, and the name was powerful enough to be briefly passed on to successor aircraft. The Supermarine Scapa was originally named the Southampton IV, and the name Southampton V was briefly used for the Stranraer—aircraft built, tested, and operated with an eye towards the legacy of the Southampton.

Today, the only piece of the Southampton legacy that survives is the hull of a solitary Mk I aircraft, which had torn loose from her moorings in November 1928 and been wrecked at Portland. The remaining hull was sold to a Mr. Kemp as a houseboat in 1929 and lingered in a pitiable state until the R.A.F. reacquired it from one Mr. Coombs in 1967 for £75. The restored hull can be seen at the R.A.F. Museum at Hendon.

Though, by even the early 1930s, the Southampton was entirely obsolete, it is well worth inclusion here for two reasons. In the first place, the Southampton was at its birth the most advanced aircraft of its kind, and as such, it is highly indicative not just of where flying boat design was in the late 1920s, but also what the roots of the even more capable aircraft of the 1930s and 1940s were. The aircraft itself would inspire successors that in some cases served the R.A.F. right until the early years of World War II, even if they bore its name only briefly.

In the second place, the Southampton was an early example of just what the flying boat was capable of. Whether in wooden, partially metal, or all-metal form, the aircraft demonstrated what was true until the 1940s: the flying boat could conquer the distances of the world, and it could do it reliably. The Far East Flights alone were a major proof of this concept, and it is small wonder that the Southampton served as long as it did. Though it is a vanished part of aviation history today, the Southampton was once a very visible symbol of the might and prowess of the British Empire, and of just how capable the flying boat could be.

37

Supermarine Walrus: A Fleet's Beloved "Shagbat"

Supermarine is, for obvious reasons, much better known today for its fighter aircraft. The Supermarine Spitfire has written itself into aviation history as a likely eternal legend—so long as there are voices to tell the stories, the Spitfire will remain a part of human memory. The cultural role of the Spitfire, at least in Commonwealth countries, is unparalleled. Even for the author of this book, it is frequently recalled, owing to a replica Spitfire in a nearby park, but also because the city's hockey team is named "Spitfires." Yet the Spitfire is not the entire story of the Supermarine Corporation, and indeed is just a small view of the overall picture.

Supermarine produced many other designs, from military craft to seaplanes that won the Schneider Trophy—and, of course, flying boats. Among the many pages of the Supermarine story would be the Walrus. The Walrus was that rare aircraft that proved so useful that it shrugged off its own successor, succumbing only to the passage of time. It would become a ubiquitous sight in the British Royal Navy, known affectionately as the "Shagbat." This remarkable biplane flying boat would write its own chapter of Supermarine's famous story, proving the durability and usefulness of flying boats for the air forces of World War II.

Specifications

First Flight: 1933
Powerplant: One Bristol Pegasus VI nine-cylinder radial engine, 680 hp
Armament: Two or three 7.7-mm (0.303-inch) Vickers K machine guns, six 100-lb (45-kg) or two 250-lb (110-kg) bombs, or two 250-lb (110-kg) Mk VIII depth charges
Top Speed: 135 mph (215 kph)
Range/Service Ceiling: 600 miles (965 km), 18,500 feet (5,650 km)
Dimensions: Length 37 feet 7 inches (11.45 metres), height 15 feet 3 inches (4.5 metres), wingspan 45 feet 10 inches (14 metres)
Number Built: 740

The Walrus certainly did not have a name that would give away how ubiquitous its role would be—walruses are neither known for their usefulness nor grace, after all. But what it did have was an aviation pedigree stretching back into the 1920s. The Walrus was descended from the Seagull series, stemming from a single-engined biplane flying boat that first flew in 1921 and was used by the Fleet Air Arm (to avoid confusion, the company built a second Seagull in 1948, though it only reached prototype phase). In fact, the aircraft that would become known by history as the Walrus originally was designated the Seagull V—it only received its more famed name in service with the Royal Navy.

The design of the Walrus was crafted to meet the requirement that it be a ship-borne, catapult-launched aircraft for the Royal Navy. As a result, the structure of the aircraft was stressed for the purpose and emerged as an extremely rugged one. The Walrus was the first aircraft to be specifically designed for this purpose. This would pay dividends to the Walrus in the many theatres in which it served, to say nothing about making it more than capable of its original design role. The wings were well adapted, using a single bay design to minimize rigging problems that were caused by the stresses of the rapid acceleration. The wheels retracted into the underside of the lower wing to further reduce drag, a first for the type.

The high pusher propeller had a pair of benefits for the aircraft. It was away from the spray and it also meant that the crew could operate in picking up moorings or manoeuvre on the sea without having to worry about a whirling propeller. It was an orthodox biplane design with an all-metal hull, and the engine served as part of the central strutting linking the top and bottom wing. The hull itself came with straight sides and a straight-vee bottom, which was something

A Supermarine Walrus in her prime. (*Photograph courtesy of Dan Shumaker*)

of a throwback to older flying boat designs. Unlike those older aircraft, the hull was made from aluminum rather than wood or another material. This was an important choice, since the designers wanted to ensure that the aircraft could work in any environment, and wood tended to rapidly rot in tropical climates. Inside the hull, the extreme forward was occupied by the open position for the gunner, equipped with a Scarff gun ring. There was a detachable cover for this position for a compartment that held the mooring equipment. Behind this was the pilot's compartment, with sliding windows for the sides and roof. Dual controls were an available feature, and behind the cockpit was a navigator's compartment. Usually, only a single pilot was carried, and the controls themselves were a little bit unusual. The column was not fixed but could be unplugged from a floor socket and just put into another. On the occasions where a co-pilot was there, a pilot wanting to hand over control quite literally handed it over! It may surprise people looking at the Walrus from the outside to realize that there was a table for the navigator's chart box, and windows for observations and data gathering. There was another gunner's position behind that. According to early accounts, despite the engine overhead, the noise was not too severe, with crew members able to call to each other without the aid of a telephone.

The aircraft first flew on June 21, 1933. It quickly was found that it behaved very well on the water, with the undercarriage strut not creating any spray. As the aircraft picked up speed, the hull design ensured the water was kicked up behind it. While it has become ubiquitously associated with the British Royal Navy, it might surprise some readers to know that the aircraft had its original impetus in 1929 as a private venture between Supermarine and the Royal Australian Air Force (RAAF) for a catapult-launched aircraft for their cruisers. Development took quite a bit of time, but the Australians were more than happy to take on the aircraft when it arrived. The design worked just as well for the British.

The durability of the design was put in stark relief when the prototype was mounted on H.M.S. *Nelson* in 1935. On a test flight overseen by Admiral Roger Backhouse, the naval commander-in-chief, the pilot attempted to land on the water with the landing gear accidentally extended. The aircraft immediately flipped over, but the pilot suffered only minor injuries, and the aircraft returned to service. Many other aircraft would have been wrecked by such an accident, and it was not a coincidence that the Walrus thereafter was one of the first aircraft to come with a gear indicator light.

The Australians were so happy with the result that they ordered twenty-four aircraft directly off the drawing board, which started to arrive in 1935. The Royal Navy took its first deliveries the year after. In addition to its "Shagbat" nickname, the aircraft also picked up the name "Steam-pigeon," named for the steam produced by water striking the hot Pegasus engine. In the Royal Navy, the aircraft equipped cruisers and some battleships, and were to be found on the monitor H.M.S. *Terror* and the seaplane tender H.M.S. *Albatross*. When the war came, an irony quickly arose. The Walrus had originally been meant to carry out spotter duties for the Royal Navy, but the nature of the war meant that rescue and anti-submarine operations took priority. In actual practice, it served as a fleet spotter only twice, at the Battle of Cape Sparviento and the Battle of Cape Matapan. The aircraft even saw limited service as a bomber in East Africa and in the Norwegian Campaign. Late in the war, they were taken off warships to open up more space, and in some cases, they operated from Royal Navy aircraft carriers. The aircraft could land slowly enough that it did not need to have a tail hook, nor did it need to use the arrestor cable.

As an anti-submarine aircraft, the Walrus proved remarkable in being one of very few biplanes ever equipped with anti-submarine radar, and in this role, they not only hunted U-boats but also German surface raiders. The main role of the aircraft proved to be air-sea rescue, as part of the R.A.F.'s specialist squadrons. The Walrus was the last aircraft in a relay for the task. Downed aircrew or sailors were found by Spitfires or Boulton-Paul Defiants, and then Avro Ansons would drop dinghies or necessary supplies, with the Walruses coming in at the finish to perform the rescue.

Especially over the English Channel, these rescues could be dangerous. One Walrus pilot won the Victoria Cross for doing so. Pilot Tom Fletcher's 2010 obituary in the *Daily Telegraph* laid out the harrowing situation:

> On October 2nd, 1942, a Spitfire pilot was forced to bail out over the English Channel, landing in the sea four miles off the French coast on the edge of a minefield. His leader orbited overhead the dinghy and transmitted an emergency call. The naval authorities at Dover considered it to be impossible to get a launch through the minefield. They also considered it too dangerous for a Walrus amphibian to make an attempt. Despite this advice, Fletcher immediately volunteered to make a rescue attempt and took off with a Spitfire squadron providing an escort.
>
> He arrived on the scene as another Spitfire squadron engaged enemy fighters trying to interfere with the rescue. He located the dinghy and landed 150 yards away and taxied towards the survivor who failed to grasp the boathook on the first pass as he fell out of his dinghy. In the strong wind and choppy sea, Fletcher made another attempt when the pilot was hauled aboard. He then taxied clear of the minefield and took off, just clearing a floating mine. Throughout the rescue, the Walrus had come under heavy fire from shore batteries.
>
> *A Dictionary of Coastal Command, 1939-1945*, pp. 132–133
> Geoff Simpson

Though it was an angel of mercy, this did not mean that it was beloved by all its pilots. One pilot serving with the Air Transport Auxiliary, Mary Ellis, had nothing but scorn for flying the aircraft:

> The only aircraft I really disliked intently was the Supermarine Walrus. A single-engine amphibious biplane reconnaissance aircraft, the Walrus flapped about all over the sky, and at times seemed almost uncontrollable. On land it was like a

> penguin, but apparently it was good on the sea and during its history it had saved many lives. It is extraordinary to think the same designer had created the beautiful Supermarine Spitfire. Yes, Reginald J. Mitchell must have had a bad day when he drew up his plan for the Walrus.
>
> I can't think of one ATA pilot who liked this aeroplane. It was like flying a deadly-heavy elephant. It wobbled about in the air like a crazy thing. In fact, the Walrus had a mind of its own. Even the ATA's most high-achieving woman pilots loathed it, including the indomitable Lettice Curtis. Indeed, it was the cumbersome, irrational, uncontrollable and rattling old Walrus that nearly killed my friend First Officer Anne Walker and made me think twice about flying ever again.
>
> *A Spitfire Girl: One of the World's Greatest ATA Ferry Pilots Tells Her Story*, p. 116
> Mary Ellis and Melody Foreman

The Walrus was the second to last biplane to enter service with the Royal Air Force, and amazingly, it had been on the drawing boards at Supermarine while the Spitfire was—a wildly different pair of designs to be pursuing at once! It rapidly became the fleet's standard catapult-launched amphibian, finding itself employed for artillery spotting, anti-submarine and convoy duties, and communications duties. In civilian use after the war, the Walrus was even put to work as a spotter for whaling activities—one even being affectionately and ironically named *Moby Dick* for the purpose. When the war came, it would take on the vital role of air-sea rescue as previously described. If this were not enough to endear it to the men who were saved and served by the Walrus, it apparently also on occasion took on the duty of ferrying beer to thirsty infantrymen. Small wonder the affectionately known "Shagbat" became a very welcome sight to those in need—and, perhaps, in thirst. Initial production of the type comprised the Walrus Mk I, with the Bristol Pegasus VI engine. There was also the Mk II with a wooden hull and similar equipment, which operated quite well in colder climates. Examples of this "wooden Walrus" served with the Royal Canadian Air Force (RCAF) from 1943 until 1947. The aircraft proved so necessary that to remove some of the production burden from the company, the aircraft would be subcontracted extensively to Saunders-Roe.

The Walrus amazingly survived her own successor, the Supermarine Sea Otter. The designs were similar, but the Otter was more powerful owing to a Bristol Mercury XXX engine. The Otter would serve alongside it rather than replace it, and the next successor to both aircraft ended up being cancelled in 1952 as helicopters took over the air-sea rescue roles. By this point, the Walrus had already done stellar service for many countries, not only serving with Australia, Britain, and Canada, but also with many other nations as disparate as Ireland and the Soviet Union. Today, there are four examples in existence. The first is in Australia, one of the original run of aircraft, located at the Royal Air Force Museum, where it has been on display since 1979. The Australians retain one themselves, at the Royal Australian Air Force Museum. A third resides at the Fleet Air Arm Museum, having been recovered from a dump in 1963 and then lovingly restored. The last was at an air museum in Southampton, before being sold to a private owner to continue its restoration process.

The Walrus was an unusual aircraft. Tough but hard to fly, a biplane with radar, a crucial rescue aircraft in the first years of jets. The aircraft was a welcome sight to many downed airmen over the years, and a ubiquitous sight in the Royal Navy's arsenal. Even after the war, it continued to be used in many different places, its durability keeping it alive far longer than a biplane flying boat might otherwise have lasted. The Supermarine Walrus was Britain's rescue aircraft much as other flying boats served in other lands during the war in the same role, but its unique story is well worth recounting.

Conclusion

As this work came to an end, what had become most striking was not only the dedication of so many people both to designing flying boats and flying them in their original contexts, but the passion to keep them alive—to make the golden age of the flying boat more than just a ghost. If there is a single thread winding through this book, it is passion. The passion of the designers who had to master not just making an excellent airplane but an excellent boat as well. The passion of the operators of these aircraft, in peace and war. The passion of the dedicated restorers, civil pilots, museum personnel, and historians and historical enthusiasts.

There is much to be owed to the era of the flying boat, and in this regard, the author disagrees with the notion put forward by some sources that flying boats were of limited utility and of little practical import in aviation history. Such a view may, with very careful framing, be possibly applied to World War II, but even there, the flying boat carved out a significant niche with every major power. As either patrol aircraft or transport aircraft, and even as bombers, the flying boat more than proved its worth. That they were overtaken by land-based aircraft cannot be denied, but this should not denigrate their overall usefulness in much the same way that the extinction of the dinosaurs should not overshadow their success before that event.

Moreover, in the larger picture, the age of the flying boats is even more important since it created the world of long-distance passenger air travel that everyone benefits from today. The flying boats were the pioneers of reliable, regular air travel between continents, and they did this when the technology needed to do so was not only brand new but also unproven. These were aircraft that operated at the sharp, front edge—true, they carried far fewer passengers than today, but nobody had carried passengers as they had before. Nor, when one gets right down to it, has anybody since. The world of the flying boat was one of comfort and, in a sense, intimacy that nothing that has come since has matched. In a world of maximized profit through minimized passenger space, the era of the Clippers and the Empire boats becomes more and more alien but should be remembered all the more as a result.

Flying boats did more, besides. They explored vast spaces, carried the flags of nations, hauled cargo, and, to this day, put out fires. Many of the aircraft in this book are still in some form of use today, either for display purposes or as historical artifacts, but also as practical and personal aircraft. It is a testament to the durability and quality of these designs that so many have lasted through the decades. Again, it is even more a testament to human ingenuity and passion. This became more prominent to the author as this book unfolded. The people who were willing to speak about their aircraft demonstrated amply how important it is that people be passionate about history. To pick just one example from the throng, the work of dedicated restorers is the only reason that there is a physical legacy of Canada's first-ever production aircraft. Had it not been for their efforts, the last vestiges of the Canadian Vickers Vedette would have been slowly claimed by the natural spaces the aircraft once mastered.

So it is that the world of the flying boat is a vanished one, but in other ways, it is not vanished at all. Like so many simple notions about history, the more one examines it, the more one finds exceptions to the rule—often glaring ones. Flying boats could practically be a case study for this concept: far from disappearing when they were surpassed in technical and practical terms, they found different niches and survived. Production of flying boats in various contexts continues to this day.

This project began as an attempt to introduce to a general audience the sense of wonder that this author first felt when looking at flying boats. They so often possess a gracefulness—to a modern eye, perhaps an unusualness—that feels unique to the casual observer, and the more deeply one looks, the more interesting the story becomes. There is so much more to the story, too, and in many ways, this work merely is a beginning. There are simply so many more flying boat stories to tell, so many other types, and so many roles and incidents. The story, in short, continues. It is highly recommended that the interested reader seeks out other books, but above all, seek out the aircraft themselves and the hands that maintain them.

In the end, this book is the result of so many dedicated hands and passionate minds—people who laboured to ensure that either in print or reality, the legacy of history's flying boats remains intact. This author is deeply indebted to the people who shared their time, stories, and efforts to make this work a reality.

Bibliography

Aaron, R., "'Home Front' issue is ugliest coin of the decade," *The Toronto Star*, (Toronto; Toronto Star, 1994)
Alegi, G., "The castle door, the mooring pylon and the Transaereo—Part 1," *WW1 Aero—the Journal of the Early Aeroplane*, (Red Hook; World War I Aeroplanes, Inc., 2006)
Algeu, K., *The Use of Seaplanes as an Advanced Weapon System* (Monterey; Naval Postgraduate School, 1988)
Allaz, C., *The History of Air Cargo and Airmail from the 18th Century* (Paris; Institut du Transport Aérien, 2004)
Allward, M., *An Illustrated History of Seaplanes and Flying Boats* (Ashland; Moorland Publishing, 1989)
Amos, H., "Mystery of missing plane is solved after 80 years," *The Independent* (London; The Independent, 2015)
Anderson, J., *Confessions of a Muckraker* (New York; Random House, 1979)
Andersson, L., *Soviet Aircraft and Aviation: 1917–1941* (Maryland; Naval Institute Press, 1994)
Andrews, C. F., and Morgan, E. B., *Supermarine Aircraft Since 1914* (2nd edition) (London: Putnam, 1987)
Australian Defence, "Stand Firm," *The Australian Quarterly*, 1(3) (Sydney: Australian Institute of Policy and Science, 1929)
"About the Mighty Mars," *Life Magazine* (Chicago: Time Inc., 1944)
"Aircraft Fleet—'The Mighty Martin Mars.'" *Flying Tankers Inc.* [viewed August 25, 2017] Available from: web.archive.org/web/20060501200714/http://www.martinmars.com/mars.html
"Beriev: An 80th Anniversary since Maiden Flight of the MBR-2 Seaplane Designed by George Beriev," *EMPNewswire*, May 4, 2012
"Beriev Design Bureau and Taganrog Aircraft Plant in World War II," *EMPNewswire*, May 15, 2015
"Breguet Bre-730/731," viewed July 5, 2017 Available from: web.archive.org/web/20080116134527/ and www.samoloty.ow.pl/str237.htm
Century of Flight: Short Empire, viewed August 13, 2017. Available from: www.century-of-flight.freeola.com/Aviation%20history/coming%20of%20age/flying%20boats/Short%20S-23%20Empire.htm
"'China Clipper' is Giant of Pacific Air Fleet," *Popular Mechanics Magazine* (California; Popular Mechanics Magazine, 1935)
"Clippers At War," *The Flying Clippers: Pan Am's Fabulous Flying Ships*, viewed June 29, 2017. Available from: www.flyingclippers.com/clippersatwar.html
"The Dornier Do. X: First Authentic Data and Particulars," *Flight* (London; Flight Global, 1930)

"Fantasy of Flight: Kermit Weeks Vision of a Military Aviation living Museum par excellence based in Central Florida," viewed August 15, 2017. Available from: www.myflorida.org.uk/htm_pages/fantasy_of_flight.htm

"Individual History: Supermarine Seagull V A2-4/VH-ALB," viewed July 15, 2017. Available from: www.rafmuseum.org.uk/documents/collections/73-A-426-Seagull-V-A2-4-(Walrus).pdf

"Individual History: Supermarine Southampton 1 N9899 Museum Accession Number 67/A/705," Royal Air Force Museum, 2014

"Introduction the Saro A1," *Flight* (London; Flight Global, 1947)

"Latécoère Laté 523," Clausuchronia, viewed August 2, 2017. Available from: clausuchronia.wordpress.com/tag/latecoere-late-523/

Translator Vanier, J., *The Latécoère 521 "Lieutenant de vaisseau Paris" Commercial Flying Boat* (French), (Washington: National Advisory Committee for Aeronautics, 1936)

National Advisory Committee for Aeronautics, *The Supermarine "Southampton" Seaplane (Observation of Bomber)* (Washington: National Advisory Committee for Aeronautics, 1926)

"Pentagon Over The Islands.... The Thirty Year History of Indonesian Military Aviation," *Air Enthusiast Quarterly*, 1976 (2) (Britain, Air Enthusiast Quarterly, 1976)

"Russia Provides Two Be-200 Aircraft on Portuguese Fire-Fighting Mission," *Sputniknews*, July 25, 2017.

"Sister Ship of Do-X Biggest in the World," *Popular Science Monthly* (New York: Popular Science Monthly, 1931)

"Six Engines Drive Big Sea Plane Over Ocean," *Popular Mechanics* (New York: Popular Mechanics, 1936)

"The Supermarine 'Seagull' Mark V," *Flight*, 1934 (13) (London; Flight Global, 1934)

The Supermarine Southampton Boat Seaplane, Mark II. (Metal Hull) (London: His Majesty's Stationery Office, 1929)

"Telltale Surface on Ocean Found by Transport Meigs" (Lowell; The Lowell Sun, 1938)

Untitled—Report of the crash of Latécoère 631 F-BDRC, viewed August 20, 2017. Available from: aviation-safety.net/database/record.php?id=19480801-1

Untitled—Report of the crash of Latécoère 631 F-BDRE, viewed August 20, 2017. Available from: aviation-safety.net/database/record.php?id=19550910-0

Untitled—Report of the crash of Latécoère 631 F-WANU, viewed August 20, 2017. Available from: aviation-safety.net/database/record.php?id=19500328-5

Untitled—Report of M.130 China Clipper Accident. *Aviation Safety Network*, viewed June 29, 2017. Available from: aviation-safety.net/database/record.php?id=19430121-0&lang=en

Untitled—Report of M.130 Philippine Clipper Accident. *Aviation Safety Network*, viewed June 29, 2017. Available from: aviation-safety.net/database/record.php?id=19430121-0

Untitled—Report of M.130 China Clipper Accident. *Aviation Safety Network*, viewed June 29, 2017. Available from: aviation-safety.net/database/record.php?id=19450108-2

Axelrod, A., *Encyclopedia of World War II, Volume 1* (New York: Facts on File, Inc., 2007)

Bacon, R., "Straight and Level" *Flight International*, July 1989

Barfield, N., "Getting the Spruce Goose off the Ground: Obituary of Rae Hopper," *The Guardian*, May 15, 1991.

Beck, C., Schofield, J., and Johnson, W., (eds) *Matériel Culture: The Archaeology of Twentieth-Century Conflict* (London: Routledge, 2002)

Bellini, C., "An Historical Perspective of Early Italian Air Medical Transport." *Air Medical Journal* 27(6), p.286-292

Bertke, D., Kindell, D., Smith, G., *World War II Sea War Volume 6: The Allies Halt the Axis Advance* (Ohio: Bertke Publications, 2013)

Bluffeld, R., *Over Empires and Oceans: Pioneers, Aviators, and Adventurers* (Ticehurst; Tattered Flag Press, 2014)

Boyne, W., *Clash of Wings: World War II in the Air* (New York; Touchstone, 1994)

Braybook, R., 'Wings Over Water', *Armada International*, 22(2), pp. 8-18 (Bangkok; Armada International, 1998)

Curtiss Aeroplane and Motor Company, *The Flight Across the Atlantic* (New York; Curtiss Aeroplane and Motor Company, 1919)
Brenard, R., "The Romance of the Air Mail to East and South Africa," *Journal of the Royal African Society*, 38(150), pp. 47-64 (Oxford; Journal of the Royal African Society, 1939)
Brown, E., *Wings on My Sleeve: The World's Greatest Test Pilot Tells His Story* (W&N, 2007)
C de R., 'The Savoia-Marchetti S.66', *Flight*, October, pp. 958-959 (London; Flight Global, 1932)
Cassidy, B., *Flying Empires: Short 'C' class Empire Flying Boats* (Queens Parade Press, 2004)
Chamberlain, P., "1945-1963: Arms Smuggling etc.," viewed July 14, 2017. Available from: http://www.haddenhamairfieldhistory.co.uk/beaufighters.htm
Chapman, H., *State Capitalism and Working Class Radicalism in the French Aircraft Industry* (Los Angeles; University of California Press, 1991)
Chun, C., *The Fall of the Philippines 1941-42* (Oxford; Osprey Publishing, 2012)
Clayton, A., *Three Republics, One Navy: A Naval History of France 1870–1999* (Solihull; Helion & Company Limited, 2016)
Cronin, M., 'Northern Visions: Aerial Surveying and the Canadian Mining Industry, 1919-1928' *Technology and Culture*, 48(2), pp. 303-330 (Baltimore; Technology and Culture, 2007)
Current, J., (ed.), *American Warplanes of World War II: Fighters, Bombers, Liaison* (Mainz; PediaPress, year unlisted)
Dancey, P., *Lufthansa to Luftwaffe: Hitler's Secret Air Force.* (Lulu.com, 2013)
Dancey, P., *The Soviet Aircraft Industry.* (Oxford; Fonthill Media Limited, 2015)
de Jong, P., *Dornier Do 24 Units* (Oxford; Osprey Publishing, 2015)
Dean, P., 'Return of the Albatross: The Revival of the Existing Fleet' *Warbird Digest*, Special Insert, pp.9 (Huntington; Warbird Digest, 2006)
Donald, D, (ed.), *The Encyclopedia of World Aircraft* (Ontario; Prospero Books, 1998)
Dornier, C., *Lessons of the Do. X (*London: Reprinted from the Journal of the Royal Aeronautical Society, 1933)
Dorr, R., *Fighting Hitler's Jets: The Extraordinary Story of the American Airmen Who Beat the Luftwaffe and Defeated Nazi Germany* (Minneapolis; Zenith Press, 2013)
Dover, (ed.), *The Long Way Home* (Self-published, 2008)
Dumas, R., and Jordan, J., *French Battleships 1922-1956* (Annapolis; Naval Institute Press, 2009)
Dunn, R., "Air-Sea Rescue Operations in Europe During World War II: Historical Perspective on a Footnote in International Law" *Air Force Law Review*, pp. 602-619 (United States; Air Force Law Review, 1979)
Ellis, M., and Foreman, M., *A Spitfire Girl: One of the World's Greatest ATA Ferry Pilots Tells Her Story* (Yorkshire; Frontline Books, 2016)
Evans, J., *The Sunderland Flying Boat Queen Volume 2* (Pembroke Dock; Paterchurch Publications, 1993)
Falke, E., *Biscarosse, home to Pierre Georges Latécoère and his seaplanes (Lieutenant de Vaisseau Paris Latécoère 521*, viewed July 9, 2017. Available from:
falkeeinsgreatplanes.blogspot.ca/2012/12/biscarosse-home-to-pierre-georges.html
Farnham, A., "The Aviator's Air Yacht," *Forbes*, viewed August 2, 2017. Available from: www.forbes.com/2005/03/08/cz_af_0308conn.html
Ferreras, J., "Why B.C. isn't using the Martin Mars water bomber to fight the wildfires," *Global News*, viewed July 11, 2017. Available from: globalnews.ca/news/3589169/martin-mars-water-bomber-bc-wildfires/
First Across the Atlantic; Bluejacket.com, 2017, viewed May 10, 2017. Available from: www.bluejacket.com/usn_avi_nc4.html
Frame, A., *Flying Boats: My Father's War in the Mediterranean* (Wellington; Victoria University Press, 2007)
Fuchs, J-V., and Perchoc, M., *Pages D'Histoire Navale* (Du Gerfaut, 2004)
Gandt, R., *China Clipper: The Age of the Great Flying Boats* (Annapolis; Naval Institute Press, 1991)

Gaunt, C., and Cleworth, R., *Cats at War: Story of RAAF Catalinas in the Asia Pacific Theatre of War* (Roseville; J.R. Cleworth, 2000)

Goebel, G., "The Beriev Be-6, Be-10, & Be-12 Flying Boats," viewed June 25, 2017. Available from: www.airvectors.net/avbe12.html

The Great Aviator: Howard Hughes, His Life, Loves & Films—A Documentary (Los Angeles; Delta Entertainment Corporation, 2004)

Gribbin, D., "Aéropostale and Air France—A Decade of South Atlantic Airmail," viewed July 26, 2017. Available from: stamps.org/userfiles/file/symposium/presentations/GribbinPaper.pdf

Griehl, M., *Airwar over the Atlantic* (Barnsley; Pen and Sword Books Limited, 2016); *Luftwaffe Over America: The Secret Plans to Bomb the United States in World War II* (London; Greenhill Books, 2004); *X-Planes: German Luftwaffe Prototypes, 1930-1945* (Barnsley; Frontline Books, 2012)

Grierson, J., "Whaling from the Air," *The Geographical Journal*, 111(1/3), pp. 33-46 (Medford; The Geographical Journal, 1948)

Griswold, W., "When Boats had Wings," *Popular Science*, June, pp. 72-79, 173-175 (Harlan; Popular Science, 1963)

Guttman, R., "Convair's Incredible Wet Jet," *Aviation History*, pp. 24-25 (Virginia; Aviation History, 2009)

Hack, R., *Hughes: The Private Diaries, Memos and Letters.* (Beverly Hills; New Millennium Press, 2001)

Hackett, B., and Kingsepp, S., "Operation Tan No. 2: The Japanese Attack on Task Force 58's Anchorage at Ulithi," viewed June 16, 2017. Available from: www.combinedfleet.com/Tan%20No.%202.htm

Hardy, M. J., *Sea, Sky and Stars: An Illustrated History of Grumman Aircraft* (Arms & Armour Press, 1987)

Hoffman, R., *The Fighting Flying Boat: A History of the Martin PBM Mariner* (Annapolis; Naval Institute Press, 2004)

Huber, M., "S-38 Replica Completes Historic Flight," *Flying Magazine,* 126(2), pp. 34 (Winter Park: Flying Magazine, 1999)

Jackson, R., *The Encyclopedia of Military Aircraft* (London; Paragon, 2002); (ed.) *101 Great Bombers* (New York; The Rosen Publishing Group, 2010)

Johnson, E. R., *American Flying Boats and Amphibious Aircraft: An Illustrated History* (Jefferson; McFarland & Company, 2009)

Jones, D., *Wings on the River: Flying Boats on the Brisbane River & Redland Bay* (Brisbane; Boolarong Press, 2007)

Joseph, F., *The Axis Air Forces: Flying in Support of the German Luftwaffe* (Santa Barbara; Praeger, 2012)

Höfling, R., *Blohm & Voss BV 222 "Wiking" (Flugzeug Profile 40))* (Stengelheim; Unitec-Medienvertrieb e.K, 2003)

Karant, M., "As I Saw It," *Flight Magazine*, September, p. 140 (Chicago; Flight Magazine, 1945)

Katz, E., *The Film Encyclopedia (3rd Ed.)* (New York; HarperPerennial, 1998)

de Kerston, B., "New Giants of the Sky," *Boy's Life*, July, pp. 8-9 (Irving: Boy's Life Magazine, 1934)

Ketley, B., and Thomas, G., *Luftwaffe KG 200: The German Air Force's Most Secret Unit of WWII* (Mechanicsburg; Stackpole Books, 2015)

Kightly, J., "Sunderland Survivors," *Aeroplane,* 2009.

King, H. F., "Water-based Fighters: An Outline History and a Survey of Modern Possibilities," *Flight*, 58(2186), pp. 551–555 (Winter Park, Flight Magazine, 1950)

Kohn, L., "Boeing XB-15 Super Flying Fortress: U.S. Heavy Bomber" in Merriam, R., "U. S. Warplanes of World War II," pp.69. (World War II Journal, 2002)

Kondapalli, S., "China's naval structure and dynamics," *Strategic Analysis*, 23(7), pp. 1095-1116 (United States; Strategic Analysis, 2008)

Kowalonek, J., "The Sikorsky VS-44A Flying Boat," *Igor Sikorsky Historical Archives*, viewed August 14, 2017. Available from: www.sikorskyarchives.com/S-44%20restore.php

Lepage, J.-D.., *Aircraft of the Luftwaffe, 1939-1945: An Illustrated Guide* (London; McFarland & Company Inc., 2009)

Lindstrom, R., "Sikorsky S-38 Project," *AVWeb*, viewed August 2, 2017. Available from: www.avweb.com/news/features/Sikorsky-S-38-Project-223654-1.html

Livcock, Grp Capt. G. E., "The Far East Flight of the Southampton Flying Boats, 1927/28," *The Aeronautical Journal of the Royal Aeronautical Society*, 75, pp. 327-335 (London: The Aeronautical Journal of the Royal Aeronautical Society, 1971)

Marcon, T; "Il CANT Z.501 Gabbiano," *Storia Militare Magazione*, pp. 10–21 (Italy; Storia Militare Magazione, 1995)

M.A.S., "Fighter Flying Boat," *Flight*, July 29, pp. 123-129 (London; Flight Global, 1945)

Marriott, L., *Catapult Aircraft: Seaplanes that Flew from Ships without Flight Decks* (South Yorkshire; Pen & Sword Aviation, 2006)

Mattioli, M., *Savoia-Marchetti S.79 Sparviero Torpedo-Bomber Units.* (Oxford; Osprey Publishing, 2014)

Morgan, E., "Database: Supermarine Stranraer," 29(4), *Aeroplane*, 2001

Mondey, D., *The Hamlyn Concise Guide to Axis Aircraft of WWII: the Warplanes of Germany, Italy and Japan During World War II* (England; Chancellor Press, 2000)

Morris, D., *Royal Navy Search and Rescue: A Centenary Celebration* (Gloucestershire; Amberley Publishing, 2015)

Moy, T., *War Machines; Transforming Technologies in the U.S. Military, 1920–1940* (College Station; Texas A & M Press, 2016)

Munson, K., *US Warbirds from World War I to Vietnam* (Sterling Pub. Co, 1985)

Nesbit, R., *The Armed Rovers: Beauforts and Beaufighters over the Mediterranean* (Barnsley; Pen & Sword Books Limited, 2012)

Nico, "French flying boats and amphibians," *Let Let Let Warplanes*, viewed June 25, 2017. Available from: www.letletlet-warplanes.com/2008/07/05/french-flying-boats-and-amphibians/

Niccoli, R., *Book of Flight: From the Flying Machines of Leonardo Da Vinci to the Conquest of Space* (New York; Friedman/Fairfax Publishers, 2002)

Norris, G., *The Short Empire Boats (Aircraft in Profile Number 84)* (Surrey, U.K.; Profile Publications Ltd., 1966)

Nowarra, H., *Blohm & Voss Bv 222* (Pennsylvania; Schiffer Military History, 1997)

Nugent, F. S. "The screen: Warners' 'China Clipper' at Strand documents dramatic story of a transpacific flight," *The New York Times*, August 12, 1936

O'Connor, D., "Italy's Consummate Showman," *Aviation History*, pp. 50-53 (Virginia; Aviation History, 2014)

Pan American Philippine Clipper Memorial Plaque, Hiller Aviation Museum, San Carlos California

Peattie, M., *Sunburst: The Rise of Japanese Naval Air Power, 1909-1941* (Maryland; Naval Institute Press, 2001)

Petrescue, F., and Petrescue, R., *Near the flying time* (Lulu Publishing; 2011)

Phipps, M., *Wessex Aviation Industry* (Gloucestershire; Amberley Publishing, 2013)

Pigott, P., *On Canadian Wings: A Century of Flight* (Hounslow; Toronto, 2005)

Roche, J.-M., "Histoire de la BAN Saint-Mandrier (1951-1959)," viewed July 5, 2017. Available from: www.netmarine.net/aero/bases/stmandrier/histoire/histoire05.htm

Selinger, F., "Meteorological Operations in the Arctic 1940-1945" Lecture, War in the Arctic 1939-1945, Arkhangelsk, August 29–September 2, 2000.

Sikorsky, I., *The Story of the Winged-S* (New York; Dodd, Mead & Company, 1938)

Sikorsky, S., *The Sikorsky Legacy* (Chicago; Arcadia Publishing, 2007)

Simkin, J., "Owen Brewster," *Spartacus Educational*, viewed: August 2, 2017. Available from: spartacus-educational.com/JFKbrewsterO.html

Simpson, G., *A Dictionary of Coastal Command, 1939-1945* (South Yorkshire; Pen and Aviation, 2017)

Skaarup, H., *Canadian Warbirds of the Second World War* (Lincoln; Writer's Club Press, 2001); *RCAF War Prize Flights, German and Japanese Warbird Survivors* (Lincoln; iUniverse, 2006)

Smith, C., *Supermarine: An Illustrated History* (Gloucestershire; Amberley Publishing, 2016)

Smith, V., and Wright, V., *Open Cockpit over Africa.* (Lincoln; iUniverse.com, Inc. 2001)

Soviet Transports: Beriev Be 6, *Oldwings*, viewed June 25, 2017. Available from: www.oldwings.nl/st/beriev_myasishchev_sukhoi.pdf

Stage, A., "Second Raid on Pearl Harbor," *World War II*, 13(5), pp. 30 (World War II, 1999)

Stearns, D., "New Planes for Ocean Travel," *Popular Science*, September, pp. 81-83 (New York: Popular Science Monthly, 1941)

Stroud, J., *European Transport Aircraft since 1910* (New York; G.P. Putnam's Sons, 1967)

Szigeti, M., "Dornier Do X: Legendary Flying Boat," *Flug Revue*, pp. 16 (Stuttgart: Flug Revue, 1999)

Tatara, P., "Articles: China Clipper," *Turner Classic Movies*, viewed August 21, 2017. Available from: www.tcm.com/tcmdb/title/1214/China-Clipper/articles.html

Tobin, J., *To Conquer the Air: The Wright Brothers and the Great Race for Flight* (New York; Free Press, 2004)

Trimble, W. F., *Attack from the Sea: A History of the U.S. Navy's Seaplane Striking Force.* (Annapolis; Naval Institute Press, 2005)

Ulrich, J., "Größenwahn hoch X," *Spiegel Online*, viewed July 16, 2017. Available from: www.spiegel.de/einestages/luftfahrtgeschichte-a-948453.html

Van Doren, C., "Pan Am's Legacy to World Tourism," *Journal of Travel Research*, 32(1), pp. 3-12 (Thousand Oaks: Journal of Travel Research, 1993)

Vosilla, J., "1930: Grumman Takes Flight," *Long Island Business News,* January 9 (Long Island City, Long Island Business News, 2004)

White, R., *Into the Black* (London; Bantam Press, 2017)

Whiting, K., *Soviet Air Power, 1917-1976.* (Alabama; Air University, 1976)

Wilson, J. A., "Civil Aviation in Canada," *Queens Quarterly*, January, pp. 294-312 (Kingston: Queens Quarterly, 1929)

Workman, R. B., *Float Planes and Flying Boats: the U.S. Coast Guard and Early Naval Aviation* (Annapolis; U.S. Naval Institute, 2012)

World Heritage Encyclopedia, *Canadian Vickers Vedette*, viewed August 24, 2017. Available from: www.self.gutenberg.org/articles/Canadian_Vickers_Vedette

Yenne, B., *Seaplanes of the World: A Timeless Collection from Aviation's Golden Age* (California; O.G. Publishing, 1997)

Zichek, J., "A Detailed Look at the Fabulous Boeing 314," *Airpower Magazine*, pp. 14-27 (Sarrebourg; Airpower, 2005)